Kautilya today

Kautilya today

Jairam Ramesh on a globalizing India

India Research Press
New Delhi

Published by

{

India Research Press
B-4/22, Safdarjung Enclave, New Delhi – 110 029.
Ph.: 4694610; Fax : 4618637
e-mail : bahrisons@vsnl.com
www.indiaresearchpress.com

2002

Publication Rights : India Research Press
2002 © Jairam Ramesh

ISBN : 81-87943-37-8

Cataloging in Publication Data
Kautilya Today
Jairam Ramesh on a globlizing India
by : Jairam Ramesh

Includes bibliographical references and index.
ISBN : 81-87943-37-8
1. India 2. South Asia 3. Globlization 4 . Economics
5. Politics 6. Title 7. Author

*Published by Anuj Bahri for India Research Press
Printed at Focus Impressions, New Delhi – 110 003.*

In Tribute

Jairam Ramesh is an unusual, indeed an extraordinary, politician. He has terrific commonsense, an acute intellect, an insatiable intellectual curiosity, boldness of vision and articulation in speech and writing. It is a tribute to our political process that he has managed to hold high office in the Congress Party, which has profited in consequence from his willingness to think big and to fly in the face of little men who do not.

It is *India Today*, a leading Indian magazine that must also be congratulated for signing him on to write a regular column. Writing often is demanding and almost impossible to manage unless you are a full-time columnist. You have to be relevant, interesting and feisty. If you had asked me whether Jairam Ramesh, a full-time politician in the highest echelons of the Congress Party, could have pulled this off, I would have said: no way. But he has done the impossible.

This collection demonstrates beautifully what I say. Its range is immense; its sparkle undying, unlike the fizz of champagne. It also provides a vivid recall of the issues that we have faced in India, of our accomplishments and of our shortcomings. Like Oliver Twist, we can only ask for more. Unfortunately, he got less, but we are going to be luckier. For Jairam Ramesh continues to write and his column *Kautilya* finds a new abode at *The Times of India*. We can therefore look forward to reading many more of his columns and then, let us hope, also seeing him collect them afresh in a sequel.

Buy, borrow or steal this collection. And do not just put it on your coffee table. Read it: it belongs to the coffee table or the bookshelf only after you have savoured its entertaining and instructive contents.

Jagdish Bhagwati
Professor of Economics
Columbia University
June, 2002

Praise for Kautilya

"I have always read Jairam Ramesh through 'Kautilya' where he explores a wide spectrum of issues – political, economic, educational and social – and sets them forth in their myriad, glowing hues. His vibrant personality and intellectual brilliance are reflected in every one of his columns. He convinces the readers with incisive arguments and irrefutable logic, and he provokes thought with his in-depth analysis. Jairam is a true statesman who has consistently transcended narrow political alignments..."

– Narayana N. R. Murthy, Chief Mentor,
Infosys Technologies

"As an avid reader of the Kautilya columns I am delighted that they are being brought out in book form. They represent a remarkable concurrent commentary on economic political and social developments in India that are made all the more important because Jairam has been an insider, an activist agent of change, and a consistent advocate of economic reforms through the 1990s and indeed even earlier. I always found the Kautilya columns to be especially enjoyable because Jairam invariably managed to adhere to the standards of intellectual honesty one wants in a columnist one reads regularly, even though the compulsions of partisan politics must have made it inconvenient at times. A must read for any one wanting to relive or research the flavour of the past decade."

– Montek Singh Ahluwalia, Director, Indpendent
Evaluation Office, IMF, Washington

"Jairam's articles are excellently researched, clearly and pointedly written and are really first-rate. In some ways, the articles are quite unique in India and are world-class. They show a superb thinker, practioner and co-communicator at work."

– Bimal Jalan, Governer, Reserve Bank of India

vii

"(T)hese are some of the best-informed, cogently-reasoned and most outstanding personalities in Indian public life. Jairam lights up Indian politics and economics and how he keeps up with such a range of issues with consistent brilliance, I always wonder !"

– Arun Shourie
Hon'ble Union Minister for Dis-investment

"The only Indian writer currently writing a world class column with an internationalist perspective..."

– Nayan Chanda, Center for the Study of globlization,
Yale University

"It is utterly refreshing to read a column so full of thought, brilliance and reflection every week..."

– Ashutosh Varshney,
Director, Centre for South Asian Studies
University of Michigan

"Beyond the specific circumstances of the subcontinent, Mr.Ramesh's argument captured well a wider sentiment. India, like many countries..... wants to rebuff or keep at bay American pressure or influence."

"The Economist"
Global Survey on America's world trade
June 29th, 2002

CONTENTS

I. Macro Economy: The Big Picture

A. *Growth*

B. *Employment*

C. *Poverty*

D. *Inflation*

E. *Trade*

ix

II. Public Finances: India's Edifice Complex

A. *Centre*

B. *States*

III. Farms and Factories: Hot Air, Cold Facts

A. *Agriculture*

B. *Public Sector*

V. In Praise of Federalism: The State of the States

VI. Partisan Politics: Prayer to a Jogi

VII. Foreign Relations: Not For the Birds

A. Americas

B. China

C. East Asia

D. Europe

E. Pakistan

X. Notables: Men & Matters

XI. Different Takes

A First Word

This book is a collection of the weekly columns I wrote for *India Today* between April 1998 and April 2002.

In December 1997, I had quit as Adviser to the then Finance Minister P. Chidambaram and joined the Congress Party as a full-time apparatchik. Looking for legitimate sources of income — a contradiction in terms in Indian politics perhaps — I casually asked my friend Prabhu Chawla who was then *India Today's* Executive Editor whether I could start writing for the magazine. He told me that there were already two "star" columnists—Tavleen Singh and Mani Shankar Aiyar—and that to accommodate a third might be difficult. Nevertheless, he still promised to try.

In March, 1998 Prabhu got back to me and asked me to start writing from April. I never asked him what prompted him to agree to my request after his initial hesitation. I was a bit nervous since this would be the first time I would be writing for a diverse audience. Previously, I had written a weekly column for *Business Standard* (1994-96) and a fortnightly column for *Business Today* (1995-96) but the readership of that newspaper and magazine, though restricted, was specialised and professional. *India Today*, by contrast, catered to a wide variety of tastes and its readership, though large, was basically lay as far as economics was concerned. At least, that was my perception.

Prabhu told me just one thing: don't write like a Congressman. I said that it was not my intention to do so and that I would even differ with my party if the need arose. As it turned out, this policy frequently landed me in trouble with the party "High Command". Prabhu and I also agreed that I would, as far as possible, stick to economics, although he did want me to occasionally write on political issues. I then had to find a name for the column. For years, as an addict of *The Economist*, I had dreamt of writing a Bagehot, a Lexington or a Charlemagne. But the format in that magazine is different: a columnist's name never appears unless it is by special invitation. Even so, I felt that it was important to create a "brand". I asked Prabhu's colleague and the resident wit of *India Today*, Sumit Mitra for ideas. He immediately suggested *Kautilya*.

I then went back and had a fresh look at L.N. Rangarajan's master-piece of editing, translation and commentary: *Kautilya's The Arthashastra*. Rangarajan writes that the *Arthashastra* is the most comprehensive and earliest available treatise on statecraft of classical times. It deals with economics in its widest sense. It is a practical work and its author's view is always sane, moderate and balanced with his advice rooted in *dharma*. Rangarajan emphasises that Kautilya was not only an original thinker but he was a great teacher as well. Re-reading Rangarajan, an IFS officer-turned academic, I was more than convinced that the column should be called *Kautilya* (even though Kautilya when referred to by his other name of Chanakya is often derided as a wily Brahmin!)

I have been fortunate that *Kautilya* has received an enthusiastic reception in many parts of the world. That is a tribute to *India Today's* awesome reach and credibility. I would often get letters asking me to put together all the columns in one volume. In September 2001, my young friend Rahul Sagar who considers himself as my protégé of sorts put together a website to bring together these columns in one place. The website proved to be very popular and one common subsequent request was for such a book. Mahesh Rangarajan, one of India's sharpest political commentators, Arunabha Ghosh one of the most promising students of international relations at Oxford, Karthik Muralidharan a brilliant economics student at Harvard, and Pavan Ahluwalia who is keeping the Ahluwalia dynasty in economics alive, all put pressure on me to complete the book. Shashank Jaitley provided valuable technical assistance toward this end and I am also grateful for his tremendous support with the website. Furthermore, Ashok Malik and Babar Zaidi, both with India Today, were sounding boards during the period I wrote these articles and vastly improved their readability. I am privileged and grateful to have Jagdish Bhagwati associated with this volume. He has been a *guru* in more respects than one ever since we met at MIT over two decades ago.

A book of columns is necessarily dated and is therefore never popular with publishers. But Anuj Bahri who runs one of Delhi's best and most visited bookshop in Khan Market, *Bahrisons,* is clearly an exception and welcomed this idea very positively. I may have written the columns but it is Rahul Sagar now a doctoral student in political philosophy at Harvard University *in international relations* who put it together. Without him, this collection would not have materialised. He is, in many ways, the *sutradhar* of this volume.

I wrote the column for the general public. Many articles may therefore appear low-brow for the specialist, but I make no apologies for this because I was always thinking of the reader in Tiruppur or Chandigarh when writing, and not of the pundits in Delhi. Moreover, writing a 830-word column on complex contemporary issues demands discipline and forces you to focus on the essentials. Many of the columns therefore deserve a more lengthy treatment but I leave that task to others better qualified than myself.

Finally, the columns have not been re-written. They have been regrouped into broad themes and are not presented chronologically. I was advised that the latter option would not "sell", but I was keen to preserve the flavour of the times which provided the backdrop to the columns. Each column took an issue of political economy that was current then and made a comment. Much against the advice of my young friend and the publisher himself, the columns appear here as they did originally. I hope the reader vindicates my choice.

Kautilya is now a fortnightly column in *The Times of India*.

Jairam Ramesh
New Delhi
June 2002

xix

I

Macro Economy : The Big Picture

This section has five broad themes: growth, employment, poverty, inflation and trade. Trade issues reappear in a later section on international institutions where I deal with the WTO, a subject on which there is much misunderstanding both here and abroad.

The growth articles both celebrate and criticise India's growth performance, especially in the 1990s. The four articles on poverty consider the debate that has taken place over the past two years on the official poverty estimates. While the debate remains incomplete, I have tried to greatly simplify the technical issues underlying the debate in order to make this important matter more accessible to the general public. Similarly, the controversy over the employment numbers refuses to die down. I have written about the Montek Ahluwalia report that was attacked by George Fernandes and disowned by the Planning Commission of which Ahluwalia was a member when he presented his analysis. The article on McJobs—an allusion to low-paid, casual jobs in the services sector—invited considerable comment from economists such as K. Sundaram and sociologists like Gail Omvedt.

The inflation piece – *Core to RBI, Sore to Others* – evoked responses from the Reserve Bank of India (RBI) and I got a nice letter from Bimal Jalan himself agreeing with my findings. The article on gold in the trade sub-section is important since I believe one of the most significant steps taken in the 1990s has been the liberalisation of gold imports. This has destroyed the black market and brought in a large volume of workers' remittances from overseas into the official banking channel. It is no surprise that "invisibles" earnings in the balance of payments account show a very large spurt from 1997 onwards.

A. Growth

BLINKERED VISION 30/60
Understanding BJPnomics:
NAG's goal okay—but numbers don't add up

The BJP-led Coalition's first intellectual missile, NAG (National Agenda for Governance) is loaded with philosopmhical paydirt that is guaranteed to send all intended victims into a state of stupor. But somehow, two very pin-pointed warheads have sneaked in. NAG calls for a 30 per cent domestic savings rate and 60 per cent plan investment in agriculture and rural development. What to make of this 30/60 vision?

Investment comes from savings. Growth arises out of investment. Equity is sustained through growth. This is the simplest reason why savings rates matter. Yet, India's fundamental problem now is not low savings but inefficient investment. South Korea grew twice as fast as India in the '60s and '70s, even though the savings rate in the two countries was identical. Our methodology for estimating savings is deeply flawed. For example, official figures for household savings do not include assets like jewellery and gold. Even so, India's overall savings rate of about 25 per cent of GDP is remarkable for a poor country. At around 19 per cent of GDP, our household savings rate is comparable to that prevailing in east Asia. Our private corporate savings rate is rising and is currently around 4 per cent of GDP.

The villain is public and government sector savings. This is what differentiates India from countries that have high investment and high growth rates. Public saving is less than 2 per cent of GDP, with the savings of government administration actually close to -3 per cent of GDP—hence the use by economists of that awful term, "dissavings". What is needed, therefore, is a strategy for increasing public savings. Without this, we will just not be able to increase investment levels in the economy. There is absolutely no evidence to suggest that conventional fiscal incentives actually result in increased savings rates. The payoffs are greater if we concentrate on boosting public savings through privatisation, full commercialisation of railways, posts and telecommunications, better recovery of costs in power, irrigation, higher education and transport and a cut in the size of the government at all levels. Politics will undoubtedly influence the course of public savings. In the short term, there may well be electoral setbacks to chief ministers who pursue fiscal reform seriously. N. Chandrababu Naidu, J.B. Patnaik, Bhairon Singh Shekhawat and Bansi Lal—all of whom have been pursuing tough fiscal policies—have been badly bruised in the recent elections. Political management will thus be the key to sustaining such reforms.

But there is another route for boosting savings that does not depend so critically on the vagaries of electoral politics. This is bolder and faster financial liberalisation. The monopoly of LIC and GIC must be broken. The pensions and insurance industry must be opened up to new players. UTI should be reorganised to inject effective competition in the mutual funds industry. The provident fund system must be reformed in a manner that provides alternatives to the existing fully funded, defined-contribution schemes. Accelerated financial liberalisation and increased public savings will help take domestic savings rates to over 30 per cent of GDP. Also, increased GDP growth itself will increase savings rates. And in the short term, a doubling of the current level of foreign investment inflow will bring investment rates to around 30 per cent of GDP.

The other NAG figure—60 per cent of public investment in agriculture and rural development—makes no sense. Is it public investment in agriculture and rural development, narrowly defined? Or is it public investment in a whole range of rural-oriented activities that go beyond agriculture and traditional rural development and also include irrigation, rural power, rural education, rural health, rural water supply, rural roads and rural communications? If we go by what NAG says, then we will see a jump from something like 15 per cent to 60 per cent. This is untenable, even unwise, given the competing demands on public investment. However, if we interpret NAG in terms of all public investment in rural areas, then we are already at about 55 per cent, which is perhaps what it should be. Hopefully, this is indeed how Jaswant Singh will redefine what he initially wrote.

Agricultural research and education specially require greater investment. But overall, agriculture has suffered not so much because of insufficient funds but more because industry has been pampered. Ashok Gulati, the noted economist, has shown that industry has enjoyed a 45 per cent tariff protection while agriculture has been taxed at 22 per cent. Unfortunately, NAG is sympathetic to more protection to our corporate zamindars. This is simply inconsistent with its concern for farmers.

Key to getting the maximum out of public investment in rural areas is the financial empowerment of pan-chayat institutions. To begin with, all rural development funds—currently about Rs 8,000 crore a year—must be transferred directly from the Centre to zilla parishads and panchayats. Sadly, NAG is silent on this. Fortunately, this Government has a great champion of panchayats in Ramakrishna Hegde. Given his experience in Karnataka, Hegde now has a historic opportunity: to help energise panchayat bodies, particularly in north India.

13/04/1998

WHY LOW GROWTH
Understanding the roots of Indian industry's woes

Indian Industry has clearly been going through troubled times. Industrial production grew by 8.4 per cent in 1994-95 and by a whopping 12.8 per cent in 1995-96. But thereafter it has been downhill— 5.5 per cent growth in 1996-97, 6.6 per cent in 1997-98 and perhaps no more than 4 per cent in 1998-99. The fall in farm output in 1995-96 and 1997-98 adversely affected industrial demand in 1996-97 and 1998-99 respectively. But the growth in money supply has been such that the constraints on industrial expansion arising out of the decline in farm output have not been as severe as one might expect. So, why the slowdown?

First, the credit squeeze supposedly imposed in late 1995 by the government, battered by an inflation rate of 10.8 per cent in 1993-94 and 10.4 per cent in 1994-95. This argument is not convincing. True, as against an average increase of 16.5 per cent per year between 1990-91 and 1995-96, the increase in bank credit to the commercial sector, however limited a measure of total flows, was just 10.9 per cent in 1996-97 and 15.1 per cent in 1997-98. The fact is by 1995-96, the capital market had begun to sputter.

This meant companies could not raise equity. If they could not bring in money, there was no reason for banks to lend. Banks themselves were under pressure to fund only projects that met global criteria for economic viability. What is probably more valid is that tough action against non-banking financial companies (NBFCs), particularly from 1996-97 onwards, has caused financing problems for specific industries like commercial vehi-cles and consumer goods. Also, the credit-delivery mechanism has choked, what with the bankers' dread of the CBI and the CVC.

Second, high interest rates that persist because of the high fiscal deficit are hurting private investment. This is not persuasive at all. Investment boomed even when interest rates were high and as industrial growth has declined the prime lending rate has also come down from 16.5 per cent to 13 per cent. Nevertheless, even though it has not caused the slowdown, interest rates must reduce. But as long as banks are owned by the government, this will not happen.

Third, import liberalisation. This is a bogus argument. As Montek Singh Ahluwalia shows in a soon-to-be published paper, between 1991-92 and 1995-96, as industrial growth accelerated, the import-weighted average customs duty rate fell from around 87 per cent to 27 per cent—with a depreciation in the real effective exchange rate providing the compensating cushion. Ironically, this average has increased to 30 per cent as industrial growth has slackened. Imports as a proportion of total consumption in many industries have fallen; in steel, it has come down from 9 per cent when industrial growth was at a peak to about 6 per cent now.

Fourth, global deflation and export deceleration. From 1996-97, world export growth and prices began declining and this had its effect on segments of industry. But the roots of export collapse are more domestic than foreign. As long as small-scale reservations continue, India will never emerge as a major exporter in industries that count, like garments and consumer goods. We are even losing market share in growth areas like leather (6.3 per cent to 3.5 per cent), tea (22 per cent to 11 per cent) and drugs (1.2 per cent to 0.5 per cent). The export boom of 1993-96 was largely the result of the two devaluations of July 1991 and the trade liberalisation of 1991-92 that substantially undercut the incentives for under-invoicing of exports. Once that effect petered out, export growth came to a screeching halt. Will another one-shot exchange rate adjustment help? Probably not, since according to the

RBI, the rupee is actually undervalued in relation to the dollar by about 2.5 per cent and the overvaluation with other currencies is just 3-4 per cent.

A fifth explanation for the slow-down is restructuring that is good for investment in the medium-term but has negative effects on growth in the short-term. Corporate India is in the midst of a long overdue phase of clean-up. A good example of this is the ce-ment industry, where 56 companies are producing 91 million tonnes per year. However, the industry profile is changing and in the past 18 months, there have been nine acquisitions worth almost $850 million. Most industrial markets, however, are still far too fragmented. The answer to the excess capacity problem is simply to allow a shake-out and permit exits more freely, albeit humanely. It is also obvious that in a number of consumer industries companies simply underestimated the price sensitivity of the Indian market and overestimated the Indian consumer's willingness to pay a premium for brands.

Finally, industry has been affected by a slackening ingovernment investment programmes at the Centre and, more importantly, in the states. The fiscal deficit has to be cut substantially. But finance ministers must be allowed to do it in an investment-friendly manner. In areas that create demand for industry, like power, irrigation, roads and construction, physical additions to capacity have come down. Private-sector projects have got bogged down. In power, the country added 4,200 MW per year during 1992-95, just 2,124 MW in 1995-96 and 1,624 MW in 1996-97. More than the quantity of state spending, it is the quality that is impeding growth. Governments are spending on the wrong things and demand-stimulating investment has become a casualty. An increase in public spending without structural reforms is not the way out of the morass.

05/04/1999

◆———◆

SAVE MORE GROW MORE
A higher rate of economic growth will be constrained
by the rate of home savings

An Embattled finance minister is thinking bold. In Bangalore on June 5 he talked about going beyond a 7 per cent growth perspective.

On June 6 in Delhi, during his discussions with the visiting IMF chief, he talked of an 8-10 per cent rate of economic growth. But sadly, reality appears to be a little different. In 1998-99, economic growth at constant 1993-94 prices clocked 5.9 per cent. True, 1994-95 saw a 7 per cent growth, 1995-96 7.3 per cent and 1996-97 a peak 7.5 per cent—the first time when we have seen a 7 per cent hat-trick. But it has been downhill since then.

Is this mere quibbling over numbers? The difference between 6 per cent and 8 per cent is, after all, a mere 2 percentage points. But this is not the way to look at it. These are *compound* annual growth rates. Thus, India growing at 6 per cent per year will double its per capita income in 17 years, while this doubling will take 12 years with an 8 per cent growth rate. For a civilisation that has had little respect for time this difference may look trivial but it matters in a most fundamental sense.

No doubt, technology, productivity and efficiency will be crucial to attain a higher growth rate. But we also need a higher rate of investment. And for a higher rate of investment we need a higher rate of savings. Further, given the imperative to keep the current account deficit at about 2 per cent of GDP, domestic savings will be the major determinant of investment even as we take steps to increase the contribution of foreign savings.

The importance of savings rates alone, however, must not be overdone. In 1960, South Korea and India had roughly the same rate of domestic savings. But thereafter, South Korea's growth rate was over twice that of India's. India has suffered less from insufficient savings as much as it has from inefficient investments. There is also new econometric evidence reported in a January 1997 IMF working paper prepared by Martin Muhleisen that the causation goes from growth to savings and not from savings to growth as has been the Indian theology.

Even so, savings rates have to go up. Assuming that in view of the huge infrastructure backlog that has to be met, the incremental capital-output ratio (ICOR) remains at its recent historical average of between 4 and 4.5 (meaning that to generate one extra rupee of output an additional Rs 4-4.50 of investment is needed) the total savings rate has to be between 32 and 36 per cent of the GDP in order to trigger an

8 per cent rate of economic growth and to keep it going. This means the gross do-mestic savings rate has to be at least 30 per cent of the GDP. Compared to this, right now we are floundering. In 1998-99 the gross domestic savings rate had fallen to 22.3 per cent of GDP. The highest has been 25.5 per cent of GDP in 1995-96.

There are three components of the domestic savings rate—household savings, public savings and private corporate savings. Household savings are broken up into household financial savings and household physical savings, while public savings comprise savings of government administration, departmental enterprises like railways and non-departmental enterprises like SAIL, NTPC and other PSUs. As with most of our statistics, savings rate data are severely flawed. For example, the household financial savings do not cover gold and jewellery. Household physical savings are derived as a residual. Household savings include those of small-scale industry, the estimates of which are very difficult to come by. Corporate-sector savings are based on an out-dated sample. Investment estimates are based on outdated production coefficients.

But let us accept the estimates as they are. What has happened in 1998-99 is simply that public savings have fallen to zero from 1.4 per cent of the GDPin the previous year. Thus, increasing public savings is the single most important step to be taken to increase overall savings rates. This is where control of the fiscal and revenue deficits, tax management, privatisation and reduction in the govern-ment's establishment expenditure assume special significance. If the quantity and the quality of the fiscal deficit of both the Central and state governments continue as at present and if high real rates of interest persist, then there will be an investment famine in the country with disastrous consequences for sustained growth. Financial-sector reforms with focus on the provident fund, insurance and pensions market will stimulate greater private long-term savings, as will price stability.

The savings rate has been the hardiest perennial in Indian economic planning. That hallowed status must continue but a whole new perspective on how its halo has to be regained and how it can stimulate an investment boom is called for.

19/06/2000

NOT A FALSE DAWN
Growth and sentiment are recovering,
investment not yet

For the past few weeks, the question uppper-most in the minds of economy watchers in the country has been: is there a sustained economic rebound and are we back on the growth track after almost 36 months of industrial sluggishness? Economy watching reminds Kautilya of the old story of the pessimist who says he cannot imagine anything worse than the present—and the optimist who says he can.

Before giving his verdict, Kautilya wants to enter five lessons of caution. The first is not to look at monthly data. For example, industrial production in October 1998 grew by a measly 0.1 per cent. This was the bottom of the cycle. Octo-ber 1999, therefore, will show a very healthy growth if pre-sent trends continue. It might even be double digit growth. However, this is the low base problem that vitiates comparison of one month in one year with the same month the previous year.

The second lesson is simply not to look at just one or two indicators like diesel consumption or housing finance loans. In May, one pink newspaper blared the headlines that since diesel consumption had increased by 10 per cent in April, the economy was on the mend. The same newspaper kept silent in June and did not comment when diesel consumption fell sharply in May. Similarly, it went to town some weeks back saying that first quarter results of corporate India showed a strong recovery. But just a few days ago it moaned that while sales are up margins are down substantially, wondering whether a recovery is actually on or not. The US has a very sophisticated system of leading indicators that are watched meticulously every month to keep track of what is hap-pening to the economy. The Ministry of Finance has engaged a private research outfit to develop a similar set of leading indicators for India. The work should be complete by December. Industry associations are not of much help since their surveys of business confidence and outlook are too qualitative rather than analytical.

The third lesson is indicators that may have worked in the past will not necessarily still be relevant. Import growth is one of the best indices of buoyancy in our economy. But with what has been happening to the world economy and with the global price deflation in these past few years, we may not witness huge growth in import values even as we record higher growth rates.

The fourth lesson is we must distinguish sentiment from actual performance. Undoubtedly there is a "feel good" factor, particularly among foreign institutional investors who seem to have discounted the future and are betting on it. But there is also a lot of hype as far as sentiment is concerned. True, sentiment will be positive or negative depending on perceptions of future prospects. But the stock market has a peculiar logic and momentum of its own. Even in the US, there is now a revival of the "random walk" hypothesis. This basically says that the stock market does not reflect fundamentals and that the link between economic performance and stock market behaviour is tenuous at best.

The fifth lesson is that we must come to grips with cyclic-ity in performance brought about by changes in the economy's structure. Monsoons and levels of public investment induced earlier cycles, which were of short durations. Now, increasingly, it is private consumption that is driving the eco-nomic cycle. The most recent downturn from peak to nadir lasted 24 months, normal by world standards. This cycle has yet to be fully understood and this is one of the reasons why we have not come up with effective counter-cyclical policies to spur growth these past three years.

With all these caveats, what's the scene? We now have data for the entire first quarter of this financial year and for the entire first half of this calendar year. Kautilya has poured through this data and concludes that a mild recovery is on. With three-month data on production, exports, sales, output of cement, steel, aluminum and com-mercial vehicles, sales of consumer goods like televisions, refrigerators and washing machines, retail invest-ment in mutual funds and tax returns, it can be said with some confidence that we have long passed the bottom of the cycle. However, much as Kautilya has applauded the pragmatism and re-formist intentions and actions of Atal Bihari Vajpayee's government, he will not attribute this to any great skill in economic management. The recovery just had to happen.

Growth has certainly picked up. But investment has not. That is the real cause for worry. Public investment that can stimulate demand and that is needed to sustain both farm and factory growth has reached its limits. This is because of the very structure of government expenditure, both at the Centre and in the states. Private investment is in the doldrums not just because of the demand constraint but also because of high real rates of interest and the moribund primary market. Policy barriers like reservations for small-scale industry and an extremely lackadaisical approach to privatisation are aggravating the investment famine. For its part, Indian industry is now in need of more Nirmas that will radically redefine the price-quality-performance equation and create a whole new generation of consumers.

16/08/1999

INDIA AHEAD OF GERMANY
Between 1996 and 1998, India became the world's fourth largest economy

A pot of good news on India's macro-economy. According to the World Bank's annual data treasure-house *World Development Indicators (WDI)* that has just been released, between 1996 and 1998 India overtook Germany and became the world's fourth largest economy behind the US, China and Japan. At current rates of growth, India will cross Japan in 2010. But the gap with the US and China is large and will remain.

International comparisons of the size of economies are done looking at GNP figures. GNP stands for gross national product and is the broadest measure of a country's income derived from both resident and non-resident sources. GDP or gross domestic product is the value of output of final goods and services produced within a country. GNP is GDP plus the net income earned (by foreigners). When GDP exceeds GNP, it means that, for example, the stock of Indian capital abroad, both human and physical, is less than the capital stock of foreigners in India. In 1998-99, India's GDP was higher than its GNP by a very small 1 per cent. For all purposes other than international comparisons of size and standards of living, GDP is used since it is a more appropriate measure.

However, international comparisons are very tricky. This is because the exchange rates that are used to convert, say Indian data in rupees to the international yardstick currency of the dollar, do not fully reflect differences in relative prices. That is why GNP estimates of countries are converted into globally comparable dollars using what are called purchasing power parity (PPP) rates. The World Bank calculates these PPP conversion factors from price surveys that are conducted once in every five years by various international agencies. The last such survey was completed in 1996. A PPP dollar will buy the same basket of goods and services all over the world. Although for some reason, the *WDI* does not report it, the ratio of India's PPP rate to the dollar exchange rate works out to around 22 in 1998; this means that a bundle of goods and services that cost $100 in the US cost only $22 in India in that year. When conventional GNP figures are used, India ranked 11th in the world in 1998, up from 14th position in 1996. But when PPP dollars are used, the picture changes dramatically. India's position jumps to 4th in 1998. In 1998, China too has jumped upwards from 7th rank based on GNP to second position based on GNP (PPP).

Why should countries like India and China stand to gain from PPP comparisons? Very simply because the price of services, called "non-tradeables", is very low, both relatively and absolutely, in our countries. Steel and fertilisers are classic tradeables. These can either be produced at home or purchased from abroad. But what about a haircut? This is a quintessential textbook case of a non-tradeable since we neither import barbers nor do we go abroad for haircuts. Restaurants, education and healthcare are other examples of non-tradeable services. In general, most manufactured goods and commodities are tradeable, while most services are non-tradeables, although this is changing and services is one area of our global strength . Prices of these services are very low in developing countries both in relation to that in richer countries and to the price of tradeables in the developing nations themselves.

Why should this be so? In a classic *Economic Journal* article written in 1984, Jagdish Bhagwati argued that poor countries have more labour relative to capital. This labour is cheaper and is used intensively in providing non-tradeable services. As a result, services are cheaper in coun-tries like India than in the US. Another explanation is that of Paul Samuelson and Bela Balassa who say that in countries like India, the productivity of labour in the tradeables sector is lower than in countries like the US. This means lower wages in poor countries that, in turn, results in lower price of non-tradeables.

Even though it is a step forward, the PPP has its own drawbacks. It has also become the object of some analytical amusements. *The Economist* generates a quarterly Big Mac Index where currency strengths are calculated based on PPP principles—the common basket being the standard MacDonald's hamburger! Alas, the Big Mac is not sold in

India and hence we have to make do with using the Maharaja Mac as a surrogate. When this is done, it turns out that the rupee is undervalued in relation to the dollar by a whopping 57 per cent whereas according to the RBI the undervaluation currently is just 2 per cent. This is , perhaps, more a reflection of MacDonald's marketing strategy and the structure of our fast food industry than of macroeconomic fundamentals!

29/05/2000

◆——◆

THE MOMENTUM OF DRIFT
The economy is now suffering from the QSQT effect—Quarter Se Quarter Tak

Remember tl e hit hindi filim of the late 1980s—Qayamat Se Qayamat Tak, popularly known as QSQT. The economy is going through what can be called the QSQT effect—quarter se quarter tak. The summer of hope has become the winter of gloom. Compared to the first quarter last year when real GDP growth was 6.9 per cent, this year's first quarter (April-June) has seen 5.8 per cent growth. Of course, it is entirely possible that these figures will be re-vised later but for now the gospel is that the economy has lost its fizz. But a 6 per cent growth being defined as a slowdown is a remarkable tribute to the new level of as-pirations created by the reforms programme.

It is a mixed picture. Exports are growing very healthily and the current account deficit is in a safe zone. Overall tax collections, particularly those of direct taxes, are buoyant. Housing finance trends are robust. Current bank credit growth is over 20 per cent. The inflation rate has gone up as a result of in-evitable hikes in administered prices but it is not spinning out of control. Tough decisions on telecom deregulation and particularly on oil prices have been taken by the Government. New private insurance companies have finally been given the green signal.

But on the flip side, the monsoon has been less than normal in six states, industrial production appears to have slumped even after allowing for statistical aberrations, interest rates have increased across the board and the rupee has depreciated vis-a vis the dollar by almost 5 per cent since April 1, 2000. Investment continues to be extremely sluggish and business sentiment is unusually depressed.

The response of industry has been predictable: increase import duties; speed up privatisation and increase government spending. Of these three, the most dubious is the recommendation relating to import duties. In fact, it could well be argued looking at the data that the Indian economy has moved to a lower growth path since 1997-98 precisely from a time when the downward trend in import duties was reversed first under P. Chidambaram and later by Yashwant Sinha. Moreover, when the rupee depreciates, imports immediately become costlier giving protection to domestic producers.

As far as privatisation is concerned, A.B. Vajpayee's Government has taken bold steps although only one deal relating to the sale of Modern Foods to Hindustan Lever has been consummated so far. Many more transactions are on the anvil but these must go through the process of due diligence. There is no point short-circuiting this process and giving privatisation a bad name just to deal with some short-term hiccups. And while on privatisation, the government cannot escape its responsibility for eroding the market value of a number of blue-chip PSUs by half-baked pronouncements and actions.

The third option is the standard Keynesian prescription for reviving an economy during a depression. But we are not in a depression. Keynes' solution of more govern-ment spending was made when governments in the West followed conservative fiscal and balanced budget policies. What he would have recommended in a situation when an economy's overall fiscal deficit is around 10 per cent of the GDP is something worth speculating about. Former RBI governor C. Rangarajan put it well in his JRD Tata Memorial Lecture in Delhi in July 1988: the argument that borrowing by the public sector for the purpose of capital expenditure which create assets is not harmful, loses much of its validity in India, since the rate of returns on these assets is nowhere near the interest rate paid on the borrowings. Government spending on infrastructure like power, roads, irrigation, railways and housing must undoubtedly increase. But it cannot as long as government expenditure is consumed by salaries, pensions, subsidies, bailouts and debt servicing. Neither the Central budget nor the state budgets can sustain any increase in investment expenditure. Thus, additional public investment in infrastructure must come from re-structuring existing government expenditure consistent with the need to reduce both the fiscal and specially the revenue deficit.

In developed countries, interest rates are raised to cool overheating or lowered to revive decelerating economies. We have yet to reach that stage. But we must move faster towards creating a framework that allows interest rates to be used as an instrument of macro-economic management. Meanwhile, what can be done to deal with QSQT pains is to maintain an overall policy stance to keep sentiment bullish. Vajpayee has allowed drift to gather momentum. It is this, more than anything else, that is causing nervousness. It is not enough to like business. You have to be business-like to be taken seriously and for investment psychology to be positive.

06/11/2000

GLOBAL COOLING NOT WARMING
India's message—don't do anything, nothing will go wrong—can't continue

Hardly has the dust settled on the debate over global warming kicked up by the US's withdrawal from the Kyoto Protocol than we are in the vortex of what is being called "global cooling". This has also raised fears of a contagion of the type that rocked the global economy during 1998-99.

In the quarter ending June this year, the US GDP grew at a seasonally adjusted annual rate (that is, over the same quarter in 2000) of a measly 0.7 per cent, the slowest in the past eight years. The "deepest investment slump in a generation" has intensified and personal consumption growth has also slackened. The US slowdown is having its most direct impact on east Asia—Singapore, Malaysia, Indonesia, Philippines, Hong Kong, Taiwan and South Korea. Forty per cent of their exports to the US are IT-related. These countries do have a healthy level of foreign exchange reserves and are running current account surpluses. But currencies are taking a sharp tumble and growth forecasts have been slashed. To make matters worse, Japan, the world's second largest economy, continues to be in the doldrums.

Meanwhile, Argentina totters, weighed down by a continuing recession and huge fiscal deficits. Its woes are beginning to have an impact on Chile and on Brazil, which had been bailed out just two years ago. The country's currency, the real, has depreciated in value by almost a quarter over the past six months. When a currency loses value sharply, the value of dollar-denominated debt increases. In addition since governments seek to prevent the slide by boosting interest rates, the economy also slows and prices shoot up. Mexico may escape the ill-winds from Argentina but it is unlikely to be insulated from the American deceleration.

Gloom is spreading in Europe as well and Germany, its motor, is expecting no more than a 1-1.3 per cent growth this year. Russia which grew at 8 per cent in 2000 has been unable to sustain that pace. Poland looks vulnerable. Turkey is also in dire straits with a plum-meting lira, runaway inflation, weak banks, spiralling real interest rates and a huge debt to be serviced. Turkey is in a peculiar bind. Its policies have drawn appreciation from the IMF but the markets have been unimpressed. In an unprecedented move, the outgoing deputy managing director of the IMF, the redoubtable Stanley Fischer, made a public appeal on July 13 to markets to take positive note of what Turkey is achieving. But it is not just markets which have reacted Turkey's most respected economists, Oktay Yenal, who incidentally had a long association with India while he was with the World Bank, dubbed the IMF as the Irresponsible Monetary Fund for what he calls the dubious analyses and cavalier changes in policy prescriptions.

The only robust performer is China which keeps going on its 7-8 per cent growth trajectory buoyed by booming domestic demand, deep reforms and an export basket comprising largely of consumer goods which, unlike that of its east Asian counterparts, is not as vulnerable to the business cycle in the US. But even though China's growth continues unabated, it will not, for some years at least, be able to fill the regional and global gap caused by Japan's sclerosis. With a good monsoon, India will probably clock a 5-6 per cent plus rate of economic growth this year. But what is most worrisome is that Indian industry is in the midst of a severe growth slowdown since December 1999, with the growth rate declining for six consecutive months to May 2001. However, it is being spared the Turkey and Argentina-type disasters mainly due to five factors: the structure of our for-eign debt and its magnitude (as a proportion of the GDP and of exports) are dramatically different and the volatile short-term debt as a pro-portion of foreign exchange reserves is vastly lower; the overwhelming pro-portion of portfolio (FII) capital is in equities; the current account deficit is under control not only due to software exports and remittances but also because of growth stagnation; our exchange-rate management strategy of a "dirty float" has been very pragmatic; and we still retain a variety of controls on the free entry and exit of capital, specially for domestic residents.

But the fact is also that the anaemic pace of reforms itself may have protected India from any "external" collapse. But this external/ internal dichotomy should not be overdone; for example, the failure to sustain import liberalisation is impacting on industrial growth. The conse-quences of homoeopathic reforms in UTI, IDBI, IFCI and other financial institutions are also unfolding. And for how long can we ignore the serious crisis caused by stagnant investment in physical and social infrastructure on account of astructure of public expenditure that bears no relation to pressing socio-economic concerns and challenges?

13/08/2001

◆——◆

NO RESPITE IN SIGHT
The Indian economy was in slowdown mode
well before September 11

India has been showing signs of a growth-fatigue. In the four quarters of 1999-2000, inflation adjusted GDP growth rates averaged 7.3 per cent, 6.2 per cent, 6.1 per cent and 6 per cent. In 2000-01 these numbers were 6.1 per cent, 6.2 per cent, 5 per cent and 3.8 per cent. The latest news for the first quarter of 2001-02 (April-June) is still gloomy with real GDP growth averaging just 4.4 per cent. The fallout of September 11 will make life more tough. The macro-economic impact will be transmitted via five main channels—trade, equity investment, capital flows, exchange rate and oil prices.

Since our exports constitute about 10 per cent of the GDP, of which around a fifth are to the US, we are certainly not as badly off as countries like Malaysia, Taiwan and South Korea. But if American consumer confidence remains low, India will not remain unaffected. Already, there have been some reports of buyers from New York, which is the hub of the US garment pro-curement network, cancelling orders from India. However, it is safe to assume that the Bush Administration will go out of its way to boost sentiment by tax cuts and by "pump priming" through additional expenditure on construction in New York and on defence. In addition, the US Federal Reserve has continued on its aggressive interest rate cutting spree and the key rate is now down to 2.5 per cent. A matter of special concern to us is whether the US outsourcing to Indian software companies would decline. There are fears that the growth rate of soft-ware exports would halve in 2001-02 to 15-18 per cent. There are also concerns that some companies would cut billing rates. This would be disastrous when the recovery takes place, realistically, in the latter half of 2002.

Equity investment or foreign direct investment (FDI) is not influenced by short-term considerations. If we provide lucrative market opportunities and world-class infrastructure and if we are perceived to be a safe place to invest, investors will come. More than September 11, FDI prospects will be influenced by how we are seen to be handling Enron in Maharashtra and AES in Orissa. Regulatory uncertainty and the perception of "rule rigging" by politically savvy Indian companies are deterring foreign investors in telecom. Elsewhere, privatisation has brought in large FDI. But in India privatisation is stuck, for which the primary blame lies with the Centre itself.

Portfolio capital inflows through foreign institutional investors (FIIs) come into the stock market over-whelmingly as equity investments. The calendar year 2001 has been a bumper year with about $2.6 billion coming in so far compared to $1.5 billion in 2000. However, in September 2001, FIIs sold more than they purchased, the difference being about $113 million. December 2000 was the last month that witnessed such a trend. Here again, if the perceptions of the regulatory process remain negative and given their compulsions to mobilise cash, FIIs could start taking money out. Already, Janus, a major FII, has started liquidating its India portfolio in very large measure.

The exchange rate is a matter of demand and supply. Demand for dollars being what it is for a growing economy like ours, any downward pressure on the supply of dollars will drive up their value and would mean a depreciation of the rupee. Since September 11, the ru-pee has fallen by about 1.2 per cent in relation to the dollar. The RBI will certainly intervene to prevent any precipitous fall in the rupee's value vis-a-vis the US dollar. But there are limits to such interventions as Brazil dis-covered to its chagrin three years ago.

Barring a spike for a day or two after September 11, oil prices have actually fallen by about $6 a barrel in the past three weeks. The prospect of a global recession is putting downward pressure on oil prices. OPEC has repeatedly stated its intention to maintain prices in the $22-28 a barrel band and is meeting on November 14 to decide on its strategy. Saudi Arabia has undoubtedly played a key role in ensuring that the oil markets are not turbulent. The geopolitics of Central Asia has changed dramatically after September 11 and the entry of Caspian oil and gas into world markets could have a salutary impact.

In his address to the nation on September 14, Prime Minister A.B. Vajpayee promised tough measures to revive the economy. The only "tough" decision his Government has taken so far was when on September 18 it gave an unwarranted bonanza to Central government employees and pensioners as cost-of-living adjustment with effect from July 1, 2001. The additional expenditure in 2001-2 on account of this fiscally retrograde move will be about Rs 791 crore. The result will be further erosion of the already fragile capacity of the Government to boost investment spending. We can then bid goodbye to any sustained economic recovery.

15/10/2001

—◆——◆—

GAIN IN PAIN
The global economy is in serious trouble but India should move ahead boldly with reforms

The world economy is passing through very turbulent times. But there are some silver linings—a new round of trade liberalisation is to be launched, inflation is low, interest rates are declining, many budgets are in balance, equity markets are showing signs of hope, oil prices are depressed, exchange rate regimes are becoming more flexible and, barring Argentina, emerging market volatility appears to be in check. But all these are over-shadowed by the dark clouds of recession.

Technically, a national recession is defined as two con-secutive quarters (six months) of declining economic output as measured by inflation-adjusted (real) GDP. There is no accepted definition of a world recession since some countries can be in a recession while others could be growing and overall, the world eco-nomy could show positive growth rates. That is what is happening now with the US, Japan and Europe dragging world growth rates down and China, India and Russia pushing them up. On balance, the orld economy may still show a positive 1-2 per cent growth in calendar years 2001 and 2002, a growth performance previously seen in 1975, 1982 and 1991.

The last time the world economy was in recession in the sense of a negative growth was in the depression-hit 1930s. A more accurate description of what is happening in the world now is a "synchronised downturn" in the Big Three—the US, Japan and Europe—and a "growth recession" in the global economy. Actually, Japan has been a write-off for the past decade. So what we have to worry about are the other two, specially the US which is the engine of world growth. It will be a time before China replaces Europe and Japan as the rear engine.

A recent International Monetary Fund paper, "The Impact of US Economic Growth on the Rest of the World: How Much Does It Matter?" by Vivek Arora and Athanasios Vamvakidis quantifies the US role. In 2000, US GDP was equivalent in size to about a third of world GDP measured at market exchange rates. The US accounted for nearly a quarter of the expansion during 1992- 2000. However, this analysis captures only part of the overall impact on growth since it is confined to merchandise trade. The influence of investment and capital flows, stock-market performance and business confidence and sentiment is not included in such an analysis. Even so, countries like Canada, Mexico, Malaysia, Singapore and South Korea are crucially dependent on US growth. India is much less so since its overall exposure to the US is around 4 per cent of GDP.

In the third quarter of 2001, US real GDP registered a decline of 0.4 per cent and it is widely expected to repeat this performance during October-December 2001 as well confirming that it is indeed in a recession after a decade of unprecedented expansion. GDP data is available only quarterly and continually revised. That is why th : Cambridge (US)-based National Bureau of Economic Research, which tracks business cycles, looks at monthly indicators specially on employment. By this measure, the US is already in a recession and in October alone it lost about 415,000 jobs, although that month's joblessness rate of 5.4 per cent was the same as the figure registered in December 1996.

Why is America in recession? September 11 is not the cause. The real reason is the overinvestment and overbor-rowing spree of the

1990s that could not be sustained. Unrealistic forecasts of productivity growth created an atmosphere of "irrational exuberance". In a way, therefore, the current slowdown is a welcome corrective to the excesses of the 1990s. The expectation of most analysts is that the US economy will show signs of recovery by the second half of 2002. The Bush Administration will use both fiscal and monetary policy aggressively to ensure that this indeed happens, although its predilection fortax cuts instead of public spending could blunt the efficacy of the stimulus package. There are two other worries. First, the volume of international trade is not expected to grow in the next year. This could intensify the effect of a recession. Second, when real GDP and inflation are falling as at present, nominal GDP growth also plummets. This increases fears of a deflation and raises the spectre of the 1930s. Paul Krugman, the celebrated economist, in his 1999 book, *The Return of Depression Economics*, wrote that while the world economy may not be in a depression, depression economics has staged a stunning comeback.

For India, while we need to be concerned about the global economy, it is not disaster or devastation time. Of course, the world slowdown will be used by the government as an alibi for our growth deceleration. But the present pause gives India yet another opportunity to push through its domestic reforms agenda and restore its growth momentum.

26/11/2001

B. Employment

JOBS AND INDIANS
Ten million new jobs a year? Perhaps more, with the right policies.

The creation of 10 million jobs a year has become a mantra for all political parties. Are we on track Data on employment in India comes from two sources—the decennial census and the quinquennial estimates of the National Sample Survey (NSS). The most recent census information was obtained in 1991 and the most recent NSS survey is for 1993-94.

The Planning Commission uses this data to calculate what economists call employment-GDP elasticities—the statistical relationship between growth in output and in employment—for different sectors of the economy. The elasticities are then used to project employment, based on anticipated GDP growth rates. Using this method, it transpires that between 1978 and 1983 the economy created, annually, about five and a half million jobs. This increased to an average of about seven million per year between 1983 and 1994 and to around 10 million between 1994 and 1997. The conclusion is clear. The daunting employment challenge can be met only if the GDP and export growth recorded in 1994-95, 1995-96 and 1996-97 is maintained.

What is the level of unemployment in the country? According to the NSS data, the unemployment rate as understood and de-fined internationally is 2 per cent of the labour force. As on April 1, 1997, the Planning Commission estimate was 1.9 per cent. But traditional concepts of unemployment have little relevance in India. The bulk of the workforce here is self-employed and largely (65 per cent) in agriculture. That is why underemployment is also estimated by the NSS. In 1993-94, this affected 8.6 per cent of the labour force. Underemployment, however, seems to have declined sharply. The 1993-94 level was about half that in 1978. Nationally, 60 per cent of the increase in employment is coming from agriculture. But in states like Gujarat, Haryana, Kerala, Punjab, Maharashtra and West Bengal, non-agricultural activities are the real job creators. Four factors have contributed to the growth of employment in recent times.

Agricultural growth is high in the resource-rich but laggard region east of Kanpur. This area has high emloyment elasticity in agriculture. Its share in incremental foodgrain output has doubled since the mid-'80s. However, it still suffers from weak physical and financial infrastructure, untapped irrigation potential and incomplete land reforms.

The non-farm rural sector has been dynamic. It already accounts for a quarter of rural employment. Now it also absorbs three-fourths of the new entrants into the rural labour force. Output in unregistered manufacturing has grown at almost double the rate than in registered manufacturing. The fast-growing export sectors of garments, diamond cutting and polishing and leather processing are largely in the unregistered sector. The bad news is in the past two years, export growth has all but collapsed. Since the mid-'80s, there has been sub-stantial investment in special rural em-ployment programmes like the Jawahar Rozgar Yojana (JRY). Today, the outlay for such schemes is Rs 5,000 crore.

In its Ninth Plan document, the Planning Commission has analysed the regional dimensions of unemployment over the next decade. Category I includes Andhra Pradesh, Gujarat, Haryana, Karnataka, Maharashtra, Tamil Nadu and West Bengal. These show de-creasing unemployment and low growth of labour force. Category II includes Assam, Madhya Pradesh and Orissa. These show decreasing unemployment and high growth of labour force.

Category III includes Kerala and Punjab. These show increasing unemployment and low growth of labour force. Category IV includes Bihar, Uttar Pradesh and Rajasthan. These show increasing unemployment and high growth of labour force. States in categories III and IV are clearly a priority. The popular belief is that illiterates predominate among the unemployed. This explains the emphasis on programmes like the JRY. However, the 1991 census revealed almost 47 per cent of those jobless had finished secondary school. The NSS put this figure at 64 per cent. To see it another way, a quarter of those registered with em-ployment exchanges are graduates.

This reflects a fundamental mismatch between what the educational system supplies and what the economy demands. Vocational and technical education needs massive inputs from the private sector. Existing labour laws which are hampering faster job-creation in industry need to be modified. Trade policy reforms must remove all biases against labour-intensive activities.

The vitality of financial institutions and easy access to venture capital can facilitate new jobs in small enter-prises and in the self-employed sector. Technology has made decentralised production economically viable. The key barometer of growth is productive employment. The challenge of generating 10 million jobs year after year is formidable. Since the mid-'80s, the economy has been generating close to eight million jobs annually. India can do better; in fact, it must.

17/08/1998

Sick Solutions
A humane exit policy will actually benefit labour

The big B has been much in the news these past few days with the problems he has been having repaying the Rs 12 crore he owes Canara Bank. Amitabh Bachchan has followed in the footsteps of many of India's top industrialists who, when faced with mounting debts, simply get themselves declared what is called a "BIFR case". Once you get this stamp, you are free from the clutches of your creditors. In this instance, a judge of the Bombay High Court in his interim judgement of April 26 ruled that since ABCL, the Big B's collapsed enterprise, has already approached the Board for Industrial and Financial Reconstruction (BIFR), Canara Bank couldn't take possession of Bachchan's mansion in Mumbai. If you ever wonder why there are no sick industrialists in India while there are sick companies, you have the answer.

The quasi-judicial BIFR came into being in May 1987 under the Sick Industries Companies (Special Provisions) Act, 1985, commonly called SICA. This law was meant to be an instrument of industrial revival. Any company whose net worth has been completely eroded becomes a "sick" company and falls under SICA's purview. BIFR then gets into the act, examines the prospects for revival and suggests a rehabilitation plan where feasible.

Since May 1987, BIFR has accepted 2,404 companies for further scrutiny under SICA, of which 157 are state and Central PSUs. Of these 2,404 companies, 606 have been recommended to the high courts for winding up but only in 40 cases have winding-up notices actually been issued by the courts. In another 637 cases rehabilitation schemes have been approved by BIFR.

SICA has many infirmities. It does not capture incipient sickness. It only embraces the terminally sick as revealed by the fact that less than 10 per cent of the companies scrutinised by BIFR are no longer "sick". BIFR itself has become like a civil court, whereas industrial revival demands a professional and managerial approach. It has become a post-retirement sinecure for government officials. Delays have become endemic and the average delay in BIFR is around 24 months, enough time for influential owners to secure a favourable deal for themselves. Over half of BIFR's winding-up orders have been challenged in the appellate tribunal by managements, showing that the board is seen by industry as an instrument of filibuster and as a trigger for a slew of fiscal incentives.

In May 1997, the United Front (UF) government introduced a whole new bill to replace SICA and facilitate a timely turn-around where revival is possible, quick closure where closure is inevitable and to protect the interests of secured creditors. This bill has many innovative features and alters the definition of bankruptcy to a default on debt in any two quarters out of four. The existing SICA provides for an automatic stay on all legal proceedings. The new bill does away with this open-ended provision.

The BIFR's role in the new legislation is that of a facilitator, which enters the picture only when negotiations between management and secured creditors break down. Thereafter, the bankruptcy procedure is clearly defined and subject to a regimen of transparent rules so that a company exits from BIFR in no more than 150 working days. Unfortunately, this bill has become a victim of political instability and has lapsed. The new government will have to start all over again.

But it is not enough to have a new SICA. Major changes have to be introduced simultaneously in the Companies Act, 1956, as well to quicken the process of liquidation. Sixty per cent of the companies under winding up in courts have been there for over 10 years. Again, the comprehensively new Companies Bill introduced in Parliament by the UF government in November 1997 had far-reaching provisions to transform and expedite liquidation proceedings. But like the new SICA draft, it lost its champion with the departure of P. Chidambaram. Deliberately, he had introduced the new Companies Bill in the Rajya Sabha. This means it is still active and has not lapsed. There are other barriers to faster industrial restructuring. The Urban Land Ceiling Act has prevented companies from disposing of their most valued asset—namely, land—and using the proceeds for golden-hand-shake packages and new economic activity. Fortunately, this Act was repealed by the Centre a few months ago. Now the onus is on the states.

The Industrial Disputes Act—specifically sections 25 and 25-O—while designed to protect labour has actually worked against labour's interests by resulting in illegal shut-downs, lock-outs and haphazard exits. In the absence of a pro-labour exit policy, economist Omkar Goswami has estimated that 35,000 textile workers who lost their jobs in the late '80s were deprived of their terminal benefits and arrears. The conclusion he and Rakesh Mohan, another expert on industrial restructuring, have reached is unambiguous: labour laws in India have resulted in inflexible labour deployment with niggardly compensation. According to a World Bank study, employment security regulations may have caused a 17.5 per cent reduction in employment in India.

An exit policy does not necessarily mean blind hire and fire. Properly designed and humanely executed, it will actually be an essential component of a policy that aims at faster growth, greater employment and industrial renewal—all of which India so very badly needs.

17/05/1999

McJOBS ARE EXPANDING
The latest employment survey throws up both disquieting and encouraging trends

Hardly has the dust settled on the controversy over poverty numbers in the 1990s generated by the surveys of the Central government's National Sample Survey Organisation (NSSO) than the agency's numbers on unemployment are kicking up a storm.

The census done once every 10 years provides reliable data on employment. But the NSSO surveys carried out once every five years are the ones that are more frequently used. The NSSO's most recent survey was for July 1999 to June 2000. The first detailed analysis of the survey's data has been done by India's pre-eminent scholar on employment K. Sundaram of the Delhi School of Economics and was published in the Economic and Political Weekly three weeks back. His main conclusions are that in the 1990s:

- using the most comprehensive measure, the overall unemployment rate—that is, proportion of the labour force unemployed—worsened;
- worker-population ratios —that is, the proportion of the population which is work-ing— reduced sharply, implying that the labour force's growth rate was lower than the population's

growth rate.

- age-specific worker-population ratios also fell considerably in the 5-9, 10-14, 15-19 and 20-24 age groups, indicating that school and college enrolment is up in substantial measure;
- for the first time since Independence, the absolute number of workers in agriculture declined, although its share in total employment is just below 60 per cent;
- barring construction, labour productivity grew significantly, translating into a growth of over 3.2-3.6 per cent a year in average inflation-adjusted wage earnings per worker both in urban and rural India;
- two sectors, (i) construction and (ii) trade, hotels and restaurants, increased their respective shares in the workforce with the latter emerging as the third largest employer, after agriculture and manufacturing.

In India, there is an inverse relationship between poverty and unemployment. The poorest states—Bihar, Uttar Pradesh, Rajasthan and Madhya Pradesh—have the lowest unemployment rates while the relatively better-off and unionised states like Kerala, Tamil Nadu and West Bengal have the highest unemployment rates. This is not surprising for two reasons. First, the poor just cannot afford to remain unemployed for long. Second, the more educated you are, the more choosy you get about the type of employment you want.

Undoubtedly, we can expect to see Sundaram giving more insights as he engages himself in more data-bashing, particularly at the statelevel. In addition, the Centre's Task Force on Employment chaired by Planning Commission member Montek Singh Ahluwalia is expected to submit its report by the end of this month. Given the intellectual prowess of its chairman, the task force's report would definitely be authoritative and will certainly generate much discussion. What it has to say on organised-sector employment will be of special significance. These are jobs that are sought after by all but actually gained by a tiny few—only 7 to 8 per cent of total employment in India is in the organised sector but the pay, privileges and perquisites of this minuscule minority occupies centre-stage of policy and politics. The task force's calculations reveal that organised-sector employment grew by 1.59 per cent per year in the 1980s but fell steeply to 0.86 per cent between 1991 and 1997. The task force attributes this deceleration to the sharp fall in the growth rate in public-sector employment from 2.22 per cent in the 1980s to 0.38 per cent in the 1990s; the growth rate of private-sector employment actually went up from 0.16 per cent to 2 per cent during the same period. The fall in public-sector employment was not compensated by the growth in private-sector employment since the private sector's share in organised-sector employment was only a third. Even so, the experience of the 1990s is reassuring and if rigid labour regulations and laws are liberalised andwe put in place a pro-labour exit policy, the growth in organised private sector jobs will be even more impressive. The lack of a timely and humane exit policy has actually hurt labour and only benefited industrialists—hence, the paradox of a lot of sick industry but no sick industrialist in India.

The task force will come out with a detailed sectoral agenda for accelerating employment growth. At its most aggregate level, India's employment challenge is to generate 10 million jobs every year. A sustained 7-8 per .cent rate of GDP growth is an absolute must. While this will call for an increase of an investment rate by about 3 to 4percentage points to about 29-30 per cent of the GDP, the main focus has to be on increasing investment efficiency. This, more than lower investment rates per se, is our Achilles' heel.

16/04/2001

——◆——◆——

AHLUWALIA'S LABOUR LOST?
The Employment Task Force's report demands urgent attention and action

The report of the planning commission's Task Force on Employment Opportunities, chaired by the distinguished economist Montek Singh Ahluwalia, is now out. This report, intensive in data analysis and extensive in policy recommendations, was prepared by a team that included the late Pravin Visaria and K. Sundaram, two of India's authoritative scholars on employment. Its main message is that employment strategy can no longer be dissociated from the process of accelerating economic growth and bringing about structural changes in the economy.

Based on the five-yearly surveys conducted by the National Sample Survey Organisation, the report conclude that the growth of employment has dropped sharply from 2 per cent per year between

1983 and 1993-94 to less than 1 per cent between 1993-94 and 1999-2000. Does this mean we are having "jobless" growth? Not necessarily, for three important reasons.

First, the growth of the labour force has reduced from 2.3 per cent annually between 1983 and 1993-94 to a little over 1 per cent between 1993-94 and 1999-2000. Unemployment being defined as the proportion of the labour force unemployed, the lower the labour force, higher the unemployment. A smaller labour force particularly in the younger age groups means that more young men and women are in schools and colleges. Second, the growth of total employment has declined mainly because for the first time, farm employment has come down in absolute terms from about 243 million in 1993-94 to about 238 million in 1999-2000. This, too, should not be entirely unwelcome since the essence of growth is to get people out of low-productivity primary-sector occupations to high-productivity industrial and service-sector employment. Third, public-sector employment has also fallen from 19.44 million to 19.41 million be-tween 1993-94 and 1999-2000. But there has been a sharp rise in private-sector employment growth from just 0.45 per cent per year between 1983 and 1993-94 to 1.87 per cent annually between 1993-94 and 1999-2000. These trends, again, are not undesirable in themselves.

Annually, about nine million new jobs have to be created over the next decade. This means that the present rate of productive employment growth has to virtually treble. In addition, the quality of existing employment has to improve significantly. For achieving both these objectives, the report suggests a fivefold strategy:

- Accelerating the GDP growth rate to at least 8 per cent annually, particularly in the populous but poor states, through higher rates of investment and its efficient use, privatisation, infrastructure expansion, financial sector reforms and enhanced credit for the informal sector;
- Pursuing sectoral policies in agriculture, industry and services (that alone will account for 70 per cent of the new jobs), with emphasis on increasing public investment in irrigation, removal of controls on agricultural trade, development of food processing, revamp of small-scale industry and a boost to tourism, IT, construction, housing and real estate, road transport and retail trade;

- Improving the efficiency—with focus on building durable community assets—of special employment-generation schemes for the rural and urban poor on which the Centre spends close to Rs 9,000 crore annually;
- Upgrading the quality of the workforce through a completely revamped and vastly expanded network of technical education, voca-tional training and skill development;
- Ensuring that the policy and legal environment encourages creation of new jobs specially in the organised sector which today accounts for barely 7 per cent of total employment.

Vindicating the early fears of no less a person than the guru of Indian planning P.C. Mahalanobis himself, labour laws have become the biggest impediment to the creation of new jobs. Is it any surprise that Kerala and West Bengal have the highest un-employment rates? The lack of an effective and timely exit policy has only protected industrialists. Reservations for small-scale industry have prevented India from be-coming a global power in labour-intensive mass manufacturing that would, in turn, create millions of factory jobs at home, as it has in China. Special employment pro-grammes do have a crucial role to play but require re-structuring so as to be able to fulfil their objectives. However, when the educated constitute about 60 per cent of the unemployed, the impact of such schemes is limited.

Predictably, the report has drawn flak from leftists and the RSS. The Planning Commission itself finds it too radical. But we ignore the report at our own peril. The prime minister should simply push ahead by building a coalition of chief ministers who have to deliver on jobs, not peddle obsolete ideologies and cling to shibboleths. The author is with the Congress party. These are his personal views. The Employment Task Force's report demands urgent attention and action.

10/09/2001

C. Poverty

REFORMS AND THE POOR
Poverty is still high—but it is declining like never before

Nowhere is poverty so grinding, dehumanising and degrading as in India. It is visible on every street. In these circumstances, to expend intellectual energies in "measuring" what is obvious may appear heartless and in-sensitive. But it is required to get a broad picture of poverty trends and see where we are headed. This is particularly necessary because the popular perception is liberalisation and reforms are increasing poverty.

Two of our technically most accomplished econo-mists—Amaresh Dubey of the North-East Hill University and Shubhashis Gangopadhyay of the Indian Statistical Institute, Delhi—have published the results of 20 months of painstaking study. They have produced what must rank as the most rigorous and detailed study on poverty trends in recent times. Their monograph, Counting the Poor, has been issued by the government after months of wrangling. The delay occurred because the finding that poverty is falling went against the personal convictions of the United Front's Planning Commission. Even now, there is extreme reluctance to give the report wide publicity.

Poverty in India has different dimensions. For example, there is education poverty: over two in five females above the age of seven are illiterate. There is nutrition poverty: three of every five children are underweight and malnourished. The poverty used for policy purposes is "expenditure and consumption poverty". It is estimated through five-yearly surveys of consumer expenditure. These are carried out by the government's National Sample Survey (NSS) Organisation. The poverty line is defined as a level of expenditure incurred by an individual to obtain a certain minimum daily calorie intake. This is 2,435 calories in rural areas and 2,095 in urban ones.

Dubey and Gangopadhyay break with past practice and calculate different poverty lines for rural and urban areas in 25 states and seven Union territories. In terms of monthly consumption expenditure, the average poverty line for rural India in 1993-94 ranges between Rs 186 and Rs 214 and for urban India between Rs 245 and Rs 279.

For the first time, the NSS parted with its raw data—collected for the years 1987-88 and 1993-94. The two economists used this data to estimate different indices of poverty. The simplest of these is the head count ratio: the proportion of people with a monthly expenditure below the minimum stipulated as the poverty line.

The conclusions on magnitudes vary; those on direction don't. In 1993-94, anywhere between 29 and 40 per cent of India was below the poverty line as officially defined. But all indicators of poverty show a decline between 1987-88 and 1993-94. The decline is of the order of about 1.25 per-centage points per year. This is double the rate of decline in the '70s and '80s.

Thus, poverty is declining at a faster rate. But this rate is not good enough. It will take at least another 25 years to bring all Indians above a modestly-defined poverty line. The analysis shows that rural poverty is declining broadly at the same pace as urban poverty. Average per capita expenditure of the poor has gone up by over 3 per cent—after adjusting for inflation. This matches other evidence about improved living standards. Terms of trade are moving in favour of agriculture. Average real wages for unskilled farm labourers have also increased.

For the first time, the number of poor has declined in absolute terms as well—the reduction being over 25 million between 1987-88 and 1993-94. Since 1991-92 was a year when GDP growth was a paltry 0.8 per cent, the magnitude of this achievement becomes even more striking. Moreover, the human face of reforms—for example, increased expenditure on rural development, urban employment programmes and social security schemes—became public only with the 1993-94 budget.

Given India's size and diversity there will always be regional and group variations. Dalits, Adivasis, agricultural and casual labourers are most vulnerable to poverty. Contrary to national trends, poverty has increased in the North-east, the east, Haryana and Himachal Pradesh.

In the North-east, increased migration is surely adding to the poor population. The pace of decline in West Bengal is not very substantial, intriguing given extensive land reforms and rising foodgrain production there.

On the other hand, reduction in the poverty ratio in Rajasthan and Madhya Pradesh have taken place at about double the national rate. This indicates two things. One, the large poverty base in these states to begin with. Two, the positive impact of development programmes.

The next NSS consumption expenditure survey will be ready by July 1999. It will provide data for the crop year 1998-99. If this data is also subjected to independent analysis by professionals like Dubey and Gangopadhyay, then we will be better placed to draw the links between reforms and poverty. Even on the limited evidence so far, it seems clear that reforms are not wors-ening poverty. That, by itself, is a significant conclusion. Hopefully, it will spur even bolder reforms.

27/07/1998

◆━━━◆

POVERTY OF NUMBERS
The debate on poverty numbers is stoked again
but there are no definite trends

An article fitted "Has poverty declined since economic reforms?" published recently in the *Economic and Political Weekly* is causing a flutter since it shows that rural poverty may have increased since 1991. The article is authored by Gaurav Datt, a World Bank economist. Critics of reforms are gloating, while the defenders of the faith have become sullen. Both are wrong.

Datt uses statistical data from the government's National Sample Survey (NSS) Organisation. During the pre-reform period of July 1989-June 1991, 35.37 per cent of the rural population and during the post-reform period of July 1995-December 1997 36.47 per cent of the rural population were estimated to be living below the poverty line. Urban poverty ratios, however, fell from 33.08 per cent to 29.02 per cent over the same period. Datt hedges his case by saying "there is no evidence to suggest that this has been due to an inegalitarian growth process".

All poverty estimates after 1993-94 are based on a "thin" sample of 20,000 households. This "thin" sample is considered unreliable for drawing any definitive conclusions. Every five years, the NSS surveys a larger sample of around 115,000 households. The last year for which data based on this larger sample is available is 1993-94. The next reference point is July 1999-June 2000, the results of which will be out only in December 2000.

Ironically, the World Bank's own annual economic report on India, released five weeks back, admits that "inconsistencies in statistics raise questions about how much of the slower poverty reduction is a statistical artefact". The survey highlights the growing gap between the figures of per capita consumption on which poverty estimates are based, with the NSS indicating a downward trend and the National Accounts Statistics (NAS) revealing just the opposite. Morever, falling per capita consumption, especially of cereals, does not automatically imply growing poverty.

Meanwhile, a detailed analysis of prices and poverty in India till 1993-94 has just been completed by Angus Deaton and Alessandro Tarozzi of Princeton University, US. Officially, rural poverty fell from 39.18 per cent in 1987-88 to 37.21 per cent in 1993-94. Deaton and Tarozzi estimate that the ratio in 1993-94 may well have been 32.94 per cent, showing that rural poverty may have declined at a faster rate than is officially put out. Officially, the estimate is that urban poverty has increased from 22.56 per cent in 1987-88 to 32.62 per cent in 1993-94. The duo calculate that urban poverty may have instead fallen to anywhere between 18.11 per cent and 21.36 per cent. The state-level estimates are also different. For example, Andhra's rural poverty was officially just 16 per cent in 1993-94, the second lowest in the country after Punjab but the Princeton dons show that it may be more than double that figure.

Poverty is very sensitive to price indices. The base year for prices is 1973-74. This is then updated by the Planning Commission using the Consumer Price Index for Agricultural Labour for rural areas and the Consumer Price Index for Industrial Workers for urban India. Both are indices that suffer from many flaws. The commission has now stopped computing all-India poverty lines. It calculates only state-level lines, from which implicit national poverty lines can be deduced. The implicit rural poverty line in 1996-97 was Rs 266, the monthly expenditure each person required for a daily intake of 2,400 calories; in urban areas it was Rs 353 for a daily intake of 2,100 calories.

One factor that may have impacted adversely on rural poverty in the '90s is the slackening in agricultural growth. But if the new GDP data is used, the growth rate does not seem to have decelerated. What has retarded reductions in rural poverty is food inflation—cereal prices increased faster in the '90s at over 10 per cent per year as compared to around 6.4 per cent in the '80s. This inflation was fuelled by huge increases in the minimum support prices for paddy and wheat between 1991 and 1995 and from 1996 to 1998. On the other hand, these increases helped turn the terms of trade in favour of agriculture after a long time.

Sadly, we spend more time quibbling over largely dubious numbers instead of tackling more critical issues like improving the effectiveness of anti-poverty pro-grammes on which the Centre alone spends close to Rs 20,000 crore annually. We also either glorify or vilify liberalisation without appreciating that real social infrastructure-stimulating and poor-oriented fiscal reforms have yet to be launched. Nevertheless, we still need to get a broad fix on the numbers and their trends since they have acquired a great political purpose and dimension.

23/03/2000

◆───◆

NUMBERS OF POVERTY
Four new papers on the movement of the poverty ratio in the 1990s

It is a cruel crime to reduce the poverty issue in the country to a game of largely bogus statistics but since these numbers have acquired great political significance such an exercise is unavoidable.

Kautilya had earlier discussed two papers, one by Shubasish Gangopadhya and Amaresh Dubey ("Reforms and the Poor") and the other by Angus Deaton and Alessandro Tarozzi ("Poverty of Numbers"), both of which had concluded that official statistics are overestimating poverty ratios considerably. These papers had shown how sensitive poverty ratios are to the price indices used. Now come four more studies by very eminent Indian economists.

The first is by Pravin Visaria, now director of the Delhi-based Institute of Economic Growth. Ironically, Visaria is also chairman of the governing council of the Government's National Sample Survey Organisation (NSSO) which carries out the quinquennial consumption expenditure surveys used by the Planning Commission to calculate poverty ratios. Visaria points out that poverty data are based on surveys on food consumption with a recall period of 30 days. Most other countries collect data for consumption seven days preceding the date of survey. To a lay person, this would appear more realistic. For January-June 1998, if the recall period is 30 days then the rural poverty ratio as revealed by the National Sample Surveys (NSS) is 42.6 per cent.

But if the recall period is shortened to seven days then this ratio falls sharply to 23.6 per cent, marginally up, however, from 22.8 per cent in January-June 1994-95. The second paper is by Deepak Lal, Rakesh Mohan and I. Natarajan. Lal is with the University of California, Los Angeles (UCLA) while the other two are with the Delhi-based National Council for Applied Economic Research (NCAER). NCAER has been carrying out MISH—Market Information Survey on Households—since 1985-86. MISH covers three lakh households, almost thrice the size of the "full" NSS. It is a survey of ownership of manufactured goods. It does not collect data on food consumption like the NSS does but it provides income distributions. The poverty ratio "P" is first taken as officially estimated in 1987-88 and then the income level below which "P" lies based on MISH is calculated. According to this, the poverty ratio that was 38.85 per cent in 1987-88 had fallen to 26.2 per cent in 1997-98 as compared to 37.6 per cent revealed by official data. More than the actual ratios, what is important is the trend. The authors also point out that the NSS seriously underestimates non-food consumption expenditure. The third study is by Surjit Bhalla, one of our most rigorous econometricians who now runs his own research outfit in the capital. Bhalla's painstaking analysis shows that in 1998 the poverty ratio may have been between 13 per cent and 19 per cent as against 42 per cent indicated by official sources.

Incidentally, Bhalla is perhaps among the very few who have successfully challenged Nobel laureate Amartya Sen. This episode took place in the late 1980s. The Great Man wrote that Sri Lanka's public expenditures were responsible for its stunning social indicators. But Bhalla showed that what happened in Sri Lanka in the 1960s and thereafter was simply a continuation of historical trends and, if corrected for initial conditions, was not as miraculous as Sen was making it to be. After this pat, Sen stopped using Sri Lanka as an exemplar and started using Kerala instead!

The NCAER and Bhalla studies make a detailed critique of the NSS estimates in the 1990s and say that downward biases have crept in particularly in the richer states. The growing divergence in consumption estimates between those provided by the NSS and those thrown up by another government source, namely the National Accounts Statistics (NAS) is, in their view, damaging enough to call into serious doubt the very reliability of the poverty numbers derived from the NSS. The final paper is by K. Sundaram and Suresh Tendulkar, both professors at the Delhi School of Economics. Without questioning the basis of the poverty surveys which are based on a "thin" sample of 25,000 households after 1993-94, the dons conclude that rural poverty has not declined at all in the 1990s. This is because of high foodgrain prices and a deceleration in value-addition in agriculture.

They add that the reduction in poverty during 1981-91 resulted predominantly from agricultural growth and not from expanded coverage of anti-poverty programmes. The full survey for 1999-2000 is over and the results will be out by the year end. Meanwhile, what is abundantly clear is the need to restore dynamism to broad-based agricultural growth. The failure to do so thus far is because fundamental fiscal reforms to enhance the investment capacity of the Centre and states have yet to take place.

31/07/2000

◆——————◆

A NEW ROUND OF CONTROVERSY
Rural poverty is down, perhaps due to the changes in the way it is calculated

The debate on poverty numbers has just got murkier. So far, the Planning Commission was saying that rural poverty had gone up in the 1990s. Its latest calculations show exactly the opposite. Contrary to popular belief, there is no explicit national poverty line. What we now have, instead, are state-specific poverty lines from which an all-India poverty line is derived implicitly. The rural poverty line is the monthly consumption expenditure of a person so that he or she can get a daily intake of 2,400 kilocalories.

Every five years, the government's National Sample Survey

Organisation (NSSO) surveys some 1,20,000 households across the country for getting data on con-sumption expenditure. Based on these surveys, the poverty ratio, that is the proportion living below the poverty line or the nutritionally minimum consumption expenditure level, is estimated by the Planning Commission. The last such full survey whose results have been officially published was in 1993-94. In that year, the national rural poverty ratio was 37.3 per cent. For subsequent years, however, we have only "thin" sample data covering only 20,000 households. This is never used for deriving definitive conclusions. Even so, the "thin" sample data reveals that the national rural poverty ratio in January-June 1998 had increased to 42.5 per cent.

The NSSO was to do a full sample survey in 1999-2000 (June-July). This has been completed and the results for the first six months or for the first two rounds have just been made public. Using these results for household consumption expenditure, the Planning Commission estimates that the all-India rural poverty ratio in 1999-2000 was between 24.5 per cent and 27.5 per cent, a very sharp decline since 1993-94.

In 1993-94, half the sampled households were asked for their consumption expenditure based on a 30 day recall and the other half was asked based on a seven day recall. In 1993-94 and in subsequent years, consumption expenditure as revealed by a seven-day recall was almost 16-17 per cent higher than that revealed by a 30-day recall. This means that a seven day recall survey will show significantly lower poverty than a 30 day recall survey. Incidentally, this 30 day reference period is used, perhaps, only in India and traces its origin to a study done way back in 1954 in 76 West Bengal villages covering 1,254 households. There was no difference in this survey between data based on recall of a month and a week. It is only since 1993-94 that the seven-day recall is also being experimented with.

In 1999-2000, however, the same households were asked for consumption expenditure based first on a seven day recall and then based on a 30-day recall. Surprisingly, the difference between the two instead of being significant as it was in previous years, turns out to be just around 3-4 per cent. This is the first puzzle. Then consider the fact that there has been an extraordinarily sharp decline in rural poverty in Bihar, Uttar Pradesh and Rajasthan. This fall is counter-intuitive and needs a closer look. The figures are also extraordinarily sensitive to the way price indices are constructed. Angus Deaton of Princeton University shows that Andhra Pradesh's rural poverty ratio in 1993-94 could be anywhere between 16 per cent and 34 per cent.

Pravin Visaria, one of India's most respected economists who is also the chairman of the NSSO's Governing Council, feels that the 1999-2000 survey is a step forward. He also believes that it would be wrong to mechanically compare poverty ratio data for different years and derive policy conclusions on whether reforms have accentuated or alleviated poverty. He is right. We could do without the political (ab)use of the poverty numbers. Some Planning Commission pundits, however, feel that the 1999-2000 survey was contaminated because the same household was asked the seven-day/30 day question in that order.

When the 1987-88 quin-quennial survey of the NSSO showed that poverty had reduced significantly over 1983-84, there was an outcry. In response, the Planning Commission set up an expert group in September 1989 under the chairmanship of the noted economist D.T. Lakdawala to review the methodology for estimating poverty. Now under similar circum-stances when 1999-2000 shows lower poverty numbers, the Planning Commission is setting up another expert group to study the figures. The survey results for the full year 1999-2000 will be available by March next year. They will provide a better picture on poverty trends.

There is really no mystery as to what it takes to reduce rural poverty: sustained agricultural growth, low food prices and investments in physical and social infrastructure. But the present structure of public expenditures at the Centre and in states prevents this from happening.

30/10/2000

D. Inflation

ARE YOU SERIOUS, MR SINHA?
To fight poverty and promote growth,
keep fighting inflation

So far, the finance minister has been the epitome of sobriety and sound economic sense. That is why his recent outburst on inflation is at once perplexing and disturbing. Yashwant Sinha seems to think that a tight money policy is being followed. He believes this has choked growth. He adds he is not one who believes in controlling the inflation rate at the cost of growth.

The finance minister is a politician. He need hardly be reminded that in our country, where the organised sector accounts for less than 15 per cent of the workforce, an anti-inflation strategy is the most powerful pro-poor policy any government can adopt. After all, inflation hurts workers and families in the unorganised sector the most. Sinha will surely not disagree with this. He will not disagree that in a vigorously democratic and increasingly media-driven society like ours, the tolerance levels for Latin American or east European-type inflation rates are very low. Double-digit inflation is a spectre dreaded by all knowledgeable occupants of North and South Block.

Where Sinha will disagree is with the reasons why the current inflation rate is low and just refuses to rise. It is now well below 5 per cent. This has come about not because of cyclical factors arising out of a tight money policy but because of structural reasons. In recent times, the money policy of the RBI has been anything but tight. In 1996-97, money supply grew by 16.2 per cent and in 1997-98 by 17.1 per cent. In 1997-98, the total credit flow from banks to industry doubled over the previous year. The momentum has been kept up in 1998-99 as well.

India is now more open to international trade than it was a decade ago, though not as open as it should be. This has worked to the advantage of the Indian consumer. It has forced producers to keep their prices low, since the domestic buyer now has the option of imports in case the do-mestic producer persists with keeping his prices high. Before 1991, industrial recessions or slow-downs accelerated inflation rates. This is no longer true, a positive fall-out of the trade liberalisation initiated in 1991.

The openness and the relatively comfortable foreign currency asset position of over $26 billion has also provided the Government with an opportunity of resorting to the threat of imports. Sometimes, the credible threat of imports has a disciplining effect on domestic prices. The most recent example of this is the wheat market, where the import window has helped dampen speculation and driven down domestic prices.

World prices in many industries are in check because of over-capacity and recessionary conditions in major exporting countries. International prices of raw materials, intermediates and finished products are at all-time lows. Oil prices have fallen. For the first time, falling diesel prices in international markets have been translated into lower prices at home.

Reduction in inflation rates helps not just the poor. In managing our international competitiveness, what matters is not the nominal exchange rate but the real effective exchange rate. This is the exchange rate in relation to a basket of currencies of our major trading partners, adjusted for differentials in interest rates. Reducing our inflation rate has the same effect on competitiveness as a depreciation of the rupee.

Inflation rates in India are low not just because of an open macroeconomy but also because price adjustments haven't been carried out. The issue price for foodgrains is about 40 per cent of the economic cost for consumers below the poverty line and about 70 per cent for those above, as identified by state governments. If issue prices are raised, the inflation rate may increase by at least a percentage point. Inflation rate averaged 9 per cent in the '70s and 8 per cent in the '80s. In the first five years of this decade, it was around 10 per cent. There was also pressure on the rupee. A tight money policy was needed to prevent the flow of funds from the domestic money market to the forex market. This was the background to the anti-inflation measures adopted by Manmohan Singh in 1995-96, to which Sinha seems to have reacted.

Rather than fall victim to the explanation blaming the 1995-96 policy for the contemporary industrial slow-down, Sinha will do well to read the Sukhamoy Chakravarty Committee report on monetary policy. It had targeted 4 per cent as the acceptable rise in prices that could meet the objectives of growth and social justice.

Sinha would also do well to recognise it is not the RBI's tight money policy that is hurting industry and trade. It is the unwillingness of public-sector banks to lend that is. This will persist as long as the Government continues to be the majority owner. Sinha must focus on reforming the credit-delivery system and not under-mine the battle against price stability and inflation. It takes years to dampen inflationary expectations. But no time at all to rekindle them.

Industry and Murli Manohar Joshi want a loose fiscal policy.

Sinha does not seem to be averse to a loose mone-tary policy. This is a dangerous brew. The cocktail of a lax fiscal and a lax monetary policy will spell doom for us. Be an inflation hawk like your predecessors, Mr Sinha.

11/05/1998

◆ ◆

EYE ON PI
Demystifying the current 1.85 per cent rate of inflation

In India the inflation rate, that is the rate at which the price level is increasing, is commonly measured by movements in the wholesale price index (WPI). The index is a basket of 447 commodities and the base year taken for giving weights to individual commodities is 1981-82. The lag is usually two weeks. The base year will soon be changed to 1993-94.

There are two WPIs. The first is called a point-to-point annual rate, which tells us what the rate of change in wholesale prices is in a particular week or day in one year as compared to its level in the same week or day the previous year. The other is what is called the annual average WPI rate, which is a 52-week average.

A second set of inflation indicators is based on the consumer price index (CPI) put out monthly by the Ministry of Labour. Three CPIs are published—for industrial workers (CPI-IW) for urban non-manual employees (CPI-UNME) and for agricultural labour (CPI-AL). The CPI that is watched with the greatest interest is the CPI-IW, since it is used to calculate the dearness allowance (DA) to be paid to employees in the organised sector. Its base is 1982 and it covers 260 commodities. Data is collected from 70 centres around the country. The lag is usually a month. Attempts to change the base year to make the CPI-IW more reflective of changes in the economy have been scuttled in the past. The CPI-UNME's base is 1984-85 and the CPI-AL's is 1986-87. But the CPI-IW's base remains unchanged. This is pressure politics exerted by government unions and their political patrons. If the base year changes the CPI-IW will be much lower.

The third inflation indicator is the GDP deflator. This is the ratio of the national income in a given year in current prices to that in constant prices. But since it used to be calculated on an annual basis and was available only with a lag of a year, its policy relevance was marginal. That has changed and the GDP deflator is now available quarterly with a lag of just two quarters, with 1993-94 as the base.

The differences among the various inflation indicators have fluctuated around a narrow band. However, since May 1995 something remarkable is taking place that has gone unnoticed. The CPI-IW and the WPI have started diverging by increasing margins. In an econometric analysis published recently in RBI Occasional Papers, G.P. Samanta and Sharmishta Mitra conclude that differences in the commodity basket and the base year explain only part of the growing divergence. Other factors like price quotations and differences in market structures could be playing a more significant role. But the truth, which no economist will ever admit, is that we really do not know what is happening. India's leading monetary economist, who is right now vegetating in Hyderabad's Raj Bhavan, should put his mind to this and enlighten all of us.

But what to make of the low WPI in recent times? Could it be reflecting stagnation and lack of demand in the manufacturing sector, which has a weight of 57 per cent in the WPI? Or could it be a statistical artifact since last year's base, on which this year's rate is calculated, was high? It is here that the distinction between point-to-point and annual average rates becomes crucial. The point-to-point rate has plummeted but the average is still around 6 per cent, broadly consistent with the rate of increase in money supply.

There are other structural factors at work. Increasing rural prosperity is leading to a greater monetisation of the economy. This means that a high rate of money supply need not necessarily lead to a higher inflation level. The world is also going through very low inflation and since we are integrating with the rest of the globe, we cannot be immune to this trend. Since our economy is more open now than it has ever been, there is no room for Indian manufacturers to jack up their prices.

However, the vulnerability to domestic crop failures remains. But even here, had the government imported onions in time, the 1998 fiasco would have been averted. The WPI inflation in 1979-80, a bad drought year, was 17 per cent. But it also saw the second oil price shock. By contrast, WPI inflation in 1987-88, when we had the last bad drought, was 8.2 per cent. With $31 billion in the forex kitty, with expanding irrigation coverage and with sensible import policies, we could withstand crop failures without an inflation boom.

However, to sustain low inflation, the syndrome of what economists call "high long-term inflationary expectations" has to be addressed. In simple language what this means is that the level of expected inflation, as Venugopal Reddy, the learned deputy governor of the RBI, never tires of pointing out, has been much higher than actual inflation in recent years. This demands a credible anti-inflation stance. Real interest rates have also to move southward. This will happen when the interest rates on small savings, relief bonds and provident funds are set at more realistic levels, government equity in banks falls below 50 per cent so that banks can lower their spreads and when the overall fiscal deficit is brought under control.

09/08/1999

◆――◆

RBI SIGNALS ITS INTENTIONS
The central bank's bi-annual credit policy is more than a ritual

A mid all the political shenanigans last week, that citadel of continuity and stability, the RBI, announced the credit policy for the first half of 1999-2000. This is a bi-annual event that takes place every mid-April and mid-October. Till 1997, mid-April was billed as the slack season policy and mid-October as the busy season policy. This slack/busy distinction reflected the crop cycle of cotton, sugarcane and other farm commodities and was a throwback to the times when the bulk of bank lending was for agricultural trade.

Since 1997, however, the intellectual justification for this half-yearly event has changed. The budget is usually presented by the end of February. March is the busiest financial month and the nation's books close on March 31. The mid-April monetary policy takes into account budget expectations and the performance in the previous year. The mid-October announcement is a mid-term review of sorts after 75-80 per cent of the government's borrowing programme gets completed and the commercial sector's appetite for credit picks up.

If inflation is raging, credit policy tries to arrest the growth of money supply and in normal times, it seeks to expand the availability of credit for business and trade. The two main instruments it uses are the statutory liquidity ratio (SLR) and the cash reserve ratio (CRR). The SLR stipulates the amount that banks have to invest in the securities that the government issues to raise money to meet its expenditures. The CRR stipulates the amount banks must park with the RBI.

Before the 1991 reforms, 40 per cent of the increase in a bank's deposits was pre-empted by the SLR and another 25 per cent by the CRR. Since then, however, the SLR has declined to 25 per cent and last week the RBI reduced the CRR from 10.5 to 10 per cent. Thus the government's pre-emption of incremental deposits, that is, the yearly increase on deposits, has reduced from 65 per cent to 35 per cent in seven years.

Herein lies the significance of the fiscal deficit. Simply put, lesser the fiscal deficit lower will be the pre-emption of bank deposits by a profligate government—leaving more resources to be made available for lending by banks to agriculture, trade and industry.

The RBI influences credit availability. It cannot by itself do much about credit delivery, which is the bottleneck today. The choke in the credit delivery system can be gauged from the fact that banks are holding over Rs 56,000 crore in government securities over and above the RBI stipulated level. Sometimes, a credit policy that appears routine may actually be the harbinger of a paradigm shift. For instance, the October 1998 credit policy stipulated new norms for capital adequacy for banks. To meet these norms, over the next two years the public-sector banks have to mobilise around Rs 26,000 crore of fresh capital, assuming 75 per cent of the non-performing loans are written off. Recap money can no longer come from the government's budget which, over the past six years, has already provided Rs 20,000 crore for recapitalisation. This money will have to be raised from the market. But as long as the government retains over 50 per cent equity, these public issues will not command the needed premia. This makes the privatisation of banks a financial imperative. Last week's policy disappointed industry since it did not herald a cut in interest rates. But there is more to private investment than interest rates. In 1992-96, interest rates were high but private investment zoomed. In 1996-98, interest rates declined but private investment was stagnant, showing the "demand" factor's importance.

But can interest rates be "cut" by the RBI when they are mostly deregulated? The RBI controls only the interest rate on savings deposits, on loans up to Rs 25,000 and on export credit. Interest-rate controls now apply to just 20 per cent of the commercial portfolio of banks. The only instrument the RBI has is its own reference bank rate—the rate that it charges the banks for loans. But this is really a signalling device. This explains last week's focus on the "transmission mechanism", so the preference for lower interest rates is actually trans-lated into practice by banks.

The most masterly exposition on the complex issue of interest rates has been by Y.V. Reddy, the erudite deputy governor of the RBI, in the July 1998 RBI Bulletin. He identifies five factors that cause an upward pressure on real interest rates.

- the high levels of government borrowing, especially the persisting revenue deficits
- the stickiness of spread between the deposit rate and the lending rate of banks brought about mainly on account of government ownership
- the interest tax that the Centre imposes on banks, which is passed on to customers
- the high effective rate of return offered on small savings, relief bonds and provident funds
- the lack of depth and efficiency in the government se-curities and money markets

Reddy's most fundamental point is that as long as expectations of inflation do not fall—and they have not— real interest rates will continue to be high, even though inflation may itself decline.

03/05/1999

◆——◆

RBI TALKS TOUGH

A no-nonsense, poll-time pre-emptive move by the central bank

Right through the through the Kargil the rupee fell by about 60 paise in relation to the dol-lar, the RBI maintained restraint. Suddenly it has shed its shyness as markets perceive the demand for dollars is increasing at a time when there is uncertainty on their supply, reflected, say, in the foreign institutional investors (FIIs) turning net sellers in August after five months of hectic buying.

On August 9, substantial buying of dollars by Reliance for importing crude for its Jamnagar refinery appears to have sent the rupee falling in intra-day trading by 12 paise in relation to the dollar. The RBI immediately intervened on that day and the rupee closed seven paise up. Then there was a mild fall on August 11 following the downing of the Pakistani aircraft the day before. But this did not trigger any RBI action. The third blow was delivered by markets on August 20 when they reacted to the G-8 countries' response to India's nuclear doctrine that was released for debate on August 17. The G-8 announced that sanctions imposed in May 1998 for non-humanitarian projects in India would continue.

Markets reacted the same day and hit a new intra-day low of Rs 43.70 to the dollar, before settling at Rs 43.57, a fall of nine paise. Expecting further pressure, the RBI moved swiftly on August 22 and announced that it would not hesitate to use foreign currency reserves to pay for our oil imports and meet our external debt which together adds up to nearly $800 million every month. In effect, what this does is reduce the market demand for dollars.

What causes panic in government are big, bold banner headlines in the dailies that scream "rupee slumps", "rupee falls to new all-time low", "rupee takes a beating", "rupee plummets sharply", "rupee on skid row", "rupee slammed down" or "rupee reeling again". Such headlines are completely misleading but have their effect. Few are aware that even in the old era of fixed exchange rates, a variation of 2.5 per cent either above or below the par value was considered normal by the IMF. This means that at current values of the rupee in relation to the dollar, under the old fixed parity system, a variation of plus or minus one rupee would not need IMF approval. But we get flustered if the rupee falls by even a few paise even though we are in a market-determined exchange rate system since February 1993.

The RBI's was a pre-emptive move prompted by a recognition that during election time the exchange rate always comes under pressure through a variety of ways—for example, by exporters who do not bring back dollars and by importers who rush to cover ahead. The RBI has spent something like $400 million defending the rupee these past few days. Clearly, this is tenable only in the short-term although the type of currency attacks by Soros-types as has happened elsewhere is not possible here since the rupee is not fully convertible and severe restrictions are placed on forward market operations. To be fair, the RBI's statement says it will use reserves to meet dollar demand in full or *in part and over the next few weeks*. What the bank is betting on over the year is a manageable current account deficit (and, by definition, a capital-account surplus). But in these times, sentiment and perceptions are equally crucial as fundamentals and both have to be managed. Today, the perception is that the rupee can do with depreciation although in terms of fundamentals the five-country real effective exchange rate is roughly on a par with what it was in 1993-94.

In a world of mobile capital flows, instant communica-tions and rapid changes in financial technology, exchange-rate management has become very complex. Montek Singh Ahluwalia analysed this complexity briefly in a paper that he presented at a recent seminar organised at the Delhi-based research organisation ICRIER. He argues that:

- A country can opt for exchange-rate stability and monetary indepen-dence but then it must introduce capital controls.
- Exchange-rate stability can be combined with full capital mobility but only if a country gives up monetary freedom.
- A country may opt for full capital mobility and monetary independence but then it must opt for free floating rates.

The essence of successfully managing an open or an opening up macroeconomy is to improve the tradeoffs among the three elements of what has come to be called as the "impossible trinity". Of course, as Ahluwalia himself argues, flexibility does not imply indifference to wild fluctuations. But flexibility means living with frequent movements. Over a medium term it is true that the rupee has not been excessively defended. Since April 1 this year there has been a depreciation of slightly over a rupee or around 2 per cent. The real question is about the best judgement of when to intervene in the very short term. Kautilya's belief is that our political economy influences the judgement of the RBI in such matters. Monetary policy has been used to manage exchange-rate stability in a regime of flexibility but in India, the efficacy of the interest rate instrument is blunted because of the artificially high rates of interest on small savings, provident funds and other special deposits.

06/09/1999

CORE TO RBI, SORE TO OTHERS
The RBI governor says that core inflation is comfortable—what does it mean?

On January 15, while speaking at the Conference of Bank Economists in the capital, RBI Governor Bimal Jalan said, "At present core inflation is 3.4 per cent and is comfortable." Just the previous day, the Government's own press release revealed that the "annual point-to-point inflation based on the Wholesale Price Index (WPI) for the week ended December 30, 2000 was 8.16 per cent".

This is for the first time that the concept of "core" in-flation has been officially used in a policy sense. The RBI did draw attention to the concept in its 1996-97 Annual Report. Later, an econometric study on the subject by an RBI analyst G.P. Samanta appeared in the summer 1999 issue of RBI Occasional Papers. Subsequently, the RBI's scholarly Deputy Governor Venugopal Reddy discussed it in a lecture he gave in Hyderabad in August 1999.

The inflation rate measures the rate at which prices are increasing. If the inflation rate is down it does not mean that prices are falling: all it means is that the rate at which prices are increasing has declined. In India, we have five different measures of the inflation rate—the WPI, the Consumer Price Index for Industrial Workers (CPI-IW), the Consumer Price Index for Agricultural Labour (CPI-AL), the Consumer Price Index for Urban Non-Manual Workers (CPI-UNME) and the GDP Deflator. Of these, it is the WPI that is the most frequently used. It gives weekly inflation rates with a lag of two weeks. The CPI-IW is important because it is used to calculate dearness allowance (DA) for organised sector employees. It is available monthly with a lag of two months but, unlike the WPI which covers the entire country, it is constructed for 40-odd cities and towns. The GDP Deflator is the most comprehensive measure of inflation since it covers services and non-tradeable commodities as well but it is a statistically derived measure (ratio of GDP at current prices to GDP at constant prices) and is not used in popular discourse as it is available only annually.

The WPI which uses 1993-94 as the base year and covers 435 items is called the "headline" rate of inflation since it is the rate that captures news every Monday. There is a point-to-point measure which calibrates the rate of increase in a particular week or day of a particular year over the same week or day the previous year. The other is the 52-week average. Both are used but the weekly point-to-point is what dominates headlines.

A current inflation rate has both a permanent and transient segment. Transient components arise from sudden shocks—like when the prices of onions or crude oil shoot up or when the prices of edible oils come crashing down. As Reddy says, core inflation has only a permanent component. It is the future underlying rate of inflation anticipated by economic agents that does not change with changes in output—either up or down.

While there is no clear-cut definition and Reddy himself admits to some discretion or judgement in its mea-surement, Samanta calculates four different indices to calculate core inflation.

- Core 1: WPI minus primary food articles and administered price commodities;
- Core 2: WPI excluding primary food articles, primary non-food articles (like cotton, sugarcane and oilseeds) and administered price commodities;
- Core 3: WPI excluding primary food articles, manufactured food products and administered price commodities;
- Core 4: WPI excluding primary food and non-food articles, administered price commodities and all other seasonal items;

After detailed statistical analysis, he concludes that Core 2 is the least volatile and the most superior measure. Presumably, Jalan had this in mind, although it appears from the figures he quoted that he may have used Core 5—WPI excluding administered prices. Hopefully, there will be some clarification forthcoming from the RBI soon.

Core inflation could be core to the central bank's monetary policy but it certainly is not core as far as the government or consumers are concerned. If you are going to exclude increases in primary food articles with a weight of 15.4 per cent in the WPI, primary non-food articles whose weight is 6.6 per cent and administered price items whose weight is 16.4 per cent,then you are really not reflecting real world concerns. When the inflation rate zoomed in the latter half of 1998, core inflation was not high. But it was this inflation spike that, more than anything else, caused the debacle for the BJP in the assembly elections at the time.

True, both inflationary expectations and inflationary experiences need to be tackled. But it would be wrong if fighting core inflation rate were to be the core of an anti-inflation strategy. Food-price inflation is the true core inflation that we should be fighting.

05/02/2001

◆――――◆

E. Trade

WRONG NUMBER MR HEGDE
Get rid of this hi-tech fixation; the key to exports is low-tech

The export-import policy for 1998-99 is a homeopathic dose of reforms. But it is significant because it punctures the anti-WTO rhetoric of the BJP. Power obviously moderates, just as the absence of power unhinges. Commerce Minister Ramakrishna Hegde has continued from where his predecessors have left off. The process of dismantling quantitative restrictions is on track, although it has been arbitrarily done. Import liberalisation is on course, although Hegde has allowed free imports of bindis, sindoor and kumkum, while the import of crude oil is still canalised and subject to licensing.

But will Hegde's policy deliver a 20 per cent growth in exports? Most definitely, it will not. Quite apart from the fact that the growth rate in world trade is now half of what it was in the mid-'90s, the real issues that bedevil our exports have not been addressed.

Import liberalisation is necessary to provide an im-petus to exports. At the same time, export liberalisation will certainly not hurt us. This is not just to liberate all exporters from the tyranny of forms and procedures but also to help realise the full export potential of important sectors in the economy. The most notable example of a sector still hamstrung by export controls in the form of quotas, bans and stopgo policies is agriculture and agro-industry. Yet, it is Indian agriculture that stands to gain the most from the new WTO regime.

The years 1993-94, 1994-95 and 1995-96 were a boom period for Indian exports. Exports in dollars, grew by 20, 18 and 21 per cent respectively. Part of the explanation for this is that world trade growth itself was very buoyant. It grew by 10 per cent per year in these three years. But the more important reason was the change in the value of the dollar from Rs 18 in June 1991 to Rs 31 by January 1993.

True, compared to early 1993, when we first moved over to a market system for determining exchange rates, the real effective exchange rate had appreciated by about 14 per cent in August 1997. Since then there has been a substantial correction and the quantum of appreciation has come down to just about 4 per cent. Faster import liberalisation is the best way to deal with the negative effects of an appreciating currency in an open economy.

But compared to June 1997 in real terms, that is after adjusting for inflation rates, the rupee is now up 8 per cent against the Thai baht, 35 per cent against the Malaysian ringitt, 18 per cent against the South Korean won, 23 per cent against the Philippine peso and 152 per cent against the Indonesian rupaiah.

In the short term, the rupee's appreciation against the east Asian currencies could adversely affect our export prospects in areas like gems and jewellery, textiles, engineering and pharmaceuticals. Given the exchange rate policies of our competitors and given the slow growth in world trade itself, it would be foolish to adopt a fundamentalist line on the exchange rate. This, particularly if the market perception is that the exchange rate is still overvalued and the market "expectations" are that of a depreciation.

No policy has hurt the cause of exports more than the ill-conceived reserving of over 830 items for exclusive manufacture in the small-scale sector. These include textile products (like garments), leather products, plastic products, engineering components, toys, electrical appliances and sports goods. Right through the '80s and '90s, the industries where world trade expanded fastest—garments, consumer goods and light engineering—were all reserved for the small-scale sector. They were thus deprived of new investment and technology, given the way we have defined the small-scale sector.

In 1985, India's export of socalled low-tech items amounted to $2.5 billion. China's was marginally more at $3 billion. By 1995, while India's exports of these lowtech items increased to $13 billion, China's zoomed to $72 billion. Pick up any consumer item in any American department store. Chances are it will be marked "Made in China". This is where we have lost out, particularly in textiles and electronics, because we cling to an outmoded idea of the small-scale sector. Elsewhere, the small-scale sector is a technological and commercial reality. In India, it is a fiscal artefact.

Trade and investment are closely interlinked. Here too we have lost out. A growing proportion of international trade—now about 30 per cent—comprises intra-company sales. Such sales take place when these companies make investments in different countries and use these countries as manufacturing platforms.

For India to emerge as a global production base, we must realise that the critical element of competitive advantage in today's world is time. We may have all the skills that MNCs need but if these companies are not able to evacuate things made in India out of India in a matter of hours, we will continue to be beaten by the Irelands and the Spains. The "hassle" factor of doing business in India, apart from our continued ambivalence on foreign investment in the consumer goods, textiles and electronics industries, is costing us dear.

Hegde plans to exhort big Indian corporates to export more. His energies would be spent more profitably interacting with foreign companies already in the country—and helping them make India a global resource base.

04/05/1998

IMF ITCH AGAIN ?
After 1981 and 1991, another BoP crisis looms

India's trade deficit worsens: so blazed the news headlines this past week. During the six months of April-September 1998, exports were $16.3 billion and im-ports were $21.3 billion. Thus the trade deficit, that is the difference between imports and exports, was $5 billion. In April-September 1997, this deficit was $2.5 billion.

Should we lose sleep over this deterioration? Not necessarily. The continued deceleration in exports is cause for concern. The slowdown in the world economy is hurting us. But there are home-grown contributory factors as well. Reservations for small-scale industry in sectors where we have tremendous export potential—like garments and consumer goods—poor infrastructure and delays in customs clearances are all adversely impacting on exports.

But the trade deficit is only part of the picture. A truer measure of our external vulnerability is what economists call the current account deficit.

The trade deficit deals only with merchandise flows, where there is physical movement of goods and commodities. It does not include, for example, dollar earnings from software exports and from tourism which come under the category of "invisibles". Remittances from Indian workers overseas also add to our dollar kitty; this too is shown in the invisibles category.

The trade deficit adjusted for these invisibles yields the current account deficit. It is the growth in the invisibles that is saving us from external collapse. For 1997-98, the trade deficit is estimated at 3.7 per cent of GDP. But the current account deficit would probably be around 1.6 per cent of GDP because we had over $11 billion in invisibles earnings. These earnings are well below what is possible. Tourism alone has vast untapped potential.

To get an even more complete picture of our international transactions, we must look at our BoP or balance of payments position. BoP has two components: the current account balance and the capital account balance. As explained earlier, the current account balance includes imports and exports of goods and commodities, other dollar earnings through software exports and tourism and remittances and dollar outflows on account of interest payments, dividends and profits. The capital account balance includes all borrowings abroad minus the repayments that have to be made, foreign aid and investments and NRI deposits.

In 1997-98, India's capital account showed a surplus of about $11 billion, while our current account showed a deficit of about $6.3 billion. As long as the capital account surplus exceeds the current account deficit, we are safe. But if the overall balance turns out to be negative, then we have to go to the IMF or dip into our foreign exchange reserves.

In simple English, a current account deficit of 1.6 per cent of GDP means we borrowed over $6 billion from the world in 1997-98 to balance the economy's books. This is because our savings, while growing, were not sufficient to meet our increasing investment needs. Our households save, and save as much as in east Asia. What drags us down is the low level of public savings born out of poor public-sector returns and excess government expenditure on itself.

It is not immediately apparent but the current account deficit is the sum of the savings gap in the private sector and the fiscal deficit in the government sector. Thus the internal and external sectors of an economy are closely interlinked, the consequences of which are not always grasped and understood. Part of the blame for the disastrous 3.2 per cent of GDP current account deficit that we had in 1990-91, the year of collapse, has to be laid on the high fiscal deficit we ran in the mid-'80s.

Actually, 1998-99 may turn out to be a most troubling year with the current account deficit being projected at between 2.3 and 2.6 per cent of GDP. This is well above the 2 per cent of GDP mark that the RBI considers the danger level. This is the amount that can be financed easily with normal capital inflows.

There are two risk factors on the external front— short-term debt and current account deficits. East Asia was killed by both. Our short-term debt is well under control and is just over a quarter of our foreign exchange reserves. But we are becoming vulnerable on the current account deficit. To make matters worse, the capital account is expected to show a visibly lower balance because of lower foreign investment inflows, lower external borrowings and lower external assistance. The net result is 1998-99 could see a negative overall balance of $2-3 billion. It may increase in the next two years.

In terms of crisis indicators, 1998-99 comes close to 1990-91. The silver lining is we have $27 billion in foreign currency assets now, as against less than a billion then. But if the next six months are like the past six, and today's loose monetary and lax fiscal policy continues, we may be forced to go to the IMF for the third time-after 1981 and 1991. This could well be the tonic needed to unleash a second wave of big bang reforms of the type introduced in 1991 and 1992—on whose strength we have survived so far. Our political system has shown that it wakes up and responds only when confronted with a crisis. Thus even if a crisis does not exist, it may be better to engineer one! Brazil's example is before us. It has gone to the IMF with almost $45 billion in reserves. The imminence of a grim BoP position must also impel the Government and the entire political class to take pragmatic decisions on issues like CTBT.

23/11/1998

OUR GREAT GOLD (C)RUSH
India's yellow fever requires new policy medicine—now

India's trade deficit, the difference between imports and exports, during April-October 1998 was $5.8 billion, as compared to $2.7 billion in the same period in 1997. Over $2 billion of the increase in the trade deficit is on account of surging gold imports.

India's appetite for gold remains as voracious as ever. In calendar 1997, the Geneva-based World Gold Council (WGC) reports that India consumed 737 tonnes of gold worth around $7 billion, more than that in the US and China combined. This year demand will probably be well over 825 tonnes. Three-fourths of demand is met through imports, the rest through recycling and scrap. Domestic production is a paltry two tonnes. The amount spent on buying gold in 1997 was a little more than the total amount spent on cars, two-wheelers, refrigerators and television sets combined.

International prices of gold have fallen sharply over the past decade from something like $450 per ounce to around $290 per ounce. This reflects the falling status of gold world-wide. Central banks have been selling their gold stocks. Other hedging mechanisms through specialised derivative markets now offer superior alternatives. But India remains a glittering exception. Gold remains the "safe haven" investment option for all Indian families. Other than land, gold is the only other form of social security that families in this country buy for themselves. Venugopal Reddy, deputy governor, Reserve Bank of India (RBI), estimates 70 per cent of gold jewellery is sold in rural areas and most of the gold sales are by way of jewellery. The WGC itself puts the rural:urban break-up of gold demand at 60:40.

The year 1992 was a watershed for gold in India. The draconian Gold Control Act was scrapped and non-res-idents were allowed to import 5 kg of gold every six months. The Act had only succeeded in creating a vast underground market. Domestic price premia were 80-100 per cent above international gold prices. This provided a tremendous incentive for smuggling and other illegal transactions in foreign exchange. October 1997 was the next landmark. Eleven authorised agencies, comprising public sector and foreign banks and state canalising organisations, were allowed to import gold freely at about 5 per cent duty and sell it locally.

India's official holdings of gold with the RBI amount to 396 tonnes worth some $3 billion. But the total private holding is placed at close to 10,000 tonnes, valued at about $100 billion. In a country where social insurance is virtually absent for the vast majority (just about 7 per cent of the workforce has provident fund coverage), private holdings of gold should not be dismissed as being "unproductive". They also help sustain a Rs 25,000 crore gold industry that employs around five lakh goldsmiths but that has never received sustained policy support and whose export potential is waiting to be realised. Exports of gold jewellery in 1997-98 were around $840 million, less than 1.5 per cent of the world market,a share that has doubled in the past six years but which can be increased even further.

Even so, a strong case exists for using our growing gold stocks more innovatively. Four attempts have been made since 1962 to bring out private gold stocks and use them for "development". These attempts have all failed. The most recent scheme was in 1993. It mopped up just 41 tonnes and yielded only Rs 1,540 crore to the exchequer.

We need a fresh look at gold banking and associated tax issues. Turkey, where private stocks are half those in India, has attracted new savings in gold and mobilised gold holdings by converting them into gold-denominated deposits. We could also now experiment with a scheme of gold monetisation managed by the SBI or the UTI.

Investors would have the option to tender gold as well as money. The units would be denominated in grams of gold. The gold principal would remain intact and the capital appreciation on gold would remain with the investor earning a nominal return for him or her. Liquidity has to be provided at all times. The concept of bearer gold units for tapping unaccounted gold could also be introduced.

With exports collapsing, unabated gold imports may tempt the Government to reimpose controls. This would be disastrous. Liberalisation of gold policy carried out by both Manmohan Singh and P. Chidambaram has destroyed one of Dawood Ibrahim's main businesses. The spread between London and Mumbai average prices of gold was around 60 per cent in 1990. It has tumbled to just 6 per cent.

Gold imports have been "officialised". Remittances are now being transferred by overseas Indian workers through official channels. Since 1992-93, private transfers in our BOP have spurted by $8 billion. This is largely on account of the liberal gold policy and has helped keep our current account deficit at manageable levels. For the first time India is seeing the strange spectacle of a slight discount on the dollar in the hawala market. The time for consolidation and the next phase of gold policy reforms is now.

28/12/1998

This section deals with India's most serious and intractable economic problem, namely the fiscal and revenue deficits of both the central and state governments. Here we have both a quantity and quality problem. Not only are our deficits unsustainably high but they largely arise out of non-productive expenditure that does not add to the nation's investment capacity. Three articles deal with defence expenditure and it is a matter of some satisfaction that the article "War and Costs" has been discussed in the new book by Amartya Sen and Jean Dreze, *India: Development and Participation*. I have also been a great supporter of Chandrababu Naidu, the Chief Minister of Andhra Pradesh – a stance that has landed me repeatedly in trouble with my own party colleagues. One piece here is very critical of him and the stance he took on the recommendations of the Eleventh Finance Commission. Incidentally, my position in this piece also went against the position of the government of Karnataka when I was serving as Deputy Chairman of its Planning Board.

II

Public Finances:
India's Edifice Complex

A. Centre

Watch that Deficit
The state of the economy depends on
the economy of the state

How times change. Less than a decade ago, Indian industry was saying that we should cut back on the fiscal deficit and rein in government expenditure. Today, the unanimous view in industry is that the fiscal deficit does not matter. If getting out of the current "recession" means a higher fiscal deficit for the Centre than the current 6.1 per cent of GDP, so be it. This is not a cry in the wilderness. It has powerful backers within the Government itself, most notably Murli Manohar Joshi, the patron saint of the "Swadeshi Jargon Bunch".

The current industrial slowdown is not a "recession". It is an essential phase of transition and restructuring. You cannot have a fiscal reform programme and hope to post double-digit growth rates year after year. At some point of time, the pains have to show. Indian industry is not facing a recession. It is facing the white heat of competition. Deficits hit growth. They are bad for private investment. They raise domestic real interest rates. They lead to current account deficits and overvaluation of currencies. And they make public investment non-sustainable.

Is there a "right" level of fiscal deficit? In perhaps the most analytically rigorous and policy-oriented sections of the Ninth Plan document bequeathed to Jaswant Singh by Madhu Dandavate and company, levels of sustainable fiscal deficit under varying assumptions have been estimated. The underlying premise is that the Government debt to GDP ratio and the interest payments to tax revenues ratio should at least remain the same as they are today and, if possible, show a decline.

Assuming the GDP grows at 7 per cent per year in the next five years, nominal interest rates remain at 11.5 per cent and the average rate of inflation is 7 per cent, then the sustainable level of fiscal deficit for the Centre works out to 5 per cent of GDP. The sustainable level of fiscal deficit for the states is around 2 per cent of GDP, as compared to the present level of 3 per cent of GDP.

What the Planning Commission has not done is estimate the deficit for public-sector enterprises as well. If this is done, the fiscal deficit for the entire economy is now around 10 per cent of GDP, as compared to a sustainable level of about 7 per cent. This is at the core of India's economic malaise. If nominal interest rates rise, then the sustainable level of fiscal deficit goes up. The downward movement of the fiscal deficit will itself ease the pressure on interest rates. But the real answer to this is a reduction in interest rates on the various small savings schemes run by the Government. The second Joshi-industry mantra is to increase capital expenditure and cut revenue deficit. Easier said than done. Cutting revenue deficit is tough. Money for rural development, education and health are part of revenue expenditure. Everybody wants such expenditure to increase, indeed it has. Some 40 per cent of the increase in revenue expenditure in recent years is on account of increased spending in the rural development and social sectors. Surely this should not be cut. But there are other elements of revenue expenditure which must be curtailed, most notably interest payments. This year, these will eat up 50 per cent of the Centre's revenue receipts and about 30 per cent of the revenues of the states. There is only one way of dealing with this problem: privatise, sell assets like land, and use the proceeds to repay debt.

Reforming the Food Corporation of India and taking away the affluent from ration shops will cut food subsidies. The replacement of the irrational factory-wise retention pricing system by one based on longrun marginal costs will contain fertiliser subsidy. Next, by not filling vacancies that arise out of the 3 per cent normal retirements that take place annually, establishment costs of the Government can be kept in check.

The Government could well decide to find another Rs 5,000 crore-Rs 6,000 crore to push into the economy to spur industrial demand. Will this "pump priming" help? Hardly likely. It will only push up fiscal deficit and jack up interest rates. Many sectors, particularly power and roads, have reached the limits of absorptive capacity. Public investment cannot increase unless costs of supply are actually recovered. Take the National Thermal Power Corporation, already owed Rs 6,000 crore.

Further, the system of awarding contracts in the public sector is extremely time-consuming. Clearances from various ministries—Finance and Environment are just two examples—add six to 12 months to the project cycle. In irrigation, over 75 per cent of the outlay is eaten up by salaries and establishment expenses, leaving little money to place orders that will spur demand.

More than expenditure by the Centre, it is expenditure by state governments that creates industrial demand. But the state governments are bankrupt and will get deeper into the red when they implement the Fifth Pay Commission's report. Reform of state finances, therefore, is imperative. Perhaps the Jaswant-Yashwant (Sinha) duo should restructure the Centre-state financial relationship so as to ease the fiscal adjustment by states. That may be the way out of the tunnel.

27/04/1998

INDIA'S EDIFICE COMPLEX
Why public expenditure figures are an exercise in self-deception

One of the few good but unheralded ideas in the recent budget was to set up a task force to review the present system for categorising public expenditure. This may sound an academic idea, of relevance only to accountants. It is not so. This opportunity could be used to make our public accounts more transparent for informed public debate, more relevant for legislative review and executive action and more comprehensive in disclosures. Otherwise, better macro-economic management will be difficult. Finance Minister Yashwant Sinha's predecessors took steps in this direction. Manmohan Singh initiated the historic move to end the Reserve Bank of India's automatic monetisation of the Central government's deficit. P. Chidamabaram issued guidelines for better cash management. Sinha can go further.

At the very core of our fiscal malaise is the growing use of capital borrowings to meet revenue expenditures. This is compounded by the increasing diversion of development funds for non-development purposes. These have come about because the demands on public expenditure have multiplied just as the capacity to mobilise funds has shrunk. The system for reporting and managing public expenditure has exacerbated the problem.

India measures progress by the growth in Plan expenditure—that is, the expenditure on new schemes. But by combining the revenue and capital components in one omnibus category called Plan expenditure, we have created an in-built tendency for diverting borrowings to meet revenue expenditure. The revenue and capital components of Plan expenditure should be treated and matched separately. This will help alleviate fiscal sickness.

The pressure is to show large Plan expenditure. It is generally believed that Plan expenditure is "good", while non-Plan expenditure is "bad". But this is mis-leading. For example, almost 60 per cent of the Centre's expenditure on agriculture and 40 per cent of the expenditure on education is non-Plan. Moreover, the very distinction between Plan and non-Plan creates a bias against consolidation, maintenance and upkeep. In one five-year plan period, investment in new school buildings and new primary health centres will be Plan expenditure. In the very next plan period, the money needed to run these schools and health centres will be non-Plan. Once it is put in the non-Plan category, it gets starved of funds. No wonder health centres without medicines are common all over the country. There is no reason why we should view salaries of teachers and doctors as non-developmental expenses.

The only relevant categorisation is between revenue and capital expenditure. But here too we are the victims of perceptions. Just as Plan is considered "good", revenue spending is considered "bad". This will have to change. All expenditure on agriculture, rural development, education and health is on the revenue account. Grants to states too. In the past few years, almost 40 per cent of the increase in Central revenue expenditure is because of increased spending on the social sectors, defence and grants to states. In fact, with more economic reforms, revenue expenditure should multiply.

The focus in Indian economic policy, the late L.K. Jha used to lament, is on outlays, not on outputs. If we spend more, we think we are doing a great job. This must change. An annual performance review of public ex-penditure both at the Centre and in states is essential. How much is spent? What results? Who benefits? This is different from the audit of spending that gets carried out mechanically.

Over time, we must move to zero-based budgeting. This is a ruthless annual review of all expenditure. Ten years ago, Madhav Godbole had introduced this in Maharashtra when he was finance secretary. Bureaucrat Sanjeevi Guhan did similarly in Tamil Nadu. But these efforts did not get institutionalised. The economic environment then was not con-ducive to such radical thinking.

But things have changed. Governments follow the cash basis of accounting that recognises a transaction only when cash is received or disbursed. This does not disclose fully the current and future costs of the operating decision. Nor does it allow an evaluation of the Government's ability to live within its means. This is required for a healthy fiscal system. Countries like the US and New Zealand, which have moved from fiscal deficits to fiscal surpluses, have made accrual based commercial accounting systems mandatory. In other countries, public accounts involve a mix of accrual and cash concepts. This is the path for us.

Greater openness in presenting government ac-counts will create pressure for change. A former inhabitant of South Block, who had earlier served in North Block, once said that subsidies in India are not too large. According to budget documents, they are only at about 1.3 per cent of GDP. He was taken aback when he was told that all subsidies put together amount to about 15 per cent of the GDP. Only better informed rulers can bring about change.   20/07/1998

———◆——◆———

JOB HALF DONE
Reforms have led to lower diesel prices for consumers

Governance is a continuing business. What one regime sows, another reaps. During much of 1995 and early 1996, the Congress government formulated the policy for phasing out the administered price mechanism (APM) in the oil sector that was standing in the way of attracting new investments, had led to unnecessary subsidies and price dis-tortions and was eroding the financial health of the oilrefining and marketing companies like IOC. This was fine-tuned during H.D.

Deve Gowda's tenure and in November 1997, it was the Gujral government that actually took the bold and far-reaching decision to phase out the APM. The BJP can now claim credit for slashing diesel prices, which it did a few days ago.

For over two decades, we had a complicated APM. Stripped of its complexity, what it involved was a subsidy for LPG, kerosene and diesel—the fuels supposedly used by the poor. The subsidy was defined as the difference between the cost of importing the product and its consumer price. The benchmark is import prices since oil and oil products are what economists describe as "tradeables" and India is a major importer anyway. The subsidy bill was met largely by selling aviation fuel and petrol at more than their import parity price. Petrol provided what is called a "cross-subsidy". An oil-pool account that had both an inflow and outflow was created. This compensated the public-sector oil companies for the costs they incurred for refining and marketing oil products.

Cumulatively, the account showed a deficit of a high Rs 5,700 crore by 1995-96. But 1996-97 was a disaster year when the cumulative oil-pool deficit shot up to an astronomical Rs 15,976 crore. The immediate cause for this was the sudden increase in oil prices in the later half of 1996 following skirmishes involving Iraq. But the problem had been building up and P.V. Narasimha Rao's government failed to carry out the necessary price adjustments in 1994. Deve Gowda summoned the courage to increase oil prices in July 1996. But this was insufficient and in January 1997 the cumulative oil-pool deficit for 1997-98 was projected to touch Rs 18,000 crore. The Finance Ministry pushed for another round of price adjustments but this was resisted by the Petroleum Ministry and the United Front's Steering Committee.

As the crisis was building up, Arjun Sengupta, a member of the Planning Commission with close personal ties with the CPI(M) met the finance minister some time in May 1997 and volunteered to find a solution. Finance minister P. Chidambaram was not concerned with the motivation for Sengupta's back-channel activism. Sensing an opening, he setup a three-man committee under Sengupta's chairmanship and comprising the revenue and petroleum secretaries. The group submitted its report by July 1997 and suggested that the money owed by the government to the oil companies be converted into "oil bonds". The government would write out a cheque in favour of the oil companies for the cumulative oil-pool deficit amount. The oil companies would then invest this money in government securities carrying a 10.5 per cent rate of interest and redeemable over five years. The main advantage of this solution to the government was that it avoided an immediate price increase. To the oil companies, the gain was that balance sheets were cleaned up and a huge liability was converted into an asset.

These "oil bonds" would take care of the "stock" of the oil-pool deficit. But what was to be done to stem the "flow", that is control the annual additions? It was here that the Gujral government followed the Rao-Deve Gowda recipe. After announcing the oil bonds in September 1997, the Gujral cabinet in its last act in November 1997 took one of the boldest decisions ever—to abolish the Rs 1.80 subsidy on a litre of diesel and align Indian diesel prices with global prices. In addition, it announced the phased dismantling of the APM. Inevitably, the finance minister played a key role but an unlikely hero was Mulayam Singh Yadav, without whose backing his Samajwadi Party colleague who was petroleum minister would not come on board.

The Gujral package was comprehensive. A five-year duty structure was finalised. Prices of products like naphtha, fuel oil and bitumen were de-controlled and lowered immediately. By 2002, the 66 per cent subsidy on kerosene was to be brought down to 25 per cent and the 33 per cent for LPG was then to be reduced to 15 per cent. By then, all subsidies would be ex-plicitly provided for in the general budget. Petrol would continue to be priced at well over global prices in order to cross-subsidise kerosene and LPG.

However, the present subsidy on LPG of almost Rs 76 per15-kg cylinder is totally unwarranted. Kerosene is consumed by the poor both as cooking and lighting fuel and some subsidy, well tar-geted, is in order. But the current subsidy of about Rs 5.40 a litre is high and encourages adulteration.

Diesel prices on a full import parity basis should have been reduced by about Rs 2.50-3 a litre. They have been reduced by about a rupee a litre. This is because import parity has to be "adjusted" so that the oil-pool account generates money to amortise the oil bonds. Half of the bond value has already been redeemed in less than nine months, as against the original expectation of about two to three years, thanks to the bonanza that the BJP has got on account of declining oil prices.

This windfall should spur it to compress the timetable bequeathed by the Gujral government and complete the APM restructuring by 2000 itself.

25/01/1999

◆――――◆

NEW SUBSIDY RAJ
The PDS has been reformed but problems remain

If Kautilya were Atal Bihari Vajpayee's spin doctor, he would have encouraged the prime minister to say something like this: We are a responsible Government and so we cut subsidies but we are also a responsive Government and so we rolled back the cuts. No tears need be shed for sugar and LPG consumers, who have been enjoying huge subsidies that are simply not justifiable. But what about subsidies on the staples, rice and wheat?

There is a popular belief in this country that the public-distribution system (PDS)—the network of 4.3 lakh fair price ration shops that distribute essentials like wheat, rice, sugar, edible oil and kerosene—works in the interest of the poor. The PDS started off in the mid-'60s, but not as an instrument of supplying cheap food to the poor. It began as a buffer-stocking operation and was meant to stabilise prices for vocal urban consumers. Over time, governments began to see it as a poverty-alleviation programme.

If poverty were to be the criteria, Uttar Pradesh's share in the PDS subsidy should have been 18 per cent, whereas it has been around 8 per cent. Similarly Bihar's share should have been 16 per cent, while it has actually been 5 per cent. The major beneficiaries of the PDS are:

* Kerala which has drawn 10 per cent of the subsidy while its "poverty" share should be 3 per cent.
* Andhra Pradesh which has drawn 13 per cent of the subsidy as against a "poverty" share of 5 per cent.
* Gujarat and Karnataka are also major gainers. Ironically, Gujarat is among the country's largest producers of edible oil and also among the largest users of edible oil from the PDS.

There have been any number of studies to show that the PDS,

which is based on the principle of universal coverage, does not reach the truly poor, except perhaps in Andhra Pradesh, Kerala and Tamil Nadu. These states also run subsidised food schemes and nutrition programmes of their own and manage the PDS more effectively. Some economists have argued that open market prices would have been lower but for the PDS. R. Radhakrishna and his colleagues at the Centre for Economic and Social Studies (CESS), Hyderabad, have shown that the impact of the PDS on nutritional status and on poverty has been minimal. They have found that the PDS is not cost-effective since the Centre spends over Rs 4 to transfer Re 1 of income to the poor.

Wage-programmes like the Jawahar Rozgar Yojana and Maharashtra's Employment Guarantee Scheme as well as the Integrated Child Development Services are better in-struments of poverty alleviation. Nearly a third of the total food subsidy, according to the CESS study, is the carrying cost of buffer stocks—which, as agro-economist G.S. Bhalla has calculated, is 8-10 million tonnes over optimal levels. Offtake of sugar and kerosene from the PDS has been high. But for rice and wheat, the gap between allocation and offtake has fluctuated. In 1994-95 and 1995-96, offtake of wheat was just 55 per cent of the allocation. In 1992 P.V. Narasimha Rao launched a Revamped PDS or RPDS. It first attempted some changes by providing for special subsidies and increased allocations for the poorest 1,750 blocks of the country. But the RPDS was not successful. Total offtake from the PDS declined between 1992-93 and 1995-96, even though infla-tion in years like 1993-94 was high.

P. Chidambaram's July 1996 budget proposed another major restructuring of the PDS. After that it was a fierce battle between those in the United Front who wanted increased open-ended subsidies and those like the then finance minister who wanted the subsidies to bear some relation to poverty. He got a calculation done that was never made public since it was a political hot potato. This calculation showed that in 1996-97 Uttar Pradesh's poverty-based share of the food subsidy should have been Rs 1,031 crore, while it would have been Rs 375 crore if distri-bution was based on the prevalent criteria of the previous year's offtake. Corresponding figures for Bihar were Rs 923 crore and Rs 143 crore, for Madhya Pradesh Rs 575 crore and Rs 220 crore. But there would have been losers. Tamil Nadu's share would have fallen from Rs 625 crore to Rs 495 crore, Kerala's from Rs 623 crore to Rs 166 crore and Andhra Pradesh's from Rs 622 crore to Rs 392 crore.

After seven months of negotiations and based on state-wise Planning Commission estimates the new subsidy package was unveiled in February 1997. It was based on the BPL (below poverty line) and APL (above poverty line) concepts. BPL helped Uttar Pradesh, Bihar and Madhya Pradesh. APL protected the southern states. Each BPL family was to get 10 kg of foodgrains per month at subsidised prices. The subsidy for BPL families was to be 50 per cent and for APL families 10 per cent. Today it is 66 per cent for BPL and 20 per cent for APL families. Subsidy here refers to the difference between the economic cost of supply and the PDS issue price. The Targeted PDS—or TPDS—is a major step forward. This, even though it remains centralised and has been criticised for the uniform 10 kg-a-family norm and for the fact that the retail outlet sells the same commodity at two different prices, an inbuilt incentive for "leakages".

The TPDS is also silent on how to improve the unwieldy Food Corporation of India, the procurement and distribution agency. It also depends very critically on the infrastructure of the state government to identify the poor and distribute the foodgrains. Since one year of the TPDS has passed, it is time for a concurrent evaluation system to be instituted.

15/02/1999

❖

SO THERE'S LIFE AFTER DEBT
How India has escaped being East Asia—at least thus far

The burden of external debt has created a severe economic crisis in countries like Indonesia, South Korea, Thailand, Malaysia, Russia, Brazil and Pakistan. But although it is among the top eight indebted countries in the world, India has escaped the contagion. This is largely due to its prudent external debt management strategy—conceived and implemented by Manmohan Singh and consolidated by P. Chidambaram.

Memories are short. We have forgotten India faced an East Asia-type crisis in 1991. Our short-term debt—debt which has to be repaid within a year—had zoomed to 146 per cent of our foreign exchange reserves. Today, this is down to about 25 per cent. In mid-1997, when the East-Asian collapse began, the figure was 206 per cent in South Korea, 170 per cent in Indonesia, 145 per cent in Thailand and 60 per cent in Malaysia. Singh's external debt management strategy had many facets:

- pushing export growth;
- phasing out volatile NRI deposit schemes;
- monitoring all external commercial bor-rowings (ECBs);
- discouraging foreign loans of maturity less than seven years;
- limiting short-term credit to finance trade;
- ceasing to ask public-sector companies and financial institutions to borrow abroad on be-half of the government;
- facilitating non-debt creating inflows;
- a market-determined exchange rate system.

Many top economists and politicians advised P.V. Narasimha Rao, then prime minister, to take the default option and seek debt rescheduling. Rao was momentarily tempted. Fortunately, his finance minister prevailed. Singh's stand was one of both fiscal and moral rectitude.

There were many pressures on Singh and Chidambaram to liberalise ECB approvals. They did so in a measured manner, all along accused of being conservative. Events have vindicated their caution. The high point of debt management was reached in early 1997, when India discharged large repayment obligations amounting to about $2.5 billion with-out correspondingly increasing its external debt. Before the 1991 reforms, 95 per cent of foreign exchange inflows created a debt obligation. Today, this is down to 50 per cent. It must decline even faster.

The RBI's recent annual report places our external debt at $94 billion as on March 31, 1998. This is an increase of just $3 billion since 1990-91. It debunks the myth that our foreign exchange reserves have increased by incurring heavy debt obligations. The structure of our debt is different from that of other countries—half is comprised of debt on concessional terms and rupee debt to Russia. The World Bank adjusts the external debt of all countries to reflect the differences in structure of debt. Its adjusted value of external debt for India is now at about $75 billion.

There are no absolute rules for judging the sustaina-bility of a country's external debt. The debt service ratio—the proportion of export earnings and remittances consumed by repayments—is one index. This was 30 per cent in 1990-91, 19 per cent in 1997-98 and is projected to fall to 15 per cent by the turn of the century. The World Bank uses two indicators of sustainability. The first is the present value of debt. If this exceeds 50 per cent of national income, then the country has to worry. This ratio was 22 per cent for India in 1996, the latest year for which the World Bank has published calculations. Thus, on this score India is a less indebted country.

The second indicator is the value of debt as a percentage of exports. This sends us into the moderately indebted category. The ratio was 152 per cent for India in 1996. Anything below 130 per cent is considered low indebtedness. China's external debt is 40 per cent more than India's. But it is classified as a low indebted country on both counts. Our basic problem, therefore, is not high external debt per se—but poor export performance. This has been brought about by policy cobwebs of our own making.

India's external debt statistics are now among the most transparent in the world. Just how transparent they are is revealed by the fact that the Washington-based Institute of International Finance (IIF) puts out its own assessment of our short-term debt. According to it, our short-term debt is a little more than double what the RBI states.

Definitions vary. For example, the RBI calculates short-term debt on the basis of original maturity. The IIF calculates it on the basis of residual maturity. It also includes some NRI deposits that the RBI excludes. Given its influence, it would be prudent not to ignore what the IIF is saying. India too should be accounting for guarantees, contingent liabilities and the full costs of NRI deposits.

Clearly, we have managed our external debt better than most countries. But in a world increasingly governed by sentiment as much as fundamentals, there is the possibility of the external debt knell being sounded again. This may well happen if policy-paralysis continues, if reform-fatigue persists and if we insist on misreading the current global turmoil as a justification for slowing down liberalisation.

28/09/1998

JALAN NEEDS TO START WORRYING
India's high fiscal deficit is a cause for great concern

Bimal Jalan, the affable Governor of the Reserve Bank of India (RBI), is most careful about what he says and does. That is why his reported statement in Washington DC that India's fiscal deficit should not be a cause for external worry is most puzzling. This is not what the RBI as an institution has said in the past or is saying now. Jalan was addressing foreign investors. He told them to worry more about the current account deficit than the fiscal deficit. A current account deficit means the country is borrowing from abroad. The current account deficit, projected to be 2 per cent of GDP in 1998-99, is still well below the danger level because of lower economic growth. But the fiscal deficit is already at unsustainable levels.

India's crisis of 1990-91 was characterised by the highest overall fiscal deficit of 12.3 per cent of GDP and the highest current account deficit of 3.2 per cent of GDP. But in actual practice the relationship has not been direct and unidirectional. Countries like Malaysia, South Korea and Thailand and Indonesia were destroyed by unmanageable current account deficits, even as they ran very low fiscal deficits. A high fiscal deficit will result in a high current account deficit. But no fiscal deficit does not necesarily mean no current account deficit.

If we want short-term funds, then the Government is right in highlighting the importance of the current account deficit. But Kautilya thought our objective was to discourage short-term investors and attract long-term ones. If this is still the goal, then the fiscal deficit is crucial. Kautilya is putting himself in Jalan's place and trying to think like him in order to make sense of his statement. If the argument is that the fiscal deficit is not important at all, then the governor is wrong. The fiscal deficit matters. The sustainable level of deficit in the country as a whole is around 7 per cent of GDP, whereas today the combined deficit of the Centre, states and public enterprises is 9-10 per cent of GDP.

But let us assume this isn't what Jalan meant. What he wanted to say was not that fiscal deficit didn't matter but that the nature of financing the deficit mattered more. True, but how do we judge this, specially since this year the governor himself—aided by the chief economic adviser—has convinced the finance minister not to indicate the level of monetisation of the deficit in the budget?

Let us also assume the governor did not wish to convey that the fiscal deficit is unimportant but that what is more crucial is the use the fiscal deficit is put to. Surely, here India has a huge problem. Half its fiscal deficit finances the revenue deficit—the gap between current receipts and current expenditures like interest payments, subsidies and establishment costs. As long as this situation persists, the ability of the Government to invest more in physical and social infrastructure is going to remain severely constrained. This should worry all investors.

Another argument Jalan may have had in mind is that fiscal deficits should matter more when savings rates are low. When the savings rate is, say, 10 per cent of GDP—as in much of the West—then a fiscal deficit of 3 per cent of GDP is a recipe for disaster. Jalan may feel that since India's savings rate is 26 per cent of GDP, the country can sustain a higher level of fiscal deficit.

The flaw in this argument is simply that in the developed countries of the West almost all the savings are financial savings. In India, household savings comprise 20.3 per cent of GDP and are made up of both financial and physical savings. Financial savings alone are 11.4 per cent of GDP. If from this figure, 9-10 per cent of GDP is being pre-empted by the Centre and the state governments to meet their deficits, then clearly our capacity to increase productive investments is limited. Actually, this whole external-internal distinction that is implicit in the governor's remarks is untenable. Imbalances in the domestic account manifest themselves in imbalances in the external account. Among key policies that discriminated against India's agricultural sector in the pre-1991 era were the overvalued exchange rate and high import duties on industrial products.

Often, external liberalisation has lower start-up costs and energises internal liberalisation. Also, all investors look at the same macro-economic and micro-economic indicators before taking a decision. East Asia was killed externally by the fragility of its internal banking system. A top economic administrator told Kautilya that the correct version of the governor's point may well be that the fiscal deficit is not a cause for external worry provided monetary policy is tight. In that case, interest rates will shoot up, spending will be reduced and imports will come down. Apart from its impact on growth, this is a purely short-term, ad hoc view.

Kautilya would suggest that the governor forget his firefighting mandarin years in Delhi, where he had to be sensitive to the political economy. Instead, he should follow in the footsteps of his distinguished predecessor who had declared intellectual autonomy from his friends and colleagues in Delhi.

19/10/1998

◆——◆

SLIM DOWN OUR BABUDOM
More pay and less work in government is leading to fiscal collapse

In his recent budget speech, finance minister Yashwant Sinha very rightly criticised the predecessor United Front regime for ignoring the recommendations of the Fifth Pay Commission on the restructuring of government. Against the advice of the then finance minister and cabinet secretary, I.K. Gujral's cabinet abdicated all sense of proportion and responsibility by providing a huge pay hike to around 3.9 million Central government employees. The total expenditure on this huge army in 1999-2000 will come to about Rs 32,000 crore as compared to a plan outlay of Rs 27,400 crore in the energy sector and of Rs 17,400 crore in the social sectors. And this excludes the annual pension bill of over Rs 10,000 crore.

However, Sinha is being a trifle unfair. In 1997, there was no politician who had the courage to take a stand publicly against the pay hike. In fact, leaders cutting across party lines addressed rallies almost daily in support of these recommendations and none came to the support of P. Chidambaram, who, seeing the writing on the wall and being subject to a daily barrage of slogan- shouting in his office, threw in the towel pretty easily.

But what is Sinha himself up to? His ministerial colleagues are busy trying to re-negotiate settled pay and allowance packages. Worse, Sinha himself took an atrocious decision in January that flies in the face of expenditure control. He made the basic pension of all those government servants who retired before 1.1.96, which presumably includes himself, equal to at least 50 per cent of the minimum of the revised pay scales, making the pension more than the salary ever drawn. This is a wholly undeserved bonanza.

And just as he announced the "abolition" of four secretary-level posts in his ministry, right under his nose two defunct additional secretary-level posts in the Central Boards of Direct Taxes and Excise and Customs are being revived. Kautilya lauds Sinha for at least using dreaded words in his budgets. In 1998 he used that perilous P word: privatisation. This year, it is the dangerous D word: downsizing. Two aspects of government employment will determine the nature and speed of downsizing. First, the overwhelming bulk of employment and expenditure is in just five areas—railways (40 per cent), police and paramilitary forces (14 per cent), civilian defence (13 per cent), posts (9 per cent) and telecom (9 per cent). Thus around 85 per cent of establishment expenditure is in what may be called "operational" areas, as opposed to the other 15 per cent, which is in purely "administrative" areas.

Second, 94 per cent of employment and expenditure is in group C and D posts—that is stenographers, clerks, assistants, peons, postmen, daftaries, police constables and so on. Government employment has great social value in these two categories. Something like 20 per cent of group C and 28 per cent of group D employees and 68 per cent of sweepers belong to the SC/ST category. One option for down-sizing may well be to abolish the approximately 3.2 lakh vacancies that exist. But this will have to be tempered to reflect the nature of the vacancies. Blind abolition if the posts are reserved for SCs and STs will be neither desirable nor feasible.

The protection that government employees get under Article 311 of the Constitution and under the rules framed following various judgements of the Supreme Court make it impossible to impose any form of performance-based employment in government, a prerequisite for any downsizing. These rules should be amended. In addition, the logic of having the "operational" segments of the railways covered by laws like the In-dustrial Disputes Act needs a relook.

Perhaps keeping in view that about 3 per cent of employees retire every year, the Pay Commission had suggested that a 30 per cent reduction in government employment be carried out over 10 years. By then, the Sixth Pay Commission's recommendations will be implemented. This is a worthwhile objective but requires detailing. The commission says a freeze on recruitment alone can do the job. This is unrealistic. So other options like mergers and abolitions of ministries, the transfer of Centrally-sponsored schemes to states in areas like agriculture, education and health and the introduction of a liberal "golden handshake" after 20 years of service to supplement the existing VRS assume greater importance.

Often, the smokescreen of parliamentary accountability is used to justify the continuation of unnecessary departments like banking and insurance, both in Sinha's own bailiwick. Such arguments have to be brushed aside. A beginning could be made in downsizing the 5,510-strong Planning Commission. It costs the exchequer over Rs 70 crore a year. The "operational" areas, specifically railways, posts and telecom, must also be reorganised into fully commercial entities. Finally, will Sinha have the courage to change the structure of allowances? Going by past trends, the overtime bill alone in 1999-2000 will come to about Rs 640 crore, health and education allowances to Rs 270 crore and the leave travel concession to Rs 160 crore. And while we are at it, how about a six-day week as some return to the nation in terms of extra work for the pay windfall?

22/03/1999

NEW SET OF FISCAL RULES
Legislation to introduce fiscal responsibility at the Centre is tabled

The government introduced the fiscal Responsibility and Budget Management Bill, 2000 just before Parliament adjourned on December 20. This is a major step forward, although just five days later the prime minister, defying the Finance Ministry and the Planning Commission, made a complete mockery of the bill by grandiloquently announcing three new schemes.

The bill commits the Central government to:

- a fiscal deficit of 2 per cent of GDP by 2006, from the 5.1 per cent of GDP budgeted for 2000-01.
- a revenue deficit of zero by 2006, from the 3.6 per cent of GDP budgeted for 2000-01.
- total internal and external liabilities at 50 per cent of GDP by 2011, from the present level of about 56 per cent of GDP.
- prohibition of borrowings by the Central government from the RBI after 2004 except under special well-defined circumstances.
- expenditure cuts whenever there is a shortfall of revenue or excess of expenditure.

Interestingly, Article 292 of the Constitution already provides for fiscal austerity. In the Constituent Assembly de-bates, Babasaheb Ambedkar had occasion to remark, "... I even concede that there might be an Annual Debt Act made by Parliament prescribing or limiting the power of the executive as to how much they can borrow within that year." Hopefully, our MPs will ensure the passage of this bill by April-May 2001. Indeed, if the Government is serious, why not issue an ordinance straightaway and have that ratified later.

Our economic malaise arises from the fact that the revenue deficit comprises the bulk of the fiscal deficit—up from two-fifths to two-thirds over the past decade. The revenue deficit is simply the difference between revenue receipts and revenue expenditure. A revenue deficit means that ·we are not living within our means and are borrowing to meet daily consumption needs. However, one caveat is important here. Spending in vital sectors like education, health and rural development is classified as "revenue" expenditure. This has to actually increase. It is the other "non-productive" segment of revenue expenditure, comprising subsidies, interest payments, defence and establishment costs, that needs to be controlled. This segment now constitutes about 70 per cent of revenue expenditure.

The fiscal deficit is the difference between total receipts (revenue plus recovery of loans) and total expenditure. This is a comprehensive measure of the government's borrowings from all sources. As the scholarly former RBI governor C. Rangarajan points out in his new collection of speeches, Perspectives on Indian Economy, if you have a household financial savings rate of around 10 per cent of GDP and a fiscal deficit of around 9-10 per cent of GDP for the country as a whole, it means that almost the entire pool of financial savings is being appropriated by the public sector broadly defined. Upward pressure on interest rates, and thereby a downward push on investment rates, is then inevitable. The single most important task before the country is to increase the rate of public and private investment in industry, agriculture and physical and social infrastructure. That will just not happen with the present structure of public expenditure, both at the Centre and in states.

Countries like the US, Germany, New Zealand, Canada, Brazil and Argentina have the balanced budget rule—revenues and expenditures have to balance annually. The European Union has a debt ceiling rule which places a limit on the stock of public debt as a proportion of national income. A third type of rule is the borrowing rule that places a limit on gover nment's borrowing from its central bank. Such rules have deli-vered unprecedented prosperity in countries like the US but in other instances like Brazil and Argentina, have been unable to stem economic disasters. East Asia practised fiscal prudence without legislation. Having legislation is one thing, having the desired outcome is quite another. Would the country have been saved from the Fifth Pay Commission disaster in 1997 had such legislation been there? Certainly not.

Implicit in the bill is tight expenditure control. However, we also have a revenue problem. Gross tax revenues of the Central government have declined from 10.8 per cent of GDP to slightly over 9 per cent now. Better tax administration and expansion of the tax base itself will be needed to reverse this trend. Rules on revenue management must go hand-in-hand with rules on expenditure management. To this extent, the present bill is incomplete. Also, in our federal set-up, fiscal management has to be a continuing joint venture between the Centre and the states. As a starter, the states will need to enact similar legislation and be in sync with what the Centre is doing.

08/01/2001

---◆—◆---

TIME FOR ARTICLE 360

COLA—cost of living allowance—is taking the fizz out of the economy

On september 15, 2001, the Prime Minister addressed the nation over Doordarshan and spoke about the inevitability of taking hard decisions on the economy. Three days later, his Government sanctioned a Rs 800 crore bonanza for Central government employees by way of a DA increase. On February 28, 2002, while presenting his fifth budget, the finance minister waxed eloquent on expenditure discipline. Nineteen days later, his Government sanctioned yet another round of DA payment to its employees and pensioners. This time the cost to the exchequer was over Rs 1,800 crore. At a time when the inflation rate has been declining, such largesse is inexplicable. At a time when the Centre's finances are so badly stretched and half of its revenue receipts go toward interest payments alone, such a bounty is inexcusable.

At a time when there is an urgent need to step up growth-stimulating and equity-inducing public investment, particularly in physical and social infrastructure, such a blatantly political move is anti-poor. But who is to protest? Yashwant Sinha blames his predecessor for destabilising public finances by accepting the recommendations of the Fifth Pay Commission. But he forgets that no political party had opposed the recommendations in 1996-97. Yet it was the same Sinha who linked pensions of those retirees prior to January 1, 1986 to the vastly enhanced "revised" pay scales.

DA stands for dearness allowance and is the compensation given to government and public-sector employees for cost-of-living increases. These employees account for around 5 per cent of India's workforce of over 300 million. But it is their pay, perquisites and privileges that are not only well protected but continually enhanced. DA is calculated using the Consumer Price Index for Industrial Workers (CPI-IW) with 1982 as the base. Unlike other price indicators like the Wholesale Price Index, the CPI-IW has not been re-structured to keep up with the times as it should because of pressure from government employee unions. Hence it is the only one that reveals increasing inflation in 2001, apart from showing the highest rate of increase in the past decade by a substantial margin.

For the financial year 2002-3, the DA bill for the Centre is budgeted at a whopping Rs 12,500 crore, while the salary bill is pegged at around Rs 18,000 crore. Before the Fifth Pay Commission, the rate of neutralisation was 100 per cent for Class III and IV employees, 75 per cent for Class II and 65 per cent for Class I employees. The commission changed this to a uniform 100 per cent for all employees. Even if there was political pressure, the least Sinha could have done was opt for a lower rate of neutralisation keeping in view the benign inflation position.

P. Chidambaram did make one valiant attempt to manage the DA burden. But the Law Ministry opined that DA could not be tampered with without the consent of employee unions and that the only way to manage the salary bill was by declaring a financial emergency under Article 360 of the Constitution. This provision allows for reduction in salaries and allowances when "a situation has arisen whereby the financial stability or credit of India or any part of the territory thereof is threatened". Chidambaram did not pursue the matter further. But the Law Ministry may have been a bit too cautious; after all, some states like Maharashtra and Assam have announced a freeze on DA. And what about the precedent of July 1974 when, following the first oil price shock of October 1973 and a monsoon failure, the inflation rate in 1973-74 had crossed 20 per cent. Indira Gandhi had turned to the then chief economic adviser in the Finance Ministry for some radical ideas to control the spiralling price rise. This economist came up with bold measures which, among other initiatives, froze wage and salary increases and 50 per cent of the DA payments in the organised sector. The inflation rate fell steeply to minus 1 per cent in 1975-76 and 2 per cent the following year. It was this achievement, incidentally, that made Manmohan Singh's reputation.

There is one view that the salary bill of the Central government is not unsustainable judged from the fact that salaries, allowances and pensions now average about 2.4 per cent of the GDP, no different from the proportion a decade ago. But to argue that the government's establishment expenditure is not having debilitating consequences is to run away from harsh realities. In Uttar Pradesh and Bengal for instance, the revenue is not enough to pay even the salary of state employees. Automatic indexation, which is what DA is all about, is accentuating the fiscal woes of the states. It is high time Delhi practised what it preaches. Otherwise, it will undermine what some reformist chief ministers like Digvijay Singh, A.K. Antony and Tarun Gogoi are trying to do. Actually, truth be told, the situation envisaged by B.R. Ambedkar himself while conceiving and piloting what became Article 360 is already here.

08/04/2002

◆——◆

BIG BOMBS, BIGGER BILLS
The Buddha's smile may turn out to be the finance minister's frown

For the post few days, we have been preoccupied with the external costs of sanctions. More critical are the internal economic implications of going nuclear. May 11 has, in the words of Lt-General V.R. Raghavan, one of our most distinguished armymen, an inexorable logic that will confer strategic benefits. This demands that we look at costs and benefits objectively.

The nuclear establishment all over the world is shrouded in extreme secrecy. Data is withheld, costs are underestimated and what comes out is doctored. Even in an open society like the US, the real cost of the nuclear weapons programme has never been revealed or investigated. That is, till earlier this month. For the very first time, the Brookings Institution in Washington has conducted a detailed study on the costs of the US nuclear arsenal. Main findings are now available on the Internet (http://www.brook.edu). The cost of the US nuclear weapons programme is placed at $5 trillion, that is $5,000 billion, over the period 1940-95. The Brookings study shows the cost of building the bomb itself is not very high. It forms just 8 per cent of the overall cost of the nuclear arsenal. The main costs are in delivering the bomb (40 per cent) and in commanding, controlling and defending against the bomb (20 per cent). In addition, there is the burden of environmental and waste management.

Obviously, if we follow the American or the Soviet route, the Indian economy will be destroyed. The alternative that suggests itself is a scaled down version of what the Americans did. But scaling down by what factor? Even doing so by a factor of 100 will imply that the cost of India going nuclear is about $1 billion per year.

However, if we have just a 10-year perspective, then we could be looking at a figure of around $5 billion or about Rs 20,000 crore per year. This too is clearly untenable. The moral is obvious. If we are going to be a nuclear state following American-style doctrines and even scaled-down versions of American hardware build-up, then we are doomed. Our society will just not be able to stand the strain of devoting such a large chunk of public expenditure to a nuclear programme. Already, about 17 per cent of the Central Government's expenditure that is made public is on defence and 45 per cent of all science and technology expenditure is on defence, atomic energy and space. Agriculture research and development is treated on a par with atomic energy. The only option is to follow an affordable strategy that in the words of Kanti Bajpai and Varun Sahni—two young defence thinkers—will be both secure and solvent. We must decide on the level of spending that can be sustained and on our strategic doctrine. Only then can we decide what our nuclear weapons portfolio should be.

Security does not come from mere numbers. China has 14 missiles pointed at the US, the US has 1,400 aimed at China. Yet there is deterrence. Security will also not come by blindly copying the western doctrine of deterrence, which is based on certainty. K. Subrahmanyam—doyen of Indian strategic thinkers—has argued that a civilisation which has produced a Trishanku and an Ardhanareeshwar can and should live with a deterrence doctrine based on uncertainty.

All plans and budgets must be based on one truth: nuclear weapons serve no military purpose whatsoever and are absolutely useless except to deter one's opponent from using them. If this is followed, then the issue is what type of minimum nuclear deterrent capability needs to be built up: warheads, test facilities, ballistic missiles, land-, air- and sea-based delivery systems, long-range aircraft, nuclear submarines, radar warning systems, satellite communication systems, airborne surveillance systems and command centres. In 1985, Rajiv Gandhi had set up a committee on defence expenditure. Headed by Arun Singh, it had reportedly worked out the costs of a nuclear weapons programme. However, its report has never been made public.

But Brigadier Vijay Nair, a key staff member of this committee, later published a book in which he methodically calculated that a nuclear weapon systems programme would cost India Rs 7,000 crore over a 10-year period. A large number of costs, like that on nuclear submarines, manned aircraft and Airborne Warning and Control Systems (AWACs) were treated as sunk costs. Some of the brigadier's assumptions need a second look. A few figures need to be updated in light of the new revelations on the American costs. Some of the sunk costs may well have to be included. Additional costs will be incurred by our space and atomic energy establishments as well. Exchange rates have changed.

Nuclear weapons may not be substitutable for conventional weapons. Therefore, the argument that a nuclear weapons programme will mean lower costs for conventional defence is overdone. Thus, a reasonable conclusion is a nuclear weapon system programme will entail an additional expenditure of at least Rs 3,000 crore per year over the next decade. That too, only if our doctrines are sensible and the hawks are kept at bay.

01/06/1998

◆━━━◆

TACKLING POKHRANOMICS
The 1991 reforms equipped us to defeat sanctions.
More reforms will arm us better.

Sanctions imposed on India following Pokhran II will undoubtedly have some effect. Half a billion dollars of Japanese aid is in jeopardy. German aid negotiations have been called off. Indo-American collaboration in some projects, such as for the light combat aircraft, faces an uncertain future. The US Exim Bank's lines of credit may not be available for infrastructure projects.

World Bank and Asian Development Bank projects totalling almost a billion dollars have been put into cold storage. Indian companies making overseas borrowings will have to bear higher interest costs amounting to nearly $40 million (Rs 160 crore) per year. There is a silver lining. Despite the impact of the sanctions, the economy will not be crippled. We will be saved simply because we are more of an open economy now than we were a decade ago, because we are more trade-oriented than aidoriented. A growing number of foreign companies have an expanding stake in India's prosperity and there's an increasing number of Indian companies with global stakes.

Mercifully, there seems to be a breeze of pragmatism blowing across the saffron curtain. Although it is doing so in a kneejerk manner, the Government is clearing many joint ventures in oil exploration and production and in mineral prospecting. This flurry of activity should not peter out. There are other areas, like in-surance, where the Indian market can be used as a bait to entice well-connected foreign companies. For instance, one of the most influential men in Washington is Hank Greenberg of the American Insurance Group (AIG). Allowing publications like The Wall Street Journal and Time to publish in India— as they have been trying to do for the past few years—will provide us new champions. We must carry forward liberalisation not just be-cause it will help us beat sanctions, but also because it is in our economic and technological interest to do so.

Investment by itself does not gain us lobbies. Trade does so instantly. True, investment and trade are interlinked. If more MNCs invest in India, it will trigger more imports and exports. This, however, is in the long term. In the short term, it is pure and simple trade that matters.

China's leverage comes from a voracious appetite for imports. China buys eight times the amount of goods from the US than we do. This, more than anything else, gives China that extra leverage. Over 200,000 American jobs are dependent on trade with China. Fourteen per cent of Boeing's sales are to China alone. The localisation of Win-dows software in Chinese has created a multi-billion dollar market for Microsoft; India remains merely a source of cheap manpower for the company. We must continue with trade policy reforms. Small-scale reservations are hampering faster export growth in industries that matter, like textiles, consumer goods, toys and light engineering.

The United Front government had agreed to a six-year phase out of quantitative restrictions (QRs) on 2,700 odd goods, commodities and products by March 31, 2003. By this date, all these will be freely importable into India but at certain tariff levels. India and the US are, however, locked in a dispute over this at the WTO. A solution is at least three to four months away. It is in our interest to settle it by offering to front-load 200-300 items of significant interest to the Americans.

Meanwhile, India should seize the initiative and boldly declare it is removing all QRs over the next four years. Instead of year-by-year announcements, the entire four-year schedule should be made public straightaway. This will also give time to domestic producers to brace up for international competition.

There are other pressing WTO obligations that have still to be met. We have yet to carry out changes in our patent laws even though we have lost all appeals at the WTO and have just another 11 months to meet the obligations. Again, these changes are needed not just to meet WTO commitments but because a world-class system for protecting intellectual property rights will strengthen Indian science and technology—which has found a latter-day Nehru in Atal Bihari Vajpayee.

Japan requires careful handling. Manmohan Singh and P. Chidambaram had invested a great deal of personal effort and time on Japan. It had begun to pay dividends. But this has now received a setback—and we are not helping ourselves by foot-dragging on the Maruti-Suzuki dispute. Japanese sentiments have been hurt. It will require painstaking diplomacy to restore India's image.

Finally, the Indian diaspora in the US will play a key role in managing the fallout. It is rich and influential. When the then finance minister faced difficulty in meeting Senator Jesse Helms in October 1997, it was Swadesh Chatterjee, a well-connected North Carolina-based Indian-American, who delivered.

Among all political parties, the BJP is best organised to mobilise the ABCDEFGHIs (American Born Confused Desis Emigrated from

Gujarat, Hindu Indians). But this should be a national and not a partisan effort. And it must be part of a well-orchestrated plan for building long-term relationships—and not just a short-term damage control exercise.

08/06/1998

◆————◆

WAR AND COSTS
Kargils can be managed by having more Cargills

The continuing military operations in Kargil are aising serious economic concerns. Some industry captains are worried about the fiscal deficit coming under pressure. These are largely exaggerated fears that arise because of a failure to distinguish between "sunk" costs and "incremental" costs. Most of the costs have already been incurred and the extra costs would not be astronomical. The 1965 war, for example, cost something like Rs 50 crore extra while the 1971 operation is estimated to have entailed an additional expenditure of around Rs 350 crore. And these were full-scale wars fought on many fronts.

A second concern is what pro-longed tensions will do to market sentiment. As long as the language is one of peace and the action is seen to be contained within the Kargil sector, the markets will not be unduly disturbed. But at the same time if eco-nomic indicators do not improve and if the pace of liberalisation does not accelerate, then market sentiment will surely turn negative. The rupee has come under pressure in the past few days but the downward adjustment may not be totally unwelcome. International pressure on India has been most benign but we should not bank on this continuing. Kashmir will remain on the world's radar screen and one way of increasing our leverage is by pushing faster investment and trade liberalisation.

What is, however, more unsettling is a third concern that has been voiced to Kautilya by some military friends. This has to do with the level of defence expenditure. The criticism is that economic reforms and liberalisation have eroded India's defence capability. In the '80s, India's defence budget averaged 3.2 per cent of GDP annually. In the '90s, this has declined to an annual average of about 2.6 per cent of GDP. But does this explain Kargil? Or are there more deep-rooted reasons like failures to gather, analyse and act on intelligence, political complacency and the complete ineffectiveness of the National Security Council (NSC)?

Without doubt, defence expenditure has been under a tight leash in the '90s as indeed has all government expenditure. This is because of the necessity of bringing the fiscal deficit under control. This pressure has been heightened because of the unwillingness and incapacity of governments to control growth in the numerous open-ended subsidies that serve little social purpose and in the size of the administration and expenditure on privileged government employees, as also because of their failure to privatise a public sector that has clearly outlived its technological and investment utility. Even today, there is absolutely no sense of austerity to reflect the long-term impacts of Kargil. Who will pick up the courage to say that 50 per cent of all future DA instalments to government employees will be paid in cash and the balance invested in, say, 20-year, zero-interest Defence Bonds?

What the critics also fail to point out is that in Pakistan too the defence budget has declined from an annual average of 6.5 per ent of GDP in the previous decade to about 5.7 per cent in the '90s. Similarly, in China the decline is around 25 per cent in the past decade and defence spending is now slightly over 4 per cent of GDP. There is no question that the defence establishment is subject to greater budgetary control in India than in Pakistan and China. India's annual defence budget would have gone up by about 10 per cent annually had the Defence Ministry got what it wanted. But defence is not unique. The same could well be said about education, health and irrigation.

The defence budget is yet to reflect the nuclear dimension fully. But even within the conventional military framework, is the present level of defence spending disastrously low? The Institute of Defence Studies and Analyses (IDSA) calculates that a defence expenditure of around 3 per cent of GDP is sustainable, although others like Vice-Admiral K.K. Nayyar point out that India needs a defence budget in the region of 5 per cent. This presumably incorporates the nuclear component. There are many in India who believe we must escalate defence spending because this will then cause Pakistan to do likewise— and forcing it into the same trap that the erstwhile Soviet Union fell into vis-a-vis the US. What the proponents of this view do not fully appreciate is that if this happens, the possibility of India too going the USSR way cannot be discounted.

The problem with our defence budget lies more in its structure and the way it is spent. Pay, allowances and pensions, growing at over 10 per cent per year, consume the annual increments and now account for almost half of defence spending. Equipment modernisation and systems upgradation do not get more than 10 per cent of the total outlay. Worse, modernisation tends to be, in IDSA chief Jasjit Singh's words, cyclical and is undertaken, if at all, in spurts. Delays in actual procurement due to aggressive claims made by proponents of indigenisation or competitive pressures imposed by rival import lobbies and their local patrons further put off modernisation. Even if money is kept aside, decisions do not get taken. It's 10 years now but India has yet to decide on acquiring the advanced jet trainer. K. Subrahmanyam, the doyen of our defence experts, argues that as important as modernisation of equipment is the modernisation of the organisation structure at all levels, a task attempted only once in the past by the late General K. Sundarji. For maximum effectiveness, both modernisations have to go hand-in-hand.

◆——◆

B. States

NEW SINGLE TAX POOL
In a pro-states move, Parliament approves
a new system of tax devolution

Om May 9, the Lok Sabha finally passed the 89th Amendment to the Constitution that creates a single divisible pool of Central taxes. This is a historic step. Till now, only income tax and Union excise duties have been shared with and devolved to the states under articles 270 and 272 of the Constitution. The share of states for the past 15 years or so has been 85 per cent in the case of income tax and 45 per cent for excise duties. The buoyant taxes, that is the taxes that have shown higher rates of growth, namely corporation tax and customs duties, have not been shared. Now these four and some other taxes will be pooled by the Centre and 29 per cent given to the states and Union Territories. The 29 per cent share would be made effective from April 1, 1996 and will be reviewed every five years by successive Finance Commissions. Historically, around 27 per cent of all taxes of the Centre have been devolved. Thus, the states have gained. More important than specific shares, however, is the principle that states will share in the overall tax buoyancy. That is why Finance Minister Yashwant Sinha has said that the bonds of "cooperative federalism" would be strengthened with this change. Tax reforms in the country will also be facilitated.

The Tenth Finance Commission recommended the concept of a single divisible tax pool in November 1994. P. Chidambaram announced the acceptance of this recommendation in his July 1996 budget. Discussion papers were then prepared for deliberations in the Inter-State Council which gave its green signal in July 1997. Legislation was also finalised but then the United Front government fell in November 1997. It is a sign of the changing polity that Sinha accepted this idea in his very first vote-on-account in March 1998. He has changed "gross" to "net" proceeds but that is only a technicality since the difference between the two is being made up through another transfer window. This creates a confusion that states have lost but the reality is otherwise. While the continuity should be applauded, it is a telling commentary on our decision-making processes that 46 months have elapsed between a radical budget announcement and its implementation.

States will, however, not be completely happy even though their share has gone up from 27 per cent to 29 per cent. Some of them were demanding a share in excess of 40 per cent. They will also not be totally satisfied with the coverage of the pool itself. They would be unhappy that surcharges and cesses have been excluded from the sharing pool. Article 268 of the Constitution gives the power to levy certain taxes to the Central government but these are collected and retained by the states. In the interest of uniformity, these taxes have been kept out of the single pool and rightly so. Central sales tax and consignment tax have also been excluded. Indeed, both these taxes are, in themselves, undesirable as they have fragmented and distorted the domestic economy and prevented the emergence of an Indian common market. Some states have also been suggesting a constitutional amendment so that states could levy service taxes since the contribution of the services sector to their economy is approaching 50 per cent. Many of these issues will, no doubt, engage the attention of the Constitution Review Commission which should ponder over the paradox of provinces in China enjoying greater financial autonomy than in India. But what is true of the states in relation to the Centre here is equally valid for local bodies vis-a-vis the states themselves.

The states should accept 29 per cent as a first milestone and move on. Their main problem is not just in-adequate funds flow from the Centre. It is also true that states need urgent debt relief. Besides, it is incontestable that the Centre's Fifth Pay Commission recommendations have destroyed state finances. But their fiscal mess is largely the creation of the states themselves and arises from poor management of both tax and non-tax revenue—enormous leakages in sales tax and state excise duty collections, unwillingness to reform power and irrigation water pricing and recover user charges and in a wholly distorted pattern of public expenditure, a significant chunk of which is consumed by salaries, pensions and interest payments. Power holds the key and if this one sector alone is reformed and run along commercial lines, between half and three-fifth of the revenue deficit of most states would vanish and more resources would become available for primary education, public health and nutrition. Some states like Orissa, Andhra Pradesh, Karnataka, Uttar Pradesh, Rajasthan and Haryana have embarked on power sector reforms. But there is still a long, long way to go.

22/05/2000

◆—◆

FALLOUT OF FAROOQ
The issue of greater fiscal autonomy for states is very much alive

Farooq Abdullah's demand for autonomy to Jammu & Kashmir (J&K) may have been rejected in its present formulation but the issue will not go away. The state is, of course, sui generis—unique, one of a kind—and will have to be tackled as such. But the colourful doctor-politician's sentiments on autonomy, specially as they relate to economic matters, have evoked support from many other state chief ministers.

Economists use a term called "vertical imbalance" to denote the mismatch between revenue raising capacity and expenditure needs as far as different levels of governmental units are concerned. To some extent, vertical imbalance is built into any federation since the Central government has a comparative advantage in raising revenues while the states are better placed to spend money more effectively. Even so, among all federations or unions of states, India has the highest degree of vertical fiscal imbalance. In a paper prepared for the Asian Development Bank recently, India's leading scholar of inter-governmental fiscal relations, Bangalore-based economist M. Govinda Rao estimates that:

—states in India now raise 38 per cent of current revenues but account for 57 per cent of total expenditure;

—from the revenue sources assigned to them, states finance just 47 per cent of their total expenditure.

Among all federations and unions of states, Rao points out that fiscal centralisation is the maximum in India. Of course, what is true of the states vis-a-vis the Centre is also true of rural and urban local bodies vis-a-vis the states themselves. Paradoxically, even in communist China, provinces seem to have greater freedom—they collect about 60 per cent of total revenues. While rejecting the J&K autonomy proposal, the Vajpayee Government has sworn by the Sarkaria Commission on Centre-state relations. The commission was set up in March 1983 in the backdrop of the Akali agitation on the Anandpur Sahib Resolution and amidst clamour for autonomy by non-Congress chief ministers. The chairman was Justice R.S. Sarkaria, a retired Supreme Court judge, and the members were the noted economist S. R. Sen and the redoubtable administrator B. Sivaraman.

The commission did not have an easy task. The political context was vastly different from what it is today. It sent out a detailed questionnaire to political parties in January 1984 asking for a response in three months. months! In the first two years of its working, only 10 states had replied. But the commission laboured hard and submitted its report in the middle of 1987. It made a number of workman like recommendations on legislative, administrative and financial relations, planning, agriculture and forests, mines and minerals, inter-state water disputes and civil supplies. But the basic framework was kept intact even as the states were given more room for manoeuvring.

The economic landscape has been transformed in the 1990s necessitating a whole new look at the Centre-states- local bodies triangle. Three far-reaching developments have already taken place for which successive governments—Congress, UF and NDA—deserve credit. First, instead of sharing just income tax and excise duty, now the Centre will share all the taxes with a slightly in-creased share for the states. Second, barring Bihar and Pondicherry, all the states now have uniform floor rates of sales tax. Third, the states have agreed to move over to a value-added tax system by April 1, 2001. The deadline will slip but the principle has been accepted. In addition, the institution of a State Finance Commission is in place although the mindset is still largely one of mere delegation rather than of decentralisation of functions, functionaries and finances.

There are many issues being raised by the states that relate to matters like interest rates, overdraft clearing period, loan-grant mix, externally-aided projects, release of Finance Commission grants, ceilings on profession tax, small savings, royalty rates on natural resources and Centrally-sponsored schemes that can be decided upon by the government if it wants to. It must do so quickly. But there are other larger issues—like the power to tax the growing services sector and the freedom to borrow from overseas like companies do—that will require amendments to the Constitution. It is, therefore, timely that the Constitution Review Commission has set up an expert group chaired by former finance secretary M. Narasimham to prepare a new fiscal framework. This offers an opportunity of reforming the present structure of inter-governmental economic relations so as to promote cooperative federalism, the essence of which is sound fiscal health of the Centre, states and local bodies.

17/07/2000

◆　　◆

THE FLOW OF FUNDS
The fiscal dentists have submitted their report
on filling of budgetary cavities

Just as the debate on greater autonomy for states is raging, the 11th Finance Commission chaired by the noted and that most urbane of economists, A.M. Khusro, submitted its report to the President on July 7. Article 280 of the Constitution lays down that the Central government shall set up a finance commission once every five years to recommend how the taxes collected by the Centre should be shared with and among the states and how grants from the Centre should be provided to the states. The framers of the Constitution had the Australian Commonwealth Grants Commission as a model. Babasaheb Ambedkar described the finance commission as a quasi-arbitral body whose function is to o justice between the Centre and the states. By and large, successive finance commissions have realised this vision. Granville Austin writes in his monumental Working a Democratic Constitution that with-out the finance commission, the distribution of revenues would have degenerated into something like open warfare. In a tribute of sorts to the very concept of such a mechanism, Article 280 was amended in 1992 to provide for state-level finance commissions as well to strengthen the finances of local bodies.

There are three main channels for transfer of resources from the Centre to the states. These are the Finance Commission, the Planning Commission and the Central ministries—through what are called "Central-sector projects" and Centrally spon-sored schemes. If the word "transfers" includes tax shares, loans and grants, then the Finance Commission transfers account for around 38 per cent of all Central inflow to states, with the Planning Commission accounting for 40 per cent and Central ministries for another 22 per cent. But if "transfers" are taken as just tax devolutions and grants, as indeed they should be since loans have to be repaid at some time or the other, then the Finance Commission's share increases to around 60 per cent. Central transfers, in turn, account for 40-45 per cent of the states' current expenditures.

The Planning Commission deals with what are called "Plan" expenditures while the Finance Commission is empowered to deal only with "non-Plan" revenue expenditures. This distinction has become completely artificial and untenable. The building of a new school or a primary health centre is considered a Plan investment but its running and maintenance is reckoned as non-Plan spending. Interest payments on loans taken for implementing Plan projects are considered non-Plan. Not all Plan schemes are good or developmental, just as not all non-Plan are bad or unproductive.

Yet, this myth persists. Successive finance ministers, both in Delhi and in state capitals, have recognised the havoc this dichotomy is causing but have been unable to do away with it and take a consolidated view of finances keeping in perspective the interdepen-dence of Plan and non-Plan expenditures. Worse, there is no synchronicity between the two commissions. The Ninth Plan runs from April 1, 1997 to March 31, 2002 while the 11th Finance Commission's award is for the period April 1, 2000 to March 31, 2005. And for some strange reason the Vajpayee Government broke with tradition and did not appoint a member of the Planning Commission as a member of the Finance Commission which would have ensured some coordination at least.

Economists Govinda Rao and Tapas Sen in their Fiscal Federalism in India have called the Finance Commission's approach "fiscal dentistry" that fills in budgetary cavities and gaps in the states. This dentistry has had deleterious impacts on state finances. But this is inherent in the way the Finance Commission has been conceived. Only the 9th Finance Commission was given a bold new mandate—to make a normative assessment of each state's revenue-raising capacity and its expenditure needs and then recommend transfers. This departure proved very controversial and was buried thereafter. The 11th Finance Commission has been asked to suggest a link between fiscal reforms by states and transfers of non-Plan revenue grants. States will undoubtedly raise a ruckus over this. Another innovation this time is that the commission will indicate the quantum of transfers from the Centre to local urban and rural bodies also.

Although it has followed different norms for tax devolutions and for grants-in-aid, the Finance Commission has been unbiased. But there is now need for fundamental reform. The Finance Commission needs to be made permanent and professional. Apart from this, the entire system of inter-governmental transfers needs a relook to enable a comprehensive perspective on state finances and to make the transfers themselves more purposive and effective particularly in relation to the needs of the poorer and fiscally disabled states.

24/07/2000

◆——◆

THE CENTRE MUST HOLD
Defending New Delhi in the debate on greater fiscal autonomy to states

In the wholly welcome debate on centre-state economic relations that is currently taking place, much is being said in favour of greater fiscal autonomy for states. One hardy perennial is the role of what are called Centrally-sponsored schemes. This is an important channel of resource flow: roughly one-sixth of the gross transfer of resources from the Centre to the states inclusive of tax devolutions, loans and grants takes place through such schemes.

These are projects or programmes funded either fully by the

Central government or on a matching basis and im-plemented by the states themselves. There are 185 such schemes run by ministries in the Centre. In 1999-2000 these schemes involved a budgetary expenditure of around Rs 19,000 crore. Almost half of this expenditure was accounted for by rural development schemes alone like water supply, employment assurance, housing, wage employment and asset creation. Rural development programmes are usually funded on a 75:25 basis between the Centre and states. Another 15 per cent was for the national family welfare and planning programme, yet another 15 per cent for primary education and a further 10 per cent for child development projects. The family planning, primary education and child development programmes are funded fully by the Centre. Thus, around 90 per cent of the expenditure is involved in about 15 national projects. This is completely in the form of grants, that is, it does not have to be repaid.

Let there be no mistake about it—given the all-perva-sive fiscal bankruptcy, if these projects are transferred to the states, the money will simply be diverted to meeting salary and pension bills and for debt servicing. That is why champions of panchayati raj are clamouring that all rural development funds go directly from the Centre to elected panchayat bodies although there is a contracynical view that what this will do is strengthen the foundations of decentralised leakages! Be that as it may, such transfers have begun—funds for the erstwhile Jawahar Rozgar Yojana, now restructured as the Jawahar Gram Samridhi Yojana, go directly to village panchayats. This year, that is in 2000-01, Rs 1,485 crore will be provided to almost 2.3 lakh village panchayats directly.

Each of these schemes has an economic or social rationale. In fact the criticism should be that there are not enough Centrally-sponsored schemes, especially in the poor regions. One initiative that will transform populous north Bihar, for example, is flood control and drainage. This is beyond the capacity of the state Government to support and will require Central intervention.

The Planning Commission is also criticised by advocates of states' autonomy for discretionary support to states. Much can be said against the Planning Commission but this is one charge that is unfair. There are three channels for distributing Central assistance to state plans. The first is called formula-based Central assistance, the second is Central assistance for externallyaided projects and the third is specific earmarked sectoral or area-based schemes.To the extent that there is no explicit formula governing transfers through the second and third channels, there is undoubtedly an element of discretion but project preparation and implementation capacity is a more crucial determinant. In 1999-2000, the formula-based channel accounted for about half of Central assistance, the externally-aided channel for about 15 per cent and earmarked programmes for the balance 35 per cent.

The formula is called the Gadgil formula after the deputy chairman of the Planning Commission under whose stewardship it was first formulated almost 30 years ago. Thirty per cent is set aside for the "special category" states of Assam, Arunachal Pradesh, Meghalaya, Manipur, Mizoram, Nagaland, Tripura, Sikkim, Himachal Pradesh and Jammu and Kashmir. The balance 70 per cent is then apportioned among the remaining 15 states based on weights comprising the 1971 population (60 per cent), per capita income (25 per cent), fiscal performance (7.5 per cent) and special problems (7.5 per cent).

All states, apart from the Centre itself, are in a fiscal mess but the special category states are a case apart. They do not have a debt problem since 90 per cent of the money they get from the Centre is in the form of grants. But 5 per cent of India's population getting a 30 per cent share of Central assistance for state plans and much more by way of non-Plan grants is simply not sustainable even after accounting for the special characteristics of these states. Dependence on the Centre is staggering—gross transfers account for between two-third and three-fourth of aggre-gate disbursements. Actually, in the name of special category, corruption engendered through such liberal Central transfers, has become a mode of cohesion.

07/08/2000

NAIDU'S WRONG
It is sad to see a dynamic chief minister play
partisan politics and forget India

In the past few days, nara Chandrababu Naidu has created a stir over the recommendations of the Eleventh Finance Commission (EFC). He claims that "reforming" and "performing" states have been penalised. Even though he frequently allows hype to overtake him, Naidu is energetically trying to redefine politics. But on this issue of the EFC he is wrong.

The finance commission is set up once every five years under Article 280 of the Constitution. It recommends to the Central government how much of the tax and duty revenues collected by the Centre are to be shared with the states and how that share is to be distributed among the states based on a transparent formula. It also recommends how much maintenance and special grants each state should get. For all states as a whole, these statutory transfers constitute about 60 per cent of all transfers (that is, money given by the Centre that does not have to be repaid). But the importance varies: share of Central taxes provides a fifth of all revenues in Andhra and a third in Uttar Pradesh.

Thanks to P. Chidambaram's July 1996 Budget, the EFC has created a single, divisible pool of taxes and duties and made all transfers transparent. During 2000-05, Rs 4,34,905 crore will be transferred to the states, of which roughly 87 per cent will be the share of taxes and duties and the balance the share of grants.

Naidu claims that some states have "lost". He compares the share of taxes and duties during 2000-05 with those during 1995-2000. But why take 1995-2000 as sacrosanct? Each commission is different. A look at the accompanying table shows what happens when a comparison is made over a longer period. States that "lost" earlier have now "gained" and vice versa. But all these comparisons are simply notional.

The formula for determining the share of states worked out by the EFC is based on population (10 per cent), per capita income (62.5 per cent), area(7.5 per cent), infrastructure (7.5 per cent), tax effort (5 per cent) and fiscal discipline (7.5 per cent). Per capita income works thus: the average of Maharashtra, Punjab and Goa, the richest states, is first computed and then the distance of each state from this average is calculated. Obviously, the poorer states will gain. But that is precisely the purpose of the finance commission since richer states are in a better position to attract private investment, borrow more and mobilise more external aid.

Redistribution from the rich to the poor is at the very core of federal transfers. Naidu forgets the crucial role that Central investment has played in the development of south India, specially Hyderabad and Bangalore. He is silent on how Kerala with 3 per cent of India's poor has enjoyed 10 per cent of Central food subsidy. Governance in Uttar Pradesh and Bihar is awful but these two states—home to one in four Indians—still groan under historical, cultural and geographical burdens. And Naidu overlooks how in the past the Central government had eroded the comparative advantage of east India by making the price of steel the same across the country. Further, if states are to get more money, the Centre's fiscal position itself must improve. You cannot oppose subsidy cuts and privatisation, as Naidu has done, and hope this will come about.

The distinction between "reforming" and "non-reforming" states is invidious. Andhra Pradesh is certainly reforming. But Naidu's cohorts—Punjab, Assam, Kerala and Ma-nipur—are certainly not. Uttar Pradesh, Madhya Pradesh and Rajasthan—three states not in Naidu's chosen category—are as reforming as Andhra Pradesh and Karnataka. Maharashtra has turned prosperity into bankruptcy. And the EFC report itself shows that under Naidu, his state's reliance on its own resources has declined.

The very basis of our public finances—the Planning Commission concerned with "plan" or new investments and the finance commission dealing with "non-plan" revenue expenditure—needs a complete change. The current system has, contrary to what Naidu claims, worked to the advantage of the richer and better endowed states. But setting this aside, the EFC can be criticised: it is the first finance commission not to have a member of the Planning Commission. It assumes that the non-plan revenue deficit of states like Andhra Pradesh, Karnataka and Tamil Nadu will be zero from this year itself. Lest these states howl, the same assumption is made for states like Bihar and Madhya Pradesh as well. But it is an apolitical body that does a professional job under the most trying of circumstances. Its recommendations are always accepted. This is the first time such high-voltage drama has been enacted. Buffeted within the state on the power tariff issue—on which he deserves support—Naidu has embarked on a dangerous course. India will be the loser.

04/09/2000

III

Farms and Factories :
Hot Air, Cold Facts

This section directs our attention away from the big picture and toward the sectors that constitute the Indian economy. There are six pieces on agriculture and my only regret is that only 3% of my columns dealt with this most important subject. The public sector is very much in the news as regards disinvestment and privatisation and therefore finds frequent comment in these columns, once again not always in consonance with the official view of the Congress Party. This is particularly true of denationalisation of banks. I also deal very extensively with industry. I have written on just four specific companies—Infosys, Reliance and Enron and GE, although the article "One Truth, Many Path", deals with the different approaches different companies have taken in the pursuit of global excellence. This article elicited wide comment from captains of industry and industry associations such as the Confederation of Indian Industry (CII). There are also a few sceptical pieces on the "new economy", which were considered by many to be unduly pessimistic and critical when they first appeared. Needless to say, my doubts stand vindicated by recent events.

A. Agriculture

KILLER COTTON
Reform cotton policy and rural
credit—or face more farmer suicides

A suicide contagion has swept the cotton farming community in the Deccan. The last time there was such a spate of deaths was in 1981-82. These suicides reflect deep policy and institutional ailures, particularly as they relate to the cotton economy and to rural credit—specially to small and marginal farmers.

There is, as usual, a debate on the numbers. The Andhra Pradesh Government has admitted to 60 such deaths. Local newspapers and research bodies place the number at around 170. Maharashtra's Vidarbha region has also not been spared this tragedy. Over 20 farmers in adjoining northern Karnataka too have taken their lives. These were, however, largely cultivators of tur dal, chillies and tomatoes.

There have been several explanations for this tragedy. In some places, the administration claims the media has exaggerated and sensationalised the suicides. Some district collectors have attributed the deaths not to crop failures but to family problems. Another view is that when such a "wave" strikes, like it did during the anti-Mandal agitation in 1990, people with personal problems go over the brink so as to be seen as martyrs for a grand cause. A third and more appropriate view is that farming in these arid and semiarid regions imposes heavy risks on poor cultivators.

Even though canal irrigation has spread in the past decade in districts like Andhra Pradesh's Warangal, cotton cultivation in the Deccan is predominantly unirrigated. This apart, there is something in the very agronomy of cotton that gives it an element of risk. Cotton is the most pesticide-intensive crop. Something like 40 per cent of all pesticide use in India is by cotton farmers. Pesticides alone account for 35 to 40 per cent of the operational cost per hectare.

The pesticide formulation industry has mushroomed in the past few years without any quality control and discipline. Andhra has over 90 known pesticide companies. Farmers in Guntur district, for example, have suffered enormously from the use of spurious pesticides.

The growth of the pesticide dealer network by itself is not the problem. What has happened is that this growth has taken place just as the agricultural extension service has all but vanished. Further, the institutional credit network has failed the small and marginal farmers. The pesticide dealer has become the source not just of the input but also the supplier of technical advice and of working capital.

G. Parthasarathy, noted economist, has published a detailed analysis of the suicides in a recent issue of the Economic and Political Weekly. He points out that the growth of lease holding in cotton has aggravated the adverse condition of cultivators. But, fundamentally, the inaccessibility of credit from primary agricultural credit societies and dependence on the pesticide dealer for funds at high rates of interest constitute the main problem for cotton ryots in Andhra. But there is more. Although India was the first to start a hybrid cotton industry, cotton cultivation has been starved of modern science and technology inputs. This is all the more surprising since cotton is our most important commercial crop. India has roughly 20 million acres under cotton cultivation, the largest acreage in the world.

Trade policy has gone against cotton farmers. Stop-go and restrictive export policies have contributed to low growth rates in productivity. What we have done by denying our farmers free access to world markets is provide an implicit subsidy to our organised textile mill owners. Cotton is characterised by significant price fluctuations. Cotton prices can be stabilised by imports and exports. But because quotas, open to manipulation, dictate imports and exports, cotton prices fluctuate with domestic output. Farmers are denied benefits international trade can bring to smoothening price fluctuations. Also, cotton markets within India are not integrated; another mechanism for smoothening price variations is lost. The policy bias against private trade has meant a heavy government presence in trading. This is something the public sector is inherently unsuited for. Elsewhere, futures markets are used to manage seasonal fluctuations in prices of agro-commodities. India allowed forward trading in cotton between 1958 and 1965. Thereafter, it was banned. The 1997-98 budget had proposed a resumption of domestic futures in cotton. It is still awaited.

More generally, the rural credit delivery system must be reformed at once. Commercial banks are important but as far as farmers are concerned, the primary agricultural credit societies are the lifeline. They account for about 60 per cent of short-term loans to farmers.

But the system is in an extremely precarious condition. Only about 55 per cent of the 90,000-odd primary agricultural credit societies are viable. Recapitalisation must be initiated. But this must be subject to prudential norms: state governments giving commitments not to interfere and, say, the RBI or NABARD being made responsible for enforcing financial discipline. Innovations like the Grameen Bank, that has transformed Bangladesh, must also be introduced so that small and marginal farmers get adequate and timely credit. Otherwise, expect more suicides

04/09/2000

—◆——◆—

SOW SEEDS OF SUCCESS
Presenting a reformist blueprint for the second Green Revolution

One of the hardy perenials in our economic policy is the terms of trade: the relative prosperity of agriculture vis-à-vis industry. Conventional wisdom is the terms of trade is weighted against agriculture. The Commission on Agricultural Costs and Prices (CACP) calculates the terms of trade annually. The terms of trade is defined as the ratio of the index of agricultural wholesale prices to that of industrial wholesale prices. Setting the value of the ratio for the triennium ending 1971-72 at 100, the CACP estimated the ratio in 1990-91 at 90 and in 1996-97 at 88.9.

Our pre-1991 macroeconomic and trade policies definitely worked against the interests of farmers. Overvalued exchange rates, absurdly high import duties on industrial goods, and export bans and quotas for farm products caused the discrimination. But the idea that the terms of trade is still moving against agriculture is wrong. Three years ago, a committee headed by the noted agro-economist A.S. Kahlon submitted its report on a revised methodology for calculating the terms of trade between agriculture and industry. His committee made two significant recommendations.

• Given the changes in production and consumption patterns, the base year should be the triennium ending 1990-91 and not 1971-72.

- Indices normally used do not fully capture the nature of farm activity or its economy-wide linkages. So a more comprehensive index to measure the terms of trade should be used. Kahlon's committee calculated the terms of trade as the ratio of the index of prices received for farm products to the index of prices the farmer pays for farm inputs, his own food and capital investment.

If Kahlon's ideas are incorporated, then it turns out that the terms of trade has been moving in favour of agriculture through the 1980s—and sharply since 1991. For example, the index was 93.9 in 1984-85 and 101.9 in 1990-91. By 1994-95, it had risen to 106.6. True, favourable terms of trade does not automatically mean high profitability. But what is clear is the discrimination against agriculture is being whittled away. Private investment in agriculture has grown in real terms, despite a decline in public investment. All this would not have happened had the terms of trade gone against agriculture. Unfortunately, the Kahlon methodology is contrary to the prevailing mindset. That is why his report lies ignored. Continuous hikes in procurement prices have, no doubt, boosted the terms of trade in favour of agriculture. But this benefits only those who have a market surplus to offer— barely 15 per cent of all farmers. Since all governments find it hard to raise issue prices for consumers after increasing procurement prices for producers, food subsidies keep burgeoning. Investment, productivity and technology have to drive and sustain the terms of trade in favour of farmers. A five-point "refarms" agenda suggests itself.

First, over the past decade, farm subsidies have grown at three times the rate that farm investment and infrastructure expenditure has gone up. This is crazy. Investment in rural areas for roads, power, irrigation, research, education, technology transfer, storage and marketing is the only way to accelerate agricultural growth. It may also be the solution to poverty, particularly in eastern and central India. But investment in agricultural science and technology is now one-third that of defence and nuclear energy. This is a clear case of misplaced priorities.

Second, the vitality and viability of the rural financial system, destroyed by years of competitive populism, have to be restored. It is not the cost of credit but its timely, adequate and convenient availability that matters. A majority of our small and marginal farmers do not have access to institutional credit. Annual flow of farm credit has to almost treble in order to meet demand.

Third, a special programme for irrigation has to be launched. Just about 37 per cent of the total cultivated area is irrigated. Currently only the wheat and sugarcane crops are assured of near-complete irrigation. Irrigation departments must be converted into farmer-owned corporations and put on a sound financial footing. Fourth, agricultural decontrol must be pushed forward. The 1997-98 budget made a beginning by abolishing an-tiquated laws like the Ginning and Pressing Factories Act, 1925, the Rice Milling Industries (Regulation) Act, 1958 and the Cold Storage Control Order, 1964.

It also deserved some items from exclusive production in the small-scale sector. Next it allowed futures trading. Freeing both domestic and international trade in agriculture will enrich farmers. Fifth, even today only one crop is grown in over two-thirds of the net sown area. Diversification is imperative for farm prosperity. Also, given the pressure on land, nonfarm employment in rural India must be given a new thrust. Forestry, animal husbandry, afforestation, construction, agroprocessing, sericulture, leather: these are only some of the areas which hold potential.

31/08/2000

HOT AIR, COLD FACTS
The parliamentary debate on agriculture only contributed to global warming

A few days ago, parliament was exercised over the plight of farmers. Alas, the debate was marked more by political rhetoric and less by economic literacy with many of the arguments flying in the face of facts.

The developed countries subsidise their agriculture very heavily; so should India. True, the US, the European Union (EU) and Japan spend billions of dollars subsidising their farmers. But they can afford to. Moreover, in these countries the farm population constitutes no more than 5 per cent of the total unlike in India where the proportion is around two-thirds. The reason why we have to target sub-sidies better is because we are bankrupt and subsidies means money taken away from more essential investment in infrastructure, a trade-off that does not exist elsewhere.

The level of farm subsidy in India is negative and hence we can afford to increase it. The WTO uses a concept called the aggregate measure of support (AMS). For India, this AMS has been calculated at minus 31.1 per cent of the value of agricultural production for the year 1995-96, as compared to a plus 3.1 per cent for the US, 32.5 per cent for Japan and 22.9 per cent for the EU. The minus sign for India simply shows that our farmers receive output prices that are below global prices. Many farmers' organisations would agree to subsidy cuts if Indian farmers get world prices. One of India's most distinguished economists, Y.K. Alagh, has recently outlined a roadmap to halve our AMS.

Imports are killing Indian farmers. The only instance of excess imports is edible oil. What happened was that the import duty of 15 per cent was fixed when the international price was ruling at around $600 a tonne. These prices crashed to around $200 a tonne but the Government took time to adjust the import duty to 65 per cent. This points to the need for a trigger mechanism to automatically adjust import duties to fluctuations in global prices and for a better system of timing for imports.

Low import duties on farm products are destroying our farmers. Low import duties are very often fixed so as to protect the interests of consumers as in the case of edible oil or where domestic production is stagnating as in the case of pulses. India is committed to a maximum import duty (the "bound" rate) of 100 per cent for primary products and commodities, 150 per cent for processed items and 300 per cent for edible oil. These are absurd rates that weaken our capacity to demand cuts from developed countries. As opposed to this, the actual import duty rate, as estimated by Ashok Gulati, India's top agrieconomist, now averages 38.5 per cent. For items like rice, maize and skimmed milk powder, the bound rate was zero because when these rates were fixed in 1948, India was an importer. These rates have been re-negotiated recently. India must unilaterally set an actual import duty rate of 50-60 per cent across the board for agriculture. This will also give us the moral authority to lead WTO negotiations on agriculture, from which Indian farmers have a great deal to gain.

Agricultural production has suffered on account of liberalisation. True, the rate of growth of foodgrains production has declined from 2.7 per cent in the 1980s to 1.9 per cent in the 1990s. But GDP from agriculture and allied activities, a measure of value-addition, has averaged an annual growth rate of 3.5 per cent in the 1990s as compared to 2.9 per cent in the previous decade because of the growth that is taking place in sectors like horticulture, dairy, poultry and fishing. But infrastructure to support this diversification is woefully inadequate. Investment in agriculture is falling alarmingly. In constant 1980-81 prices, public investment in agriculture has fallen. But this measures only expenditure on irrigation, leaving out spending on other rural infrastructure like roads, power, markets, research and storage. Falling public investment in agriculture reveals the growing bankruptcy of state governments. However, private investment has picked up. In the 1990s, private investment has accounted for about 80 per cent of total investment in agriculture, up from its historical average of 65-70 per cent. Private investment has increased because the terms of trade, that is the ratio of prices received for farm output to the prices paid for farm inputs, for family consumption and for capital investment, have moved in favour of agriculture in the 1990s. This is a direct consequence of the 1991 reforms of reducing import duties in industry, of moving to a market-determined exchange rate and hefty increases in procurement and minimum support prices.

In the past, Parliament has adopted special resolutions reflecting an all-party concern on national issues. These non-binding resolutions help crystallise consensus. The least our lawmakers should have done was to pass a special resolution outlining an agenda to revitalise Indian agriculture that faces many challenges and opportunities.

18/12/2000

RICE OF THE FUTURE

Exciting times for rice research but new varieties are still some years away

Two significant development took place recently concerning our staple food, rice. On January 19, the Manila-based International Rice Research Institute (IRRI) receivedthe first research samples of "golden rice" from the scientists and companies who had originally developed it. Second, on January 26, two private companies from Switzerland and the US unveiled the complete map of the rice genome. New varieties are, however, at least five years away.

Golden rice is genetically modified rice invented by two scientists—Ingo Potrykus, a Swiss, and Peter Beyer, a German.Although it provides about a third of our daily calorie intake, normal rice is low in vitamin content. Through modern genetic engineering techniques, Potrykus and Beyer have incorporated three new alien genes into the conventional rice plant—two from daffodils and another from the earth bacterium Erwinia. The colour of this transgenic seed is yellow—hence, the name golden rice. It contains beta-carotene and other carotenoids which break down into Vitamin A.

Vitamin A deficiency causes blindness and is endemic amongpre-school chilren in the poorer regions of India. We do have a national programme whereby infants in the nine-36 months age group are to be provided with massive Vitamin A doses. But actual coverage, particularly for follow-up doses, is low. IRRI, which is a publicly funded laboratory, will now mount a global effort to further investigate golden rice, using local rice varieties. Remarkably, a Humanitarian Board chaired by Potrykus has been set up to further the application. This points to howpublic-private partnerships in biotechnology can be structured. IRRI has a strong India connection—it was headed by none other than M.S. Swaminathan himself during 1982-88 and for the past three decades its top breeder has been the legendary Gurdev Khush. Incidentally, the world's leading wheat and maize breeders are Sanjaya Rajaram and Surinder Vassal at IRRI's sister lab-oratory CIMMYT in Mexico, from where we got the wheat seeds in the mid-1960s to launch our Green Revolution. Although the genetic code of rice has been sequenced, the exactfunction of eachgeneis notknown. The next step is to determine what each of these 50,000 genes do. It would then be possible, for example, to develop new rice varieties tolerant to drought. IRRI is establishing a global network for functional genomics research and Khush believes India should play a leadership role in this network.

Over half the births in India are of markedly underweight babies brought about by maternal malnutrition aggravated by iron deficiency. In January 1999, five Japanese scientists reported the development of a transgenic rice based on the transfer of the soyabean ferritin gene. This transgenic rice contains two to four times the iron normally found in rice. Since anaemia is widely prevalent among pregnant and lactating women in our country, ironfortified rice is of special significance to us. A third new transgenic rice variety is called Bt rice. This is rice that produces a protein toxic to insects and pests by the injection of a gene from the microorganism Bacillus thuringiensis. In1915, a scientist had isolated this toxin from a dead moth in the German region of Thuringen—hence the name of the bacterium. Bt rice is still in its infancy unlike Bt cotton which has taken major strides. About a third of the cotton area in the US is under Bt cotton. In India small field trials are on. Bt cotton is of great importance because the cotton crop now consumes about 60per cent of all chemical pesticides used.

Way back in 1954, two scientists at the Cuttack-based Central Rice Research Institute, S. Sampath and H.K. Mohanty, were the first to draw attention to the possibility of developing hybrids involving two separate parental lines for a self-pollinated crop like rice. But it was China that surged ahead. Around 40-45 per cent of China's rice area is under hybrid varieties. India too has been experimenting with hybrid rice. A. Janaiah of IRRI, who has been studying the socio-economics of hybrid rice, believes that while hybrid rice gives higher yields of at least 15-20 per cent over high-yielding varieties, it results in lower profitability. This is because of three main reasons: lower market prices on account of poor grain quality and higher risks of pests and diseases. While we keep abreast of the latest in rice science, there are many immediate production challenges. As Swaminathan has pointed out recently, Punjab must diversify from rice to agro-forestry, fodder crops, quality protein maize and legumes. In arid regions, low-yielding rice has to give way to other lucrative opportunities like tree crops. Eastern India has to see a fuller development of its substantial groundwater resources. Finally, there are big yield gaps—between potential and actual—that need to be bridged.

26/02/2001

PLANT BIOTECH TAKES A PAUSE
Plans to sell new transgenic cotton varieties to Indian farmers are put on hold

In an allusion to the potential of biotechnology (BT) to transform Indian agriculture, it was the veteran politician Mohan Dharia who remarked that while IT reflected India Today, BT represented Bharat Tomorrow. But it is not going to be smooth sailing. The Central Government has just postponed, for at least another year, the commercial use of Bt cotton, a genetically engineered variety that increases yields and pest-tolerance significantly.

Bt stands for the micro-organism Bacillus thuringiensis. The bacterium was isolated by a German scientist from a dead moth in the

Thuringia region of Germany, hence the name. Bt cotton is cotton into which a gene obtained from this soil-based bacterium has been introduced. This gives the cotton plant the capacity to produce its own protein which is toxic to specific pests like bollworms. Some 70 per cent of all chemical pesticides used in India is just on cotton. Over one-third of this is in Andhra Pradesh alone. Another two-fifth is accounted for by Karnataka, Gujarat and Punjab. Not coincidentally, the maximum number of farmer suicides have been that of cotton cultivators in Andhra and Karnataka.

India has the maximum area under cotton in the world followed by the US and China. However, our productivity is the lowest. Over half the cotton area in the US is under transgenics, that is plants into which genes from unrelated species have been introduced to give them desirable characteristics. China too has moved forward on its own. In India, field experiments with Bt cotton first started in 1996-97 and were continued in 1997-98 and 1998-99. Large-scale research field trials and seedproduction took place in 2000-01. The Jalna-based Maharashtra Hybrid Seeds Company (MAHYCO) is responsible for the field trials in India. MAHYCO is a research-driven company led by Dr B.R. Barwale, the 1998 recipient of the World Food Prize, considered the Nobel Prize in agriculture. The US multinational Monsanto has a 26 per cent stake in MAHYCO and it is Monsanto's Bt gene that has been introduced into MAHYCO's hybrid cotton and is under test.

Encouraged by the preliminary results of the experiments and the field trials on about 12 hectares, the Department of Biotechnology moved the Genetic Engineering Approval Committee (GEAC) under the Ministry of Environment and Forests for permission to have Bt cotton seeds sold commercially to farmers. The committee has denied this request and now wants further large-scale field trials on another 100 hectares under the supervision of the Indian Council of Agricultural Research before taking a final decision. Proponents of Bt cotton feel that the influential pesticide manufacturers lobby is at work. Some progressive farmers' organisations are upset while NGOs have welcomed the GEAC's move.

Undoubtedly, Monsanto's involvement has mobilised opposition to Bt cotton. It has been dubbed the Frankenstein of Foods out to destroy the world through genetic manipulation. But Monsanto apart, five specific fears have been raised about Bt cotton. First, we could develop immunity to specific antibiotics like streptomycin. Second, the bollworms themselves could soon develop immunity to the toxin. Third, animals fed with Bt cotton seed could develop toxicity and serious allergies and soil micro-organisms could be adversely affected. Fourth, the Bt cotton pollen might flow beyond a safe zone and begin to impact on other crops. Fifth, the Bt cotton seed might contain the "terminator gene" which means that farmers will have to buy seeds year after year from the market.

The Department of Biotechnology believes that these fears are unfounded and that MAHYCO's experiments and trials yield robust data to substantiate this position. Many scientists also agree but few others have raised doubts—The Hindu has been carrying a debate on this.

The only way to inspire confidence is to make all results of the trials under Indian conditions public and have them subjected to scientific peer review. Even though highly complex scientific issues are involved, the debate has to be conducted in easy-to-understand language without clouding public concerns in some technical mumbo-jumbo. A bit of humility on all sides—on the part of both gung-go scientists and self-righteous and scare-mongering NGOs—will also help. India desperately needs to harness the undoubted potential of transgenic plants.

At the same time, risks have to be managed through a transparent and effective regulatory regime. We could also profit from innovative public-private partnerships and a greater role for public-sector research, of the type that triggered the earlier Green Revolution. And speaking of the Green Revolution, it was the wildly enthusiastic acceptance by farmers that turned the tide. It is this that will make or break plant biotech.

23/07/2001

◆——◆

TAKING STOCK OF STOCKS
Understanding the reasons why India's foodgrain
stocks are now mounting

India's granaries are over flowing. The safe level of buffer stock of foodgrains (that is, rice and wheat) is about 24 million tonnes as of July 1 every year. Pre-1999, stock levels were not abnormal. But foodgrain stocks were about 34 million tonnes on July 1, 1999, around 43 million tonnes on July 1, 2000 and approximately 62 million tonnes on July 1, 2001. Almost half of the foodgrain stocks are held in Punjab, one-fifth in Haryana, one-tenth in Uttar Pradesh and about 6 per cent in Andhra Pradesh. And what about their vintage? A 1999 World Bank report placed half the stock as being at least two years old and another 30 per cent being two to four years old.

In the 1970s, procurement of foodgrains by the Food Corporation of India (FCI) averaged about 10 million tonnes annually. In the 1980s, it averaged around 18 million tonnes per year. Between 1990-91 and 1998-99, procurement averaged about 23-24 million tonnes annually. But in the past two years procurement has zoomed: 31 million tonnes in 1999-2000 and 36 million tonnes in 2000-1.

Punjab, Andhra Pradesh and Haryana account for over 80 per cent of rice procurement. Andhra Pradesh's performance has been particularly striking: a half of the rice output is being procured now as compared to just one thirds five years back. Punjab, Haryana and Uttar Pradesh account for 90 per cent of the wheat procurement. Procurement is Punjab's lifeline; here, over half of the wheat and three-fourths of the rice out-put is purchased by the FCI. The Central government pushes the procured foodgrains through the Public Distribution System (PDS), a network of about 4.6 lakh ration shops across the country. On an average, in the 1970s about 11 million tonnes and in the 1980s around 16 million tonnes were pushed through the PDS annually. Thus, the balance between procurement and PDS supply was more or less maintained. This balance continued pretty much in the 1990s also. But in 2000-01, PDS supply fell sharply to 11.7 million tonnes.

Thus, foodgrain stocks are overflowing because procurement has increased very sharply and the supply to the PDS has plummeted. The increase in procurement clearly has had a far greater impact. This raises further questions. Why has procurement skyrocketed and why is the PDS selling vastly lower quantities of foodgrains?

The NDA allies in Andhra Pradesh, Punjab and Haryana are pressurising the Vajpayee regime to procure more foodgrains and to relax quality norms. The 1990s has also seen very liberal increases in the minimum support price (MSP) taking them higher than in the 1980s and what would be justified on considerations of inflation. For instance, the Commission on Agricultural Costs and Prices (CACP) had recommended an MSP of Rs 465 per quintal of paddy in the 1999-2000 crop year. But the actual price was Rs 490 a quintal. For wheat, as against the CACP recommendation of Rs 490 a quintal, the actual procurement was at Rs 550 a quintal. Such a support price policy has also priced Indian rice and wheat out of international markets.

On PDS, the H.D. Deve Gowda government in February 1997 introduced the Targeted PDS (TPDS) that distinguishes two categories of consumers to be identified by the states: below poverty line (BPL) and above poverty line (APL). This was done to introduce a pro-poor bias into a PDS that had hitherto been universal in coverage and had been benefitting mainly the better-off peninsular India and West Bengal. In the TPDS, Uttar Pradesh and Bihar have received significantly higher allocations of foodgrain as they must. But the BPL/APL distinction has proved to be unworkable, specially since it is the same retail outlet that sells to both categories. In any case, dual pricing always leads to leakages. The Vajpayee Government worsened the situation by introducing new schemes and by increasing APL prices to a level where they are now higher than even the market prices. As a result, PDS consumers are now buying better quality foodgrain from the market.

A massive food-for-work programme is certainly needed in the ecologically vulnerable regions to provide both employment guarantee and food security. But this will absorb at most five million tonnes of foodgrains. The problem of mounting stocks can be addressed only when we muster up the courage to (i) diversify Punjab's agriculture out of the wheat-paddy cycle; (ii) introduce a more realistic MSP policy; (iii) reform the entire foodgrain marketing system presently built around a high-cost and inefficient FCI; (iv) remove policy-induced inefficiencies in private-sector storage, milling, marketing and trans-port operations; and (v) simplify the PDS by doing away with dual pricing but keeping the pro-poor state bias in allocations. If this is not done, we will continue to confront a crisis of plenty while our mindset is still tuned to managing a crisis of shortages.

17/09/2001

B. Public Sector

PSUs WITHOUT A USP
Privatisation is now an overriding economic compulsion

The public sector has served the nation well. It has built a technological capability in key areas like energy and manufacturing. It has served as a nursery for managerial and technical manpower. It has opened up backward areas. But it has now run its course. The public sector was set up on the assumption that private entrepreneurship was not available in India. This is no longer true. The public sector expanded on the belief that private companies could not mobilise resources for mega projects. This is no longer valid.

The public sector continued its dominance in the belief that there are "natural monopolies" and scale economies. From telecom to fertilisers, new technology is making this irrelevant.

Today, apart from arguments based on security, there is really no economic, entrepreneurial, technological or financial basis for a public sector. But we persist in our faith—and at great cost. On a total investment of around Rs 1,50,000 crore in 237 companies owned and operated by the Central Government, the profits and dividends are less than Rs 3,000 crore per year. Each year, the Union budget outlay to these companies is more than what is spent on agriculture and rural development. It is even worse in the states. On an investment of close to Rs 40,000 crore in about 860 companies, the annual losses are over Rs 8,000 crore. This is four times what we spend on family planning.

There have been four major attempts to reform the public sector. The first was in the '70s, which saw the experiment with holding companies. Pretty soon the bureaucracy, seeing the holding company as a threat to its powers, finished off the experiment. Moreover, what good are holding companies if the companies they are holding are themselves sick?

Next came the experiment with the memorandum of understanding (MoU). This was a non-starter. How can an MoU work if the CEO can be fired for non-performance, but the concerned administrative ministry cannot be held accountable?

Then came disinvestment. But disinvestment was and is only an easy way of raising money for the exchequer. Around Rs 10,000 crore has been raised by disinvesting government equity in 39 companies. This has made no difference to corporate governance in the public sector.

Finally, there was the Chidambaram-Maran effort in 1997 with the navaratnas and the mini navaratnas. These gentlemen fought a lonely battle against their ministerial colleagues and their own mandarins to push for greater autonomy. On paper, the autonomy package looked grand. In practice, it has already been buried. There is one lesson that stands out from over 20 years of attempts to reform the public sector: our bureaucracy, politicians and Parliament will just not allow true commercial autonomy. As a result, the public sector has ceased to attract top-flight talent.

Up to a point, forcing competition on public enterprises will make them more efficient. Indian Airlines is a good example. But only up to a point. For enterprise to flourish, the Government must cease to be the majority owner. Of course, whether the sale of government equity should be to a strategic partner or to the public at large depends on the specific company.

The routes to privatisation are diverse. Wherever it is not so—like in banks and telecom—government pres-ence in business must come under the Companies Act as a precursor to privatisation. In some cases, the public enterprise could be split into compact business units and some of these sold outright or spun off as joint ventures. This can be done, for example, in the case of tractors in HMT, drilling services in ONGC and transport equipment in BHEL. In some cases, particularly in the service and consumer goods sectors, the company itself could be privatised. Maruti and ITDC are cases in point.

The challenge remains of the companies that cannot be turned around. There are about 50 such companies in the Centre's portfolio. Collectively, they have some three lakh employees, no small number. Many of them are located in the region east of Kanpur. Over the next five to six years, growth buoyancy in such locations has to be triggered so as to manage the restructuring. In many cases, the sale of land will generate adequate resources to launch this process.

As the fiscal squeeze gets tighter, states will privatise. But it is not enough to sell only loss-making units. And unfortunately, privatisation in the states has often meant sale to cronies of those in power. The Orissa model of privatising power distribution is a model to follow.

Interest payments alone now eat up 50 per cent of the Centre's tax revenues and account for around 30 per cent of its total expenditure. No development and no significant step-up in investment in education, health and social programmes is possible if this continues. The only way of getting out of this mess is to retire debt. This is possible only through a bold programme of privatisation, spread over, say, a five-year period and carried out professionally and transparently. Such a programme can reduce the fiscal deficit by at least 2 per cent of the GDP. In sum, privatisation is now not just an ideological imperative but an overriding economic compulsion.

25/05/1998

WHEELS AND DEALS
Having made peace with Suzuki, Sikandar Bakht should privatise Maruti

How times change. A year ago, Murasoli Maran was being hailed by the BJP as the champion of swadeshi and being applauded for showing the Japanese that Indians could not be taken for a ride. Today, the BJP has turned around completely and made peace with Suzuki. Maran and his friends are crying foul but the prime minister, Jaswant Singh and Sikandar Bakht must be congratulated for arriving at an out-of-court settlement. Undoubtedly, Pokhran II has imparted an urgency to building bridges with Japan. But from the day he took over, Bakht had signalled his desire for a quick solution.

Actually, Maran's behaviour, even granting for Suzuki's insensitivity and arrogance, was completely uncharacteristic. As a minister, he was a bold liberaliser and reformer. All his actions, other than in the Suzuki episode, bear this out. Why he took on Suzuki in the manner he did remains a mystery.

One explanation could be that his hands were tied by decisions taken by his predecessor, who had damned the man now designated to take over as managing director (MD) of Maruti in January 2000. Another explanation may be that Maran was a prisoner of his coalition partners who wanted a particular individual, unacceptable to Suzuki, as MD. Yet another reason could be that Suzuki's initial choice for the post of Maruti's chairman was a red rag to many MPs belonging to the United Front.

All this may well be true. But it does not explain the virulence of the antagonism between Maran and Suzuki or Maran's continued refusal to seek a compromise. Maruti has transformed Indian industry. But it has also enjoyed special privileges not given to other companies. Soon after taking over as industry minister in June 1996, Maran found himself in confrontation with Suzuki. Facts supported Maran. He had four substantive charges against Suzuki. First, that Suzuki was not introducing new models fast enough and was content in raking in royalties from the 800 cc model. Second, that even after 10 years of collaboration, Suzuki had not transferred the technology for making gearboxes. Third, Suzuki was inflating project costs. As an example, Maruti's paint shop and presses cost anywhere between 25 and 40 per cent more than what may be reasonably expected through competitive bidding. Fourth, Maruti was incurring a loss of over $ 2,000 on every Zen exported and, even then, Suzuki was selling it under a different brand name: Alto.

Expectedly, Suzuki denied the charges. Next, Maruti's expansion got stuck, with Suzuki wanting equity financing and Maran insisting on the debt route. As it turns out, the expansion will cost less than what Suzuki estimated and is being financed through neither debt nor equity but through internal resources.

Beginning November 1996, following the then finance minister's visit to Japan, Maran began to seriously consider the possibility of the government selling off its stake. More than once he expressed the view that the government should not be in the business of making cars and that without complete disinvestment, Maruti would be at a competitive disadvantage vis-à-vis its South Korean and other rivals.

However, when it came to the crunch, Maran was naturally very cautious. In the ruling coalition of the day, only the finance minister and prime minister supported him. Informal talks were initiated with Suzuki for a mutually beneficial deal: for example, Suzuki to invest in a gearbox plant and new car factory in return for the government selling its equity. Sometime in February 1997, it was decided to pursue the privatisation option. But soon H.D. Deve Gowda fell and this proposal was buried.

Finally, all hell broke loose in August 1997 when Maran decided to take a tough stand on the appointment of a new MD. His stand was the joint venture (JV) agreement gave an absolute right to each of the two partners to appoint an MD by turn. Since in 1997 it was India's turn, he was only exercising that right. Suzuki's stand was the agreement provided for consultation and concurrence before the appointment of an MD. Finding Maran unrelenting, Suzuki took India to the International Court of Arbitration, where hearings were expected to commence on July 8.

Since the sorry saga is over, it is time to think ahead. For one, Maran's substantive criticism of Suzuki remains valid. More important, now that the finance minister has said privatisation is on the agenda, Maruti should be the first candidate.

The government's equity is 49.3 per cent. This could be sold to Suzuki or to the public. The government's investment in Maruti is around Rs 65 crore. A few months ago, it was estimated the Government could rake in some Rs 6,000 crore by selling its stake. This is a fantastic return by any standards. In October 1997, the chairman of General Motors had indicated as much to the then prime minister.

Since he has demonstrated that he carries no baggage, Bakht should now appoint a financial adviser or get the Disinvestment Commission to chart out the road map for the privatisation of Maruti. He will earn himself a place in the history books.

22/06/1998

◆━━◆

LIVE AND LET DIVEST
The winds of privatisation have started blowing slowly but surely

Kautilya has become suspect among his political colleagues because he has been publicly applauding the two coalition governments since May 1996 for significantly advancing economic reforms. It would have been intellectually dishonest and churlish not to acknowledge these contributions. Now one more step has been taken. Last week's issue of The Economist carried a full-page announcement of the proposed privatisation of IPCL—the Indian Petrochemicals Corporation Limited.

IPCL's market capitalisation is at present around $600 million. The government's equity share in IPCL is at 59 per cent. A fresh 25 per cent share as well as management control is now being offered to a strategic investor. This sale will bring down the government share to 34 per cent. There is a convertible bond due for redemption in early 2001. If investors decide to convert to equity—and this will depend entirely on market conditions—then government holding will rest at 26 per cent, which is the minimum needed under our Companies Act to block a shareholder's resolution.

But this 26 per cent may or may not materialise. It is better to go to 26 per cent straightaway or even better to zero per cent—and have a separate agreement giving the government a single "golden share" that could be triggered in the national interest, clearly defined. This is how successful privatisations have taken place elsewhere in the world.

The Central Government owns and operates 237 companies. IPCL is one of the five being offered for privatisation or "strategic sales", as we insist on calling it. The other four are Bharat Aluminium (BALCO), Modern Foods Limited (MFL), Kudremukh Iron Ore Company Limited (KIOCL) and India Tourism Development Corporation (ITDC). Taken together, these five privatisations, which should be complete by this time next year, could generate upwards of $1.5 billion. These revenues should be used for retiring the stock of internal debt and reducing the mounting burden of interest payments.

The privatisation is being carried out on the basis of the recommendations of the Disinvestment Commission set up by the United Front (UF) government in August 1996. After a great deal of debate, the UF government accepted the recommendations regarding BALCO, KIOCL, MFL and ITDC, while the BJP government went ahead in regard to IPCL. Very recently, a decision has been taken to reduce government holding in Air-India and Indian Airlines too to 49 per cent.

IPCL is actually the most significant since the prevailing theology in India has been that only public-sector companies in low-tech areas or those making losses should be privatised. IPCL is neither. In February 1997, P. Chidambaram's budget had identified it as one of the navaratnas—the nine super-profitmaking, globally competitive enterprises. IPCL will also present an interesting problem to the government in case Reliance bids for the 25 per cent—which it will surely do—and finally wins the beauty contest in competition with global majors like Shell and Dupont.

In the US and Europe, a Reliance taking over an IPCL would immediately trigger anti-monopoly investigations and action since such a combine would wield formidable market dominance. Some years ago, management gurus Michael Porter and C.K. Prahalad created a stir in this country when they publicly criticised the government's ap-proval of GE's joint venture with Godrej for refrigerators saying that this was not adding to competition.

But we do not have effective competition and what the Americans call "anti-trust" laws, laws that helped break up AT&T and are now being used against Microsoft. Till we have such laws, the answer to Reliance IPCL type situations is to sharply cut import duties to no more than 5-10 per cent, so market discipline is enforced by imports or their threat.

Privatisation, in the sense of transfer of existing assets and ownership from the government to private companies, is still a bad word in this country. Examples of successful privatisations are few and far between. The first instance was that of Allwyn Nissan, a truck unit of Hyderabad Allwyn that N.T. Rama Rao sold off to Mahindra and Mahindra in 1988-89. The deal was professional and transparent, quite unlike how Mulayam Singh Yadav tried to sell off UP Cements to his industrialist friends. Jyoti Basu has been trying to entice French investors to buy out Great Eastern Hotel. Maharashtra has privatised its industrial promotion company, SICOM. Orissa, Andhra Pradesh, Haryana and Uttar Pradesh have all embarked on privatising power distribution. Technically Maruti has been privatised but the government still retains around 49 per cent. This is serving no social or economic interest. The Cement Corporation of India has sold its Yerraguntla cement plant to India Cements and a German company has acquired Andrew Yule's steel belting unit at Kalyani without a murmur from the workers. HMT has been trying to sell its tractor and bearings plants. Buyers are also being wooed for Scooters India, Hindustan Photo Films and other companies. What we are learning is that divestiture is an extremely demanding, time-consuming and meticulously detailed task that calls for professional expertise of the highest standard.

14/06/1999

TIME TO SELL

Three eventful years of the Disinvestment Commission

On August 20, The Disinvestment Commission that was set up by the United Front (UF) government to recommend what to do with the Central government's shareholding in the public-sector companies it owns and operates completed its initial term of three years. The incoming government will have to decide immediately on the future role of the commission.

P. Chidambaram, the UF's finance minister, was responsible for the ap-pointment of distinguished civil servant G.V. Ramakrishna—"GVR" as he is better known—as the commission's chairman, as well as that of four other members. Because of his reputation for unim-peachable integrity, his track record of being a strong propublic sectorwallah and the larger-than-life image he had acquired as chair-man of SEBI, GVR commanded respect across the political spectrum.

This weighed most heavily in his automatic choice by a finance minister fully aware that public-sector reform is more a political activity than a technocratic exercise. As it turned out, while GVR maintained excellent relations with the media, trade unions and political leaders, the commission and the government were not always on the best of terms. Very often Kautilya had to play the peacemaker's role.

The commission has submitted 12 reports so far on 58 public-sector companies. Its most important contribution has been to propagate the concept of "strategic sale". For example the Congress, which is extremely allergic to the very word "privatisation", pledges in its manifesto to implement the recommendations of the commission on strategic sales professionally without delays. In a strategic sale, the government sells a part or whole of its equity shareholding to one investor who either takes over management control—depending on whether government equity has fallen 50 per cent—or who remains a management partner with minority equity in the hope of eventual management control.

In 37 of these 58 companies, the commission has rec-ommended strategic sale. In some cases, the government's shareholding comes down to zero, but in most cases it rests at 26 per cent, the minimum needed under the Companies Act to block a shareholder resolution and, in the commission's view, ensure that the national interest is protected. A minimum of around $5 billion could be raised by the sale of shares in these 37 companies. Another $2 billion at least would come in by way of new investment by the strategic partner. The process of privatisation of four companies—IPCL, Modern Foods, Bharat Aluminium and Kudremukh Iron Ore—has been initiated. For two more—ITDC and Madras Fertilisers—bids for appointing global advisers have been issued.

There are three other streams of activity that have a bearing on disinvestment. First, 67 loss-making companies have been referred to the BIFR. The BIFR has recommended winding up of 14 and has sanctioned revival schemes for another 18. Second, the Department of Heavy Industry has initiated the process of finding joint venture partners who will take over or revive the companies under its "control". Thus, for instance, the Yerraguntla cement plant of the Cement Corporation of India has been sold to a private company and the steel belting division of Andrew Yule has been spun off as a joint venture with a German company holding 74 per cent equity. Efforts are on to find similar partners for HMT's tractor unit and for Scooters India.Third, there are ad hoc announcements. Chidambaram's budgets announced disinvestments in companies like IOC, GAIL, MTNL and VSNL, while Yashwant Sinha's 1999 budget proposed the privatisation of Indian Airlines. Maruti stands as a case apart where the government still holds, needlessly in Kautilya's view, 49.3 per cent equity. The sale of this equity could generate at least another $1 billion.

It should take a new Disinvestment Commission another two years at most to complete the exercise of recommending disinvestment options in the balance of the public enterprise portfolio. More critical is to bring a sense of coherence and urgency to the implementation process. It has taken over 24 months to get ITDC's privatisation just partially off the ground simply because the concerned ministers and civil servants have been arguing that ITDC is fulfilling a strategic, social purpose. The sale of HMT's bearings unit to Sundaram Fasteners got tossed around between ministries for almost two years till the private company got fed up and withdrew its offer.

In a new implementation structure, all disinvestment proposals must go to a cabinet committee on disinvestment. Once this committee has decided, the Finance Ministry—and not the administrative ministry—must be given complete and clear responsibility for implementing the disinvestment recommendations. For its part, the Finance Ministry has to carve out a separate, full-time privatisation task force staffed by market-savvy professionals.

The Disinvestment Commission should be given overall responsibility for managing the disinvestment process, while the responsibility for giving the green signal on the final sale price could still rest with the Cabinet committee. In addition, to enhance coordination and commonality in approach, all disinvestment proposals must be reviewed by the Disinvestment Commission. Once the commission has made its recommendations, it should not take the government more than eight weeks to get the implementation process going.

30/08/1999

◆——◆

NEW STEPS FOR SSIs
The small industry needs a completely fresh mindset and policy framework

On economic policy, the Atal Bihari Vajpayee Government has been pragmatic and shed most of its shibboleths. But in one area, it remains a prisoner of the past. Of course, in this it is not alone. A few days ago, it reduced the limit for investment in plant and machinery that is used for defining small-scale industry from Rs 3 crore to Rs 1 crore. This is a retrograde step but reflects the pulls and pressures that governments experience. On April 27, 1999, Vajpayee spoke to the Confederation of Indian Industry where he waxed eloquent on the need to have a modern mindset. The very next day he spoke to an outfit called the Laghu Bharati Udyog and surprised his speechwriters by announcing that the investment limit for small-scale industry would be reduced! That promise has now been fulfilled.

In most other countries, small industry is defined by employment size. We define it in terms of capital employed in plant and machinery. Progressively this limit which defines small-scale industry (SSI) has increased. In 1997, the United Front government took a bold step and put the limit at Rs 3 crore, up from the existing Rs 60 lakh. Over the years, the SSI has enjoyed numerous tax and other benefits which have encouraged entrepreneurs to remain in the "small" category. In other countries small graduates into medium and large. Only here, there is a vested interest in continuing to be classified as small. There was a time when even companies like Nirma were reckoned as being small.

Our definition has prevented new investment and new technology in the small-scale sector. It has prevented vertical growth of small enterprises into competitive-sized units and resulted in horizontal proliferation and fragmentation of production capacities. This has denied the country economies of scale in production, research and marketing. To make matters worse, we have followed a completely illogical policy of reservation. Overnight, George Fernandes—in one of his previous incarnations as industry minister in 1978—increased the number of items reserved for exclusive manufacture in the small-scale sector from around 150 to almost 850. This has had no economic or commercial logic. It was this coupled with our definition of small that prevented India from deriving full benefit from the great global export boom—and continues to do so. India's exports of a basket of reserved products like garments, sports goods, toys and electrical and electronic appliances increased from around $2.5 billion to $13 billion over the mid-80s to the mid-90s, while that of China shot up from around $3 billion to $70 billion. Next time, you wonder why "Made in India" is not ubiquitous in department stores and retail outlets in world markets blame our small-scale policies. Ironically, almost 550 items can be freely imported but they cannot be manufactured by anybody other than the so-called small sector.

Things are changing but very slowly. In April 1997, the UF government dereserved 15 items including ice cream, rice milling and biscuits. In February 1999, the BJP government dereserved another 10 items that included some agricultural implements and machinery. But the growth of the textile industry in particular continues to be shackled by small-scale reservations. Scientific instruments, light engineering, leather and agro-processing are other industries which are not witnessing major expansions because of continued reservations. Very recently India agreed to phase out all non-duty restrictions on imports of all products and goods by March 31, 2001. It makes sense to phase out reservations as well by this deadline. The damage value is vastly exaggerated since only 68 items in the reserved list account for some 80 per cent of the production value and for the physical number of producing units. If there is compulsion to manufacture in small enterprises, the market will automatically ensure this as has happened in garments elsewhere—but small not as we define it.

Small-scale industry in India has been largely a fiscal artefact rooted in romance. It must now become a technological and market reality. For this to happen, the supply of venture capital has to expand manifold. A Limited Partnerships Act as it exists in other countries would enable access to more funds. Allowing large industry to take equity stake of more than the 24 per cent they are currently allowed will facilitate greater investment, technology and marketing linkages. Greater sub-contracting by large firms will stimulate the growth of small enterprises.Since small industry is clustered in 50-60 locations, area-specific programmes will have great utility. And the SSI must give way to SEs (small enterprises) or SBs (small businesses).

17/01/2000

◆——◆

FEAR OF JET FLYING
Privatisation of Modern Foods—but not that of
Indian Airlines—is a step forward

On the eve of Republic Day the Government announced the sale of the public-sector company Modern Foods, manufacturer of bread, other bakery products and energy foods, to Hindustan Lever. Completing a three-year process, this is a step in the right direction and reflects the recommendation made by the erstwhile Disinvestment Commission in its very first report way back in February 1997. The sale will yield a revenue of Rs 106 crore. Rs 106 crore is Rs 106 crore. It is, for instance, an amount spent in the past 10 years by the Central government to computerise all land records to benefit around a 100 million farm families—a most socially useful application of infotech. The sale proceeds could be put into a revitalised national land records modernisation programme to be called Modern Foods Land Records Scheme to remind the country about the link between privatisation and social needs.

But it is the other decision that invites comment. Indian Airlines (IA) is to be privatised. Twenty-six per cent of the airline's equity is to be sold to a strategic investor, 25 per cent to employees, financial institutions and the public, with the balance 49 per cent to be held by the government. So far so good. However, the 26 per cent cannot be held by anyone remotely connected with any airline. This is bizarre. But the Atal Bihari Vajpayee Government alone is not to be blamed because this decision reflects a policy mindset that was in vogue during the earlier Congress and United Front regimes as well. Incidentally, the first announcement of IA's privatisation was made in Yashwant Sinha's budget of June 1998. Nineteen months later, the same government reiterates that decision and calls it forward movement!

Jet Airways is evolving into a world-class airline and its promoter Naresh Goyal is a most engaging and entrepreneurial personality, though the structure of Jet's ownership is still shrouded in mystery. It would be churlish to deny him credit for building, in just five years, a fleet that is already half IA's size and is equal to that of Air-India (AI). But alas, Goyal is also an influential man with links to heavyweight politicians cutting across parties and to politically well-connected film stars and journalists. He has single-handedly ensured we have a domestic aviation policy that provides for a role for foreign investors alright, but not for foreign airlines in any manner. This means that foreign airlines can buy into AI but not into IA.

This policy was approved in October 1997 in the teeth of opposition from the then finance minister P. Chidambaram and the then industry minister Murasoli Maran. The Congress did not oppose this stupidity and the BJP too has embraced it. Goyal was determined to keep Singapore International Airlines out and in order to accommodate him, this policy that exists nowhere else in the world was implemented. Jet itself fell in line and the two foreign airlines that had equity in it—Gulf and Emirates—ostensibly sold their stake to Goyal. But for five years, he had enjoyed the benefits of foreign equity. Goyal is behaving rationally in managing the environment; it is successive governments who should be hauled up for succumbing to his pressures and charms.

The whole idea of a "strategic partner" is to bring in an investor who not only has deep pockets but also has technical and managerial expertise. What the Government should have done is to formulate a new aviation policy that allows foreign airlines entry subject to an equity cap, as in the insurance industry. All that the government needs to protect its interests is a 26-per cent stake. Goyal would want to buy IA. But this would decrease competition, however little of it that exists. Goyal would also like Jet to ply on international routes. This makes sense when AI and IA are both privatised.

Privatisation, mergers and takeovers should proceed faster. At the same time, there is clear need for a transparent competition policy so as to check the abuse of dominant market power and protect consumer interests. Some feel that what India needs is unbridled competition and that a competition policy would be a hindrance. This is not true and without such a we will all be at the mercy of monopolies and oligopolies. In capitalintensive industries giants are inevitable and the best way to discipline these giants—such as Reliance-IPCL, if and when such a marriage takes place—is through liberal and very low-duty imports. But a liberal trade regime by itself is not adequate. Some form of a market-friendly, professionally staffed Competition Authority along the lines of those existing in the US or UK will be also needed to ensure that competition is both free and fair.

07/02/2000

* * *

COAL NEEDS A CLEAN-UP
A bill to denationalise India's coal industry is finally introduced and the fight begins

Life and its delicious ironies! Twenty-eight years ago, the Kumaramangalam brothers—Mohan and Gopal—spearheaded the nationalisation of India's coal industry. On April 24, 2000, Mohan's son and Gopal's nephew, Rangarajan, who holds additional charge of the coal portfolio in A.B. Vajpayee's Government, introduced a bill in the Rajya Sabha to herald the denationalisation of the coal industry. In July 1991, the same Rangarajan had helped undo another of his father's legacies—the Monopolies and Restrictive Trade Practices Act that placed severe controls on the growth of big business houses.

The Congress government made a feeble attempt to reform the coal sector in 1993 when it allowed the mining of coal by private companies for specified captive consumption. Then in February 1997, the

United Front government prepared a comprehensive legislation to end the public-sector monopoly in coal production. But it panicked when the CPI and CPI(M) threatened to lead a strike. I.K. Gujral buried the bill.

The battle will be bitter and acrimonious. But it is imperative that the bill be passed because the future of India's most important energy resource is crucially dependent on new investment being mobilised,on new technology flowing in and on new organisations and management being put in place. This will not happen as long as the coal industry remains a public-sector monopoly and as long as mafias blessed by political parties rule the roost. And denationalisation will result in new investments in Bihar, West Bengal, Orissa, Madhya Pradesh and Andhra Pradesh. Tamil Nadu and Rajasthan will also benefit since they are rich in lignite.

Coal reserves in the country are presently assessed at over 200 billion tonnes. However, just about 35 per cent are proven, showing the enormous exploration challenge ahead. But even with the current level of proven reserves, at prevailing growth levels of consumption, these reserves will last for over 200 years. Coal provides security of supply as well—unlike naphtha that needs to be imported in a volatile price environment and which, in any case, is too valuable to be burnt in power stations. For power plants in peninsular India, even imported coal is a better option than petroleum fuels although a case could perhaps be made out for the import of LNG. Lately, another major coal-related resource has emerged. This is the gas located in between coal (and lignite) seams called coal-bed methane (CBM). CBM's proven reserves are now placed at about 850 billion cubic metres which is about 40 per cent more than the proven reserves of natural gas itself. Six years ago, the American company Amoco wanted to make a major investment in Bihar to develop CBM. But it left India in September 1996, frustrated after waiting for two years for the Indian government to decide whether the Ministry of Coal or the Ministry of Petroleum would be responsible for CBM! It took P. Chidambaram as finance minister to finally call a halt to this nonsense and to formulate a CBM policy. But by then Amoco had left. It now appears that companies like Reliance are eyeing this resource seriously.

Indian coal has low sulphur but high ash content—almost half of our total reserves contain over 35 per cent ash. This presents two other challenges—how to clean or "beneficiate" the coal before it is used in power stations and how to improve the efficiency of combustion itself so that more energy is produced and in an ecologically sustainable manner. The West wants us to use less coal. This pressure must be resisted at all costs. But we will strengthen our case if we are able to demonstrate higher energy and environmental efficiencies. This will call for publicly funded research and development. Indeed, coal must form one of the key areas of Indo-US science and technology collaboration as well. One of the most immediate projects would be to put out the fires that have been raging in the Jharia coalfields around Dhanbad for the past few decades, resulting not just in the loss of good quality coal but also in environmental devastation.

Like in the case of insurance and banks, coal nationalisation may well have had an economic and social rationale when it took place. But over the years this logic has lost its relevance. Circumstances, contexts and challenges change. The private sector assumes new strength. Technology moves on. The investment bill mounts. And most of all, the crippling, insurmountable limitations of a public-sector environment become painfully evident. Twenty-eight years ago, if you did not support the father you had no heart. Today, if you do not support the son you have no head.

08/05/2000

◆———◆

DON'T BANK ON THE CII
An excellent report on banks undeservedly generates heat

In March 1999, the Confederation of Indian Industry (CII) set up an expert group to recommend solutions for the bad-debt problems of India's financial sector. The group submitted its report to the finance minister on December 13. The report was publicly released on December 15. All hell broke loose on December 16 particularly on one of the 26 recommendations made in the report—that the three chronically sick banks, Indian Bank, UCO Bank and United Bank of India be closed down forthwith. MPs egged on by unions shouted foul. Rival industry associations, always eager to embarrass each other, took potshots. The media, unable to focus on details, screamed away. The finance minister then put pressure on the CII to withdraw its recommendation on closure. On December 20, the CII, eager to be on good terms with the Government, obliged. The report was buried. Nobody got hurt.

This is a pity since the CII's "Report on Non-Performing Assets in the Indian Financial System: An Agenda for Change" is actually an analytical, first-rate study. Its main author is India's most flamboyantly iconoclastic but among its most accomplished economists, Omkar Goswami. His co-authors were finance professionals from the ICICI and the CII.

The most widely used indicator of the health of banks is their non-performing as-sets (NPAs). In India, NPAs are advances on which interest has been overdue for over 180 days while in other countries, this period is around 90 days. Elsewhere, NPAs are shown as a proportion of total assets but since a substantial proportion of assets in Indian banks is in zero-risk gilts, NPAs in India are shown as a proportion of total advances. The other difference is between gross NPAs and net NPAs. This is applicable only in India because our banks are not allowed to write off the NPAs and because loan recovery is inter-minable. From the country's perspective, gross NPAs makes more sense but if comparisons are to be made over time, net NPAs also become relevant. Our NPAs are about two to three times the global prudential norms.

At the end of March 1999, gross NPAs of the 28 public- sector banks were Rs 51,710 crore. The RBI estimates that roughly 44 per cent of this is on account of bad loans in the "priority sector"—agriculture, small industry, transport operators, anti-poverty and rural development programmes, etc. Thus, if the NPAs of financial institutions like IDBI are also added, then the bad loans on account of industry alone are about Rs 38,000 crore.

What is to be done about the NPAs? Venugopal Reddy, deputy governor, RBI, puts it well—repayment of dues in India is at best a moral obligation, seldom a legal compulsion and may not even be a normal response on the part of a rational borrower! Systemic changes are required. Making the list of defaulters public is really no solution. It is also perverse today that there is every incentive for an industrialist to get his company declared sick. That is why the CII report suggests a radical overhaul of our bankruptcy, liquidation and labour laws. The other major reform recommended is in loan recovery through a complete transformation in the functioning of the debt recovery tribunals. This is the key. True, over the past three years Indian banks have somehow made cash recoveries to the tune of Rs 25,000 crore. This is impressive but only a fraction of what is desirable and possible.

Eight weeks ago, the RBI had released a broadly similar report prepared under the chairmanship of M.S. Verma, a former chairman of the SBI. It selected seven parameters covering solvency, earnings capacity and profitability to identify weak banks. The conclusion was that Indian Bank, UCO Bank and United Bank of India were systemically weak banks in spite of having received Rs 6,740 crore of government funds for recapitalisation in the past seven years. It recommended that the Government provide another Rs 5,500 crore over the next three years for re-structuring and also set up a privately managed asset reconstruction fund (ARF) which would buy the impaired loans from the banks and recover or sell them after some repair. The ARF has pluses but perhaps has more minuses. The CII rejects the ARF and plumps for closure at a cost of about Rs 10,000 crore.

Let there be no illusions. Bank reforms will be resisted by the million-strong white-collared employees. But at some stage, we have to bite the bullet. Fundamental reforms are possible only when banks are converted into companies under the Companies Act and government equity is reduced to below 50 per cent. After insurance, this is the next battle waiting to be fought in Parliament.

10/01/2000

◆——◆

BANKING ON DILUTION
Reduction of government shareholding in public-sector banks is inevitable

A big battle is brewing over banks. The Government will introduce legislation in Parliament shortly to reduce its shareholding in the 27 public-sector banks to a minimum of 33 per cent. This is being seen as privatisation and has been opposed by bank employee unions. The Congress, which nationalised the banks through the Banking Companies (Acquisition and Transfer of Undertakings) Act of 1970 and 1980 and then amended the Act in 1994 to set the minimum government shareholding at 51 per cent of paid-up capital, will also resist this initiative.

But is this actually privatisation? According to the Companies Act of 1956 it certainly is—any company in which the government owns less than 50 per cent equity is a private company. However, the public-sector banks are not governed by the Companies Act. They are governed by special laws made by Parliament. Thus, government holding can decline to 33 per cent and the public sector character of the banks can still be retained if the law is so defined. Technically, however, the law does not permit the sale of government shares. It only allows the issue of fresh shares. Thus, strictly this isn't disinvestment but diversified ownership.

Banks have to double their capital base roughly every five to seven years to maintain their business share, to provide security to their depositors and comfort to the regulator, that is, the Reserve Bank of India (RBI). In the last seven years, successive governments have pumped in a total of Rs 20,446 crore to improve the financial position of nationalised banks. This has come through the Central budget. Now, at least another Rs 15,000 crore is needed over the next four to five years. The Government will find it impossible to provide this level of support, given its precarious fiscal position as also the competing pressures on public expenditure. Thus, banks have no alternative but to raise money from the capital market. The Government has promised safeguards to ensure that no single party garners a substantial chunk of shares. It must also ensure that cross-holdings among the banks themselves do not predominate. This is most likely to happen.

Today, the government holding is 100 per cent in Allahabad Bank, Andhra Bank, Bank of Maharashtra, Canara Bank, Central Bank of India, Indian Bank, Punjab & Sind Bank, Punjab National Bank, UCO Bank, Union Bank of India, United Bank of India and Vijaya Bank. These banks have sufficient flexibility to go to the market. The real problem arises in the case of the State Bank of India (SBI), where government holding is 59.7 per cent, Bank of Baroda (66.9 per cent), Bank of India (77 per cent), Corporation Bank (68.3 per cent), Syndicate Bank (73.5 per cent), Indian Overseas Bank (75 per cent), Dena Bank (71 per cent) and Oriental Bank of Commerce (66.5 per cent). For these banks specially, the existing floor of 51 per cent government ownership will constrain their ability to raise resources and get good value for their shares.

Further, there is nothing special about 33 per cent. The minimum might as well be 1 per cent for that matter. But 33 per cent gives the impression of substantial government presence which 1 per cent does not convey. Indeed, the 33 per cent has as much logic as the prevailing minimum of 51 per cent.

Will development lending by banks be hit? No. Priority sector lending has nothing to do with ownership. Public sector banks provide 40 per cent of their advances to government-specified sectors that include agriculture, rural development, small-scale and agro-industry, small transport operators, self-employed, software, venture capital, etc. Private banks also have the same stipulation, whereas foreign banks have to set aside 32 per cent mainly for credit to exports and small industry. Nationalisation has ensured a geographical spread. Around 44 per cent of the about 46,000 branches of the 27 public-sector banks are in rural India (rural being defined as a place with a population of less than 10,000). Up to 45-50 per cent of the institutional credit flowing into agriculture annually is through these commercial banks. This too is an important achievement, although it also reflects the failure of regional rural banks and cooperative banks to expand rural lending.

But nationalisation has also created a work environment that is just not conducive to efficiency. Our public-sector banks can be transformed and be in a position to meet the challenges they confront only if they are converted into com-panies under the Companies Act. This gives them managerial flexibility impossible for parliamentary creatures. Government equity can then be set at any level. For instance, there is a case for retaining strategic control in SBI and in banks that serve poorer regions. But for most banks, 26 per cent government share will be sufficient. Even that may not be necessary since there is an independent regulator whose job is to protect the public interest.

13/11/2000

---◆──◆---

C. Enterprise

WOO BRAINS NOT ONLY BUCKS
India's NRI policy is economically and socially skewed

The success of the Resurgent India Bonds (RIBs), albeit at high cost, and Amartya Sen's Nobel prize have once again focused attention on Indians living abroad. They are clubbed together as non-resident Indians or NRIs—a term that has become pejorative. The true overseas

Indian (TOI) community—the diaspora—is probably around 15 million strong. These 15 million fall into five broad categories: roughly five million in Nepal and Sri Lanka, three million in Mauritius, Fiji, South Africa, Trinidad, Guyana and Surinam, three million in the US, UK, Canada and the Netherlands, 2.5 million in the Middle East and 1.5 million in east Asia.

Economic reforms started in China 20 years ago. Since then that country has received some $250 billion in foreign investment. About three-fourths of this has come from the overseas Chinese, a vast prosperous community numbering about 55 million. Estimates say about one-third of Chinese exports are from the investments being made by the overseas Chinese. Indians are following three broad routes to bring dollars into India. The first involves parking their savings in Indian banks. For this, the government offers attractive rates of interest. Excluding the $4.1 billion of the five-year RIBs, NRI deposits are now about $20.4 billion. This is one-fifth of our external debt. But short-term NRI deposits account for about two-fifths of the volatile component of our external debt. The second route is through actual equity investment. NRI investment approvals since 1991 comprise a little over $3 billion, just 6 per cent of the total. The third route is through annual remittances, which in 1997-98 may well have touched $10 billion. Fifty to 60 per cent of this comes from Indians in the Middle East. The big spurt in remittances came in 1993 and 1994, when we moved over to a market-determined exchange rate system and the incentives for the hawala route diminished substantially.

Maximum policy attention and incentives have been focused on the deposit schemes. There are now five such in operation. How much of these deposits is genuine savings of overseas Indians, how much is the money of businessmen becoming NRIs for FERA and income tax purposes and how much is actually Indian money under an NRI garb is hard to fathom. Such deposits have proved costly in the past. Their withdrawal triggered the financial crisis of 1991. Deepak Nayyar, the noted economist, has estimated that between October 1990 and March 1992 there was a net outflow of NRI deposits amounting to more than $2 billion. In addition, the Reserve Bank suffered a loss of over $3 billion on these schemes in 1990-93 because it provided an exchange rate guarantee. For some schemes, the guarantee is now provided by the Central government, while the banks assume the exchange rate risks for others. The Indian workers in the Middle East are the true heroes. They have saved Kerala and some other parts of the country. But the government, the airlines, the banks and the emigration, customs and immigration officials all treat them like second-class citizens—since they come from a different socio-economic strata. Yet, their remittances keep climbing—whatever the economic conditions here, with-out any special incentives. They do not add to our debt and contribute to keeping our current account deficit within manageable limits. The use of remittances for consumption is good and to be welcomed. But at the same time some attempt has to be made to "guide" them towards productive investment.

Clearly, the overseas Chinese is richer and has greater investible surpluses than the overseas Indian, who, largely speaking, is either in retail trade or is a salaried employee or a professional. But it is also clear that the emotional ties of the non-resident Chinese to the mother country are far more enduring, durable and deep than they are for the overseas Indian. Our policy towards global Indians must change from chasing their money to leveraging and networking their professional skills. Indians abroad are distinguishing themselves in a large number of fields like science, engineering, medicine, management, economics, informatics, biotechnology, agriculture, finance and energy. But this segment, which has the potential to transform and revitalise our educational, research, financial and manufacturing systems, has been largely ignored.

With faster liberalisation, many Indians will be returning to work in India. When we have a world-class patent system, we will be in a position to sell India as an attractive R&D destination. Just imagine how many top-flight Indians could return if institutions like Bell Labs were to set up shop here. Diaspora mindsets also need to change. Jagdish Bhagwati, a prospective Nobel laureate in economics, had earlier proposed a "brain drain" tax. Poor India has subsidised the education of professional overseas Indians by at least Rs 10,000-15,000 crore over the past three decades. There has to be some spark of public service in our profes-sional diaspora, some element of risk taking, some sense of self-motivation. Many of them belong to the privilegentsia—and can do without inequitous sops like dual nationality.

09/11/1998

KNOW WHAT NOT TO DO

Global excellence depends on understanding core incompetence

Eight years ago, an India-born management professor created a stir in the pages of the venerable Harvard Business Review (HBR), the world's pre-eminent management journal. C.K. Prahalad along with his colleague Gary Hamel put forward the theory of core competence. This article has become the 15th most influential in the past 75 years of the Review. Prahalad wrote that the world's most successful companies are highly focused, have developed expertise in one or two inter-related technologies or lines of businesses and do not hanker after diversification. Prahalad went on to become a global guru. Faced with a whole new world after the 1991 reforms and seeking global pastures, some Indian CEOs quickly became proteges of Prahalad.

But now the core competence theory has come under attack from two young Indian dons at the Harvard Business School, Krishna Palepu and Tarun Khanna. Drawing on a variety of cases in India, South Korea and Japan, Palepu and Khanna warn in a recent issue of the HBR that in emerging markets and developing economies focused strategies do not make sense. They present evidence that diversification can be financially profitable, add value and help beat competition. The timing of the Palepu-Khanna article could not have been worse. Hugely diversified conglomerates like Samsung and Daewoo are widely believed to have caused the financial mess in South Korea. Japan's Mitsubishi has long held a fascination for Indian corporate houses but what is not realised is that Mitsubishi reflects the peculiar political and social economy of Japan. Further, the examples of diversified and effective conglomerates in India given by Palepu and Khanna—the Tata and RPG groups—are themselves fighting for survival and are being forced to effect a fundamental mindset change. The Indian companies on the global threshold—Reliance, Bajaj Auto, Hero, Ranbaxy, Sundaram Fasteners, Infosys, Arvind Mills, Dabur, to name a few—have all stuck to their knitting. But a number of Indian businessmen have never hidden their disdain for Prahalad. One Indian CEO who is in consumer electronics, white goods, oil and power once told Kautilya that his core competence is to start new businesses. Another top CEO who is in steel, power, telecom, shipping and mining told Kautilya his core competence is the ability to raise money for mega-projects.

Believing technology and management expertise could be acquired at the drop of a hat, Indian companies went on a dizzy, wholly unfocused diversification binge in the early '90s. This is at the root of our current industrial malaise.

True, it takes a while to develop a core or a set of core competencies. So what do Indian entrepreneurs do in the interim? Kautilya recommends a strategy drawn from ancient Indian thought. Our seers, when asked what truth was, replied neti, neti, neti—not this, not this, not this. By this process of trial and error, the seeker of salvation was supposed to find the Ultimate. The ability to define core incompetence—what not to do—is perhaps more fundamental than the ability to delineate core competence.

But for this to materialise in real life, policy has to be right. First, exits have to be timely. They should be a purely bilateral issue between the management and labour. This is no prescription for a blind "hire and fire" approach. But haphazard exits are not protecting the interests of labour and are fuelling social tensions. The lack of a flexible, growthoriented exit policy is only benefiting owners who find it profitable when their companies become BIFR cases. Hence we have sick companies but no sick industrialists. The Urban Land Ceiling Act is preventing generation of resources which can take care of labour affected by restructuring.

Second, mergers and buy-outs must be freely allowed, subject only to the discipline of the transparent takeover code that is in place. Contrary to fears, such a code has not led to a flood of hostile takeovers. Even so, there is pressure from Indian industry to dilute its provisions. With buyback of shares on the cards, such a dilution would be totally uncalled for. And in takeover cases, the regulator, namely SEBI, must not take sides, a simple maxim it has forgotten in the Sri Vishnu Cements case.

Third, the way the Government and courts in the US have gone after giants like AT&T, IBM and Microsoft is a reminder that a market economy is based on laws which ensure that competition is both free and fair. India needs professional regulatory agencies that will enforce clear pro-competition rules and deter monopolistic, restrictive and un-fair business practices.

Fourth, the floating stock in Indian companies is low. Even in Reliance, the most widely traded scrip, it is no more than 25 per cent.

One of the reasons why the floating stock is low is because public financial institutions like IDBI and UTI continue to hold substantial chunks of equity in private companies. A three-year programme of divesting these holdings will not only subject the companies to greater market discipline but also perk up the capital market.

05/10/1998

◆——◆

NET SOME SAVVY
Hi-tech luddites: what do they know of IT who only IT know?

Five years ago, while speaking at a seminar on employment in Calcutta, Kautilya remarked that there is a great fascination with computer chips in this country but what will create more jobs and add more local value are potato chips. This, Kautilya thought, was a colourful way of saying that it is not the development of hi-tech but its use and diffusion that counts. But Ashok Mitra, former finance minister of West Bengal and now an MP, was not amused. He took Kautilya to task for this blas-phemy in an article in a national daily. Not content with that, Mitra summoned Kautilya before Parliament's Standing Committee on Industry, of which he was chairman. Subsequently, the swadeshi brigade turned the quip around and declared: potato chips, no; computer chips, yes. Kautilya cannot help recalling this, not to belatedly claim copyright but to place the current hype over information technology (IT) in its proper perspective.

It was Rajiv Gandhi who ushered India into the information age. He was criticised by today's IT champions as being elitist and not in tune with "Indian realities". Rajiv took the first steps to overhaul our policies in the telecom, electronics and computer industries. But unlike the present lot, he was concerned primarily with the application of IT. He launched the technology mission to use satellites to locate water sources in hard-rock villages. He started the computerisation of railway reservations, a project that now brings convenience to over half a million passengers daily.

Sam Pitroda was Rajiv's IT charioteer. At a time when telecom planners were obsessed with increasing telecom density—the number of telephones per 1,000 people—Pitroda stressed improvements in telecom accessibility. The result is public call offices (PCOs) have now become ubiquitous. At a time when people were unaware of our IT potential, Pitroda took steps to entice global companies to use India as a software base. GE was the first major company to do so.

Pitroda also helped establish the Centre for Development of Advanced Computing in Pune. It has been in the news for developing India's first supercomputer. One of Pitroda's pet projects—which unfortunately didn't take off but has the potential to transform rural India—is the application of IT in revenue administration and modernising land records. IT is not an end in itself. When the prime minister met his Industry and Trade Council recently, he asked Parvinder Singh of Ranbaxy to prepare a blueprint for knowledge-based industries This is the wrong approach. The real challenge is to apply knowledge-based techniques in all industries. So-called sunset industries like steel and textiles are being transformed by the use of sunrise and knowledge-based technologies. Productivity in the world oil industry has increased by 20 per cent due to IT use. IT can revolutionise our education and literacy programmes. But such public domain applications lack influential and aggressive champions. The IT industry too has shied away.

Kautilya cannot help wondering about the social roots of our obsession with IT at the cost of other critical industries like textiles and agro-processing. The progeny of many of India's ruling elite are working for the Intels, Microsofts, Oracles, IBMs and HPs. Silicon Valley is one of the largest agraharams (Brahmin ghettos) in the world. Is that why the IT industry draws policy attention and not, say, the edible oil milling industry—which is bigger and employs more Indians? IT is crucial for India's future. But we must maintain a sense of balance. IT is fundamentally a tool for decentralisaion and empowerment but can very easily degenerate into an Orwellian tool of control and centralisation. Kenneth Keniston, a professor at MIT and keen student of India's IT, points to the rise of a new ruling class: the "digirati". He identifies India's key IT challenge as the localisation of software to Indian languages. According to him, the Chinese are far ahead of India in this area. Keniston says he is struck by the radically different and incompatible approaches to localisation in this country.

The Government's high-profile IT task force has been fixated on fiscal incentives. What is needed is a national information infrastructure, an intra-India Internet as it were. Ajay Shah, a young Mumbai-based engineer and economist, has worked out the configuration of this infrastructure in great detail. He has published his blue-print in the Economic and Political Weekly, a journal that, alas, the IT types and globalisers don't read. Shah proposes IndiaNET as a purely public service and wholesale vendor of bandwidth in units of two million bits per second. The key to expanded domestic connectivity is a change in telecom policy. For instance, interconnections between networks are prohibited. For its part, the Indian IT industry will need to move away from selling gadgets to offering solutions. It will also need a whole new approach to retailing and marketing if it is to transit from being an outpost of the US economy to being an agent of change in India. Savvy Hi-tech luddites: what do they know of IT who only IT know?

26/10/1998

◆━━◆

WHAT'S ON THE ANVIL?

Amidst the knowledge euphoria, let us not forget good old manufacturing

It was Georges Clemenceau who is supposed to have quipped that America is the only nation in history which miraculously has gone directly from barbarism to degeneration without the usual interval of civilisation. Could India be like Clemenceau's America as far as the structure of the economy is concerned? Countries initially have a high share of agriculture in national income. This share keeps falling as a country industrialises. Then after industrial growth has established itself, the services sector takes over. What is happening to India is that it is experiencing a sharp fall in the share of agriculture in GDP all right, although on a national scale not in terms of employment. But instead of becoming an industrial giant it is catapulting itself straight into a services superpower.

According to internationally comparable World Bank data, in the last 20 years, the share of agriculture value-added in India's GDP has kept declining from 38 per cent to 25 per cent in 1998, just as the share of manufacturing value-added has moved sluggishly from16 per cent to 19 per cent and that of services from 39 per cent to 45 per cent. In China now, the share of manufacturing is a huge 37 per cent while that of services is 33 per cent. Amongst all major countries, India has the lowest share of manufacturing. In addition, the structure of manufacturing itself in India is different than that in China and other countries. We have the highest share of chemicals—19 per cent of total manufacturing value-added as compared to 10 per cent in China. This is because of our import duties which have made investments in feedstock-based industries more attractive than in metal-based ones. Also, India has a lower share of agro-processing and textiles in manufacturing value-added—24 per cent as compared to 28 per cent in China.

Figures apart, the point is very simple. India cannot afford to neglect good old, traditional manufacturing in its current obsession with IT. Sadly, the champions of IT have done a great disservice by propagating the com-pletely bogus concept of "knowledge-based industries", as if the jute, rice-milling and garment industries do not require knowledge inputs. True, the very nature of manufacturing itself is changing thanks in very large measure to IT. But the fact that we need a new vision for and thrust on manufacturing should in no way suggest a second-class status as it appears to be enjoying these days. The next wave of manufacturing must be engineered with the right policy framework and economic environment. In the past we have seen manufacturing largely in the context of capital goods. This is still important but it is consumer goods that will set the pace with low cost, high quality. The name of the game is to be internationally competitive with no more than 10-15 per cent tariff protection. This will entail major changes in the structure of domestic taxation. The movement to VAT (value-added taxation) should help producers.

India must also aggressively seek to become a global subcontractor not just on the basis of low wages but more critically on the basis of skills. Possibilities are endless if we shed our disdain for low-tech. There is no great shame in becoming a global supplier of radiator caps as the Chennai-based Sundram Fasteners has become. Even within IT there are niche areas where we can become an international production platform provided we adhere to global standards on time.

While private investment will be the engine of growth and this will require nurturing, technology is the lubricant. This will mean a mindset change in our technology policy. Old models have become obsolete as the impetus to technological change in a particular industry is coming from outside that industry. 100 per cent ownership to foreign firms will enhance access to contemporary technology.

Restructuring has to be made more flexible so that inefficient firms can exit, albeit humanely. But restructuring will call for a special focus on India east of Kanpur which needs new growth impulses to facilitate revival. Inevitably, the textile and agro-processing industries will demand separate attention given that they have not been subject to serious reforms in the past few year even though they are both areas of great competitive advantage for us. Small-scale policies need to be re-vamped by raising investment ceilings, phasing out reservations and allowing large firms to have larger stakes. Finally, since over half of manufacturing employment is in rural or semi-urban India programmes to improve the competitiveness of house-hold or artisan-based manu-facturing will have both profound economic and social consequences.

24/01/2000

◆━━◆

ONE TRUTH MANY PATHS
India's new eight-fold path to the nirvana of globalisation is now unfolding

Tata Tea's $370 million (Rs 1,590 crore) takeover of Tetley re-flects the growing globalisation of Indian business. It is also a boost for Ratan Tata himself, a man of the greatest integrity, decency and mod-esty who has been under siege facing numerous challenges in various Tata businesses. Indian companies are adopting different approaches to globalisation. The first is the Reliance approach. Here the Indian com-pany attains global parameters of production but its market focus is mainly domestic. Other ex-amples: Bajaj Auto, Hero Cycles, Maruti Udyog and BHEL.

Second is the Sundram Fasteners route where an Indian com-pany emerges as a global sub-contractor. The Chennai-based Sundram Fasteners is now a major supplier of radiator caps to General Motors but without any equity participation by GM. Such niche players can multiply in light manufacturing.

The third route to globalising is simply to build on India's comparative advantage and push up exports. This has been done brilliantly in the software industry by companies like Tata Consultancy Services (TCS), Infosys, Wipro, NIIT and others. But in other areas like leather and textiles such companies have not emerged because of

India's policy of small-scale reservation. If policy is unshackled, Indian textile giants could well emerge. As for TCS, a bonanza awaits it if and when Tata decides to make it go public, something that should have already been done.

The fourth approach is the one epitomised by the Tata Tea-Tetley deal itself. Aditya Birla was one of the pioneers with his petrochemical investments in East Asia. Hotels managed by Indian groups like Tatas, Oberoi and ITC are present in different countries. Ranbaxy is another company that has invested close to $85 million abroad. Since April 1994, the total approvals for Indian investments in joint ventures and wholly-owned subsidiaries overseas (equity, loans, guarantees and share swaps) amount to about $2.8 billion. In the next 18 months, Indian software companies will invest close to $10 billion in the US largely through stock swaps. Biotechnology and oil are other areas where over-seas acquisitions are crucial.

Fifth, Indian affiliates of MNCs, like GE, could emerge as major suppliers to their parent companies. Increasingly, this route will gain importance since already over one-third of international trade in many industries is intra-company sales. Daewoo is making India a major production platform for car engines and Peugeot is doing so for two-wheelers. Other MNCs that could make India their major centres include Motorola and Ford. However, we are at a severe disadvantage as a manufacturing base in competition with China. This has to do with poor infrastructure and our neglect of time as a key factor.

Sixth, new opportunities are opening up in services as well. GE Capital, for instance, has a call centre in Gurgaon where, taking advantage of time zone differences, an advantage that we have yet to fully understand and exploit, Indian girls mimic American accents and call up credit card and other customers in the US. Companies like British Airways, American Express and Swissair have already relocated a part of their back-office processing operations to India. New start-ups in medical transcription are coming up. Another area is R&D. Unilever's food research centre is in Bangalore while Dupont and GE have a number of R&D joint ventures with the Pune-based NCL. The big bang would be when we entice a Bell Labs, for which we will need world-class patent laws and telecom services.

Seventh, professional Indians emerging as CEOs and on boards of major corporations is another dimension of globalisation. Keki

Dadiseth and Victor Menezes are in the top echelons of Unilever and Citibank respectively and not a day passes without an Indian being inducted into top management of noted firms. Indians have proliferated in investment banks. Rajat Gupta runs McKinsey, Rana Talwar is CEO of Standard Chartered, Rakesh Gangwal of US Air, Rono Datta of United Airways, Arun Netrawali of Bell Labs, Sanjay Kumar of Computer Associates, Jim Wadia of Arthur Anderson, Shailesh Mehta of Providian and M. Farooq of Ethan Allan.

Finally, overseas-based Indian entrepreneurs are emerging as global players. The London-based L.N. Mittal owns over 20 million tonnes of steel capacity in different countries. An increasing proportion of hi-tech start-ups in Silicon Valley is by Indian techies, the most glitzy of them all being Sycamore of Gururaj Deshpande. Thus, globalisation has many avatars, each of which is giving Indian enterprise opportunity to flourish. No surprise really for the heirs to a civilisation that first propounded *Vasudhaiva Kutumbakam.*

13/03/2000

◆━━━◆

NOT JUST LOUISIANA
To be or not to be is the old question. To H1B or not to
H1B is the new dilemma.

First came the distinction between sunset industries and sunrise industries. Then, traditional based industries were differentiated from knowledge-based industries. Now, the hype is of the new economy versus the old economy. All these categorisations are invidious and we perpetuate them at our own peril. The prospects of India's deindustrialisation get heightened not from imports but from such pernicious mindsets which see only ICE (information, commu-nication and entertainment) as the symbol of an economically resurgent India. Deifying a Narayana Murthy is all very well but that does not mean that a Rahul Bajaj has to be vilified and abandoned.

To be sure, the new economy driven by IT is vital. It is undoubtedly an area where India can and must achieve global leadership. But the fundamental challenge is how we use the new economy to improve productivity and competitiveness in the old economy, how we use new technologies to transform conventional industries like steel, engineering, energy and textiles. India needs more manufacturing, more traditional industries. But sadly this seems to have vanished from the radar screen of the Government and of the media. One reason for this is probably that the children of most of India's ruling establishment work in the new economy. President Bill Clinton's visit will further reinforce this dichotomy.

The reason why the integration of the new and the old economy is not happening fast enough in this country is simply that the focus of the new economy is external.The IT industry's main demand from Clinton will be to raise the cap on H1B visas showing once again where the priorities of this industry lie. That dramatic changes are possible with new-old economy integration is best exemplified by what has happened in the world oil industry which has seen its drilling productivity increase by over 25 per cent this past decade with the proliferating use of IT. The use of IT has made small industry cost-effective. The garment industry is another example of a conventional business whose very nature has changed with the deployment of new economy tools and techniques.

The second challenge that awaits the new economy is the localisation of software. Access to the new economy will boom only when software is available in different Indian languages. Here, the Chinese have stolen a march over us even after allowing for the fact that China is not as linguistically diverse as India. While we should not fall prey to xenophobic anti-Englishism that manifests itself even in progressive states like Karnataka, it is clear that mass markets will develop only with the standardisation and easy availability of local language software and development of local content. More than anything else, the use of cable TV will fuel such a mass market. Already perhaps around 25 million households are cabled. But for cable to carry the traffic, the nature of the cable industry itself has to change and the set-top box that converts the TV into an interactive device should become available for no more than Rs 2000.

A third area for the new-economywallahs to showcase their potential is education. This will also help in bridging the growing digital divide in India. But here we must distinguish between IT education which the industry is concerned with and IT-based education which is the social need. Some public-spirited initiatives are springing up, like the SchoolNet project in Bangalore. Such initiatives need start-up capital and sustained sources of funding .

Finally, e-governance. The push here is not coming from the IT publicists but from politicians like N. Chandrababu Naidu, S.M. Krishna and Digvijay Singh and some of their IT-savvy advisers. If treasury operations had been computerised, the fodder scam in Bihar would not have been possible. True, the onus for implementing solutions lies with the Government itself but the search for such solutions will be facilitated if the new economy peddlers take half as much interest here as they do in stock markets. The stock market itself is pulverising old economy scrips which is further de-pressing the morale of old-economy CEOs.

The new economy should be proactively embraced. But the old economy has to be aggressively rejuvenated. The two are not mutually exclusive. The tragedy today is that the former has acquired a Brahminical halo while the latter is being condemned to a Dalit status. It is time for the Government to return to basics. Apart from interest rate cuts, what it could usefully do is set up a National Manufacturing Competitiveness Council that gives the old economy a signal that they are still considered important and are engaging high-level attention.

27/03/2000

◆———◆

IS THE NEW ALL THAT HOT?
A new research paper in the US questions the hype over the 'new economy'

We are being constantly bombarded with a great deal of hype on the "new economy". The Internet, computers and telecommunications are all supposed to transform our lives in an unprecedented fashion. But now a new paper from one of America's most respected economists pours cold water on these claims. Robert Gordon, a professor at Northwestern University, has just released "Does the New Economy Measure up to the Greatest Inventions of the Past" as a working paper under the aegis of the prestigious Cambridge (US)-based National Bureau of Economic Research. Ironically, the "new economy" has ensured its instant and wide dissemination.

Economics textbooks say that there is a trade-off between wage inflation and unemployment. Low inflation means high unemployment whereas rising prices are inevitable if there is to be low unemployment. This relationship is called the Phillips Curve after A.W. Phillips who first came up with this finding in 1958 based on the UK experience. The Phillips Curve has led to a concept called the non-accelerating inflation rate of unemployment (NAIRU)—the employment-inflation nirvana. In the 1960s, America's NAIRU was 4 per cent and in the 1970s it was 4.9 per cent. The best-selling MacroEconomics by Rudiger Dornbusch and Stanley Fischer, first published in 1978, put America's NAIRU in the 1980s and 1990s at between 5 and 6 per cent.

But something stunning has happened in the US in the past 10 years. Yes, it is running high current account deficits, and savings rates have plummeted. True, income distribution has become more unequal. But the American economy has seen unexpectedly high rates of economic growth in the 1990s. Inflation has remained low at around 3 per cent despite increasing wages and falling unemployment, which is currently at around 4 per cent. But instead of rising, the NAIRU has fallen. This profound transformation, many think, has been wrought by the dramatic gains in productivity made possible because of IT.

Gordon disagrees and points out that the spurt of 1.35 percentage points in productivity (weighted average of labour and capital productivity) during 1995-99 over 1972-95 comprises 0.54 percentage points of unsustainable cyclical effect and another 0.81 percentage points of an acceleration in trend growth. His contention is that productivity grows rapidly when output itself grows faster than its trend.

Gordon divides the US economy into a "new economy" sector that consists of computers, peripherals, telecom and other types of durables and a "traditional" sector. The "new economy" sector, according to his calculations, accounts for 12 per cent of the US economy and it has seen fantastic advances in productivity. The entire acceleration in trend growth of productivity for the overall economy has come from this 12 per cent seg-ment. But the balance 88 per cent of the economy has seen no acceleration in productivity growth. However, this "macro" result may not square with "micro" impacts: the oil industry, for example, has been claiming that drilling productivity has increased by about 25-30 per cent because of the use of the "new economy" tools.

Gordon identifies five clusters that formed the core of the Second Industrial Revolution: electricity, internal combustion engine, oil/gas/chemicals, telegraph/telephone/radio/motion picture/TV and runningwater/indoor plumbing/urban sanitation. US economists have been debating why productivity growth lagged during 1972-95. Gordon argues that we should, instead, be asking a more basic question—why is it that productivity growth was so phenomenal during 1913-72? The answer lies in the revolutionary impact of these "clusters". Against each of these clusters which transformed the world as we know it, Gordon finds the "new economy" falling woefully short. This is mainly because the Internet:

- has really not boosted demand for PCs and has not created truly new content;
- simply substitutes existing activities for other forms of information and entertainment and duplicates existing forms of commerce and information;
- triggers investment that represents competition for market share which, in turn, redistributes rather than creates sales; and
- has resulted in social returns being far less than private returns.

Undoubtedly, the "new economy" has an unusually great potential and its best is yet to come. But we could certainly do with a much larger dose of sobriety and a sense of balance than what is on offer these days through the media, stock market pundits and from the IT industry gurus themselves.

28/08/2000

◆——◆

NOT JUST IT-IT IS NOW GE
Research's first century began at Schenectady.
The second opens in Bangalore.

A hundred years ago to the month, the world's first industrial research laboratory was founded in Schenectady near New York by Charles Steinmetz, that mathematical genius of the early electrical industry. This was the GE Research Laboratory that transformed America and emerged as the pre-eminent centre for innovation. A century later, on September 17, 2000, GE unveiled its second multi-disciplinary technology centre in Bangalore which, by this time next year, would be the company's largest R&D concentration globally. This is a landmark, for GE has consistently been ranked as the most admired company in the world. The centre was opened by and named after Jack Welch, GE's legendary CEO.

Welch first visited India in September 1989. The visit was largely at the prodding of his deputy Paolo Fresco, who later went on to head Fiat, and Fresco's friend K.P. Singh, chairman of DLF, the Delhi-based real-estate developer. Welch's visit was to aggressively market GE's locomotives to the Indian Railways and its aero engines to Air-India and to explore joint-venture possibilities in plastics, refrigerators and medical equipment.

Welch sought to meet Sam Pitroda who was then the prime minister's closest aide and I was the aide's aide. Both of us were aware of the visitor's truly awesome reputation and we debated how we could hook the legendary Welch on to India in some dramatic way. About this time, we had been asked by Rajiv Gandhi to prepare a strategy for boosting software exports. Texas Instruments (TI) had opened its software facility in Bangalore, something in which Rajiv had taken a keen personal interest. Rajiv's directive to Pitroda was simple—get more TIs. Sensing an opportunity with GE after doing our homework, we decided to make a pitch to Welch for an India-GE partnership in software.

A second idea struck us as we recalled our interactions with R.A. Mashelkar, one of the world's top chemical technologists and head of the Pune-based National Chemical Laboratory (NCL). Mashelkar's belief was that we must move from the "publish or perish" syndrome in Indian science to a "patent and prosper" mindset. He argued for creating businesses out of knowledge. Now that Welch was here, we felt why not also make a case for India as a destination for GE's remarkable research business as well?

The meeting was held over breakfast at the Chambers in Delhi's Taj Mahal Hotel. Welch, Fresco, Larry Bossidy and Stephen Brandon were there from GE, apart from Singh, while from our side Pitroda, Montek Singh Ahluwalia and I were present. Pitroda made the slick slide presentation in his usual crisp style. The chemistry between Welch and Pitroda was electric. After an animated discussion he announced that he would soon send a team to see how GE could leverage India's software and research capabilities.

This team came to India in November 1989 and January 1990. We fixed up meetings for the team with companies like TCS, Wipro, HCL and a fledgling unknown called Infosys. Contracts for software development were then signed. Subsequently, GE and NCL also became partners. From then on, there was no looking back. Welch returned to India in 1992 and in 1995 when he was the first to publicly declare that India was a developing country with the intellectual infrastructure of a developed country. This year, GE will source about $250 million worth of software from India making it the single largest buyer. Wipro chief Azim Premji acknowledges that the initial GE contract opened other doors for him later. The same is probably true for Infosys as well.

Over the past decade, GE has built a billion dollar business in India and invested close to $600 million, making it among the largest foreign investors in the country. It has 17 legal entities, that is, either wholly owned subsidiaries or joint ventures across a wide range covering areas like appliances, medical equipment, lighting, financial services, energy, light engineering and plastics. To those who argue that MNCs should not acquire existing companies, GE's takeover of DLF's Faridabad factory should serve as an example—last year, half a million fractional horsepower electric motors were shipped from this refurbished plant to the US. The GE-IPCL and GE-BEL joint ventures are a tribute to the capabilities that reside in our public sector. In fact, the GE-BEL joint venture along with the GE-Wipro counterpart will soon emerge as a global centre for the design and manufacture of an array of medical equipment. To be sure, there have been disappointments as well. GE's alliance with Godrej is ending in divorce. The power and locomotive businesses have not grown as expected and this has hurt India as much as GE, reflecting the way we are managing these sectors. But all in all, GE's India experience is an exemplary case for a business school case study and a corporate historian.

02/10/2000

◆——◆

AFTER IT, TIME FOR T
The New Textile Policy2000 finally dereserves the garment industry

The distinctive feature of the new Textile Policy 2000 unveiled by the Government on November 2 is the removal of garments from the list of items reserved for exclusive manufacture by the small-scale industry (SSI) sector. It has taken 15 years for this to happen. Rajiv Gandhi tried in 1985 and P. Chidambaram in 1996 and 1997 but both were thwarted.

The garment industry occupies a special niche in our economy. At about $4.5 billion (Rs 20,250 crore), it accounts for around 13 per cent of India's total exports and employs close to 4.3 million people, according to an estimate by the National Institute of Fashion Technology. But from a larger perspective, we have been left far behind by countries like China, South Korea and Taiwan, what to speak of countries like Italy. There are five main reasons why India's garment exports have not exploded.

- Around 60 per cent of world trade in garments is based on synthetic fibres, whereas about 65 per cent of our garment exports are cotton-based. Till 1991, our import duties denied Indian garment manufacturers access to cheap synthetic fibre intermediates from abroad. High excise duties made domestic supplies expensive.
- Our exports themselves suffer from a lack of balanced spread, 75 per cent being items like blouses, skirts, dresses, shirts and knitted undergarments.
- Modern, integrated mills supply just about 5 per cent of the fabric for garment exports, the bulk coming from powerlooms. This has meant that we have been at a competitive disadvantage when it comes to the supply of standardised garments made of standardised fabrics.
- The garment industry itself has been oriented primarily towards the US and western Europe which, no doubt, account for about three-fourths of the total market but also where marketing is comparatively easier because we have export quotas. Other lucrative markets like Japan have remained neglected. These quotas, incidentally, will vanish on January 1, 2005 as per the WTO agreement and then we will really have to compete, for which preparation have to start now. Quotas have saved us so far.
- Perhaps most importantly, the policy of SSI reservation has created a structure of the industry that is just not globally competitive. Reservation has prevented the induction of new investment and technology and precluded possibilities of international sub-contracting as a route for market expansion for Indian firms. Inconsistent quality of products which buyers constantly complain about and poor unit value realisations (that is, value divided by volume of exports) which we worry about are the direct outcome of this reservation policy.

The world over, garments are indeed made in small firms. But not "small" as defined in India. For most of the 1970s and 1980s, the investment limit for defining a small firm in this country hovered around a pathetically low $100,000-150,000 and in the 1990s it went up marginally to about $200,000. In actual practice, since a small-scale entrepreneur does not want to lose the many fiscal and factory law benefits of remaining small, vertical growth of firms does not take place, only horizontal proliferation does. Thus, you will find a great many garment exporters in India each exporting a little, unlike in China where fewer exporters sell vastly greater quantities. Among the late industrialisers India alone did not follow what economists call the "textiles first" strategy and we have paid the price. The reasons for this are complex. It has partly to do with our fascination with the Soviet model in the 1950s which was based on the primacy of steel and heavy machinery. It has partly to do with the Gandhian legacy that positioned mass production falsely against production by the masses and wrongly placed a premium on the latter. And there was politics. Sukhamoy Chakravarthy, one of India's greatest economists, wrote in his 1987 classic Development Planning that emphasis on textile exports would have required supporting a particular regional group of industrialists at the expense of others.

On becoming prime minister, Rajiv Gandhi remarked that the job of the textile industry is to produce textiles, not jobs. It was this that led to the bold June 1985 Textile Policy. That policy combined with the 1991 reforms has resulted in a partial transformation of our textile industry. The spinning and synthetic fibre segments in the organised sector have boomed, whereas the decentralised weaving and knitting segment has grown impressively. But the textile industry is still crippled by controls and by fiscal distortions. The new policy sets an ambitious $50 billion target for exports of textiles and garments together by 2010, up from the present $11 billion. The focus has been too much on IT. It is time to shed this brahminical mindset and move from just IT to T—textiles and give India's oldest industry a new deal. This will create mass prosperity.

04/12/2000

NEW HYPE, OLD HOPE
IT IS TIME FOR B2B—BACK TO BASICS—IN THE MACROECONOMY

India presents three appartment macro-economic puzzles. These puzzles need to be understood and addressed for the new economy to be more than an enclave and to be on a sustainable foundation.

First, all countries as they develop see the share of agriculture fall in their respective GDPs. India is no exception and now agriculture accounts for about 25 per cent of its GDP, down from around 55 per cent 50 years ago. But where India is unique is that the share of agriculture in total employment has not fallen equally sharply as has happened elsewhere. This share still remains at a high two-thirds. It is this that explains much of rural poverty in India.

Second, all countries move from having a high share of agriculture in their GDP to having an increasing share of industry. Thereafter, the share of the services sector increases. Again, India is an exception. It is moving from agriculture to services without going through and enjoying the fruits of broad-based industrialisation. World Bank data shows that in 1998, services value-added were 46 per cent of GDP in India and 33 per cent in China. On the other hand, industry value-added in India accounted for 25 per cent of GDP and 49 per cent in China.

Third, when we take just the manufacturing segment of industry alone and examine its structure, we see another Indian peculiarity. For our level of development, we have a high share of machinery and chemicals in manufacturing value-added—42 per cent as compared to 37 per cent in China. Indeed, among all late industrialisers, India stands out for not adopting what economists call the "textiles first" strategy and it has paid the price. The share of manufacturing in total employment instead of growing as in other countries has remained virtually constant at 10-11 per cent. And unlike other countries, two-thirds of our manufacturing employment is in tiny workshops as opposed to modern factories.

What explains these puzzles? India is a special case not because of history, geography, culture or climate but because of its policies and its industrialisation paradigm. The planning strategy formulated by Professor P.C. Mahalanobis in the early 1950s gave us a high share of heavy industry. Import policy in the pre-1991 period tilted the balance away from metal-bashing industries in which India had a competitive advantage to capital-intensive feedstock-based industries. The Gandhian legacy ensured that we followed policies for the small-scale sector rooted neither in economics nor in technology. And our labour laws have strongly discouraged employment expansion. Ironically, it was Mahalanobis himself who wrote in 1969 that "certain welfare measures tend to get implemented in India ahead of economic growth ... the present form of protection of organised labour ... would operate as an obstacle to growth and would also increase inequalities".

India must get its macroeconomic structure right. We have to rediscover the virtues of mass manufacturing. In a study just published in the Economic and Political Weekly, Adrian Wood and Michele Calandrino detail a vision of widespread modernisation of manufacturing brought about by diffusion of the new economy, through greater openness to international trade and by wider expansion of factory employment. India is already an attractive destination for value-added services in manufacturing like research, development, engineering and design. But it is mass manufacturing—textiles and garments, agro-processing, consumer goods, toys, electrical appliances, sports goods, components, sub-assemblies to name a few—that will create blue-collar jobs. The vision must be bifocal keeping both the domestic and global markets in mind, with both domestic producers and global companies using India as a production and sourcing base. The obstacles are for-midable, what with tight labour laws, small-scale reservation, poor infrastructure, high import duties on raw materials and intermediates and fiscal anomalies that make imports of finished products cheaper. But these have to be tackled. Yashwant Sinha's forthcoming budget should signal a changed mindset with the stress not on Indian manufacturing but manufacturing in India.

To be sure, services must be encouraged aggressively. Three segments alone, worker remittances, software exports and tourism, will bring in about $16 billion (Rs 73,600 crore) in 2000-01 and pay for about 30 per cent of imports. Economists classify services as "invisibles" in the balance of payments statistics. But their economic impact is anything but invisible. India's large trade deficit (merchandise imports minus exports)becomes a safe current account deficit only because of these earnings. But as services grow, our pressing challenge is still to restore dynamism to agriculture and buoyancy to mass manufacturing through new investments and technology. This is the new economy's trishul.

19/02/2001

INDUSTRY BADLY NEEDS A VIAGRA
No longer an emerging market, India is fast becoming a submerging market

Indian industry is in dire straits. The rate of ndustrial growth has declined for six consecutive months since December 2000. Actually, the slowdown goes way back to December 1999. Even more significant is the collapse of business confidence and investor sentiment as privatisation flounders badly and reforms-fatigue takes over.

Two types of responses to this crisis have been forth-coming so far. One view is that global economic growth itself has decelerated significantly and a 5-6 per cent rate of economic growth that India might well register in 2001/02 will still place us among the world's fastest growing economies. The other view is that we are now driven increasingly by business cycles and it is only a matter of time before the upswing starts as the effects of a good monsoon are felt.

The first argument is small consolation. India just cannot afford to grow at anything less than 7-8 per cent per year, year after year for a decade or two. Moreover, India cannot hope to prosper only on the back of a booming services sector when the agriculture sector remains indifferent and industrial, sluggish, which is what has happened in recent years. The argument that India has slowed down because the world has is also weak since our total exports constitute no more than 9 per cent of GDP.

The second view has some validity but we must take note of the fact that downturns in the business cycle are getting prolonged and the recovery less permanent. While allowing the process of restructuring to proceed apace, the Government has still an important role to play in reducing the downturn and lengthening the upturn period.

Industry has two standard suggestions: reduce interest rates and increase import duties. The investment boom of 1992-95 took place when interest rates were very high. In the past year, interest rates have softened. Moreover, with the pressure that is bound to come on the rupee on account of the depreciation of competing currencies like those of the east Asian countries, the natural instinct of the RBI would be to raise interest rates to provide stability to the rupee.

The demand for increased import duties is on dubious grounds since there is no empirical evidence to suggest that imports are surging. In the mid-1990s, industrial growth accelerated as import duties came crashing down with the exchange rate providing the compensating cushion. As industrial growth slackened, import duties have, in fact, gone up. Writing in the Business Standard, noted economist Ashok Desai showed a close connection between protection and industrial failure. This protection is also eroding our export competitiveness.

If the standard suggestions do not have much merit, what then? First, agriculture still impacts on industrial growth in many ways. Since the mid-1990s, agricultural growth has fluctuated significantly and we have not had three consecutive years of good performance. Agriculture continues to be strangulated by a number of controls on production, processing, marketing and trade. The rate of growth of subsidies is about three times the rate of growth of public investment in agriculture. It is the structure of public expenditure at the Centre and in states that is responsible for our inability to rapidly proliferate rural prosperity.

Second, while recognising that the Indian consumer market has not evolved quite the way pundits expected a decade ago, industry itself has to think of new ways of connecting with consumers. Writing in Business World a couple of weeks ago, Rama Bijapurkar, one of India's leading market research analysts, pointed out that many consumer goods industries are facing saturation in urban markets but their penetration in rural markets is still very low. Even in urban markets, the penetration of refrigerators, for example, falls sharply beyond the top fifth of the income category.

Third, "kickstarting" industry through greater investments in key sectors like railways, power, roads, irrigation and construction is a possibility specially since banks are flush with funds and inflation is under control. S.L. Shetty, writing recently in the Economic and Political Weekly, suggests a "pump priming" of an additional Rs 15,000-16,000 crore a year over the next five years in the infrastructure areas. But the key question here is whether it is feasible to step up public expenditure both at the Central and state levels when the nation's fiscal deficit is close to 10 per cent of GDP and also whether it is desirable to do so in the present environment of financial indiscipline and managerial inefficiency. Just spending more money in railways, power, roads and irrigation without fundamental reforms in the manner in which this spending takes place and in the method costs are recovered is a sure recipe for getting ourselves into a deeper mess. A new paradigm of public funding and private management needs to be developed if pump priming is to be effective.

28/08/2001

◆——◆

INFOSYS IS WESTWARD HO
At last an Indian company lists on a US stock exchange

Infosys, the Bangalore-based software trailblazer, created history on March 11 by becoming the first Indian-registered company to list on Nasdaq, one of the two major stock exchanges in the US. Technically, how-ever, Infosys is the second Indian company to list on Nasdaq, since the $30 million (Rs 126 crore) US-registered but wholly Chennai-domiciled Cognizant Technology Solutions listed in June 1998. Now the doors are open and we could expect to see at least 10 Indian information technology (IT), pharmaceutical and telecom companies follow Infosys' example over the next two years. By global standards, however, India's presence on Nasdaq will be modest. Some 80 Israeli companies and a good number of companies from Australia, Argentina and South Africa are also on Nasdaq.

Nasdaq itself was launched in 1971. Although the most widely-tracked indicator of stock market health, the Dow, is based on its rival New York Stock Exchange (NYSE), close to 60 per cent of the total share volume and listed companies in the US is on Nasdaq. It is the popular perception that it is an exchange predominantly for IT companies, since its stars have been names like Microsoft, Intel, Oracle and Netscape.

Actually, less than 20 per cent of the listed companies are in the IT industry. The bulk are in pharmaceuticals, biotechnology, banking, telecom, electronics, oil, transportation and housing. By and large, Nasdaq is home to new, first-generation, technology-driven companies. Already around 20 IT companies founded by Indian-Americans with a total market capitalisation of around $16 billion—like i2 Technologies, Microchip Technologies and Mastech—are listed on it.

It is to Infosys' credit that it has been diligently following American accounting principles for the past few years so as to make its debut on Nasdaq easy. The fact that it is a professionally-owned, one-industry company of relatively new vintage helped. Over 80 per cent of its revenues are generated in North America. But a large majority of established, family- owned Indian companies will have to rework their accounts if they wish to seek listing in the US. The American standards are ruthless. In 1993, Daimler-Benz listed on the NYSE. Its reported profit of $370 million under German rules got converted into a $1 billion loss by American standards.

The Indian GAAP—Generally Accepted Accounting Principles—differs substantially from the American GAAP. First, the US requires the consolidation of the financial statements of all majority-owned subsidiaries into the financial statements of the parent company. This is not so in India. Second, unlike India, the US requires all deferred taxes to be recorded. Third, unlike the US, India allows excess depreciation and provides a choice to the company on the method to be adopted for calculating the depreciation charge. Fourth, unlike the US, the Indian standard recognises the revaluation of fixed assets. Fifth, US accounting standards require gains or losses from foreign currency transactions to be included in determining net income. There are other differences as well—for example, the US does not allow proposed dividend to be accrued and requires current portion of longterm debt to be shown as current liability.

The London-based International Accounting Standards Committee, a private-sector body of which the Institute of Chartered Accountants of India is a member, has been pursuing the cause of core, uniform norms to be adopted around the globe. The Americans have been resisting. They argue that their standards are superior, more transparent, less ambiguous and more rigorous.

A compromise under the aegis of the International Organisation of Securities Commissions, of which the Securities and Exchange Board of India (SEBI) is a member, is in the offing. In fact the finance ministers and central bank governors of the G7 have jointly called for the early adoption of an internationally agreed set of accounting standards, practices and, most crucially, interpretations of rules.

It is therefore most timely that Parliament recently approved the setting up of an independentNational Accounting Standards Board. At the same time SEBI set up an expert committee to see how our accounting principles and practices can be brought on a par with the best global practice.

Our own Nasdaq, the Over-the-Counter Exchange of India, started a few years ago, is dead. The need is for expanding the supply of venture and risk capital. Because we have not done so, entrepreneurs have used public issues to raise venture capital, bringing grief to millions of investors in the process. To multiply Infosys, the venture capital industry and the technology financing system needs to be shaken up.

Indian venture capital companies behave like bankers, fearing failure in a business where success means a failure rate of 70-80 per cent. It is said that true venture capitalists are vulture capitalists. The hope lies with foreign venture capital and private equity companies, some of whom are already in India. They should be allowed 100 per cent foreign equity freely and be treated on a par with mutual funds for tax purposes, with the restriction that they invest only in unlisted companies. Exits and repatriations must also be easy.

29/03/1990

SELF-RELIANCE TO RELIANCE?
IPCL's sale should increase competition, not decrease it

The public sector Indian Petrochemicals Corporation Limited (IPCL), with manufacturing plants in Nagothane in Maharashtra and Vadodara and Gandhar in Gujarat, has been one of India's most successful companies. It was one of the navaratnas identified in P. Chidambaram's 1997 budget for maximum autonomy and for sustained support to emerge as a global giant.

Subsequently, in March 1998 the Disinvestment Com-mission recommended that the Government privatise IPCL since it was not in a strategic or a core area. The Government's equity in IPCL is around 59 per cent. The commission's advice was to sell off another 25 per cent of the Government's share to reduce its equity to 34 per cent and also to transfer management control to the "strategic sale" partner—that is, the private investor. Ultimately, around early 2001 after the redemption of a convertible bond and if investors decide to convert their holding to equity, the Government's equity would rest at 26 per cent. This is the minimum required under our Companies Act to block a special resolution of the shareholders and protect the national interest. The sale should fetch the Government at least $350 million. The BJP Government accepted the recom-mendation and issued global bids in the first week of June 1999. Now it appears there are four serious bidders—Reliance, the American MNC Dow, the public sector Indian Oil Corporation (IOC) backed by New York-based Indian financial entrepreneur Purnendu Chatterjee and the Japanese Mitsubishi. Two of the leading petrochemical MNCs are not bidding. Royal Dutch Shell is already committed to Nocil that it acquired from Arvind Mafatlal. British Petroleum (BP) is busy working out its merger with Amoco and Arco and is more enamoured with China. Dow too is merging with Union Carbide and what this decision means for its commitment to the IPCL bid remains to be seen

Although it has world-class managers, IPCL is bleeding. This is because of competition, because of the dwindling margins in commodity polymers and also because it still suffers from many government controls. Its profit after tax has slumped sharply from Rs 500 crore to Rs 25 crore in the past three years, although this year its profit will cross Rs 200 crore. It desperately needs at least around Rs 1,000 crore of fresh equity to keep it going. It cannot incur any additional debt. Its debt-equity ratio is around 1.5:1, as compared to 0.51 for its competitor, Reliance. The Government is broke. The only option is to look for a cash-rich partner.

IOC certainly has the cash. But it itself could do with restructuring. For example, there is no reason why its entire LPG and lubricant business should not be hived off and privatised. IOC's takeover of IPCL would mean forward integration for the former but what exactly would IPCL gain other than money? IOC's partner, the Chatterjee Group, brings no real or superior scientific and technical knowledge. Besides, if IPCL is to be privatised, why have another public sector company buy it, although from the viewpoint of IPCL's out-standing professionals there is probably no better option than to have a start-up catalyst like Chatterjee involved since he would not get into day-to-day management.

Now come to Reliance. Leaving aside its fabled clout, what if its bid is the most attractive? In the UK and other European countries, a deal involving the merger of the top two companies in the market would immediately invite the attention of the anti-monopoly authorities. In the US, the Justice Department's anti-trust division would swing into action. The key question that our Government has to ask is whether a Reliance-IPCL deal would promote competition or decrease it. Only a few days ago a committee was set up to formulate a competition policy. The existing MRTP Act is wholly inadequate.

Does this then mean that the Government should stop the sale? This is where trade policy comes in. What needs to be done is slash import duties on polymers right away to no more than 10 per cent at the most from the present average of around 35 per cent. Competition would then come from imports. Incidentally, this shows how bogus the argument of "internal liberalisation first, external liberalisation later" trotted out by the BJP and the industry associations is. Very often, external competition is quicker, cheaper and more effective, particularly in capital-intensive industries.

Originally, the last date for the receipt of bids was November 30 and the sale would have been complete by December 30. Now with a new minister and a new secretary the schedule has been thrown off gear. If we get all four bids then things are on track. But if there are only two bids then there isn't really enough competition. The whole point of a strategic sale is that we bring in a company with superior technological and management expertise. Ideally, Shell and BP should have been enticed. But that has not been possible. The Government must judge whether to go ahead or make one more effort to get these two companies to bid as well. All in all IPCL's divestment is throwing up a large number of issues that need to be addressed coolly without trying to make it a totem for our commitment to privatisation.

15/11/1999

◆━━◆

OLD DAYS ARE HERE AGAIN
North Block sings the 'Essar, Essar three bags full saar' tune

If proof were ever needed on why we must privatise our financial system quickly, it was provided last week by a government that came to power vowing to end what it called "crony capitalism" but ended up doing exactly what it criticised. In a most ill-advised move that will set a dangerous precedent, the Finance Ministry has arm-twisted financial institutions (FIs) like IDBI and UTI to finance a Rs 2,500 crore bail-out package for the cash-strapped Essar Group. The institutions will provide Rs 1,700 crore and Essar will come up with Rs 800 crore largely through the sale of its power plant at Hazira.

The institutions are livid but are not protesting publicly since they know their jobs depend on keeping their bosses in North Block happy. More such rescue gifts for steel companies like Ispat, Lloyds, Bhushan, Rajender and Mukand are reportedly in the pipeline. Is it just a coincidence that some of these companies have also been strong supporters of the BJP and of its influential leaders and enjoy the backing of self-styled economic gurus of the RSS?

If the institutions, in their best commercial appraisal, felt that such help was warranted, then there could be no serious objection. Lenders all over the world will do all to ensure that their portfolio remains healthy and Indian institutions can be no exceptions. What is wrong is the proactive involvement of the Finance Ministry in championing, formulating and coordinating the entire effort. Laying down policy is one thing, brokering deals is another. Under the garb of "sector-specific" policy packages, we are moving back to the pre-1991 era, when FIs were extended arms of the Finance Ministry.

Every bad practice in India has its counterpart good practice in a developed country. It is, therefore, being said that what the Finance Ministry has done is exactly what the once-powerful MITI, the Ministry of International Trade and Industry, did to power Japan in its high-growth phase. Apart from the fact that MITI was the by-product of a unique social system and is itself now thoroughly discredited, the MITI analogy is based on a profound misunderstanding of what fuelled the Japanese miracle.

The Essar Group has been built by the dynamic Tamil-speaking Ruia brothers, entrepreneurs for whom Kautilya has personal admiration and affection. Two years ago, Kautilya even "spoke" to one FI to look at Essar's Punjab telecom project. The institution examined it and said no. That was the end of the matter.

Like most other Indian family concerns, Essar has allowed itself to be horribly over-extended. Its corporate governance practices leave great room for improvement, to put it mildly. At one time, it had a major presence in steel, aluminium, iron ore, shipping, power, oil, telecom and commodities trading. Each of these businesses is investment- intensive. Feeling the pressure of intense competition, Essar has rightly decided to get out of non-ferrous metals and trading.

The actual damage to our steel industry from low-cost imports—one reason being given for the bailout—is vastly exaggerated. Imports as a proportion of consumption have actually declined from a peak 9.2 per cent in 1994-95, when the economy was booming, to 7.8 per cent in 1997- 98. In April-November 1998, the proportion was even lower at 5.3 per cent. The investment famine in the country is behind the steel industry's woes. The industry built up capacity in the early '90s expecting a 7 per cent rate of GDP growth in India and in the hope of world trade growing at over 8 per cent per year. In the past two years, growth rates everywhere have crashed. This has eroded the profitability of steel companies. The immediate provocation for Essar's bailout appears to be a short-term loan of about $250 million, which it has to repay in July 1999. Essar and its advocates in North Block say that if it defaults on this repayment, then there will be hell to pay for India itself. This has no economic logic. Surely it must have occurred to the pundits in the Finance Ministry that the Government's move itself could be sending the very signals.

Are there other ways of avoiding Essar's default? There certainly are. For example, over a billion dollars of the Resurgent India Bonds are parked with the SBI abroad, invested in US treasuries while supposed to be used for lending to Indian corporates in infrastructure. Essar could take a $250 million loan from SBI, London. The risk could be shared among institutions and the debt could be retired once and for all.

Essar could then work out a schedule for repaying the amount owed to the SBI. It must be forced to sell its telecom business and if need be loans should be converted into equity for a specified period by FIs. The point is simple—any bailout must be preceded, not accompanied, by fundamental restructuring of the company. In this case, the FIs must put in the Rs 1,700 crore, if indeed they have to, after Essar has coughed up Rs 800 crore. Even now it is not too late to insist on this so as to uphold the Government's commitment to cleaning up and professionalising the financial sector.

08/02/1999

SO ENROFF IS ON
After years of heat Enron will now generate light

Finally, India's most written about foreign investment has taken off. On May 25, the first phase of the Enron power project at Dabhol in the Konkan region of Maharashtra was "dedicated" to the nation. The project has had a controversial and tortuous history. Conceived in June-July 1992, work on the ground commenced in March 1995. But in August 1995, the project was cancelled by the newly elected Shiv Sena-BJP Government in Mumbai, which during the election campaign had vowed to drown the project in the Arabian Sea. After protracted renegotiations, the project recommenced in January 1997.

Personally, Kautilya was never excited by Enron and disagreed with the approach to foreign investment in power formulated and executed by then prime minister P.V. Narasimha Rao's advisers like N.K.P. Salve, A.N. Varma and S. Rajagopal, who exercised greater influence in the matter of power policy than Manmohan Singh himself. Kautilya left the Rao government in December 1994 and went public on his argu-ments against Enron. Apart from Enron's abrasive style and breathtaking arrogance, Kautilya's reservations were fivefold.

- India's power policy must be based on coal and hydel resources and not on petroleum fuels like naphtha.
- Enron was really into natural gas transportation, whose installed power capacity was just 2 per cent of India's.
- Enron had negotiated a sweetheart deal for itself; the state has to fork out Rs 140 crore a month, which is roughly 5 per cent of its expenditure.
- Enron was bringing in no great technological or managerial capability that companies like NTPC, BSES and Tata Electric could not mobilise if given the freedom.
- The deep-rooted structural problems of our power industry would not get addressed if we had quick-fix solutions in the form of Enron.

Ironically, these arguments against the project were picked up by L.K. Advani to justify the ending of the contract. Kautilya, who had left the government by then, had also applauded the decision to cancel the project as an opportunity to carry out "real" reforms—the financial and organisational restructuring of the state electricity boards, minimum tariffs in agriculture and an end to the supply of free power, the privatisation of distribution, the building of regional grids and so on.

But all this is history. The Enron episode became a long learning experience, a model of both what to do and more crucially of what not to do. Now it is Kautilya's turn to applaud Enron's sheer tenacity and perseverance. It successfully fought 26 cases in various high courts and in the Supreme Court in a span of four years. It has been lobbying aggressively in the US even while facing hurdles and criticism here. Kautilya himself was present in Houston in October 1996, when both foreign and NRI investors were bad-mouthing India only to have the Enron CEO get up and put up a stout and eloquent defence of India.

For the first phase 740 MWDabhol project, whose cost is slightly over a billion dollars, Enron and its partners, GE and Bechtel, have brought in about $280 million of equity. Enron's share is 80 per cent. When taken together with the approximately $250 million that it has brought in over the past four years for its oil and gas joint ventures with Reliance and ONGC, the Enron Group has emerged as the single largest foreign investor in the country.

The second phase of the project, which will add 1,440 MW to the grid, will cost about $1.9 billion. It will come on stream in about 24 months from now. Enron and its partners will bring in over $450 million of equity. But this has generated fears that Enron will raise money in India from Indian financial institutions (FIs) whereas the whole objective of having Enron is to get it to bring money from outside. Out of the $1.4 billion loan component, Indian FIs are providing rupee loans equivalent to about $333 million, which is a little over 20 per cent of the total loan component.

This apart, Enron has taken guarantees from Indian FIs like ICICI for its overseas borrowings. This could be legitimately criticised but we should not forget the poor ratings for India in global markets in 1998, what with the Pokhran II sanctions, Yashwant Sinha's lacklustre first budget and an indifferently performing economy. And it is not as if Indian companies were denied funding. It just so happened that Enron was a lower credit risk than many Indian companies who were (ad)venturing into power without the resources and the single-minded sense of purpose as Enron.

What next? Enron's next project will in all probability be a 513

MW power plant in Kerala, exposing the hypocrisy of the Left parties. Other investments in Tamil Nadu and Karnataka are also on the anvil. Given the difficulties Indian entrepreneurs have got themselves into with profligate and unfocused expansion, it makes sense for Enron (and for the country) to invest in existing projects that are stuck for want of funds. This will add to generating capacity quickly.

One good example of this is Essar's power plant in Hazira. Indian FIs want Essar to sell its stake in that plant as a pre-condition for bailing out the financially strapped group. Given Enron's long-term plans for developing the liquified natural gas market along the western and southern coast, it would make perfect sense for Essar to bring in Enron. More such investments could follow.

07/06/1999

◆——◆

JETHMALANI'S NEW OBSESSION
A Companies Act 2000 can and should be passed soon

Ram Jethmalani, the eminent lawyer, has been a maverick minister. In his earlier incarnation, he steamrolled the repeal of the notoriously corruption- friendly Urban Land Ceiling (Regulation) Act, 1976 although only Punjab and Haryana have since followed the Centre's lead. Now as minister of company affairs, he has another opportunity of leaving his imprint if he takes on the onerous task of getting a new Companies Act passed by his colleagues in Parliament.

In November 1997, the then finance minister, who also doubled as company affairs minister, tabled a Companies Bill, 1997 to replace the Companies Act of 1956. This comprehensively new bill had taken almost 15 months to draft and involved the collective experience and expertise of a committee of outstanding lawyers, chartered accountants, company secretaries, economists and industry managers. Unfortunately, P. Chidambaram's contribution was put into cold storage since in the earlier Vajpayee government, the company affairs portfolio was held by the AIADMK. Knowing that the end of the United Front government was imminent, Chidambaram had introduced this bill in the Rajya Sabha. Hence, it has not lapsed and can still be taken up for consideration, a process that could be compressed into four months.

It was Yashwant Sinha who first saw merit in this new bill. What he did was to take four important provisions—allowing buyback of shares by a company, liberalising inter-corporate investments, establishing a national advisory committee on accounting standards and introducing employee stock options—out of the new bill and have them passed as amendments to the 1956 Companies Act earlier this year. The provision on accounting standards is significant with the globalisation of Indian business. The accounting standards to be introduced are in the format of the balance sheet and the profit and loss account as is done interna-tionally. Unfortunately, the national advisory committee is yet to see light of day. Hopefully this will happen soon.

Jethmalani now wants to follow in Sinha's footsteps and is proposing to take some further investor-friendly provisions out of the new bill and have them also passed as amendments to the existing Companies Act during the forthcoming winter session of Parliament. All power to him. Some of these amendments will help ordinary investors immensely—passing of resolutions by postal ballot, the right of minority shareholders to have representation on the board of directors, the redressal of problems faced by those having public deposits below Rs 20,000 in a company, etc. There are other equally worthwhile changes like stipulating a minimum paid up capital of Rs 1 lakh for a private company and Rs 5 lakh for a public company, abo-lishing the concept of a deemed public company, tightening the terms of appointment of auditors, the payment of interim dividend, initial offer of securities in dematerialised form, the mandatory formation of audit committees in the board of directors, stringent conditions for the disqualification to become a director, etc.

But this still does not obviate the need for the new bill to be passed. A Companies Act, 2000 should be Jethmalani's objective. The existing new bill needs new ideas, on issues like managerial remuneration and securitisation regimes to develop the debt market. Even so, it not only cleans up the 1956 Act but also contains many innovations. It permits Indian Depository Receipts (IDRs) like GDRs and ADRs to give a fillip to the capital market. It has new provisions relating to the consolidation of accounts—mandatory in other countries—which makes for a truer and fairer picture of the accounts of a company and its subsidiaries. But since the Income Tax Act does not make group accounts mandatory, the new bill does not make consolidation of accounts compulsory. This lacuna should be rectified. Then the new bill suggests very detailed and radical changes in the way the winding up of companies is managed, something that will acquire greater significance in the future. The changes suggested will make winding up and liquidation more time-bound, professional and transparent. Rotation of auditors after five years is another new idea that has been introduced. Nonvoting shares are permitted; this would help boost foreign investment in infrastructure sectors like telecom.

For lawyers, architects, doctors, chartered accountants and other professionals, the new bill allows for an association and partnership of 50, up from the present ceiling of 20, and introduces the concept of limited liability partnerships. The new bill also has a major section on transforming the existing Company Law Board into a full-fledged company law tribunal with original and appellate powers and functions. And if you thought company law was a dry and abstract subject, think again—the new bill will allow a general meeting of a company to be held on a Sunday to enable more shareholders to participate, something not possible currently. It will also ban the giving of gifts either in cash or kind to shareholders at any general meeting, a practice that has assumed menacing proportions.

06/12/1999

REGULATE TO COMPETE

A new law is needed to ensure that competition is free, fierce and fair

The US department of Justice has taken Microsoft to court arguing that the software giant had abused its market strength. Earlier in the 1980s the Justice Department had gone after the telecom monopoly AT&T and its efforts culminated in that firm's break-up in 1984. And over 90 years ago, the target had been John D. Rockefeller's Standard Oil which was split into five separate companies.

All this flexing of muscles by regulatory agencies might appear paradoxical in the land of free enterprise. But that is the fundamental tenet of a competitive, consumer-oriented economy. Transparent and knowledge-based rules are set to ensure that competition is free and fair, that market power is not abused and that at all times the freedom of choice is available to consumers. These rules, continuously evolving and founded in law, economics and technology, are rigorously enforced.

All developed countries have such laws, going way back to the Sherman Anti-Trust Act of 1890 in the US. What the world calls anti-monopoly is called anti-trust in America since at the turn of the last century "trusts" were created by corporate barons to remote control their empires.

The finance minister had promised such a law for India in his budget speech of February 1999. An expert committee under the chairmanship of S.V.S. Raghavan, the distinguished former chairman of BHEL and MMTC submitted its report on this subject to the prime minister on May 22. The draft of the actual law is to follow.

The committee has recommended a Competition Commission of India (CCI) to implement this law. The committee's report is facing flak. The first criticism is that India needs more competition and that a competition law will only act as a brake. Undoubtedly, more competition is needed and policies that inhibit it must be ruthlessly eliminated. But no serious-minded economist, industrialist or lawyer would argue that pro-competition rules and regulations are unnecessary, although corporate lobbies are already working to kill the committee's report. These lobbies must be thwarted.

A second criticism is that India already has two competition laws—the MRTP Act of 1969 and, to a lesser extent, the Consumer Protection Act of 1986. However, these reflect a vastly different economic environment and a paradigm that are anachronisms today. Many anti-competition practices—like abuse of dominance, cartels, price fixing, bid rigging and predatory pricing—are not even mentioned in the MRTP Act. And with India taking on obligations as part of the WTO accord, domestic laws must be able to deal with new anti-competition practices. Thus, a new Competition Act is necessary along with the Consumer Protection Act which is em-powered to deal with unfair trade practices. The former's domain is producers while the latter's clientele is consumers. But it will not be easy to get Parliament to repeal the MRTP Act. Changes have also to be brought about in the Companies Act, a bill for which is pending with Parliament since November 1997.

The third and most vexatious is mergers. The committee suggests that the CCI examine all mergers above a certain minimum value and give a decision within 90 days. Mergers are just beginning to take off in this country, as indeed they should. They are already subject to clearances under the Companies Act and under SEBI's takeover code. They can also be challenged in courts. Now a third agency will look at them.

True, such prior approval for mergers is required in the US and the EU too. But there the regulatory agencies are professionally competent. In any case action is initiated in just about 2-3 per cent of cases and time limits for review are strictly followed. Even so, takeovers being examined from the point of view of how they will impact competition cannot be denied, specially in the context of on-going corporate restructuring, consolidation and privatisation.

Our fundamental problem is not so much with regulations per se but with regulators. That is why the proposed CCI gives an uneasy feeling. We start new institutions with great fanfare. But because there is no culture of professionalism, lateral entry and exit and specialisation in the public services, these institutions never take off. This is the core issue and if it is not addressed frontally, the CCI, started with all good intentions, will turn out to be yet another bureaucratic behemoth. One option is to enact the law now and have it come into force by the end of next year. This would give ample time for institutional design, orientation, training and advocacy. This is what the UK did—passed a competition law in 1998 and made it effective from 2000.

05/06/2000

IV

Global Markets :
Price and Prejudice

This section deals with markets. Dematerialisation ("demat") of shares is one of the most significant achievements in recent years in which I played a small role and this has been explained. By and large, I did not write much on stock markets but whenever there was a major convulsion, either globally or in the country, I had no option but to take note. I particularly enjoyed writing *Beyond the Mumbo Jumbo* which explains in simple English the various intricacies of a highly abstract and technical issue: exchange rates. This article was taken notice of by Star Business News when it first appeared. The section also contains a number of pieces on oil markets, whose operations have a substantial impact on the health of the India's external sector.

TWO CHEERS DEMAT
NSDL is effecting a quiet revolution
in the capital market

November 8 marks the second anniversary of the National Securities Depository Limited (NSDL), an institution that is fast transforming our capital market. NSDL is actually a giant satellite-based, integrated computer network that eliminates paper in all share transactions. It was during Manmohan Singh's tenure that the idea of NSDL was born and the broad outline worked out. But it required P. Chidambaram's formidable legal and managerial skills to get Parliament to pass the Depositories Act in August 1996 and to bring sceptical companies and financial institutions on board.

NSDL itself is quite a remarkable institution, a rare success story in which even regulator SEBI has played a proactive role. Promoted by UTI, the National Stock Exchange and IDBI, it has 100 professionals with an average age of less than 30. It combines, in the words of its senior citizen, 48-year-old CEO Chandu Bhave, the best of three things Indians are good at: trading, finance and computers. The entire world-class software has been developed by TCS and the investment so far is about Rs 50 crore.

The depository is nothing but an electronic warehouse of shares. Instead of shares being held physically in the form of certificates, they are "dematerialised"—converted into electronic balances and stored in a network of computers. A depository totally eliminates the major problem of "bad deliveries". Today, every fifth person taking delivery of stock gets securities on whose genuineness there is a doubt. Further, the risk of holding reams of paper, of losing them and of having them mutilated, forged or switched is eliminated. Whenever any transaction takes place—that is when shares are bought, sold, transferred, pledged or even when addresses are changed—considerable paperwork is involved. This is something ordinary investors know only too well.

Paperwork means delays, costs and hassles. A long-term investor who, say, buys shares worth Rs 10,000 and keeps them for five years can save over Rs 100. A trader who turns over this portfolio 10 times a year could save up to Rs 500. If these shares are lost or mutilated, the cost of obtaining duplicates could exceed Rs 500. But an investor holding shares in dematerialised form will not have to incur this cost. In addition, in a depository environment there is no stamp duty for transfer of equities or of units of a mutual fund. There is immediate transfer and registration of securities. The settlement cycle is faster, which means more liquidity for the investor and quicker disbursement of corporate goodies like rights and bonuses.

In two years, 376 crore shares worth some Rs 52,000 crore have been dematerialised. This is about 10 per cent of market capitalisation, but around 40 per cent of the floating stock. Today, 264 companies have dematerialised shares. In 32 of them, dematerialisation as a proportion of market capitalisation exceeds 25 per cent. The leaders are Infosys, Wipro, HDFC, Crisil, ICICI, Reliance, BSES, Mahindra and Mahindra, Grasim, TISCO and ACC. For the top 25-30 scrips, over 70 per cent of the delivery is in de-materialised form.

Key to the interface between the retail investor and the depository is the depository participant. This could be a bank, financial institution, custodian or broker. The depository participant is one with whom you open an account and to whom you surrender your share certificates. In about 15 days, your electronic share account gets activated. There are at present 67 depository participants with whom over 90,000 individual in-vestors have opened accounts.

This may appear a minuscule pro-portion of the 22 million-odd investor population in India but it is actually around 20 per cent of the investing population that actively trades on a day-to-day basis. The participants have opened service centres or branches in 126 towns and cities, showing how widespread the investing culture has become in India.

Trading is exactly the same in a physical or electronic environment. The Indian retail investor can keep securities in paper form or have them dematerialised. To promote the depository culture, SEBI has recently an-nounced that trading for 31 leading scrips will be in elec-tronic form for all investors from February 15, 1999. Some banks have now begun offering lower interest on advances against dematerialised shares. Even so, much more needs to be done.

Telecom policy must change to permit inter-branch connectivity for the depository participants. In addition to the six already on board, the 16 other stock exchanges must be brought into the depository network. Only five of the 24 public-sector banks offer depository services. More must do so since the reach of private banks is limited. Ordinary investors should also be able to apply for public issues through the depository. Finally, very soon another depository promoted by the Bombay Stock Exchange is expected. Competition will be all to the good.

16/11/1998

IS A GLOBAL RECOVERY ON?
Thirty days that perked up the world and its markets

A week may be a long time in politics but in financial markets four weeks is eternity, the difference between life and death. In the first fortnight of October, the world was drowning in gloom. But today the mood is markedly different. Sentiments have perked up. There is cautious optimism. Six factors have contributed to this totally unexpected turnaround.

First, on October 15 the US Federal Reserve Bank caught markets by pleasant surprise when it cut the federal funds rate (FFR) by a quarter of a point to 5 per cent. This was a repeat of what it had done on September 29. The earlier event, however, had been expected. The FFR is the overnight bank lending rate and a benchmark for short-term interest rates. The Bank of England also cut its interest rates a second time by a half-point on November 5, after a first cut on October 12. Italy, Denmark, Spain, Portugal, Sweden and Poland followed suit. These cuts have sent a powerful signal to the markets that western governments will not be found wanting in a time of crisis, even though the Germans and the French are still averse to lowering their interest rates.

Such interest rate reductions increase liquidity, put more money in the hands of investors, lower borrowing costs and bolster investor confidence. As further proof of its commitment to restore market stability, the US Fed cut interest rates a third time on November 17. What was unusual about this move was that while the FFR was further reduced to 4.75 per cent, unlike previous occasions the discount rate which is charged on emergency loans to commercial banks was also lowered by a quarter of a point—to 4.5 per cent.

Next came the US Congress' vote to provide $14.5 billion in new capital to the IMF. This had been hanging fire for months. The anti-IMF mood was strong. President Bill Clinton could not help much because of the Monica Lewinsky affair. Ultimately some persistent persuasion by Robert Rubin, the US treasury secretary, won the day. The American action will enable the IMF to mobilise a further $74 billion from other countries, including a $1 billion from India, to augment its capital stock from $193 billion to $280 billion.

Then, the Brazilians voted to re-elect President Henrique Cardoso. After East Asia and Russia, Brazil was the economy poised to go over the brink. But Cardoso was seen as the symbol of fiscal rectitude and economic reforms. His re-election, the announcement of Brazil's economic revival programme in the first week of November and the IMF's approval of a $41 billion rescue package on November 13 have soothed market nerves.

There is some good news from East Asia too. The weak-ening of the dollar has eased pressure on East Asian cur-rencies. This also means lower local currency equivalents for dollar debts. Interest rates have fallen to pre-meltdown levels and are between 7 and 9 per cent. Indonesia, Malaysia, South Korea, the Philippines and Thailand had a combined current account deficit of about $40 billion in 1997. They will post a $60 billion current account surplus in 1998, although this is more a result of import compression rather than export expansion. In November 1997, South Korea's forex reserves were down to $7 billion; today they are at $45 billion. Thailand and South Korea have begun to bite the bullet on reforms, especially in the banking industry.

Another helpful factor was that between October 17 and 20, the Japanese parliament gave the go-ahead to a $500 billion package for cleaning up its banks. Then came the Miyazawa plan worth $30 billion to help East Asia. On November 16, the Japanese prime minister went one step ahead and announced a $200 billion economic stimulus package. Serious doubts persist on Japan's capacity to go through painful restructuring. But contrary to all expectations the yen has strengthened and the dollar has actually fallen by almost 10 per cent in relation to the yen since October 1. This has also removed fears of a Chinese devaluation for the present, something the markets dread.

Finally, the US mid-term election results in favour of Clinton—who has delivered low inflation, high growth and a fiscal surplus—

prevented further erosion of market confidence. Few of us really appreciate the absolute centrality of what happens in the US to world prosperity. Indeed, no country has become an economic powerhouse after 1950 without engaging the US in a sustained and deep commercial, economic and financial relationship. India is the only country that has been going against this trend. And we are paying the price.

The global crisis is far from over. World GDP will increase by no more than 2 per cent in real terms in 1998. The IMF's current projection for 1999 is 2.5 per cent. But there are influential analysts who are putting out a much lower figure of 1 per cent. While the sentiment has perked up, fundamentals are still sick. Serious question marks remain over Japan, Russia and Indonesia. But the past 30 days have certainly provided breathing time and space for countries to revive the momentum of fiscal correction and economic reforms.

30/11/1998

FIIs ON FAST FORWARD

Emerging markets are no longer submerging markets

Stock markets everywhere have their own peculiar logic and momentum. If proof were needed for this, just consider what has been happening to the Bombay Stock Exchange's Sensex, the most widely quoted index of bourse activity in this country. On April 26, the day the government fell, the Sensex stood at 3,245. As Kautilya writes on May 20, the Sensex is at 4,124, an increase of a whopping 879 points in just about three weeks. This boom is among the sharpest in recent times and is dwarfed in its magnitude only by the spurt in stock values in February-March 1992, when Harshad Mehta was running riot.

What gives the current boom special status, however, are two factors. First, it is broad-based and not confined to the usual suspects of a few Group A scrips. Second, it is fuelled almost entirely by the much-reviled foreign institutional investors (FIIs). Between April and December 1998, these FIIs took out $634 million from the country, the first time there was an outflow since our stock markets were opened to foreign investment in 1992-93.

But between January and May 1999, $683 million has been brought in, of which $225 million was in April and $355 million between May 1-19. Total cumulative investment by the FIIs now stands at $9.5 billion, about 8 per cent of market capitalisation. The bulk of this is controlled by big names like Morgan Stanley, Capital, Jardine Fleming, Fidelity and Templeton.

It is intriguing that at a time when economic growth is still in the doldrums and when there is a policy vacuum, the sentiment on India has suddenly turned positive. It is possible that the absence of a government has perversely helped because then there is no chance of springing negative surprises on the market. Could it be that the FIIs are seeing a recovery that we, caught in the trap of politics, are missing? Could it be that the FIIs are discounting political uncertainty and are betting on reforms continuing, whatever the complexion of the government later this year?

The most immediate provocation for the FIIs' return to India is simply that they have more money to invest because the US economy is continuing to perform strongly and the New York stock market is moving up dizzily. Moreover, over the past few months east Asian economies have also shown signs of recovery. The sentiment, as important as fundamentals, is positive. This is most evident in South Korea, which may post a modest 4 per cent GDP growth this year as compared to a negative 6 per cent the previous year.

East Asia is once again showing current account surpluses. Interest rates are down to precrisis levels. Forex reserve levels have increased substantially. Currencies have stabilised. Countries like Thailand, Malaysia and South Korea are also in the midst of structural reforms that are earning plaudits from foreign investors. There are very faint signs of recovery in Japan and Brazilian and Russian equities have also performed well in the first quarter of this year.

It is this rebound after the disaster of 1998, coupled with the boom in the US, that is leading FIIs to bring back investments into Asia, particularly to commodity-related stocks. India has a 7-8 per cent weight in many funds investing in Asia (minus Japan). Thus, we are experiencing a "spillover effect". It also helps that stock-market valuations of many of our companies are still modest when viewed in an Asian context. Many Indian companies are a good buy when seen for their intrinsic strengths and that is what is happening now that the country-story is on the backburner and investors are forced to focus on both the sector and company-stories. In addition, the outstanding success of our securities depository in spreading the culture of paperless transactions is expanding the investment universe. Consolidation of the depository is the key to sustaining greater FII inflows.

Most top FII managers, like Yashwant Sinha's daughter-in-law, are very bright youngsters of Indian origin. Clearly, emotion may well be part of investment decision-making. But our own attitudes remain ambivalent. There is a general impression that FII money is "hot", short-term money that will flow out of the country at the first sign of trouble. True, there is a herd instinct but broad-based FIIs of the type who are in India are medium to long-term investors. Their presence is also a guarantee that governments will follow sensible economic policies since there is always the fear that FII money will flow out. FIIs are also adding substantial value. Their regular research reports on both Indian companies and on various aspects of the economy are unmatched in data, detail and analysis. They are slowly bringing new standards of corporate gov-ernance and disclosures in the Indian corporate sector.

But it is essential that countervailing power to the FIIs through domestic institutions be also developed through, for example, UTI, LIC and other mutual funds. More importantly, retail investors must return. A recent Jardine Fleming research report suggests there is evidence that retail activity is unmistakably picking up in the equity market. This is reflected, for instance, in the rise in the number of shares traded per day, the decline in the average number of shares per trade, the increase in the activity in stocks with small capitalisation and the increase in domestic mutual-fund collections.

31/05/1999

MUMBAI'S SENSE OF RUMOUR

What really caused the August market frenzy

Mumbai has declared autonomy from Delhi or so it would seem seeing the frenzy that has gripped the stock markets these past few days with the Sensex knocking on the 5000-mark. Markets do more than reflect current performance. They also say something about the future.

A booming market means that investors are actually very optimistic about what lies ahead. What is unusual about the August boom is that foreign institutional investors (FIIs) did not trigger it. Till August 20 or thereabouts, the FIIs were actually net sellers to the tune of about $65 million. This came after they had pumped in over a billion dollars during April-July and had helped the Sensex go up from around 3600-3700 in the first week of April to 4600-4700 in the last week of July.

The FII behaviour in these four months was caused by many factors. They had more money to invest because of the continued growth of the US economy. They were coming back to Asia seeing a recovery in countries like South Korea and Thailand, and India benefited from this. Valuations of Indian stocks were very attractive specially when seen in a regional context. And, of course, the first quarter of 1999-2000 showed definite signs of industrial recovery in India. But in the first three weeks, the FIIs were probably trying to make some money on their investments by selling more than they were buying. It was only in the last week of August after the bull run was well on its way that the FIIs turned net buyers to the tune of about $40 million.

That the August bull run was fuelled by furious speculative buying by a few brokers was reflected, for instance, in the very high carry-forward rates. Another indicator is the net long positions of brokers on the BSE—the excess of purchases over sales—which at the end of August amounted to about Rs 2,400 crore, as compared to the earlier peak of around Rs 1,500 crore over six months ago. Theories abound centring on a broker called Ketan Parekh and his connection with a particular mutual fund and with influential personalities in the ruling establishment. These may or may not be true. But certainly markets have been buoyed by opinion polls that do not indicate a hung Parliament and, Kautilya must admit, by the prospects of Atal Bihari Vajpayee's return.

Speculation apart, the retail investor is finally back. There has, for example, been a significant rise in the number of shares delivered during a trading week in the NSE. The success of the depository and of dematerialisation of shares is expanding investment opportunities. During March-July 1999, net flows into mutual funds amounted to over Rs 3,500 crore, nearly five times the accretion in the previous six months. Incremental time deposits with banks during April-June 1999 are about Rs 12,000 crore lower than during April-June 1998 showing that migration from fixed deposits to mutuals may have finally started.

The August frenzy is not an exact Harshad Mehta replay. There is, as HSBC Securities points out, a solid earnings story, a robust restructuring story and an imminent liquidity story. But three concerns remain. First, the demand for good scrips vastly outstrips supply. Supply is limited partly because the floating shares that enter markets are no more than a third of all shares by global standards. And we are reducing it even further—the cutoff level for creeping acquisitions from the market, below which the takeover code would not be triggered, has been upped from 2 per cent to 5 per cent per year. One way of increasing floating stock would be for public financial institutions to disinvest their equity in private firms that they have come to hold for historical reasons. Incidentally, the FTSE-100, the UK's market index, has just decided to weigh the market capitalisation of companies according to their free float.

Second, the movement to bring in mandatory rolling settlement has to be expedited. The international practice is what is called T+3 which means that settlement (payments made or received) is made three days after the trade day. In India this period on an average stretches up to 11 days. For some time, we have been talking about moving to a T+5 system as a starter. This would reduce risks as well as increase liquidity. Ajay Shah, India's brightest financial economist, points out that rolling settlements would make highly leveraged trading an intraday affair and yield share prices more in line with fundamentals.

Third, corporate governance in the BSE, particularly its risk management and market safety practices, has to improve vastly. Although the Securities & Exchange Board of India (SEBI) is constantly criticised for being soft on the BSE by the cognoscenti, like stock-market journalist Sucheta Dalal, the market watchdog has been trying to do its bit. A few days ago it banned negotiated and cross deals, a source of great abuse. Margin rules are being enforced, though it is perplexing that what the G.S. Patel Committee had recommended as a condition for introducing the revised badla system in 1995—25per cent of profits arising out of a carry forward position should be impounded till the outstanding position is squared off—hasn't been put into practice. Action against errant brokers also needs to be prompter and tougher. SEBI's professional expertise needs substantial upgradation too.

28/07/1997

CONTAGION TIME AGAIN?

Two countries—Turkey and Argentina—face a crisis and receive emergency aid

While the world's attention is focused on the deceleration of the US economy after an unprecedented nine and a half year expansion and its impact on global trade, exchange rates and capital flows, two other countries are in financial crisis. They have received huge bailouts coordinated by the IMF. The first to receive an emergency loan was Turkey in the third week of December. The loan amounted to $7.5 billion and came after interest rates had zoomed to over 1,000 per cent, foreign-exchange reserves were depleted by almost a fourth and the stock markets tumbled to about half the value at the beginning of 2000. The immediate provocation for the turbulence in the financial markets was a crisis of confidence in the banking system. The eruption first took place in Turkey's ninth largest private bank and soon snowballed, leading to a wider liquidity crunch as foreign investors started liquidating their assets and cut lending. What aggravated the situation was a criminal investigation into the affairs of some private banks taken over by the government for cleanup before privatisation. As corruption got uncovered, ironically as part of a process of bringing about greater transparency, investors were unnerved by what more lay hidden in the banks.

At about the same time that Turkey was going through its travails since the last week of November, Argentina also hit skid row but with a far greater intensity. Argentina has been facing numerous political problems arising out of an uneasy coalition in power at Buenos Aires and from prickly relationships between this federal coalition and the provincial governments. While 1999 was a year of deep recession, 2000 has been no better with GDP growth expected at less than 0.5 per cent but a positive growth rate nonetheless. It was the fear of default on its foreign debt in the face of continued lack of growth and political wranglings that undermined investor confidence in Argentina since October 2000. Two weeks ago, after protracted negotiations with creditors and bankers, the Argentine Government unveiled a massive $39.7 billion aid plan. Of this, the IMF's share is $13.7 billion, the World Bank and the InterAmerican Development Bank will give $2.5 billion each and private banks about $20 billion. In-terestingly as a further demonstration of its growing economic clout, Spain has chipped in with $1 billion.This package will help see Argentina through 2001. The country is being keenly watched as it accounts for about a quarter of tradable emerging market debt. Turkey invites attention since it is seeking to join the European Union.

Actually, Argentina is of interest for another reason. Since April 1991, it has adopted what economists call a "currency board" system for managing its exchange rate. Under this, the Argentine currency is fixed at a rate of one peso to the US dollar, full convertibility is established between the two currencies and the central bank is required to maintain foreign-exchange reserves totalling 100 per cent of the domestic money supply. What this means is that you cannot increase domestic money supply unless you can increase the size of your dollar holdings. In effect, what a currency board does is to shift the burden of monetary policy and to some extent fiscal policy as well to the external sector of the economy.

This currency-board arrangement is usually used by small trade-dependent economies like Hong Kong. But it is also seen as the last resort for a country facing hyper-inflation needing to signal a credible commitment to sound macroeconomics. In-flation in Argentina in 1985 was 672 per cent and as if this was not enough, it zoomed to an astronomical 3,080 per cent in 1989. In contrast, inflation in 1998 was 0.7 per cent and a negative 1.4 per cent in 1999. Thus, the currency board has helped Argentina lick its endemic hyper-inflation disease.

But there have been costs: the peso's steady appreciation, which has made imports cheaper and exports non-competitive, and growing unemployment, currently higher than 12 per cent. In addition, total external debt of Argentina has sky-rocketed from $66 billion in 1991 to about $145 billion now, showing how dependent growth has become on external bor-rowings—something that we ourselves experienced in the middle and late 1980s. Argentina may now be looking forward to America's slowing down since that could result in lower international interest rates and a weaker dollar.

Financial markets impose a punishment that is wholly disproportionate to the crimes that governments commit. Turkey and Argentina are more aggressive reformers than India. Yet they have had to bite the dust, for the time being at least. Our problem, however, arises not so much from a vulnerable external or banking sector as it does from an increasingly sluggish rate of growth in the "real" economy It is true that you fall harder when you run faster. But a homoeopathic pace of reforms also takes a heavy toll.

15/01/2001

◆━━◆━━◆

GOLDILOCKS LOSES SHEEN
After an unprecedented 114-month economic expansion, America will slow down

Since the mid-1990s, the US economy came ·to be called the Goldilocks economy. Macro-economics appeared perfect: just the right temperature of the porridge (economic growth), just the right size of the chair (low inflation) and just the right size of the bed (declining unemployment). Now, however, Goldilocks may well be losing her shine.

The US economy's performance since 1992 has been unprecedented. A nine-and-a-half year economic expansion took place. Following the "stagflation"(growth stagnation and galloping inflation) that marked the 1970s, the 1980s were a growth period for books and articles that predicted America's decline. The 1991-92 recession seemed to confirm that impression. But then in a truly spectacular turn-around, the US economy rewrote all macroeconomic theories. Not only did it have a boom period longer than usual under a normal business cycle, it demolished the inflation-unemployment trade-off.

Economists call this trade-off the non-accelerating inflation rate of unemployment (NAIRU). Before the golden 1990s, America's NAIRU was estimated at around 6 per cent. But in the past decade, this has fallen to probably 4-4.5 per cent, meaning thereby that you can have a low level of unemployment with a low level of inflation. This stunning macroeconomic record is, according to the ̃guru—Alan Greenspan, chairman of the US Federal Reserve Bank—himself, the outcome of the "new" economy. Other economists like Robert Gordon take a more sceptical view of the productivity spurt of the mid-1990s. The Fed also estimates that the "wealth effect" created by escalating stock prices has added around a percentage point to GDP growth over the past four-five years with one in two American households now hooked on to the stock market in one form or the other.

2001 will certainly see a deceleration of growth in America. There is a view that while the "new" economy made the upswing possible, it will also affect the nature of the downturn—the decline could deepen and recovery speeded. Fears of an actual recession which is defined as two consecutive quarters of negative GDP growth are perhaps exaggerated. A more realistic assessment is that the US economy may have a relatively "soft" landing this year and end up with 2-2.5 per cent GDP growth as compared to 5 per cent registered in 2000 and 4.5 per cent averaged in the past four years.

With Europe showing modest growth and Japan totally in the doldrums, America has become the loco-motive of world growth—estimates are that one-third to one-half of the world GDP growth is contributed by the US alone. America's global influence is transmitted through five main channels—trade, commodity prices, exchange rates, interest rates and capital flows.

A slowing down of such a magnitude will impact on Canada and Mexico the most. Some East Asian countries which depend on electronics exports to America will also be seriously affected, although China may not suffer as much as say, Malaysia or South Korea, since its export basket is more low-tech. India is unlikely to be affected. Oil prices are expected to remain at moderate levels, barring a flare-up in the Middle East which can never be ruled out. Oil prices hovering in the range of $22-25 a barrel will clearly benefit us al-though depressed prices of other commodities could be to our disadvantage.

The dollar will most likely weaken against the euro enabling a euro-dollar parity. This will help our exports to Europe. China whose currency is fixed to the dollar will also gain, thus making its exports even more competitive. International interest rates will, in all probability, decline. This will mean lower borrowing costs for Indian companies abroad and it will also put downward pressure on domestic interest rates—something that is urgently required to kickstart a new wave of investment.

If American stockmarkets are tepid and bond yields stay low, then we can expect greater inflows of portfolio investment. But at a time of allround negative sentiment, there might well be a "flight to safety" which means funds flowing back to the US. There is also the matter of correlation with the Nasdaq. Among all emerging markets, India has the fifth highest degree of correlation after Mexico, Brazil,

Poland and Hungary. The extent of correlation, as reported recently in The Economist, is close to 0.75 with 1 being the perfect value.

All in all, 2001 may see a world economy growth of 2-3 per cent. How India fares will, however, be dependent entirely on what it does at home. Some analysts are predicting a higher growth for us this year. That is eminently within our grasp but if and only if privatisation transactions take place, interest rates are cut and reforms by implementation—not reforms by announcements—are stepped up.

22/01/2001

◆━━━◆

MAD DOW DISEASE

An economist ignored when markets were booming
is now being rediscovered

Generally speaking, economists and financial markets do not mix well, Charles Kindleberger's 1978 all-time classic Mania, Panics and Crashes being the outstanding exception. Irving Fisher is considered to have been America's greatest economist in the first third of the 20th century and is immortal for his research on inflation. But John Kenneth Galbraith writes in his *The Great Crash*, 1929 that in the autumn of 1929 just before the onset of the Great Depression, Fisher gained enduring fame for his widely reported conclusion that "stock prices have reached what looks like a permanently high plateau". In contemporary times, we have had the example of two Nobel laureates in economics, Robert Merton and Myron Scholes, who were closely associated with the hedge fund Long Term Capital Management that rocked markets by going bust in September 1998, inviting a huge $4billion bail-out operation masterminded by the US Federal Reserve Bank. In India too, barring perhaps Ajay Shah, economists have neither worked on nor helped in understanding financial markets. That Shah has done so could be due more to his ethnic background.

Thus, when Robert Shiller's book, *Irrational Exuberance* first appeared last year, it was greeted with acclaim as a fine piece of scholarship but as a poor guide to what was happening or would happenin the real world. These were months when the Dow had crossed five digits, the Nasdaq was in the 5000-6000 range and the "new economy" mania was at its peak. When the stock markets were booming, here was a Yale University professor, no doubt brilliant as a theorist, indulging in blasphemy and heresy by suggesting, on the basis of solid empirical and unusually innovative historical, psychological, cultural and sociological analysis that the US market was overvalued by historical standards and that poor performance was inevitable sooner rather than later. Now that the Nasdaq has fallen to the 2000 zone, Shiller is being rediscovered. His hardcover book has been issued as a paperback edition—the ultimate "market" accolade for an academic economist.

The title of Shiller's work is taken from the most famous quote of Alan Greenspan, chairman of the US Fed, who in the course of a speech delivered on December 5, 1996 to a Washington think tank mused, "But how do we know when irrational exuberance has unduly escalated asset values, which then become subject to unexpected and prolonged contractions as they have in Japan over the past decade." Ironically, Shiller writes that just two days before Greenspan posed the question publicly, he had himself testified before the Fed chairman and his colleagues that market levels were irrational. When Greenspan spoke thus the Dow was hovering around 6000. By March 1999, it had zoomed to 10,000.

Shiller's main thesis is that the stock market boom of the 1990s in the US displayed all the standard features of a speculative bubble, which he terms as a "situation in which temporarily high prices are sustained largely by investors' enthusiasm rather than by consistent estimation of real value". Twelve factors are identified as having contributed to the self-fulfilling prophecy of a roaring bull market in the US. These are the arrival of the Internet, triumphalism and the decline of foreign economicrivals, born-again materialism, a Republican Congress and capital-gains tax cuts, the baby boom, a proliferation in media reporting of business news, increasingly optimistic analysts' forecasts, the expansion of defined contribution pension plans, the growth of mutual funds, the decline of inflation and the effects of money illusion, expansion of trade volumes and a rise in gambling opportunities.

There is more to stock prices than present or future earnings or dividends calling into serious question one of the tenets of modern eco-nomics— the efficient markets theory. Shiller concludes that the market was high because of the combined effect of indifferent thinking of mil-lions of investors motivated largely by their ownemotions, random attentions and perceptions of conventional wisdom and influenced heavily by the news media and market analysts enjoying a nexus with investment banks or brokerage firms. An example of such wrong thinking is the belief that stocks must always outperform other investments such as bonds over the long run. Picking mutual funds that have done well also has much smaller benefits.

Shiller argues that the eventual bursting of speculative bubbles may, on balance, be a good thing. In this light, he sees the East Asian financial crisis of 1997-98 as a sanity check. The Nasdaq's precipitous fall is a return to reality. Shiller recognises that societies cannot be protected from the effects of waves of irrational exuberance or irrational pessimism. While guarding against the latter, the challenge is to put in place policies and institutions to minimise the probability of recurrence of the former.

30/04/2001

━━◆━━◆━━

PRICE AND PREJUDICE
Exchange rate is ultimately a matter of price—not pride

Recently, the rupee was very much in the news until it was overtaken by political events. Reports of differences over the "appropriate" value of the rupee between the Finance Ministry and the Reserve Bank of India (RBI) had surfaced in the media. The finance secretary was supposed to be in favour of a weaker rupee to boost exports, while the RBI saw no need for any adjustment.

Actually, the newspapers were unfair to the finance secretary. The sequence of events was roughly like this. Kautilya, while making a presentation on the industrial slowdown to the Confederation of Indian Industry, pointed out that India's great export boom of the mid-'90s was triggered in very large measure by the two devaluations of July 1991. He also pointed out that while our current round of export stagnation predates the collapse of the world economy in 1997-98, one of the factors that may have hampered the growth in our exports after 1996 is the 6 per cent appreciation of the rupee vis-à-vis the dollar between 1995-96 and 1997-98. To be fair, he added that in 1998-99 there has been a downward movement but this has had no appreciable impact on export performance.

It is in response to this that the finance secretary said constant watch must be kept on our exchange rate so that exports do not suffer. It was an unexceptionable statement from the nation's top economic administrator. Coming on top of a statement in this year's Economic Survey that the rupee is overvalued, the newspapers flashed the news that the finance secretary is in favour of a depreciation.

Figuring whether a currency is at its "correct" level is a tricky and complicated business. It is such an arcane topic that The Economist uses what it calls the Big Mac Index to enlighten its readers on the appropriateness of a country's exchange rate. It is based on purchasing power parity (PPP)—the notion that an identical basket of goods and services should cost the same in all countries. The Big Mac PPP is the exchange rate that would leave hamburgers costing the same in the US as abroad.

Since the beeffilled Big Mac is not sold here, India is not included in this "burgernomics" exercise. A strictly-vegetarian Kautilya did some market research and found that the nearest to a Big Mac is the Maharaja Mac the selling price of which suggests that the rupee is undervalued against the dollar by a whopping 48 per cent, perhaps more a reflection of McDonald's marketing strategy and the structure of India's fast-food industry than of macroeconomic fundamentals.

More seriously, staid central banks use a concept called "real effective exchange rate" (REER). The rupee's REER in relation to the dollar is the nominal exchange rate multiplied by the ratio of the Indian inflation rate to foreign inflation rates. It is REER that is relevant when assessing a country's international competitiveness. Every month, the RBI puts out two estimates, REER-5 and REER-36. REER-5 tracks the real effective exchange rate of the rupee in relation to a basket of the dollar, mark, pound, yen and franc. REER-36 tracks it in relation to a basket of 36 currencies, including those of India's main competitors.

According to REER-5, with 1993-94 as the reference point the rupee is actually undervalued by about 2.4 per cent now. REER-36 uses 1985 as a base, which needs to be changed given what has happened to East Asian currencies in the past two years.

The choice of the inflation measure is important. Indian wholesale and foreign consumer prices are used by the RBI. What appears an undervaluation using our wholesale prices becomes an overvaluation of 10 per cent using the consumer price index. The choice of the base year is equally im-portant; 1993-94 is the normal choice since that is the year India switched over completely to a market-determined exchange rate. A little-acknowledged success story in recent years has been the smoothness of this transition, which took place with no flight of capital or no great volatility. It was the duo of Manmohan Singh and C. Rangarajan that was primarily responsible for this achievement. Rangarajan's view has always been that the containment of domestic price increases has the same beneficial effect as a depreciation of the nominal exchange rate. It is this view that informed exchange rate policy between 1995 and 1997 and has come under criticism.

While there is no analytical formula and there is always balance to be struck between promoting exports and controlling inflation, the generally accepted principle of exchange rate management is the nominal exchange rate should "depreciate" by about the inflation differential. This means that we should not panic if the rupee adjusts by about 5 per cent or about Rs 2 every year in relation to the dollar.

But in this country, even a 20 paise change is considered a wild fluctuation. If foreign investment inflows into the country this year remain at the previous year's level of around $2.4 billion—or if they fall, as might well happen— and if economic activity picks up then there will be a pressure on the rupee and we might see an automatic downward adjustment. That might just kickstart exports.

10/05/1999

BEYOND THE MUMBO-JUMBO
A simple demand-supply framework for making sense
of the rupee's movements

The rupee is back in the news. On April 1, that is at the beginning of the financial year 2000-2001, its value stood at Rs 43.6 to the US dollar. By August 2, the value had weakened to Rs 45.3 to the dollar. It is true that in relation to the euro and the pound, the rupee has actually gained but what matters most is its dollar value.

How does the lay person cut through the esoteric complexity of foreign-exchange markets? Very simply, a falling rupee means that dollars are in short supply and in great demand. A rising rupee means the reverse—an oversupply of dollars and lukewarm demand. In turn, a rupee is said to fall or weaken or depreciate when more rupees are needed to buy a dollar. It is said to rise or strengthen or appreciate when less rupees are needed to buy a dollar. Most exporters want a weak rupee but a weak rupee also means costly imports. That is why when the rupee weakens, the RBI tries to control the supply of the rupee (i.e. its liquidity) by raising its price as reflected in interest rates and by asking banks to keep money with it to decrease rupee supply (by hiking the cash reserve ratio).

If there is a sudden choking in the supply of dollars, the rupee weakens. When this happens, the RBI steps in and sells dollars from its foreign-exchange reserves. This increases the supply of dollars in the market. Conversely, when dollars are pouring in as they did most recently in 1996-97 and 1997-98, the RBI purchases dollars through a variety of means. In 1996-97, for instance, RBI's net purchases of US dollars amounted to $7.8 billion (Rs 35,100 crore). On the other hand, since April 1 the RBI has spent over $1 billion trying to shore up the rupee against the dollar.

Dollars come in through a variety of means—through, for instance, foreign institutional investors (FIIs) into the stock markets, foreign direct investment (FDI) into greenfield projects or acquisitions, repatriation of export earnings, deposits by non-resident Indians, assistance from aid institutions and borrowings by companies.

FIIs, which move in herds, have invested over $11 billion in Indian stock markets in the past seven years. But there are periods when they sell more than they buy. This was what happened in the past two months when net FII sales were around $485 million. Rising interest rates in the US have made dollar investments relatively more attractive. Also, Morgan Stanley, one of the biggest FIIs, increased the weightage for its investments in South Korea and Taiwan. This has led to a corresponding fall in India's weight.

Exporters are allowed up to 180 days to bring back their earnings. What happens is that exporters, anticipating a depreciation, keep their money out till the very last minute causing pressure on the supply. That is why periodically the RBI urges them to bring back their earnings as soon as it is realised. Companies also borrow abroad but keep the money outside for long periods. This also has led to exhortations by the government.

The demand for dollars arises from import needs, debt payments and outward remittances. Oil prices play a crucial role. During April-June 2000, our oil bill was $3.9 billion compared to $2 billion in the same quarter last year. In addition, there is a new factor adding to demand—the Reliance megarefinery at Jamnagar and the Mangalore refinery of the Aditya Birla group. From time to time the RBI funds public-sector crude imports directly to relieve the pressure on the market. There are some noted economists like Surjit Bhalla who believe that if the RBI actually allows supply and demand to operate, the rupee's volatility will be lower. This is a point of view. But what is incontrovertible is that the forex market being very "thin" (a daily turnover of around $3 billion) the effect of any supply-demand imbalance gets magnified. The growing integration of this forex market with the money market and the government securities market has meant closer linkages between monetary policy and exchange rate policies.

There is really no "right" value for the rupee. The RBI uses a five-country real effective exchange rate (REER-5) to judge competitiveness. REER is the nominal exchange rate adjusted for inflation differentials. REER-5 is a basket of the dollar, mark, pound, yen and franc. Although the REER-5 with 1993-94 as base is reported by the RBI regularly, its utility is limited in the face of capital mobility. Even so, the latest data show the rupee being "undervalued" by 0.8 per cent as of June 23. Since then, the magnitude of undervaluation has increased and is now over 4 per cent. It is interesting to recall here that in the regime of fixed exchange rates that prevailed till the early 1970s, a plus/minus variation of 1 per cent (that is, around 45 paise) was considered "normal" and did not require us to go to the IMF.

14/08/2000

◆———◆

OIL'S WELL IN INDIA
But low prices should not kill aggressive exploration

In a world mindful of momentous anniversaries, a global silver jubilee has just passed by without even a whimper. It was in October-

November 1973 that the Organisation of Petroleum Exporting Countries (OPEC) first jacked up oil prices with a bang and caused convulsions in the world economy. Since then, the world has experienced oil price shocks in 1979, when the Iranian revolution struck and in 1990-91, when the Kuwait crisis took place.

But what a strange sight stares at us today. In constant 1998 dollars, the price of oil has dropped to a 25-year low of $10 a barrel. The slow growth of the world economy in 1997 and 1998 has contributed to this unusual situation. But a powerful combination of technological factors and market forces have eroded the oil cartel's influence.

When OPEC first hit the headlines, the doomsday pundits went to town. But they were proved wrong for four reasons. First, the world is using oil more efficiently in industry and in transportation. Second, new sources of oil have sprung up—most notably in Mexico, the North Sea, the Caspian Sea and offshore West Africa. OPEC countries are sitting on 75 per cent of the world's oil and gas reserves but account for just 40 per cent of global production. Third, improvements in technology are enhancing the extraction of oil from existing reservoirs. Daniel Yergin, a noted Boston-based oil expert, says information technology (IT) has allowed companies to search for oil and make a profit at $15 a barrel, which is about half the earlier threshold. As an example, Yergin points to the adaptation of the computer visualisation techniques that Hollywood used in movies like Jurassic Park for three-dimensional seismic visualisation of potential reserves deep underground. Fourth, natural gas has emerged as a major alternative to oil. This has been particularly so in power generation.

India's degree of self-sufficiency in oil and oil products has fallen from 70 per cent to 40 per cent over 15 years. We import half our kerosene and about a fifth of our diesel needs. But the soft oil prices have cushioned the impact of these large imports on our balance of payments. Now, just one-fifth of our total imports are of crude oil and petroleum products.

Our current refining capacity is about 60 million tonnes. In the next five years alone we will add a huge 69 million tonnes of capacity. The Reliance Group is constructing the world's largest oil refinery in Jamnagar. This quantum leap in refining capacity will call for matching investments in ports and pipeline networks, something that is not happening fast enough. For example, the crude handling capacity of one port alone, Vadinar in Gujarat, has to quadruple by 2002.

Our real weak point is not oil refining but oil exploration. Oil planners use a concept called the reserve replacement ratio (RRR). At a minimum, the RRR should be equal to one. That is, for every tonne of reserve depleted another tonne is added to the reserves discovered. But now it has fallen to below one. This equation implies reserves are being depleted faster than they are being discovered.

We are horribly under-explored. India's prognosticated geological reserves of oil and gas are around 26 billion tonnes, of which just 25 per cent has been actually established. We have yet to wake up to the fact that natural gas, not oil, appears to be our predominant hydrocarbon resource. This is surprising since processes to convert natural gas to diesel, our main need, are now available commercially.

Around one-fifth of our reserves are in the troubled North-east. The development of these reserves will depend critically on our ability to deal with—in a more sensitive manner than we have demonstrated so far—political and social problems that beset the states in this region.

Technology is the key. Elsewhere, 40 per cent of the oil reserves are being extracted. But in India the figure is just around 28 per cent. Also, horizontal drilling methods are increasingly being used; these are specially relevant for the type of small and medium structures that we are now discovering.

India has yet to tap rich reserves in what geologists call the mesozoic strata. This means going to depths beyond 5,000 m onshore and over 400 m water depth in deep sea off-shore. In contrast the depth of water at Bombay High, our most prolific oilfield, is only 40-50 m.

India competes for exploration investments with countries like China, Vietnam and Kazakhstan. We are less richly endowed than these countries. We also keep the best areas for the public sector. Hence the lukewarm response to our offers. Of over 100 blocks put up for offer only 22 contracts have actually been signed so far. Our time-consuming procedures have not helped either.

Decision-making is further hampered by the fear of public interest litigation, audit reports and parliamen-tary questions. The radically new and bold oil exploration policy announced in P. Chidambaram's February

1997 budget is still waiting to be operationalised. The man behind this policy, the then petroleum secretary, is now the finance secretary. Will he seize the initiative? Or will he prove the adage that in the government where you stand depends on where you sit?

21/12/1998

◆———◆

WHY OPEC HAS RISEN AGAIN
The 1980s and 1990s began with an oil bang.
This decade too is very similar.

The 11- Nation Organisation Petroleum Exporting Countries (OPEC) whose exports account for 60 per cent of oil that is internationally traded is dramatically back in the headlines. In the past few days, crude prices have touched $38 a barrel, a level not seen since the Gulf War a decade ago. What a change from just 24 months ago when in the wake of the East Asian financial catastrophe, oil prices had plummeted to $10 a barrel. True, when adjusted for inflation, crude prices are now about a third of what they were 10 years ago. But nominal prices, that is actual prices, have more than trebled to record levels in less than two years time.

It was only six months ago in March that OPEC announced it would maintain a price band. If crude prices fell below $22 a barrel, OPEC would cut oil supplies. If crude prices went up beyond $28 a barrel, it would bring more oil into the market. The price band was widely welcomed as an instrument to impart stability to a volatile market and to balance the needs of producers and interests of consumers.

But very soon the price band broke down. A series of factos contributed to heightened panic and speculation in oil markets. Robust growth in the world economy—4.7 per cent in 2000—has boosted demand for oil substantially. On the eve of winter, always a vulnerable moment, stocks of heating oil in the US were seen to have touched an all-time low. The markets also perceived spare refining capacity for conversion of crude oil into consumer products like petrol, diesel and kerosene to be scarce. To make matters worse, Iraq once again began coveting the oilfields of Kuwait.

OPEC itself was badly split with Saudi Arabia advocating caution but being outflanked by the rest under the aggressive leadership of the Americaphobic Hugo Chavez, president of a bankrupt Venezuela. Incidentally, Chavez came to power in February 1999. It is from this date that oil prices started their upward climb. Venezuela is known for producing Miss Worlds with unfailing regularity but now it threatens to occupy centrestage for another reason. It is special since it is the second largest supplier of crude and oil products to the US, just marginally behind Canada.

To be sure, when crude prices zoomed, the cartel met in the first week of September and announced that it would enhance production quotas by about 0.8 million barrels a day or about 3 per cent of normal OPEC supply. The world expected oil prices to fall. But for three reasons this did not happen. First, the quota increase was not immediate but was made effective October 1. Second, the quota increase was to be for just two months instead of the usual six months. Third, the market perception was that the quota increase would not bring in additional supplies but would only legalise what was going on illegally—namely, cheating on quotas by some OPEC members. Also, markets could not but be aware that oil storage and tanker shipping capacity are not sufficient to handle quick additions to oil supplies.

OPEC was not bothered about this because it escaped public condemnation. In Europe, for example, where massive protests took place through much of September, the target was not OPEC itself but European governments whose taxes account for between two-third and three-fourth of fuel prices. What the protesters overlooked is that high taxes had given them protection against wild price swings, a protection not available to US consumers since taxes constitute less than one-fourth of petrol prices there. And ultimately, it is the petrol market that drives crude prices.

What finally cooled price pressures was the decision of President Bill Clinton a few days back to release about 30 million barrels from the US' strategic petroleum reserve of 571 million barrels. Thank god that this was an election year in the US! The effect was immediate and for the time being the increase in oil prices has been halted. The key to further moderation in prices lies, as always, with Saudi Arabia which is the only producer that has surplus production capacity and can bring large quantities of oil into the market at short notice.

The recent price surge means that India will have to pay an extra $4-5 billion for oil imports in 2000-01. In the next few weeks, therefore, the supply of dollars into the country has to be stepped up to keep the rupee from depreciating further and to prevent the hardening of interest rates. The quickest way to do so is to go back to overseas Indians with Resurgent India Bonds-II. This has already been announced by the State Bank of India. But servicing these bonds will be costly. If increased software exports could absorb half of the extra oil import bill, then it might be worthwhile to use $2-3 billion of our foreign exchange reserves to meet the oil import bill.

09/10/2000

◆——◆

GOOD NEWS FROM OPEC
The fourth oil shock of 1999-2000 is radically different from the previous three

Finally, what the Americans had been insisting upon and what countris like India had been hoping in relation to oil prices has happened. The 11-member Organisation of Petroleum Exporting Countries (OPEC) comprising Saudi Arabia, Kuwait, Iraq, Iran, Qatar, UAE, Libya, Algeria, Nigeria, Venezuela and Indonesia has increased its oil production by 1.45 million barrels a day to stabilise crude oil prices. OPEC has decided that if crude oil prices fall below $22 a barrel, it will cut back production and if prices cross $28 a barrel, it will increase supply. Thus, oil prices are expected to settle, for the time being at least, at around $25 a barrel.

OPEC's epitaph has been written all too frequently on the grounds that it controls just 40 per cent of global oil production. But it has shown that it still counts. What is often forgotten is that apart from controlling over three-fourths of the proven reserves that can be exploited easily and cheaply, OPEC's oil exports represent 60 per cent of the oil that is traded internationally. It is this that gives OPEC clout.

Between 1973 and 1990, the world experienced three major oil price shocks. First, oil prices quadrupled in October 1973 in the wake of the Yom Kippur war in the Middle East. Things settled down thereafter and oil prices were on a downward path when the Iranian Revolution in December 1979 triggered a trebling of oil prices. Again, after this sudden spurt, oil prices started declining through the 1980s till August 1990 when Iraq invaded Kuwait and invited American intervention, trebling oil prices once again. Repeating history, once passions subsided, oil prices started falling, and by March 1999 had reached almost pre-October 1973 levels at around $10 a barrel, after adjusting for inflation. The East Asian collapse of 1997-98 sent oil prices southwards. It was then that OPEC cut back production and by January 2000, oil prices had touched $30 a barrel. Incidentally, some economists are now arguing while dear oil caused stagflation in the 1970s and low growth in the early 1980s, cheap oil through the 1990s has provided a fillip to the growth of the "new" economy.

The recent fourth episode, however, is fundamentally different from the previous three. It has taken place when the fires of inflation have been doused and inflation rates are at unprecedentedly low levels. Oil prices trebled relatively smoothly in 1999 unlike what happened in 1973, 1979 and 1990 when there was a sudden one-shot increase. The years 1973, 1979 and 1990 were also associated with wars and political convulsions adding uncertainty and nervousness to oil markets.

In India, 1973 and 1979 also saw severe droughts and 1990 witnessed political turmoil and fiscal breakdown. But 1999-2000 has been politically benign and economically salubrious. In addition, major oil-using countries of the West have become more energy-efficient and some estimates are that in the industrialised world, 50 per cent less oil is needed to produce $1 of output than was the case in the 1970s. Crude oil prices also have a less visible impact on consumers—for example, in all developed countries except the US, taxes constitute 70-75 per cent of petrol prices. Petrol prices in the US are very low. But as long as they are so low and America imports 46 percent of her oil needs, countries like India also benefit because whenever OPEC tries to flex its muscles, America intervenes.

There was a time when OPEC was applauded in this country as a Third World organisation taking on the mighty West. That mindset worked fine in the 1970s when rich countries accounted for over 75 per cent of world oil consumption. But today, developing coun-tries themselves account for almost 45 per cent of worldoil consumption and will be the hardest hit by OPEC's actions. The West will get by since with increased revenues OPEC countries will either put their money into western banks or spend more on imports from it.

OPEC governments like Nigeria, Venezuela, Algeria, Iran and Indonesia have been under severe economic stress. Iraq, another OPEC member, has not been subject to its discipline of late. If and when Iraq decides to rejoin the international community, there might well be downward pressure on oil prices. The key really lies with Saudi Arabia which has the unenviable task of balancing the interests of consumers and producers of the black gold.

The 1991 reforms were triggered by the third oil shock. The resilience with which the Indian economy has absorbed the fourth oil shock is a tribute to these reforms which are under siege these days. Alas, if these outward-oriented adjustment policies had been adopted in the wake of the first two oil shocks, India might well have been a China today.

24/04/2000

V

In Praise of Federalism :
The State of the States

One of the great paradoxes that emerge in comparative studies of India and China has been that states in democratic India have been less powerful than the provinces in communist China. This is a reflection of our Constitution, and in many respects, the deeply unitary premises of the influential 1935 Government of India Act. While the mindset of our founding fathers was also in favour of a dominant Centre, this initial fear of "Balkanisation" has only recently begun to be put to rest. Indeed, one of the most important developments of the 1990s has been the increase in the role of states in the economy. States have also got more powers as a consequence of economic liberalisation, especially as they demanded – and gained – more financial autonomy. This section deals with state-level and regional issues: why the east is different and why the south is more advanced than the north. I would have liked to cover all states and one of my regrets is that I have not done justice to the north-east particularly.

V

In Praise of Federalism :
The State of the States

SMALL-TOWN REVOLUTION
With a little help, India's boom cities can reshape its economy and society

Tirppur is a city in Tamil Nadu with a population of a little over three lakh. Every year, it generates Rs 3,000 crore by exporting cotton and woollen knitwear products. Moradabad, Uttar Pradesh, has a population of about four lakh. It exports handicraft products worth over Rs 1,200 crore annually.

Haryana's Panipat has a population of just two lakh. It is famous in history for three crucial battles. Now it has emerged as a major centre for the durrie and carpet industry, with an export turnover of close to Rs 450 crore per year. Bhiwandi, Maharashtra, has less than four lakh residents. Even so, it houses about 25 per cent of India's powerlooms.

Tiruppur, Moradabad, Panipat and Bhiwandi are a tribute to local enterprise. There are many other export powerhouses. Agra for leather. Surat for zari, diamonds and powerlooms. Coimbatore for textiles and steel. Ludhiana and Jalandhar for hosiery, sports goods and light engineering. Rajkot for pumps.

So much for the big cities. Among the medium-sized ones, there is Aligarh for locks, Maunath- Bhanjan for handlooms, Nagaur for handtools, Jamnagar for brass, Salem for handlooms, Kanchipuram for silk, Khurja for ceramics, Bhagalpur for weaving, Mirzapur for carpets, Sivakasi for matches. The examples can go on.

These towns and cities have much in common. They are all focal points for the regional economy. They have witnessed the fastest growth of employment in the past two decades. Unlike Bangalore, Vadodara or Ranchi, they have not prospered because of public investment. They are largely self-made. Each is dominated by just one or two industries. Most important, they are neglected by way of basic infrastructure and this is limiting their growth.

This pattern of spatial concentration is not peculiar to India. Italy is known for its industrial districts which specialise in precision engineering and textiles. The US has its software mecca in Silicon Valley. China has its bicycle cities and shoe villages. What is unique about

India is the neglect of these towns. It comes at a time when there is growing global demand for the skills they have developed.

There is more than economics to these towns. Many are powder kegs waiting to be ignited. They are melting pots drawing migrant workers from across the country. Child labour is rampant. Bhiwandi and Moradabad have seen among the worst communal riots in recent times. Surat, which generates Rs 5,000 crore a year in exports, was struck by a plague-like epidemic in 1994.

The tensions are intimately linked to the pattern of spatial growth, to changing economic relationships among different communities— and to government failure to provide even the minimum physical and social infrastructure.

A beginning is being made in Tiruppur. A Rs 900-crore project, jointly promoted by the Tamil Nadu Government, the Tiruppur Exporters' Association and Infrastructure easing and Finance Services, is set for implementation. It will provide piped water and set up effluent control facilities. But it has taken four years for the project to get off the ground. This relaxed schedule has to be compressed.

Such area-based infrastructure projects are needed in each growth centre. Local industry can be invited to participate. These cities also need design and technology delivery institutions of the type that exist in Japanese prefectures. These will add value to local products and make them more marketable. Recently, thanks to the Union textiles minister being the MP from Surat, the National Institute of Fashion Technology set up shop there.

The financing of infrastructure projects will get a boost if we open up the insurance and pension funds sectors. At present, these are state monopolies. Today, LIC and GIC provide close to Rs 7,000 crore a year for water, power, housing and other infrastructure projects. What will happen if we liberalise the insurance industry? In about 10 years, each new company will be able to mobilise at least Rs 5,000 crore annually for infrastructure. The development of a municipal bond market will also help in financing such projects. Recently, the Ahmedabad Municipal Corporation became the first urban body to raise resources through the issue of bonds to the public. It mobilised Rs 100 crore, a small amount but still a beginning.

The Government supports various schemes for modernising industry. It provides funds for improving productivity in the bicycle industry. It also runs projects for providing urban infrastructure in, say, Jalandhar—which supports a large bicycle-manufacturing base. But these programmes are not inter-linked simply because different ministries operate them.

Infrastructure will no doubt reach Ludhiana. But how much better it would be if it were related to the needs of the city's economic lifeline. Social justice too can be productively linked to globalisation's imperatives. All this requires is giving economic policies the necessary area focus. Take the leather industry. Upgrading its facilities in western Uttar Pradesh can benefit the Jatavs, among the preponderant Dalit groups in north India. There could yet be a meeting point for social and economic reforms.

24/08/1998

—◆——◆—

EAST NEEDS YEAST
The pains are east of Kanpur, the gains elsewhere

The economic decay of Bihar set in long before Laloo Prasad Yadav appeared on the scene. It is actually part of a deeper malaise we have long ignored. It can be diagnosed as "EOK negative". If a vertical line were to be drawn through Kanpur, EOK—east of Kanpur—is stagnant while the western segment is buoyant.

This is not to suggest the entire WOK is advanced. Northern Karnataka, western Gujarat, central Maharashtra, north-west Andhra Pradesh and parts of Bundelkhand are all backward, although not in as stark a manner as EOK. But the essential difference between EOK and WOK is one of developmental ethos and ambience.

There is nothing genetic about it: EOK labour underpins Punjab's farm prosperity. EOK is India's most resource-rich region. It is also politically very conscious. But it remains the bowl of poverty and backwardness. State governments are primarily responsible but the Centre has contributed substantially to EOK's plight and misery. Its rejuvenation is now a national responsibility transcending partisan politics. But this will not be achieved through Article 356-type coups. Of the 243 Central PSUs, 58 are chronically loss-making. Almost 60 per cent of the workers in these companies, which just cannot be turned around, are in EOK. Similarly, there are about 2,000 private companies in intensive care, facing a slow death. Half their employees are in EOK.

What is inhibiting quick industrial restructuring is that EOK receives only about 15 per cent of new investment. When new jobs are not being created in large numbers, old and unproductive jobs cannot be phased out without exacerbating social tensions. Kanpur itself epitomises this poignantly.

Liberalisation has not created the EOK problem but only brought it into sharper focus. Fifty per cent of all public investment in industry in the 1950s and '60s took place in EOK. But the policy of freight equalisation—that equalised the price of steel throughout the country—killed the comparative advantage of EOK. The failure of India's heavy industrialisation strategy—we should have been producing 100 million tonnes of steel now instead of 22 million tonnes—resulted in huge idle capacities in EOK.

Pre-1991, 50 per cent of all industrial licences went to just four states: Gujarat, Maharashtra, Tamil Nadu and Karnataka. Disbursements by all-India financial institutions to EOK made up 20 per cent of the total in the heyday of planning. By 1991, this had fallen to just 15 per cent.

Even after 1991, it was the wrangling between two Union ministries that sabotaged the prospects of companies like Amoco investing billions of dollars in Bihar. To this day there remain barriers to private investment in the coal industry. It took 20 years to get the Haldia Petrochemicals project off the ground. The formula for sharing revenues with states in EOK for the use of mineral resources still favours the Centre. EOK is home to about 40 per cent of India's poor but gets less than 20 per cent of the food subsidy.

In the past decade, EOK has done well in agriculture. Fertiliser use has increased, as have tractor sales and energisation of pumpsets. The farm productivity gap between eastern and western Uttar Pradesh has narrowed.

But much more is required to sustain an annual 5-6 per cent

growth in agriculture. Just about 21 per cent of the major and medium irrigation potential of Assam and 43 per cent of Bihar and Orissa have been developed. Associated with this is a special thrust on agro-processing technology and marketing. West Bengal, for instance, has gone through a potato revolution but value-addition has been low.

With growing environmental consciousness in the world, jute will gain in importance. The world wants new jute-based products but all we can offer in volumes are gunny bags.

EOKneeds roads and bridges. A Calcutta Siliguri expressway will transform north Bengal. North and south Bihar are connected only by one road-cumrail crossing across 800 km of the Ganga. A string of superthermal power stations at the coal pithead will transform the power scene. But there must be fresh demand as well. West Bengal has a power surplus because there is no demand growth.

EOK's financial system needs major expansion. In north India, the average population per bank branch is 12,000. In EOK, it is almost 19,000. In WOK for every Rs 100 bank deposit credit is Rs 65-75. In EOK it is Rs 30-50. Money alone is not the answer. The Centre pours Rs 3,000 crore yearly into the North-east. But this has little effect since corruption is seen by successive Central governments as a mode of cohesion.

EOK's economic future is intimately linked to the integrated development of the Ganga-Brahmaputra-Barak basin. EOK chief ministers must demand an India-Nepal-Bangladesh endeavour to harness the eastern Himalayan rivers. Such a joint effort will bring all-round prosperity and respite from floods.

Finally, the reorientation of public expenditure at the Central level is essential for releasing more resources that could be used for social development in the EOK region. If EOK states carry out painful reform as Orissa is doing in the power sector, the Centre must transfer a share of the improvement in its fiscal deficit to make state finances viable. This is an essential prerequisite for growth.

12/10/1998

A TALE OF TWO CITIES
The Bangalore-Hyderabad rivalry is all very well but now for a Silicon Triangle

Not a day passes without news of a spat between Bangalore and Hyderabad, two of the most cosmopolitan Indian cities of roughly the same size. Actually, Bangalore has already arrived. A few years ago, the Japanese management guru Kenichi Ohmae wrote that Bangalore was India's future. Very recently, the in-flight magazine of American Airlines identified it as one of the 10 cities of the 21st century. But Hyderabad is pushing its case aggressively, at times engaging in needless hype and prickly one-upmanship. The media too is fuelling the competition.

Both are pan-Indian cities although the truly local content is higher in Hyderabad. Both are vying with each other for the Insurance Regulatory and Development Authority. Both lobbied for a visit by President Clinton. Both are bidding for an international airport. Both are on the radar screen of the World Bank. Both are showcasing themselves as global centres for knowledge-based industries. Both have embarked on ambitious infrastructure development programmes. Both have influential diasporas, although Bangalore's is perhaps more professional than commercial. And both are being led by two of the most reform-minded politicians, one a high-profile, self—styled CEO and the other a low-key but no less dynamic personality who faces a more difficult task given the nature of the political environment in which he has to function and coming as he does after years of poor governance.

There is another similarity. Both cities are creations of public investment. Without the public sector in industry, in education and in science and technology, Bangalore and Hyderabad would not be where they are today. They have not been intrinsically entrepreneurial cities in the way Ludhiana or Coimbatore have been. The impetus for the growth of Bangalore came from companies like ITI, HMT, HAL, Bharat Electronics, Bharat Earth Movers and BHEL and from scientific agencies like ISRO, NAL and LRDE. Hyderabad grew because of companies like BHEL, ECIL, Bharat Dynamics, HMT and IDPL and scientific establishments like the Nuclear Fuels Complex, DMRL, IICT, NRSA, NGRI and others. Even though in recent years both cities have attracted private investment, government- funded R&D is still sustaining them.

But there are differences as well. Within Karnataka, Bangalore commands disproportionate influence in spite of other rich centres like Mysore, Mangalore, Hubli-Dharwad and Belgaum. Its location in the deep south of the state has contributed to the neglect of other regions. The paradox is that while many of the influential politicians of the state have come from northern Karnataka, investment has tended to take place largely around Bangalore. Of late, Hubli has been rediscovered thanks to its being the birth place of the world's second richest Indian (as of now) Gururaj Deshpande of Sycamore fame. But Bangalore continues to exercise a stranglehold which is great globally but debilitating locally.

Located in the northwest of the state, Hyderabad is a little less unfavourably located vis-a-vis the rest of Andhra. And within that state, cities like Visakhapat-nam, Vijayawada, Warangal, Guntur and Rajahmundri have emerged as major centres. This is mainly because Andhra's agriculture has been more prosperous than Karnataka's—its fertiliser consumption per hectare of cropped area is double that of Karnataka. Andhra is a major rice producer whereas Karnataka is a major producer of coarse cereals, although of late it has emerged as a major horticultural centre. Twenty-four per cent of India's droughtprone areas lie in Karnataka, thus constraining its agriculture. Because of greater agricultural surpluses, Andhra has also witnessed the emergence of many local entre-preneurs who have, in turn, been nurtured by successive state governments. The focus of Karnataka since the mid-'70s has been, first, social re-engineering and, later, democratic decentralisation. Both of these have profoundly transformed its society. Karnataka's home-grown entrepreneurs are largely in liquor, banking and professional education.

Gone are the days when a chief minister of Karnataka could be someone who studied in Osmania University. That showed the composite culture which the two cities are heirs to and whose legacy should not be forgotten. Synergies are possible. E-governance is an area of colla-boration. The development of the Hyderabad-Karnatak region and of the Krishna basin will demand statesmanship on both sides. Taking an even larger perspective, an isoceles technology triangle with Bangalore, Hyderabad and Pune at its vertices could also be visualised.

PANDORA'S BOX IS OPEN
Three new states come into legislative being but there is still a long way to go

Bills to creat three new states have finally been passed by Parliament. Of these, only the formation of Jharkhand out of Bihar can be said to be the outcome of a long, long struggle. Chhattisgarh and Uttaranchal, for instance, do not find any mention in the report of the States Reorganisation Commission that was submitted 45 years ago. What is intriguing about Uttaranchal is that it has given three great chief ministers to Uttar Pradesh in the past 50 years—Govind Ballabh Pant, Hemvati Nandan Bahuguna and Narain Dutt Tiwari—and yet the region felt neglected. Similarly, Chhattisgarh produced many noted political leaders, three of whom—Ravi Shankar Shukla, Shyama Charan Shukla and Motilal Vora—became chief ministers of Madhya Pradesh.

Two other chief ministers, D.P. Mishra and Arjun Singh, contested from Chhattisgarh. Yet this region too felt unwanted. New voices are being heard. Fresh demands for Bodoland out of Assam, Vidarbha out of Maharashtra, Gorkhaland out of West Bengal and Telengana out of Andhra Pradesh are being made. And since Uttaranchal does not solve the problem of Uttar Pradesh's simply un-governable size, some cries for a further break-up of India's most populous state are also being raised.

In the early 1990s, a senior political leader would repeatedly proclaim that instead of a piecemeal approach, what India needed was a new states reorganisation commission. Good idea. Yet, this same leader speaking in Parliament a few days back categorically rejected the idea of such a body saying that its creation would open a Pandora's box. The name of this politician: L.K. Advani.

Uttaranchal is a predominantly upper-caste state where the OBCs form a very minuscule proportion. But Scheduled Castes (overwhelmingly non-Chamars) form close to a fifth of this new state's population. Scheduled Tribes form close to 33 per cent of Chhattisgarh's and around 30 per cent of Jharkhand's population, the highest proportions in the country barring Mizoram, Meghalaya, Nagaland and Arunachal Pradesh.

Going by the 1991 census, Uttaranchal's population of about seven million is 5 per cent that of Uttar Pradesh; Jharkhand's population of around 22 million is about a quarter that of Bihar; and Chhattisgarh's population of approximately 18 million is about a third of Madhya Pradesh's. If existing liabilities are shared according to population and per capita income, the debt burden on the new states, particularly on Jharkhand and Chhattisgarh will not be crippling. Approximately 60 per cent of Bihar's total revenues accrue from Jharkhand and about 30 per cent of Madhya Pradesh's from Chhattisgarh.

Jharkhand and Chhattisgarh will be mineral-rich states. Jharkhand is the nation's depository of, among other things, coal, iron ore, uranium, mica and manganese. It has steel plants, engineering factories and technical institutions. Similarly, Chhattisgarh has abundant forest resources, apart from coal and iron ore. It too has steel plants and engineering units and is home to a large number of rice varieties. In contrast, although it has hydel resources, Uttaranchal will be a markedly revenue-weak state. It is, of course, a centre of great tourist attraction and has two of India's best professional institutions—the Roorkee and Pantnagar universities. There will undoubtedly be a clamour for declaring it as a "special category" state like the seven sisters of the North-east, Sikkim, Himachal Pradesh and Jammu and Kashmir.

What is striking about the new states is the sex ratio—the number of females per 1,000 males. Kerala is the only state where this ratio exceeds 1,000. Bastar and Rajnandgaon in Chhattisgarh have a sex ratio greater than 1,000. Uttaranchal has a sex ratio of 1,000. In some of its districts like Chamoli, Garhwal, Tehri Garhwal, Pithoragarh and Almora, it exceeds 1,000. Migration of men to other regions in search of jobs explains this pheno-menon. Some ecological historians have drawn a link between women's power and the success of the Chipko movement—the antitree cutting campaign that hit the headlines in the 1970s. The sex ratio in Jharkhand is distinctly more favourable to women as compared to north Bihar although this too must be attributed to the flight of men to the rest of the country.

One in four Indians will continue to live in the reorganised Uttar Pradesh and Bihar. Governance has simply collapsed here although a valiant rescue effort has been launched in Uttar Pradesh as part of a $5-6 billion World Bank programme. Bihar needs a similar initiative. While it is necessary to hold the local leadership accountable, the challenges that confront these two states are such that they simply cannot be solved without a vastly stepped up national investment and management effort. The author is with the Congress party. These are his personal views.

21/08/2000

◆——◆

WHY BIHAR IS AFLAME

No swarg out there but certainly lots of swar and swabhimaan

Last week, the central government announced a Rs 500 crore "package" for Bihar. This is not the first of such packages. Over 10 years ago, a Rs 200 crore package code-named Operation Siddharth was launched by the Centre in the very part of central Bihar that is burning these days. Earlier in 1982 Indira Gandhi had deputed the then member-secretary of the Planning Commission, Manmohan Singh, to make a comprehensive study of the Naxalite phenomenon in Bihar. Some measures were taken following a detailed report. Going back even further, 1973-74 was declared "land reform year"

Scheduled Castes constitute about 15 per cent of Bihar's population. In the central Bihar districts of Patna, Nalanda, Gaya, Jehanabad, Aurangabad, Nawadah and Bhojpur, most affected by violence unleashed by Naxalites and the caste senas, the proportion is higher, at around 20 per cent. Central Bihar also has a substantial population of aggressive land-owning upper and backward castes like the Bhumihars, Rajputs and Kurmis.

But these provide only the backdrop. What is more significant is that farm prosperity and literacy in central Bihar are higher than in the rest of the state. Bihar's overall literacy rate in 1991 was 38.5 per cent, whereas Jehanabad's was 46.4 per cent and Nalanda's 47 per cent. Thus in some ways the violence in central Bihar is not the offshoot of stagnation and poverty but is instead a reflection of development and growth, however stunted.

Jehanabad is no stranger to violence. April 19, 1986, saw what the American historian of Bihar Walter Hauser describes as a Jallianwalla-like episode. Police opened fire on 700 men, killing 21, at Arwal. The issue was a dispute over a parcel of public land that was being claimed by landless Dalits in the face of opposition from local land-owning Dalits.

In June 1987, 18 Dalits were massacred in Nonahi-Nagawan and in August 1988, 11 more were killed in Damuha. Other central Bihar districts fare no better. Twenty two Dalits were shot down at Danwar-Bihta in Bhojpur dis-trict in November 1989. December 1991 saw the killing of Dalit farm labourers at Barasima and Main in Gaya. Pipra in Patna district witnessed the killing of 14 Chamars by Kurmis in February 1980. This is only a selective list.

The past two decades have seen the growth of a new assertiveness among long-suppressed and quiescent communities in central Bihar. Democracy may not be alleviating poverty but is certainly imparting dignity and self-respect. The election of Karpoori Thakur as chief minister in 1977 was a watershed, as was that of Laloo Prasad Yadav in 1989. Australian political scientists Oliver Mendelsohn and Marika Vicziany, in their recent book *The Untouchables*, discuss how the Musahars, the most downtrodden of the Dalits, have emerged as the symbol of insurrection. Remittances from Punjab have also helped improve the standard of housing of Dalits, something that is an eyesore to the traditionalists.

Arvind N. Das, one of the very few serious writers on Bihar, has written that legislation arouses expectations and, it might be added, also fuels aspirations. When expectations are belied, struggles start. Undoubtedly, Naxalite groups have organised the poor in central Bihar. Ironically, these groups say they derive their inspiration from that great crusader for land reforms and social justice Swami Sahajanand Saraswati, himself an upper-caste Bhumihar.

There have been many twists and turns in Naxalite politics. Right now, there are three major groups—the CPI-ML (Liberation Front), Maoist Communist Centre (MCC) and the People's War Group. The first believes in elections and the second has been used by Laloo in the past.

K.B. Sahay was almost alone in his crusade for land reforms in the formative 1950s and '60s. Bihar suffered for want of a Charan Singh from an upwardly mobile intermediate caste who would push land reforms. Even so, Bihar was the first to introduce legislation to abolish zamindari. But the Patna High Court struck down the Act, as did the Supreme Court. It was this that led an exasperated Jawaharlal Nehru to push the first amendment to the Constitution. The legislation on land ceilings was introduced in the Assembly in 1955. A watered-down version was passed only in 1959 and got presidential assent in 1962.

India's foremost authority on land reforms is P.S. Appu, a distinguished IAS officer of the Bihar cadre. In 1994, Appu put forward what he himself calls "a modest programme for the '90s". First, he suggests the implementation of ceiling laws against the 84 landowners in the state who own more than 500 acres. The Bihar Government claims to have acquired 3.85 lakh acres of surplus land, while scholars like Indu Bharati have estimated that the land that is surplus is actually 18 lakh acres.

Second, he recommends a campaign like West Bengal's Operation Bargha to secure permanent rights for bataidars and tenants. Third, since there are real limits to land reform, he advocates that the government should acquire private land and turn it over to the four million-odd landless families. Sadly, the new package does not even recognise what Appu has been saying. The police will benefit, not the poor.

12/04/1999

◆━━◆

PUNJAB'S PARADOXES
Punjab has achieved much but some puzzles remain

The tercentenary of the khalsa is a good occasion to reflect on the economic development of India's richest state. No doubt, Punjab has achieved much in the past 50 years. The achievements are doubly noteworthy when the disadvantages with which it started out are recognised. Around 70 per cent of the canal irrigation capacity built by the British went over to Pakistan. The region saw a massive dislocation of population, estimates of which vary between five million and eight million, along with horrendous orgies of killings. But very quickly Punjab went on the fast forward track under the dynamic leadership of politicians like Pratap Singh Kairon and administrators like M.S. Randhawa. Investments by the Centre, like in the Bhakra Nangal project, were crucial in Punjab's take-off. The Centre's policy of equalising steel prices all over the country benefited Punjab substantially.

In the '60s and early '70s, when India was being written off as a basketcase, it was largely Punjab that restored our self-pride. Over the past three decades, around 70 per cent of wheat and 40 per cent of rice procurement for the national public distribution system has been done in Punjab. The growth of agriculture that continued unabated even during the troubled periods of the '80s and early '90s is responsible for Punjab having the lowest proportion of people living below the poverty line—between 7 per cent and 13 per cent, depending on how you measure. Yet, paradoxes abound.

First, why is Punjab's farm prosperity not triggering faster social modernisation? This is all the more intriguing since Sikhism is so very egalitarian, Hinduism in the region has also been subject to reform movements and there has been Christian influence as well. Punjab and Tamil Nadu have about the same female literacy rates—in 1991, Punjab's was 50 per cent and Tamil Nadu's was 52 per cent. Punjab and Tamil Nadu also had the same average age at marriage for females. Punjab's expenditure on family welfare per eligible couple is 60 per cent more than Tamil Nadu's.

But Tamil Nadu has already reached the replacement level of fertility of 2.1, whereas Punjab's total fertility rate is 2.9 and it is not expected to reach the transition point till 2019. Punjab's sex ratio—the number of females per 1,000 males—is 882, much lower than 974 in Tamil Nadu and the Indian average of 927. Punjab's population of 21 million is much smaller than Tamil Nadu's (56 million) which makes the paradox even more striking.

Second, why has representative Dalit politics not taken root in the state? Among all states, Punjab has the highest proportion of Scheduled Castes in its population. The all-India figure is around 16.5 per cent, Uttar Pradesh's is about 21 per cent but Punjab's is 28.3 per cent. True, the caste system in Punjab was among the least oppressive. Even so, how Punjab has remained relatively immune to the growth of political awareness among Dalits, a phenomenon so very evident in the past two decades in Uttar Pradesh and Bihar, is a mystery.

Ironically, Kanshi Ram himself is from Punjab. But the influence of the BSP has been the maximum in Uttar Pradesh and not in Punjab. In the 1996 Uttar Pradesh assembly elections, the BSP got 17 per cent of the vote but in the 1997 Punjab assembly elections it could get just 7 per cent. Third, why is it that in spite of having an entrepreneurial ethos and an energetic diaspora, Punjab is not seeing an N. Chandrababu Naidu, a Digvijay Singh or even a Kalyan Singh? Interestingly, way back in the '70s, the famous Anandpur Sahib Resolution talked of a 7 per cent economic growth rate in the state. This was long before the country had discovered the virtues of a faster rate of economic growth.

But the dominant mindset was and remains government-centred and subsidy-oriented.

The resolution expressed its "unabated opposition to the concentration of economic and political power in the hands of capitalists". Deep down, the suspicion of a modern, market economy still prevails. Punjab's annual growth rate in 1992-97 at constant 1980-81 prices was just 4.7 per cent, as compared to 12.1 per cent in Gujarat and 9.6 per cent in Maharashtra. Economic structure does not provide the full explanation. The credit-deposit ratio of commercial banks is a woeful 39 per cent, as compared to 56 per cent nationally. This reflects the poor commercial environment in the state.

Finally, why is it that in spite of agriculture being subject to so many regulations and restrictions, Punjab has not been in the forefront of a reforms and decontrol campaign? On the contrary, in the past the Akalis have even talked of nation-alising trade in foodgrains, a recipe for disaster. Barring perhaps Bhupinder Singh Mann, there have been no great agrimobilisers from Punjab, like a Charan Singh, a Sharad Joshi or a Mahendra Singh Tikait. And why is it that in spite of the demonstrated benefits that WTO offers India in agri-exports, no public figure from Punjab has been defending it?

The land of the lions can still emerge as a tiger like the East Asian countries did. It has all the pre-requisites. But a paradigm shift in economic governance is needed. Sadly, there is no evidence of this as Punjab totters on the brink of bankruptcy, living from the threat of one default to another.

19/04/1999

———◆——◆———

SEX SKEWS IN HARYANA
The land of the Lals has made tremendous progress. Or has it?

Haryana is very much in the news, what with the BJP betraying its 1996 promise and with-drawing support to Bansi Lal. But spare a thought for Bansi Lal, a man now unfortunately remembered only for his role during the Emergency. In his past incarnation, Lal was a no-nonsense administrator who contributed substantially to building the physical infrastructure of the state. If Haryana has connected its approximately 7,000 villages by all-weather roads, if every village of Haryana has electricity and if tourism has got a boost in the state, Bansi Lal deserves what in north India would quaintly be called "the loin's share of the credit".

But as it so often happens with patriarchs, somehow the second innings is never as good as the first. Bhairon Singh Shekhawat was an outstanding chief minister during his tenure in Rajasthan in 1977-79. Sadly, the Shekhawat of the '90s was a pale shadow of his former self. Racked by illness, he allowed himself to fall victim to that dreaded Indian disease called "kin-itis". Muthuvel Karunanidhi is another example. Bansi Lal too falls in this category, although it should be said he exhibited signs of his old daring and toughness when he started the programme to reform Haryana's power sector in 1996-97. Farmers agitated, politicians protested. But Bansi Lal held firm and today, along with Orissa, Andhra Pradesh and now Utar Pradesh, Haryana is in the midst of a profound privatisation of its power industry. Its full impact will be evident five to six years from now.

Beyond the Lals and Chautalas, what to make of Haryana itself ? It is undoubtedly a puzzle—India's second richest state but the worst in terms of the sex ratio. It was an economic backwater when it was created in November 1966. Over one-fifth of its land area is arid and semiarid. But in less than two decades it had become a crucial part of India's grain basket. It had industry in Faridabad to begin with—started largely by Partition's refugees, of whom Hari Nanda of Escorts was the most prominent. But Maruti's location in Gurgaon and its proximity to Delhi ensured that Haryana's industrial growth took on an added dimension.

However, while Haryana's economy was taking off, while poverty ratios were falling because of rapid farm growth, the sex ratio—the number of females per 1,000 males—was also gradually coming down. In the 1991 Census, Haryana's sex ratio was 865, as compared to the national average of 927. Keeping company with Haryana are Uttar Pradesh at 879 and Punjab at 882. Haryana's total fertility rate is a high 3.3 as compared to a national average of about 3.1. There is no religion to blame this on since Muslims are just four per cent of Haryana's population. At this rate it will not reach the replacement level of fertility of 2.1 till the year 2025. What sets Haryana apart from Punjab is its high level of female participation in agriculture, which means the women certainly have economic utility.

Amartya Sen and Jean Dreze debunk the popular misconceptionthat female infanticide has led to low sex ratios. This is because excess female mortality in childhood occurs after the age of one. Could it be that the sex ratio in Haryana, Punjab and western Uttar Pradesh is depressed because this region draws migrant farm labour from other areas? This explanation, however, breaks down when the data for the past 100 years is examined. This region has consistently had the lowest sex ratios in India ever since the first Census in 1881. And to further counter this argument, remember that male outmigration from Haryana is itself quite substantial, for example, into the army.

The only detailed study of rural Haryana has been by Prem Chowdhry, a historian whose The Veiled Women (1994) is a fascinatingly meticulous analysis of shifting gender equations in Haryana over the past century. In her words, the ghunghat remains the most ubiquitous and potent symbol of male authority and power, which still dominate the Haryanavi woman. Chowdhry's conclusion is that even while women have made progress, Haryana has not experienced any significant democratising movement that may have a positive impact on gender relations. On the contrary, repeated attempts have been made by the state's political class to nullify any attempt at gender equality, evidenced in the efforts to amend the Hindu Succession Act, 1956, that confers equal inheritance rights to daughters, sisters and widows.

Rapid changes may be leading to ambivalence and to what Chowdhry calls the complicity of women themselves in the reconstruction of patriarchy. Translated into simple English this means that women themselves give moral sanctity and legitimacy to male domination and macho social customs and religious traditions.

The historian's conclusion is unambiguous: that the removal of this ghunghat as a symbol may perhaps constitute the first truly revolutionary step for the women of Haryana. Sadly it is clear economic growth alone will not make this happen. These are issues that have to be taken up as part of a sustained campaign of social mobilisation by political parties. Will the Sushma Swarajs take up the challenge?

05/07/1999

NEW BLOOM IN POES GARDEN
The politics of Tamil Nadu hits the headlines as a
quiet revolution proceeds

The continuing melodrama of Tamil politics is detracting from
the state's manifold contributions to the shaping of modern India.
"Periyar" Ramaswamy Naicker was one of the greatest social reformers
India has ever known and the social justice movement in the state has
been truly revolutionary. Three out of eight members of the committee
that drafted our Constitution and five out of the 25 finance ministers
that independent India has had have come from the state. K. Kamaraj
and C.N. Annadurai were among the most outstanding politicians in
the past half century. It was the Tamil trinity—C. Subramaniam, B.
Sivaraman and M.S. Swaminathan—which spear-headed the Green
Revolution.The two Indian Nobel laureates in physics—uncle and
nephew—were Tamil-ians. In the Indian diaspora, Tamils occupy pride
of place.

There is clearly a development dynamic in the state that transcends
all political shenanigans. Ranked 11th in terms of per capita inflation-
adjusted income in 1970, the state has jumped to fifth place today.
Compare it to say, West Bengal which has slipped from fifth to ninth
rank or Kerala whose rank has fallen from ninth to 10th in the same
period.

On key social indicators Tamil Nadu has done very well. In the
mid-1970s, it had a higher infant mortality rate than Karnataka, Punjab
and Maharashtra. But in just 20 years' time, Tamil Nadu had reached
second position below Kerala. However, its infant mortality rate is still
more than four times that of Kerala. The sex ratio (that is, the number
of females per 1,000 males) in the 0-6 age group in four districts—
Salem, Dharmapuri, Theni and Namakkal—is disturbingly low at below
900 (the optimal range is around 943-952) and confirms the prevalence
of female infanticide.

Kerala's remarkable success in population control has been rightly
acclaimed all over the world. But what has been applauded less is Tamil
Nadu's achievement at lower rates of female literacy. Kerala was the
first state to reach the critical replacement level of fertility of 2.1 in 1988
while Tamil Nadu was next to do so in 1993. About a generation or two
after this milestone, the population stops growing. Tamil Nadu has

accomplished this largely because of both sustained political commitment and administrative zeal of officers like R.A. Gopalaswamy and T.V. Antony.

The state routinely ranks amongst the best in imple-mentation of rural development and social welfare pro-grammes. The food security system works for the poor. Dr Manmohan Singh introduced the National Social Assistance Programme in 1995 based largely on Tamil Nadu's experience in social security. The state has pioneered nutrition programmes and the mid-day meal scheme introduced by MGR in 1982 now covers about 6.5 million pre-school and school-going children daily. Its fiscal position, reflected in interest payments as a proportion of total revenue, is the best, although public finances are now under stress and expenditure reforms are urgently called for. It supplies power free to farmers but its electricity board is the most efficient in the country with the lowest losses and the highest level of metering. No doubt, Tamil Nadu has benefited from public-sector investments in the 1950s and 1960s. This has helped diversify its economy. For instance, the state has the lowest share of agriculture in state domestic product. But it has also had a great tradition of enterprise most in evidence in its automotive, textile and engineering industries.

Unlike Bangalore and Hyderabad, Coimbatore and Tiruppur have flourished on sheer native entrepreneurship. Just five years ago, Tamil Nadu was not associated with in-formation technology (IT) even though it had a first-class network of higher education. But today, Tamil Nadu is very much on the IT map, and already leads the nation in IT application, particularly in education and governance. The title of a recent Harvard University monograph by Colin Maclay captures the new spirit—"Readiness for a Networked World: A Quiet Information Revolution in Tamil Nadu". It is also racing ahead in biotechnology. Dr J. Jayalalithaa has an outstanding legacy to build on. Her earlier tenure, though controversial,was also notable for the way she wooed Ford, Sterlite and Dupont to invest in the state and the emphasis she placed on social issues. She also kept a tight control over prices of essential commodities. Intellectually and managerially, she is one of the most impressive chief ministers. It would be a colossal tragedy if we do not get to see this side of her personality flower soon. Tamil Nadu has got all that it takes to replicate the East Asian and Chinese successes. But it also has all that it takes to become another Bihar, what with the proliferation of political parties wedded to no larger social agenda, caste violence and rampant corruption. The choice is hers and hers alone.

NORTH-SOUTH DIVIDE
The south has development in politics and the
north has politics in development

Bill Clinton's visit to Hyderabad and the continued political shenanigans in Uttar Pradesh and Bihar have once again raised the north-south divide issue. Peninsular India, a term that does more justice to reality since Maharashtra is very much like the quartet of south Indian states, does appear to be dramatically different from the Hindi heartland. Nobody can miss the developmental ethos and drive that exists in the south and that is absent for the most part in the politically more influential north. At a superficial level, the differences could well be ascribed to the fact that the south has a vibrant film industry which the north does not have. But we must dig deeper.

History and geography have shaped differences as has been analysed by distinguished historians like K.A. Nilakanta Sastri and Burton Stein. The south has had more peaceful contacts with the external world through trade. The north had been a more un-settled place being more vulnerable to invasions. The north was run on the zamindari system, while the south was ryotwari-based, which brought the administration at all levels into direct contact with farmers.

Social anthropologists, most notably Iravati Karve and David Mandelbaum have written classics on how kinshi organisation and the institutions of marriage and family have marked regional differences and worked to increase security of women in the south. The economist Bina Agarwal in her widely-acclaimed *A Field of One's Own* has argued that in the northern part of the subcontinent women were essentially excluded from land rights and that this has had a profound impact on social development. Another factor could be that the south is predominantly a rice economy. This demands a high female participation in agriculture thereby imparting a greater economic value to women. However, the rice/wheat dichotomy cannot explain Bihar, which is also a ricegrowing area.

The differing roles of Christianity and Islam must have left their impacts. Christian influences have been more extensive in the south, and through education it has been a major stimulus for modernisation. The spread of Islam in the north has largely been through the sword while its diffusion in the south has been more through Sufism and trade, making its influence there relatively more conducive to social amity. It would also be fascinating to speculate what the impact of Jainism has been on the development of south Indian society.

More fundamentally, the south has seen revolutionary social reform movements over the past century. These movements were aimed at breaking the stranglehold of the Brahmins who constituted less than 5 per cent of the population and who derived their power not through ownership of land but largely through education and professional skills. The Sanskritisation process first described by M.N. Srinivas was so strong that the intermediate and lower castes wanted to emulate the upper castes and establish equality through education. In the north, social reform movements of the type launched by Jyotiba Phule, Sri Narayana Guru and Periyar have been absent in modern times—although north India did experience the momentous Ramanand revolution in the 14th century. Here, the upper castes constitute anywhere between 20 and 25 per cent of the population and derive authority not from learning but from being land owners. It is the numeracy of the upper castes that explains, for example, why north India reacted violently to the Mandal Commission in 1990. Since the upper castes themselves have not used education as a tool of advancement, the Paswans, the Yadavs and the Mayawatis have also not made basic socio-economic issues part of the social justice agenda. The exclusive objective is political power. The role of the dominant castes like the Lingayats and the Reddys in the south has been hugely transformative unlike that of their northern counterparts. The Congress's perspectives in the north have been different than in the south—in the north, it has been a upper caste party run mostly through a central writ. The BJP is now behaving no differently, showing that national parties treat the north as an extension of Delhi-based fiefdoms.

The south has its problems too. Kerala is suffocating in the absence of pragmatic mindsets and economic growth. Tamil Nadu's social reforms have not embraced Dalits. Northern Karnataka and Telengana remain under-developed. Linguistic chauvinism and casteism are well entrenched. Bitter water disputes are holding back faster progress. The common legacy and complementarities are forgotten and fratricidal rivalry is being generated. Sure, the south is ahead of the north but is that enough?

03/04/2000

GRIM NEWS OUT OF THE RBI
A new study shows that the state of the states is precarious

Brzil is in deep financial trouble again. The IMF approved a $41.5 billion rescue package for it in October last year. Markets heaved a sigh of relief expecting the worst to be over. Suddenly, disaster has struck in a most unexpected way. On January 6, Itamar Franco, governor of the Brazilian state of Minas Gerais, one-time president of Brazil and a bitter opponent of President Henrique Cardoso, declared a 90-day moratorium on about $15 billion owed by his state to the federal government. All hell broke loose. Other state governors talked of defaults and Brazil has started tottering again. The 27 states in Brazil collectively owe the federal government about $90 billion.

Could this happen in India? After all, at the end of March 1999, the collective debt owed by the 25 states to the Centre will have crossed Rs 200,000 crore ($50 billion)—about 60 per cent of their total outstanding liabilities. The answer, strictly speaking, is no. India is not Brazil. In India, no debt can be incurred by a state without the knowledge and approval of the Centre. The RBI puts a limit on a state's ways and means advances. We also have multiple channels through which "Central" resources flow into a state—through the Planning Commission, Finance Commission and financial institutions. As long as the inflows exceed outflows, a state will not take the risk of declaring a moratorium unilaterally.

Debt servicing by states as a proportion of gross transfers to them from the Centre in 1998-99 would average 27.5 per cent, high but not at a danger level. In states like Punjab, Maharashtra, Gujarat and Goa though, debt servicing is growing steadily and consumes 40-60 per cent of gross transfers. It would be a colossal mistake to think that state finances will not impact on sentiment. A landmark analysis by RBI, carried in its February 1999 Bulletin, shows Indian states are in dire financial straits. The total non-developmental expenditure of the states in 1998-99 would be close to 36 per cent of their total expenditure, a proportion that has been rising sharply. This year, the states will be financing 40 per cent of their fiscal deficit by dipping into their provident funds, reserve funds and through deposits and advances. The fiscal deficit of the states as a whole is budgeted to be 3.68 per cent of GDP, over double the sustainable level.

The difficulties in fiscal restructuring by the states should not be minimised, specially in view of the fact that two-thirds of all expenditure on agriculture, rural development, irrigation and the social sectors is carried out by the states and will only increase. The Centre has relatively greater room for manoeuvre. At times, the states also get penalised for Delhi's profligacy as can be seen from the havoc which the Fifth Pay Commission bonanza to four million Central government employees is causing. In fact, till 1985-86, state finances were in balance. The Fourth Pay Commission triggered the rot. A Centre living with a fiscal deficit well in excess of 6 per cent of GDP and which has to resort to gimmicks like buybacks and cross-holdings in oil PSUs to cut the deficit can hardly assume the role of a fiscal evangelist. Even so, there is much the states can and must do to raise tax and non-tax revenues as well as reorient public expenditure.

One of the best things to have happened is the permission given by the Finance Ministry to the World Bank in 1996 to enter into structural adjustment loans with the states directly. These loans typically cover power, education and health but the states don't get the money unless they make irrevocable commitments to reform their finances. Andhra Pradesh was the first to get almost $3 billion. Uttar Pradesh and Rajasthan will probably be next in line. Gujarat has a similar loan from the Asian Development Bank. These loans bring financial discipline. But while such loans are welcome, other measures to introduce fiscal discipline are needed. RBI has been shouting hoarse for what it calls a "sinking fund" by states. This is a fund to which every year some money will be appropriated so as to meet future debt obligations. States say that in the presence of a revenue deficit such a fund may not have much meaning. But it is the principle and the signalling that is important. States like Rajasthan have agreed to this since it is the only way they can break out of the debt trap.

A growing source of worry is off-budget liabilities in the form of guarantees, letters of comfort and other such "incentives" that states are offering both while borrowing and attracting new investments. The outstanding guarantees of states in 1996-97, according to RBI, amounted to about Rs 64,000 crore. This may well increase as the states face a financial squeeze on transfers from the Centre as well as difficulties in raising funds from the capital market. Currently, these guarantees and contingent liabilities are not considered debt obligations. This is a prescription for disaster.

In a way, what happened in Brazil demonstrates the limits to fiscal freedom and decentralisation in a federation. The answer is not to look at the Centre and the states as fiscal adversaries as we have tended to but as partners in a painful but essential process of the reshaping of the public expenditure system—that today is neither promoting growth nor enhancing equity. This is the true essence of economic reforms.

01/03/1999

THE STATE OF STATES
A new analysis of the performance of states in the
1990s has fresh insights

In its present structure, shape and style, the Planning Commission is an anachronistic nuisance. But it can be a great intellectual watering hole for anyone with a scholarly bent of mind. And so it has been for Montek Singh Ahluwalia, India's distinguished economist-administrator who was banished to Yojana Bhavan in August 1998. Twenty-two years ago, Ahluwalia produced a masterpiece on rural poverty that is still a standard reference work. During his PMO and Finance Ministry tenure he had little time for academic output, although he did contribute to various edited volumes. Now, after producing a comprehensive and authoritative monograph on the new global financial architecture for the Commonwealth finance ministers last year, he has come up with another landmark work. This is on the growth performance of states, a paper that he presented last month at Stanford University, US. Ahluwalia concludes that in the 1990s as compared to the 1980s growth rates of gross state domestic product (GSDP) in:

- Gujarat and Maharashtra accelerated significantly.
- West Bengal, Rajasthan, Madhya Pradesh, Tamil Nadu and Kerala also increased considerably.
- Uttar Pradesh, Bihar, Orissa, Punjab and Haryana decelerated sharply. Karnataka remained at the same level while Andhra Pradesh saw a small decline.

The biggest shocker is Punjab that has all it takes to be a "tiger economy" but is bankrupt. The records of Karnataka and Andhra underscore the need to go beyond information technology while looking at this otherwise dynamic duo. Ashish Bose, the noted demographer, had coined the term BIMARU (sickly) for Bihar, Madhya Pradesh, Rajasthan and Uttar Pradesh. But Ahluwalia shows that Rajasthan and Madhya Pradesh may be breaking out of the BIMARU trap.

What influences poverty most in this country is farm growth. Ahluwalia's conclusions on the growth rate of agricultural SDP in the 1990s as compared to the 1980s is as follows:

- Punjab and Haryana have witnessed a sharp slackening but this is after over two decades of high growth.
- Gujarat and Maharashtra have shown significant step-up along with Rajasthan, Kerala and West Bengal.
- A modest to appreciable fall has occurred in Bihar, Uttar Pradesh, Madhya Pradesh, Andhra and Karnataka.
- Orissa and Tamil Nadu have seen a steep decline.

Ahluwalia calculates that inter-state inequalities have increased over the past decade although the popular notion that the rich have got richer and the poor poorer is not entirely accurate. The growth rates of per capita GDP, which is the most basic index of well-being, present a more complex pattern. Nevertheless, he is on very tentative grounds while trying to explain the differentials in growth performance. However, his failure to find a statistically significant relationship linking growth with various investment and infrastructure factors should not blind us to a very basic fact—that as long as states continue to be financially strapped, hopes of their sustaining a growth momentum are bleak. The finances of the 10 "special category" states (the seven North-east sisters, Sikkim, Himachal and Jammu and Kashmir) that are almost completely dependent on the Centre are in terrible shape. For the rest, as judged by the ratio of interest payments to revenue receipts:

- West Bengal, Uttar Pradesh, Rajasthan and Punjab are in a perilous situation.
- Orissa, Gujarat, Haryana, Bihar and Andhra are not in dire straits but their position is not encouraging either. Bihar has survived fiscal stress by not increasing expenditure while Andhra Pradesh is now experiencing it on account of growing commitments.
- Kerala, Goa, Karnataka, Maharashtra, Tamil Nadu and Madhya Pradesh have kept their debt burden down, at least for the time being. But this is little consolation. In Karnataka, for example, over half of the state's revenues are consumed by salaries and pensions (including that of teachers and police).

Ahluwalia's paper should trigger a lively debate. But this debate must not take place in an adversarial manner and the Centre must become less preachy. Undoubtedly, growth in states will be determined largely by their own governance and fiscal capability. But it will also be influenced by Central policies which determine not only the terms of borrowing through Central loans and assistance but also through loans via agencies like LIC, HUDCO and NABARD. The states are not benefiting from a lower interest rate regime while the 70:30 loan:grant mix in central assistance, fixed when the revenue component of State Plan expenditure was around 30 per cent, is clearly outdated given that this share is now over 50 per cent.

03/07/2000

STATES ARE CENTRAL
World Bank chief's visit to India reinforces the growing economic clout of states

Delhi, the Late Sanjeevi Guhan who was one of our most distinguished economic admin-istrators, once remarked, is a capital in search of a country. But the 1990s changed all that and to reinforce that trend, World Bank President Jim Wolfensohn visiting India between November 6 and 14 met the chief ministers of Gujarat, Maharashtra, Karnataka, Andhra Pradesh and Uttar Pradesh in their states and spent less than 48 hours in Delhi.

In the good old days, Wolfensohn would have spent all his time in Delhi with the mandatory weekend in Agra or Jaipur. That he is no longer doing so is, in large measure, due to a decision taken in October-November 1996 when P. Chidambaram was finance minister to have the World Bank "focus" directly on states with the Central governmen t playing a purely facilitative role. This move was opposed within the system on the ground that the Centre would lose control, but thanks to N. Chandrababu Naidu's clout in the then United Front and Chidambaram's tenacity, the opposition was overcome. Andhra Pradesh became the first focus state as also the recipient of about $4 billion in loans. Uttar Pradesh was next with around $6 billion. Karnataka is third with a portfolio of about $2.5-3 billion. Chidambaram's desire to see our states in the orbit of the World Bank came at a time when the

Washington-based development financing institution was reinventing itself with a view to decentralise its operations in major countries like India to its local office.

The World Bank package is not charity. It comes with conditionalities, the most basic being reforms in the power sector. Without this, the states will not be able to reduce their revenue deficits. Between 50-70 per cent of the revenue deficit in many states is due to power losses and subsidies. If states cannot reduce their revenue deficits, they will not be able to invest more in essential social and physical infrastructure which is the need of the hour. Other than power reforms, there has to be a commitment to reducing open-ended subsidies and making public utilities more commercial and the government's size financially sustainable. These conditionalities are not an assault on our sovereignty; they are things that we should be doing on our own in our own interest but since we do not change unless there is a crisis or there is external pressure, perfectly sensible policies are seen as "conditionalities". World Bank terms are pretty liberal for the states: 70 per cent riod is 20 years with half the loan having an initial grace period of five years.

Typically, a state-level programme begins with the publication of a white paper on finances and a mediumterm plan for fiscal management. These set out detailed roadmaps with milestones to be fulfilled. Once this is done and a credible demonstration of commitment to transformthe electricity industry is made, negotiations on specific projects take place. Karnataka, for instance, has just got Wolfensohn's nod for a Rs 12,000-crore development package covering watershed development, rural water supply, tank irrigation, roads and highways, urban water supply and power and fiscal restructuring. This money is spread over four to five years.

One criticism of Chidambaram's decision was that only advanced states would gain. Andhra and Karnataka are developed states. But the World Bank is in Uttar Pradesh in a significant way and is negotiating with Rajasthan and Orissa. However, Bihar and Assam are not benefiting. Madhya Pradesh felt it would not able to handle World Bank conditionalities and hence opted out, although it is now in dialogue with the Manila-based Asian Development Bank.

The growing interaction of the World Bank with states has made both happy but the Finance Ministry in Delhi is uneasy. Many officials feel they are now playing second fiddle, though it is ironic that these very people are champions of decentralisation when they are working for state governments. This, of course, illustrates a basic bureaucratic maxim—where you stand depends on where you sit!

The greatest danger to this new interaction lies in failure to reform the power sector and deliver tangible results in a two-three-year time frame. So far, power reforms have been seen only as increasing power rates for consumers. If this perception persists, it will be a setback. That is why there has to be a primary focus on cutting the huge transmission and distribution losses (a euphemism for theft), introducing universal metering and augmenting power supply itself. The political packaging is also crucial. That is why the Karnataka chief minister told Wolfensohn last week in Bangalore that after nature and IT parks, he wants World Bank help for a new type of PARK—Poverty Alleviation in Rural Karnataka—in which water supply, watershed and other such projects occupy pride of place.

20/11/2000

————◆————

HOUDINI OF HYPERABAD
Understanding Chandrababu Naidu's contribution to Andhra's indebtedness

Undoubtedly, N. Chandrababu Naidu has transformed mindsets and given a whole new meaning to governance. But his critics are now accusing him of bankrupting the state. Much of the noise is being generated by his opponents but of late even sober economists who have held high policy-making positions and who are not unsyathetic to what he is trying to do have started expressing their uneasiness. Are these fears justified?

Let us start with the facts as brought out by the Reserve Bank of India in its recent annual study of state finances. As of March 2000, the outstanding liabilities of Andhra Pradesh are budgeted (actuals may be higher) at Rs 27,845 crore, as compared to Rs 15,164 crore in March 1996. Thus, Naidu has almost doubled the debt of the state in just four years.

And this is not even the complete picture. It does not include guarantees and other "contingent" liabilities whose payment is contingent on the failure of the state Government or its agencies to discharge their debt obligations. These do not figure in budget documents. The RBI says that in Andhra Pradesh these guarantees have increased from Rs 4,343 crore at end-March 1996 to almost Rs 10,500 crore as of end-September 1999.

Thus, in absolute terms, Naidu is multiplying the state's indebtedness. This, however, is not the right way to look at debt. The two ratios that are commonly used to evaluate indebtedness are debt as a proportion of SDP (state domestic product or state's income) which portrays the "stock" of debt and interest ayments as a proportion of revenues which indicates its "flow".

Take debt as a proportion of SDP. The RBI estimates that in 1996-97, Andhra Pradesh's ratio was 23.9 per cent, as compared to a national average of 31.1 per cent. States substantially worse off than Andhra Pradesh include Goa (49.7 per cent), Bihar (48.7 per cent), Orissa (48.6 per cent), Kerala (40.1 per cent), Punjab (37.1 per cent), Rajasthan (34.9 per cent) and Uttar Pradesh (33.6 per cent). Andhra's debt-to-SDP ratio in 1999-2000 is probably around 26 per cent. But one caveat—the World Bank's figures are lower by about 3 percentage points and that needs to be reconciled by the Bank and the RBI.

Now come to interest payments as a proportion of revenue receipts, an index of debt servicing. In 1999-2000, Andhra's ratio is 17.3 per cent, compared to the national average of a little over 20 per cent. States in difficulty include West Bengal (35.6 per cent), Punjab (28.9 per cent), Uttar Pradesh (28.5 per cent), Orissa (27.7 per cent) and Rajasthan (24.8 per cent). And the rate of increase in these five states compared to 1990-93 is far higher than in Andhra Pradesh.

Thus, judged in relation to other states and to the Central government itself, Andhra's debt burden is not very high nor is its debt unsustainable. But this excludes state government guarantees. Andhra has been profligate in this regard, as has Maharashtra. Between the two, they account for a quarter and along with Gujarat and Punjab for half of all state guarantees. But since these liabilities are only "contingent", simply adding them to the figure of outstanding liabilities is wrong. The RBI takes a third of these guarantees and adds it to the debt. If this is done, Andhra's debt burden works out to around 29 per cent of SDP, still less than that of many states but higher than in Maharashtra and Karnataka. And if the guarantees are taken as a proportion of revenue receipts, the ratio for Andhra is around 67 per cent, as against India's 42 per cent.

It is also being alleged that the World Bank is contributing to the debt burden. Far from it. Thirty per cent of World Bank assistance is interest- free and the balance is to be repaid at around 12 per cent interest over 20 years— very liberal repayment terms.

Nevertheless, Andhra's fiscal position is deteriorating and Naidu is beginning to skate on thin ice. If the state's economic growth does not accelerate beyond the '90s average of 5 per cent per year and if revenue growth is not sustained, he's in for trouble. Naidu's defence is that debt is being incurred for development projects like roads, irrigation and power that will yield commercial returns in future. However, the temptation to use borrowings to meet government's establishment expenditure is great, specially given that Andhra is cash-strapped. Maharashtra has done this in substantial measure. What Naidu needs to do, since so much is at stake, is take both his fans and critics into confidence and produce a white paper on the state's overall debt position that also details how he proposes to manage the debt. This is the first step.

28/02/2000

◆——◆

LEAD KINDLY LIGHT

At least some states are waking up to reforms in the power sector

If There is one sector that epitomises India's economic malaise it is power. The commercial losses of the state electricity boards (SEBs) in 1997-98 exceeded Rs 10,000 crore—and this excludes the Rs 4,000 crore of subsidies provided by the state governments. Quite clearly, there is no hope for an end to India's power problems unless the SEBs are fundamentally reformed. Chasing private investment without such reforms is like chasing a mirage. More public investment will simply mean more waste of money.

Fortunately, four states have recognised this. They are moving towards the needed reforms. The chief ministers in these states are providing personal leadership and taking the political flak. The four belong to different political parties—the Congress, the Telugu Desam Party (TDP), the Haryana Vikas Party and the BJP. This shows that behind all the cacophony a consensus on doing the right thing does exist. While the chief ministers deserve credit, they could not have made much headway without the sustained support of the Union Finance Ministry and the World Bank. The World Bank has committed close to $4 billion to underwrite the reforms programmes over the next six to seven years. Rightly, it has linked disbursement to performance.

First off the block in November 1993 was Biju Patnaik in Orissa. His cabinet approved an overhaul of the state's power sector. Fortunately, his Congressman successor, J.B. Patnaik, endorsed the reforms and obtained legislative approval in April 1996. Orissa has got a commitment for over half a billion dollars from the World Bank. It has already set up an in-dependent agency to fix power tariffs. Tariffs are being revised regularly. The SEB itself has been converted into a corporation and is now being made into a joint venture company with an American firm. The foreign partner will hold 51 per cent equity. For power distribution, the state has been divided into four zones. Global bids have been invited for managing the distribution of power in each of these zones. Distribution is expected to be fully privatised by 2000. Orissa's case shows that the homework prior to privatisation itself can take two years. Without this homework, privatisation can boomerang.

The most telling criticism made initially was that sales to agriculture in Orissa are a paltry 6 per cent of total electricity sales. Hence, Orissa is atypical. The Finance Ministry and the World Bank then lobbied with Haryana, where agriculture accounts for over 45 per cent of total electricity sales and which, therefore, is more representative of the country than Orissa. Chief Minister Bansi Lal was a willing listener. In fact, he took the initiative and persuaded the World Bank—in the face of a motivated farmers' agitation—to agree to cough up around $600 million for supporting power sector reforms in Haryana. The reforms law arrived in April 1998. It is broadly similar to Orissa's: establishment of an independent regulatory agency to adjust tariffs periodically and enforce performance standards; separation of generation, transmission and distribution; privatisation of distribution.

The latest entrant is Andhra Pradesh. It has been promised $1 billion by the World Bank to support its power reforms. In Andhra Pradesh, the public education that preceded the package was much more intensive than in Orissa and Haryana. Chief Minister N. Chandrababu

Naidu spent almost two years convincing the media, trade unions, politicians and people at large.

Rajasthan is the fourth state to have woken up to reforms. But Chief Minister Bhairon Singh Shekhawat has put off the needed legislation because of the impending assembly elections. Even so, Rajasthan has not been sleeping. It was the scene of an unusual experiment in 1996-97. Farmers in Rajasthan have to wait at least 10 years for a new connection. The SEB announced that if a farmer paid 10 times the normal initial charge of Rs 5,000, the power connection could be obtained in four to six weeks. These farmers would also pay four to five times the usual agricultural tariff. Surprisingly, over 60,000 farmers in the state availed of this scheme before it was discontinued because of political pressure. The consumers didn't complain, the politicians did. Benefits of the power reforms will be visible only in six to seven years. Support for them will expand if visible gains accrue to consumers in the short term. Hence, the importance of World Bank funds upfront for replacing transformers, building new substations, improving transmission systems and billing services. These can dramatically, and almost immediately, improve power supply.

Power reforms are proving contagious. Even Uttar Pradesh is negotiating for a billion dollar restructuring loan from the World Bank. But the real question is whether these reforms can be saved from the vagaries of electoral politics. They must be. The power sector consumes some 4 per cent of GDP. All of this comes from the public exchequer. If the sector is made self-sustaining, the money saved can be used for social development. India will be enlightened, literally and otherwise.

03/08/1998

◆——◆

KALYAN FOR UTTAR PRADESH?
Talking tough on power the CM shows the way ahead

The brand equity of Kalyan Singh, Uttar Pradesh's chief minister, is that he is an OBC Lodh in an upper-caste dominated BJP. His power minister, Naresh Aggarwal, epitomises the worst of Indian politics. But this duo has just struck a powerful blow for Uttar Pradesh's very survival. Faced with blackmail by 97,000 employees of the state electricity board

(UPSEB) in the wake of the Government's plans to reform and privatise the bleeding power sector, they talked tough and acted tough. The strike was withdrawn in just two days. Against all political odds, Kalyan is negotiating a huge loan with the World Bank. It could easily top $3 billion. He knows this loan, which is needed to rescue Uttar Pradesh, is itself dependent on his delivering on power-sector reforms.

Uttar Pradesh is in an awful fiscal mess, a mess that has been comprehensively analysed in a November 1998 World Bank report on the state's finances and in the February 1999 Bulletin of the Reserve Bank. The annual losses of the UPSEB amount to about Rs 1,800 crore. Subsidies are over Rs 6,000 crore, less than 10 per cent enjoyed by the poor. In 1997-98, the financial position reached its nadir. The state's tax and non-tax revenues were Rs 8,300 crore, while expenditure on interest payments and debt servicing, police, salaries of 1.8 million employees and pensions was about Rs 10,300 crore. Sixty per cent of whatever development expenditure is taking place in the state comes from the Centre and the balance from borrowings from the market, from institutions and from, of all places, the provident and insurance funds at the state's disposal. Thus, there is absolutely no way that any meaningful development can sustain itself in India's most populous state without a fundamental reform of the fiscal system.

Just as it sits on a fiscal volcano, Uttar Pradesh is also perched on a demographic time bomb. Its annual rate of job creation has to increase at least five-fold to keep pace. Its population has already touched 160 million and is growing by over four million a year. On present trends, Uttar Pradesh won't reach replacement levels of fertility of 2.1—a precursor to stabilising population growth—till well after A.D. 2100. Even Bihar will reach this transition point by 2060. Of the state's 83 districts, 31 have social and human development indicators that bring shame to this country. Its growth rate in the '90s has been a measly 3.4 per cent a year. There are parts of the state, like the Jat-dominated western region, where agricultural prosperity is striking. But what is distressing is that this prosperity is not translating itself into improvement in the quality of life indicators, particularly as they relate to the status of women. For example, there are just 840 females for every 1,000 males in this region. This fact alone should be enough to demolish the myth that poverty is the cause of Uttar Pradesh's human and social development problems.

If a poll were to be taken outside Uttar Pradesh, it is certain that there would be a unanimous vote for its break-up. But small size is no guarantee for political stability or good governance. Take Goa and Manipur. Even so, the time has come to revisit Sardar K.M. Panikkar's lucid dissent note to the report of the States Reorganisation Commission of 1955 and ask not just whether the present size of Uttar Pradesh is in the national interest but also whether the growing regional disparities within this sprawling giant can ever be addressed in the prevailing politico-administrative structure.

Uttar Pradesh's tragedy is not lack of resources. In fact, it is too richly endowed for its own good. It is being betrayed by its political class, a class that is a different species from its counterparts in other states. Even the self-styled parties of social justice—the Samajwadi Party and the BSP—do not talk the language of development or social reform. They are obsessed with political power. In this, they are totally different from their counterparts in southern and western India. One reason for this could well be that they are emulating the values and priorities of their upper-caste antagonists, who in Uttar Pradesh have themselves never made a cause of social backwardness or human deprivation. This is the essential mindset change required.

No Uttar Pradesh politician has ever cared that the state, with 18 per cent of India's poor, draws 8 per cent of the food subsidy, while Kerala with 3 per cent of the poor draws 10 per cent of the subsidy and makes that subsidy reach the needy. No Uttar Pradesh politician has ever understood why cooperatives work so well in Maharashtra, which has really no comparative advantage in sugarcane, while they flounder in Uttar Pradesh, which has all the prerequisites. The answer is simple: in Maharashtra the cooperatives are de-mocratic and professional, in Uttar Pradesh they are controlled by politicians and run by bureaucrats.

Jean Dreze has pointed out that absenteeism of teachers, protected by political patrons, is destroying the state's education system. Their attendance rate is just about a third. The challenge before the local politician is simple: remove politics from development and bring development into politics. This has happened in other states. There is no genetic or cultural reason why Uttar Pradesh should be different.

22/02/1999

———◆——◆———

UP POWER REFORMS

The UP power strike was rightly broken but sector reforms have a long way to go

The Uttar Pradesh power strike has been broken. Two individuals—the prime minister himself and his effervescent power minister—deserve kudos for not succumbing to blackmail. The minister, however, was needlessly harsh on the unions. The real culprits are their political patrons cutting across party lines. And what a delicious irony! More than 10 years ago when a proposal for privatising power distribution in Delhi was first mooted by Kautilya to the then prime minister, the man who killed it was a Congress MP acting on behalf of the employees union of Delhi's erstwhile power utility, DESU. His name: Pronindranath Rangarajan Kumaramangalam.

Power reforms in Uttar Pradesh will now continue. Some of these reforms, like the trifurcation of generation, transmission and distribution, the privatisation of distribution and the establishment of an independent regulatory commission to depoliticise the fixing of power rates, are steps in the right direction. But haste should be made slowly. Bids have been invited to privatise distribution of power in Kanpur. Other cities are to follow thereafter. This amounts to what is called "cherry picking" by which all the lucrative and easy-to-manage areas are privatised first. Cherry picking will give distribution reforms a bad name, just as the large number of dubious MoUs and sweetheart deals have done for reforms on generation.

The Uttar Pradesh initiative is part of a nationwide power and fiscal reforms programme being underwritten by the World Bank. Orissa was first off the block in 1996, followed by Andhra Pradesh and Haryana. Then came Uttar Pradesh. Rajasthan and Karnataka have also jumped in. Karnataka has gone one step further and in addition to negotiating with the World Bank, it is poised to sign on February 12 the first-ever memorandum of agreement with the Centre on power reforms. Power reforms are crucial for financial health. In a fiscally well-managed state like Karnataka, power subsidies and losses account for a third of the fiscal deficit.

However, the privatisation of distribution is no instant panacea. The mess is so deep that it is going to take at least six to seven years before some tangible impact is made. And we should not oversell competition and pri-vatisation. In fact, competition is not on the horizon at all. We privatise simply because commercial discipline can never be enforced—and more importantly, sustained—in a public sector environment. We would, however, still have to worry about rural subsidies and how best that should be provided. Andhra Pradesh's reforms have been the most hyped. But all that Chandrababu Naidu has done so far is set up two corporations and used them to borrow more for the exchequer. Haryana promised much under Bansi Lal but under O.P. Chautala reforms came unstuck. But to be fair, a good deal of financial restructuring has been effected in both states. Such restructuring which includes asset revaluation, set-offs, write-offs, provisioning and funding of staff liabilities is essential for successful privatisation.

More has happened in Orissa. The regulatory com-mission has passed three orders to reduce subsidies and enforce norms and standards. There has also been increased transparency in reporting losses. Audited and measured losses are double the reported figures and are estimated at around 48 per cent. The SEB was broken up into two companies, the Orissa Hydel Power Corporation (OHPC) and Grid Corporation of Orissa (GRIDCO) for transmission and distribution. Then the state was divided into four distribution zones and in each zone 51 per cent of GRIDCO's stake was sold to a private company with 39 per cent being retained by GRIDCO and 10 per cent in employee trusts. Three zones have been awarded to the Mumbaibased BSES and another zone to the US company AES Transpower, which has also bought 49 per cent of the Orissa Power Generation Corporation—set up in the late '80s—for Rs 603 crore.

Orissa's experience also demonstrates that since actual losses are more than reported losses, loss reductions take time to implement, and since assumptions on tariff increases are always optimistic, companies like GRIDCO will inevitably face cash shortages in the initial reform years. By March 31, 2000, GRIDCO's cash deficit will total Rs 860 crore. How this huge cash deficit is managed will determine the pace and extent of reforms both in Orissa and elsewhere. This is where sustained support from the World Bank, the Centre and other financial institutions will be crucial. What is also clear is that as part of pri-vatisation, there is a huge agenda of internal reforms within power utilities that has to be implemented.

14/02/2000

NEW LIGHT ON POWER

Karnataka's new model: public-sector generation,
private-sector distribution

When states innovate they rarely capture national headlines. In recent days, he Karnataka Government has taken two major initiatives in the power sector that have significance for the rest of the country. First, it has entered into an agreement with the Infrastructure Development and Finance Company (IDFC) for financing a 210 MW coal-based power project of the state-owned Karnataka Power Corporation (KPC) at Raichur. Second, it has cancelled a MoU entered into with a private consortium for developing the Upper Krishna hydel power project at the Almatti and Narayanapur dams and awarded the contract to the KPC. The power plant equipment supplier for these projects will be BHEL which is a strong vote for indigenous manufacturing and that belies the propaganda that reformers are anti-public sector.

The IDFC accord is a break-through because it opens up the financing of power projects by domestic financial institutions and links that financing with reforms to be carried out by the borrower states. It is this link that marks a watershed. The IDFC and a group of commercial banks will provide Rs 500 crore of the project cost of Rs 640 rore. This agreement stipulates a number of tough conditions that the state will have to fulfil within a specified time schedule. The non-fulfilment of these conditions will amount to default. For instance, the agreement comits the state to privatisation of the distribution system and forces it to clean up the balance sheets of the KPC and the Karnataka Power Transmission Corporation Ltd (KPTCL) that transmits and distributes power. Detailed obligations of KPC and KPTCL along with those of the Government are stipulated. If we can sign such agreements with the World Bank, surely we can do so with our own institutions.

IDFC, which was conceived of and set up during P. Chidambaram's tenure as finance minister in 1996-97, was established to commercialise private-sector infrastructure projects. It has made an exception in financing a government- owned company like KPC. But it is insisting that while KPC starts the project, it must disinvest its stake after the project is completed. This is based on a recognition that the public sector's great advantage lies in starting power projects but it does not have the capability of sustaining such projects commercially.

Private companies, on the other hand, cannot bear the huge risks involved in setting up power projects as we have seen to our great cost in the past few years. But such companies can operate power networks better simply because the work environment is superior and there is no political interference.

Thus, what Karnataka is putting into effect is a new model of power development—public-sector generation and private-sector distribution, with the public sector acting as a project promoter, developer and implementer and exiting in the manner of a venture capitalist when the project is up and ready. This exit is important because that is one way of generating funds that can be ploughed back for further expansion.

As far as the Upper Krishna hydel project is concerned, it is ironical that in one of his previous incarnations as state power minister, Chief Minister S.M. Krishna had approved the MoU with a private consortium in the mid-1990s. That decision was taken when there was a lot of euphoria about private investment in power—false hopes as it turned out. The private consortium whose technical expertise was no match for KPC'S had offered to develop the 1,100 MW project at about Rs 4 crore a megawatt. When KPC offered to develop this project at Rs 3 crore a megawatt and when financial institutions evinced interest in supporting the bid, Krishna had no option but to rescind his earlier decision. The fact that this project is part of a controversial inter-state complex involving irrigation as well tipped the scales in favour of a public-sector promoter. In any case, why should cheap hydel sources be privatised? Upper Krishna power will cost less than Rs 2.50 a unit.

Karnataka is sitting on another cheap hydel re-source—the 270 MW Shivasamudram project which will yield perhaps Rs 1.50-a-unit power. But the bitter Cauvery dispute with Tamil Nadu is preventing the state from harnessing this potential. The late P. Rangarajan Kumaramangalam had suggested that the Central government-owned NHPC take up hydel projects in the Cauvery basin with a total capacity of about 1,600 MW. Indeed, the most challenging task awaiting the two states is the establishment of a Cauvery basin hydro-power authority that will develop projects that do not involve any consumptive use of river water. This would be without prejudice to either state's case on the water-sharing dispute that is presently before the Supreme Court. But whether they break the shackles of the past and seize this opportunity remains to be seen.

23/10/2000

END CAPITAL PUNISHMENT
At last some light at the end of Delhi's dark tunnel

Delhi's power system has already collapsed. This has been a collective enterprise of Delhi's political class, of its consumers and of a section of the employees of the Delhi Vidyut Board (DVB). Even assuming that Delhi's problems are peculiar because of the nature of its consumption pattern—characterised by heavy summer and winter peaks—there can be no excuse for the shocking state of affairs. Nevertheless, the ills are three-fold. First, demand for electricity outstrips supply by a wide margin. The present shortage of peaking power is of the order of some 300 MW and it will probably treble by the year 2002. Eighty per cent of the capital's energy requirements are met by supplies from the northern grid. Thus, what happens in states like Uttar Pradesh, Haryana and Punjab impacts critically on the power situation in Delhi. There has been no new capacity addition in recent years and because of the old age of plants, utilisation of existing capacity is less than 50 per cent.

Second, Delhi has a level of power transmission and distribution (T&D) losses that finds no parallel in the world. In Mumbai, these losses are around 11 per cent and in Calcutta around 19 per cent. In Delhi, they average a shocking 43 per cent; in parts of the city, like sprawling east Delhi, losses are in excess of 65 per cent. Quite clearly, T&D in Delhi stands for theft and dacoity.

Third, the financial position of DVB is in a mess. It owes others Rs 6,900 crore and in turn is owed some Rs 2,900 crore. Only 1992-93 accounts have been audited so far. Its gap between revenues and operating expenses in 1997-98 exceeded Rs 850 crore. The Delhi Government gives it around Rs 400 crore per year for managing the power system, an amount that is about one-fourth of what is needed. But the DVB cannot spend the full amount.

It is against this scandalous background that the new state Government has just issued a strategy paper for reform of its power sector. The paper lays out a detailed short-term action plan aimed at managing the power situation during the summer of 1999. A lot will depend on how soon DVB will be able to add additional T&D capacity and how effectively it is able to upgrade its maintenance. But even after doing this, Delhi will have to simply buy more power from Himachal

Pradesh and from the surplus eastern grid.

The medium-term strategy is of greater significance. To enforce commercial discipline and ensure greater accountability, the strategy paper proposes to convert DVB into a number of companies: to begin with, one to handle generation and extra high-voltage transmission and about four or five to handle low voltage transmission and distribution. The distribution companies are proposed as joint ventures (JVs).

Also part of this package is the establishment of an independent electricity regulatory commission whose main task will be to depoliticise the fixing of power tariffs, act as a licensing body and enforce performance standards. This package is very much along the lines of what is being implemented by the Congress in Orissa, the Haryana Vikas Party in Haryana and the Telugu Desam Party in Andhra Pradesh. The BJP Government in Uttar Pradesh is finalising a similar restructuring programme.

Delhi will pose the maximum transition problems. DVB's 25,000-strong labour force has strong political clout. In one of his earlier avatars as a Congress labour activist, before he started preaching privatisation from the BJP's pulpit, Power Minister P.R. Kumaramangalam opposed reforms as a union leader of DESU (DVB's predecessor). But labour can be convinced. Resistance will really come from consumers and their political patrons.

There are four types of thieves: those who draw more power than they are entitled to, those who get their meters "fixed", those who live in unauthorised colonies and cannot be given a legal connection and those who live in electrified colonies but do not take legal connections. Probably just about a fourth of the theft is in jhuggie-jhopdis. The bulk is by commercial, industrial and relatively better-off consumers in the approximately 1,255 "unauthorised" colonies. Breakdowns are maximum in areas where theft is at a peak.

Chief Minister Sheila Dikshit has her work cut out. The regulatory commission must start straightaway. Legislative sanction for the reforms must be obtained by March-April. The JV distribution companies must be in place in the next 12-15 months. A World Bank loan must be negotiated, like the other states have done, so as to get some immediate funding for modernising and expanding the T&D system.

Most critically, the war on theft must also commence in right earnest. Connections must be sanctioned on demand. Tapping of electricity by hook is already banned. This has to be strictly enforced. The strategy paper suggests that a grace period of four weeks be given to all consumers to take legal connections. Within this period, DVB should provide metered connections. The paper also suggests that DVB be given adequate police support. It is in such a tough and un-compromising anti-theft campaign that the true mettle of the Delhi Government will be tested.

01/02/1999

VI

Partisan Politics :
Prayer to a Jogi

This is a section that many wanted more of, but where I was un willing to oblige. I saw my core competence in economics and did not believe that I would add value to political issues unless I got into personalities—which I was loath to do. There are five articles on Atal Behari Vajpayee and each one of them drew a lot of comment from both within the Congress and the BJP. Readers applauded my sense of fairness but my party colleagues were unhappy that I was publicly praising the Prime Minister. Each of these articles was born not out of malice but out of a great sense of disappointment at a basically good man's failure to live up to expectations. I am told that the Prime Minister himself took these pieces in his stride and was bemused by their style and substance. I also have a piece in defence of P.V. Narasimha Rao with whom I worked very closely for 100 days in late 1991. Although I was summarily sacked from his staff and shunted off to the Planning Commission in October 1991 for reasons that are still mysterious, I felt that it was my duty to defend him at a time when he was under attack from all quarters and when his reputation had been all but besmirched. This section also contains a tribute to Ram Jethamalani for having had the courage to get the Urban Land Ceiling Act, 1976 scrapped when he was Minister for Urban Development. Mr. Jethamalani caused me endless embarrassment by his well-meaning acknowledgement in Parliament of my small contributions toward making this happen. His speech was good for my ego, but was not calculated to enhance my credibility within my own party.

HINDUTVA TO HINDUJA
Sinha's daydream budget: banking
on unreliable NRIs and unrealistic numbers

The reformer in Yashwant Sinha did come out ever so creepingly on the evening of June 1. For the first time in 50 years, a finance minister making a budget speech has had the courage to use the dreaded P word: privatisation. Sinha's statement that government stake in all non-strategic PSUs will be reduced to 26 per cent should be welcomed. The modalities of how this will be done and how the privatisation proceeds will be used should be spelt out soon. India's fundamental fiscal problem is that debt servicing consumes 46 per cent of the Centre's revenues. The only way to solve this is to use privatisation proceeds to retire debt.

Like Manmohan Singh in July 1991, Sinha has also mustered some courage to cut the fertiliser subsidy. However, he has kept more undeserved concessions, like the Rs 400 crore sugar subsidy, intact. He has also shown great political wisdom in continuing many ini-tiatives launched in P. Chidambaram's two budgets. Those, in turn, took off from the six Manmohan budgets. Continuity is here, alive and for real. But barring a few flourishes, this is a pusillanimous budget. Sinha has lost the chance to usher in another era of big-bang reforms. The budget completely ig-nores the fallout of Pokhran. Here was an opportunity of sharing the Government's assessment of the costs of the nuclear tests.

The budget assumes that net external assistance will double in 1998-99. This is untenable. Sinha has ignored the economic consequences of nuclearisation, except in his efforts at wooing fickle NRIs—like those perennial all-party favourites, the Hindujas. In any case, NRIs must remain the only species wanting sops and incentives to invest in their home country. The budget numbers are deceptive. Rs 1,600 crore of the Rs 2,300 crore step-up in the outlay for education is on account of higher education. Our priority is primary education. In the power sector, the plan outlay for PSUs has been hiked from Rs 6,400 crore in 1997-98 to Rs 9,000 crore in 1998-99. But budget support is actually down from Rs 2,500 crore to Rs 2,220 crore. In 1997-98, power PSUs were expected to raise Rs 4,500 crore outside the budget; actually they could raise just Rs 3,900 crore. This year, Sinha expects them to raise an extremely unrealistic Rs 6,800 crore. The story repeats itself in other infrastructure sectors like coal, oil, roads and telecom. In 1997-98, only 80 per cent of the funds allocated to infrastructure was spent. Thus absorptive capacity and structural bottle-necks are the real issue, not lack of funds. The budget is silent on this.

After seven years, lobbies have once again resurfaced and dictated wholly arbitrary duty changes in chemicals, steel and other industries. There are now 12 rates of customs duty and nine rates of excise duty with numerous concessions. This reverses the earlier trend towards simplification. Sinha has announced a special additional duty (SAD) of 8 per cent on select imports. SAD would have made sense if customs duty had itself declined. It has not. Actually, SAD works out not to 8 per cent but to between 12 and 15 per cent—since it is to be computed on the aggregate of the assessable value and the basic, special and additional customs duties. This is in addition to the 15 per cent extra protection industry has got over the past year because of the rupee depreciation. The effect of the rupee depreciation gets eroded with SAD. And any hike in industrial tariffs is anti-exports and, more important, anti-farmer. Also, by exempting traders from SAD, the finance minister is getting his signals crossed. He should be protecting manufacturing, not trading.

Reforms have now moved into the phase where parliamentary consensus is imperative. The repeal of the Urban Land Ceiling Act depends on the approval of at least two state governments and, subsequently, Parliament. Opening the insurance industry, even in the halfhearted manner proposed in the budget, depends on Parliament amending the LIC and GIC Acts and passing the Insurance Regulatory Authority Bill. Regrettably, the finance minister was completely silent on the pending Companies Bill. It can transform the corporate sector.

The budget's greatest risk lies in its inflationary potential. The rate of inflation, after being stable at around 5 per cent for most of 1998, has jumped to 6.35 per cent over the past 60 days. There will be new pressure on the inflation rate on account of the additional Rs 8,300 crore of excise and customs levies. In fact, with higher inflation and a depreciating exchange rate, Sinha's revenue collection targets may well be met. But at what social cost?

Finally, the budget speech was tall on Sinha's concern for the rural economy. Yet, the budget allocation for small, rural and agro-industry remains unchanged at Rs 1,016 crore. That for special rural employment pro-grammes has increased only marginally, from Rs 3,900 crore to Rs 4,000 crore. Sadly, no plans were unveiled to initiate the transfer of central rural development funds—totalling some Rs 10,000 crore in 1998-99—directly to elected zilla parishad bodies. An opportunity to revolutionise rural India was missed.

———◆——◆———

NEW CONVERT TO REFORMS
The BJP's changed thinking on insurance and patents augurs well

The two far-reaching decisions taken at the Union Cabinet meeting on November 23' show that power moderates, just as the absence of power unhinges. Exactly a year ago the BJP, then in the Opposition, had cussedly torpedoed P. Chidambaram's efforts to liberalise the insurance industry and end the monopoly of the Life Insurance Corporation (LIC) and the General Insurance Corporation (GIC). The BJP wanted Chidambaram to give a categorical assurance that no foreign investment would be permitted in the insurance sector, an assurance that the then finance minister rightly refused to give. Now, the very same BJP has decided to open up the insurance industry and offer up to 40 per cent equity to foreigners.

Again, over a year ago, a strange combination of George Fernandes of the Samata Party, Ashok Mitra of the CPI(M) and Murli Manohar Joshi of the BJP prevailed upon then prime minister I.K. Gujral not to carry out changes in the Patents Act in keeping with our obligations to the World Trade Organisation (WTO) and in keeping with what our research system needs to make it more user-oriented. Now, a government in which Fernandes and Joshi are leading lights has done exactly that. Welcome as they are, the two cabinet decisions are only the beginning. Relevant bills will now have to be introduced in Parliament. The Congress could be reasonably expected to support these bills.

Instant results from the opening of the insurance industry must not be expected. The most immediate effect will be that the Americans will be happy. We will gain powerful lobbyists on our behalf in Washington DC, where insurance companies are enormously influential. Once the bills are passed, it will take another year to actually give out the first licences to private companies.

Even so, we can look forward to more attractive insurance schemes, particularly in health and pensions. Life insurance and provident fund coverage is good although it falls far short of what is needed. For example, there are about 100 million life policies— roughly a fifth of the insurable population. Similarly, there are about 25 million workers covered by provident fund—less than a tenth of the workforce. A paltry two million have health insurance and a minuscule one million have pension policies.

In the long term, more money could be mobilised for infrastructure projects. Today, out of its annual investible surplus of about Rs 20,000 crore, LIC allocates Rs 5,000 crore per year for water supply, housing and power projects. Each private company would, in about eight years time, be in a position to generate a similar amount annually to be invested in infrastructure. Now that competition is imminent, LIC and GIC also have to be radically restructured. After a long hiatus, Chidambaram constituted the boards of these companies with eminent citizens and professionals as a first step to making them autonomous. This must be consolidated.

The Indian Patents Act, 1970, confers only process patents, that is on the method of manufacture, and not product patents in research-intensive industries like pharmaceuticals and agro-chemicals. The lack of product patents has enabled Indian companies to do what they call "innovative reverse engineering" but what the Americans, the Germans and others call "patent-busting". Initially Indian drug companies like Ranbaxy actively fought against changes in the Patents Act. But when Ranbaxy became a major exporter and a global investor and began to entertain visions of growth through R&D, it became an enthusiastic proponent of the very changes. Other drug firms like Dr Reddy's Labs are also in the same boat. According to the WTO agreement, we have to amend the Patents Act to allow for product patents before January 1, 2005. Till then, we have to open a "mailbox" into which all companies will apply for product patents in India. The mailbox is akin to the old industrial licensing system. It will establish priority dates and the applications being made will be examined for patentability.

After examination, such companies must be given exclusive marketing rights (EMRs) in lieu of product patents. The first EMR in drugs and chemicals is unlikely to be granted before January 1, 2002. The EMR will be valid up to January 1, 2005. In this period no other company can market that product in India. Initially we thought we could get away by allowing for the mailbox and EMRs through a government order. But such is our reputation for non-transparency that we have been forced by the world community to make this provision explicit in our laws before April 19, 1999.

The BJP's volte face is commendable. But while announcing these cabinet decisions the finance minister, in a needless fit of reform bravado, also declared that the Government is contemplating advancing the date for introduction of product patents to January 1, 2000. No doubt this will please the Americans. But it is ironical that a party wedded to "calibrated globalisation" is seeking to curtail a 10-year transition period won through hard bargaining at the WTO to five years. Clearly there is no convert more zealous than the neoconvert.

· 07/12/1998

THERE IS A CONTINUITY
The BJP pushes through bills drafted by the UF regime

Suddenly, it is bill season in parliament. Insurance has been denationalised. A new Foreign Exchange Management Act has replaced the dreaded FERA. New legislation to stimulate private investment in the mining industry has been passed. A bill to amend the Companies Act so as to protect the interests of investors and bring about greater transparency in company accounts is being brought forward. The Government has also announced its intention to introduce legislation to facilitate quick industrial revival and restructuring. A constitutional amendment to have a single, divisible tax pool that would increase the states' share of the Centre's tax collections to 29 per cent has also been promised.

The BJP can legitimately claim credit. Equally, the Congress is justified in claiming that the BJP's achievements are its own. But the truth is that these bills are the legacy of the 1996-97 United Front (UF) government. Many of these bills were actually either drafted by or spearheaded by its finance minister P. Chidambaram.

Barring the so-called "dream budget" of February 1997 which was to be later termed "the nightmare budget"—both appellations being totally off-the-mark—the UF government has not got the credit it deserves. It unclogged the reforms process that had slowed down in the later years of P. V. Narasimha Rao. In telecom, it was the UF government that got the Telecom Regulatory Authority of India in place and provided the fillip to the launch of private telecom services. Over 25 agreements for private investment in the oil and gas industry were finalised and signed and a whole new policy for oil exploration got introduced. Its most momentous decision was to abolish the subsidy on diesel and announce a phased dismantling of subsidies on LPG and kerosene.

The UF got some private power projects off the ground and brought forward legislation to establish an independent Central electricity regulatory commission and to attract private investment in transmission, both of which were later pushed forward by the BJP. The framework for private investment in roads and ports was finalised in early 1997. If disinvestment and privatisation have wider acceptability today, it is thanks to the credibility and work of the Disinvestment Commission that was set up in August 1996. Murasoli Maran as industry minister carried out the very first sale of a public-sector unit.

It was the UF that courageously negotiated with the WTO to phase out quantitative limits on imports by 2002-3. The commissioning of the national securities depository in November 1996 has revolutionised capital markets. A radical pro-poor restructuring of the public distribution sys- tem was effected in February 1997 when, for the first time, the concept of below-the-poverty-line and above-the-poverty-line families was introduced across the country to determine access to ration shops. Irrigation received an investment boost, perhaps reflecting the personal predilections of its first prime minister. And if the budgets of July 1996 and February 1997 are re-read today, what will stand out is the extraordinary emphasis given to science and technology. In foreign policy, the special focus on neighbours was a hallmark, reflected most vividly in the historic water-sharing agreement signed with Bangladesh.

To be sure, the UF had major shortcomings. It lacked a dominant core that could impose a discipline and give it coherence. The most disastrous episode during its tenure was the manner in which it accepted and implemented the recommendations of the Fifth Pay Commission. In its defence it should be said that not a single political leader expressed public opposition to the Commission's recommendations. But history cannot forgive I.K. Gujral and Chidambaram for the abject manner in which they caved in to pressure from their political colleagues and to blackmail from employee unions. True, neither the Congress nor the BJP would have behaved any differently. In fact, the BJP went one step ahead and conferred wholly unwarranted benefits to all pensioners by linking the basic pension to 50 per cent of the revised pay scales on a retrospective basis.

The UF is unmourned and unsung today. Some of its leading lights like Chidambaram are in political wilderness. Some like Chandrababu Naidu and Maran have made common cause with the BJP. Some like Jaipal Reddy are in the Congress, along with those like Arjun Singh, N.D. Tiwari and Madhavrao Scindia who were with the UF initially. Others like Mulayam Singh Yadav, who played a crucial role in pushing reforms in telecom and oil, want to disown their pragmatic past. The communist parties, who propped up the UF, want to forget the reforms record even as they wax eloquent on the collegial and transparent manner in which decisions were taken. But when an objective history of the '90s is written, the Congress will be given credit for initiating reforms and breaking old mindsets, the UF for taking these reforms further and giving them a new momentum and the BJP for having the foresight to swallow its slogans and build on what the Congress and the UF launched. Who runs away with the credit is immaterial. India has gained, and that is what counts.

27/12/1999

◆———◆———◆

ACT AND QUICKLY
With the budget the BJP's pseudo-swadeshi is dead

The dust is slowly settling on the last budget of this century. The budget belied the worst fears and the darkest worries. Hence the initial reaction of the markets was more than enthusiastic. Undoubtedly, there has been some manipulation. Yashwant Sinha has transferred a fiscal burden of around 1.25 per cent of GDP in 1999-2000 to the states by shifting 75 per cent of the liability of small savings to them. But this makes no difference to the overall fiscal deficit of the Centre and the states.

Sinha's interim budget of February 1991 had proposed a new

Bharat Bachat Bank to take over the small savings portfolio and to that extent reduce the Government's fiscal deficit. Those were the days when the IMF was breathing down our necks. This time too he tried to peddle this idea but mercifully the committee he appointed to rework the treatment of small savings in the Union budget shot it down Sinha has also benefited from statistical changes introduced in the estimation of the nation's income by the Central Statistical Organisation, which has jacked up the GDP figures by 10-15 per cent. His mundane allocations do not match his lofty intentions. The budget allocations for rural employment and anti-poverty programmes and for the mid-day meal scheme for primary schools is actually down in 1999-2000 even in nominal terms.

But to be fair, steps like the overhaul of the excise-duty structure, the attempt to make productive use of private gold wealth, the incentives to equity-oriented mutual funds, the write-offs to facilitate corporate mergers and demergers and the slew of measures to promote housing should be unreservedly welcomed. Sinha should also be congratulated for not succumbing to protectionist lobbies as he had done in 1998. The 34.5 per cent increase in the plan allocation for agriculture and allied activities must be commended even though this increase gets magnified because in the previous year actual expenditure was around 72 per cent of the budget estimate. Like in his previous budget, the finance minister has also rightly stressed "strategic sales"—a euphemism for privatisation, something that should come naturally to the BJP. But the track record so far has been disappointing.

For Kautilya, the most significant feature of the budget is that it commits the BJP irrevocably to the reforms and liberalisation programme launched in 1991 by the Congress and expanded by the United Front in 1996-97. By talking of phasing down of customs duties to Asian levels, albeit by 2004, instead of the earlier target of 2000, Sinha is continuing the globalising process, whatever be the RSS rhetoric. Like P. Chidambaram before him, Sinha has proposed an expenditure reforms commission. This is of paramount importance. Reorientation of public expenditure of both the Centre and the states is the very essence of economic reforms. The combined fiscal deficit in 1998-99 is probably around 7 per cent of GDP (using the new GDP num-bers). This has to be reduced to 3-4 per cent of GDP. The combined revenue deficit in 1998-99 will be about 4 per cent of GDP. This must, as the finance minister says, be phased out over the next four years.

But it cannot be done without a major political initiative. Chidambaram tried to persuade Jaswant Singh to head the commission. Jaswant was supportive but expressed his inability to take on a public stance. Sinha could either set up a committee of chief ministers drawn from different political parties under the chairmanship of that patriarch, Jyoti Basu, or get together a group under the stewardship of a veteran like Bhairon Singh Shekhawat or N.D. Tiwari. Sinha has also promised a discussion paper on the second generation of reforms. This is a good idea but he must not forget that most of the second generation reforms are critically dependent on legislative action. This is where the Government is demonstrating monumental lethargy, incompetence and cussedness. For example, Chidambaram got a team of economists, lawyers, chartered accountants, administrators and industry managers to draft a new Companies Bill to replace the 1956 Act. This bill is floundering since the minister concerned is from the AIADMK. The Insurance Bill is with the Standing Committee where only its chairman, Murli Deora of the Congress, is showing any interest. The bill to replace FERA has got through the Standing Committee only because of two former finance ministers.

If any meaningful reforms of the banking sector have to take place, government equity in the banks has to come down to below 50 per cent. For this, parliamentary approval is needed. If the Industrial Disputes Act and the Sick Industries Companies Act have to be amended, if a statutory ceiling has to be introduced on the growth of public debt, if the coal industry is to benefit from private investment, then again new legislation has to be passed by Parliament. Sadly very few MPs appreciate the urgency of new economic legislation. Worse, neither Atal Bihari Vajpayee nor Sinha has shown any enthusiasm in crafting a legislative consensus. Kautilya finds great merit in Jayalalitha's suggestion of a special session of Parliament devoted exclusively to passing important economic bills. Kautilya hastens to add that this support to the puratchi thalaivi has no political overtones nor is it a case of Iyengar blood being thicker than water. A good idea must transcend politics.

15/03/1999

NOW TO WORK
A 10-point, pre-Y2K budget agenda for the new PM

An exceptionally long and acrimonious election campaign is over. Now it is time for serious governance. The first 100 days w:ll set the trend.

First, crucial price increases have to take place. The oil subsidy has ballooned to almost Rs 5,000 crore thanks largely to increasing global prices of oil in the last six months. Diesel prices have to be increased by Rs 2-3 a litre, kerosene prices by at least Rs 2 a litre and LPG prices by at least Rs 30 a cylinder. Similarly, the economic cost of supplying wheat to ration shops is slightly over Rs 8 a kg whereas it is sold to "below-the-poverty line" families at Rs 2.50 a kg. The subsidy was not to exceed 50 per cent but it has. Likewise, sugar prices have to go up by about Re 1 a kg.

Second, the Disinvestment Commission has to be given a fresh and expanded mandate. The 37 strategic sales recommended by the earlier commission have to be carried out in a time-bound, professional manner. The Finance Ministry must be given sole responsibility for all privatisation programmes once the Cabinet gives its approval. Revenues must be used to retire debt.

Third, critical legislations must get passed in the winter session of Parliament. These include the bills to liberalise insurance and amend FERA. The government will have to decide the fate of the comprehensive New Companies Bill that has been awaiting approval since November 1997. Some other bills should at least be introduced in the winter session. These include bills to denationalise the coal industry and banks, facilitate quick industrial revival and foster congenial industrial relations.

Fourth, key commitments made in recent budgets should be met. Committees to formulate a competition policy and for revamping economic statistics have to get going. All rural development funds must flow directly to elected panchayats. An expenditure reforms commission, promised by both P. Chidambaram and Yashwant Sinha, to evolve a national consensus on public expenditure must be set up. At the same time, the Finance Ministry should issue a white paper on a Fiscal Responsibility Act.

Fifth, the new telecom policy has to be put into operation. The autonomy of the Telecom Regulatory Authority of India has to be fully respected and be seen to be respected. Steps have to be taken to begin the corporatisation of the Department of Telecommunications at all levels. Also, 51 per cent foreign equity in telecom companies should be permitted. This is the only way we will get new investment and technology. A number of investment and contracting decisions in power, oil and gas, highways and airports are awaiting finalisation and should be expedited.

Sixth, a pragmatic and proactive negotiating breif for the forthcoming WTO ministerial meeting at Seattle has to be finalised. We should be fully involved in all new negotiations but also continue to insist that commitments made by all countries in the Uruguay Round be fulfilled as pledged and also raise our special concerns on the protection of bioresources, the non-linkage between environment and trade and other issues. We have positions in common with the Americans vis-a-vis the Europeans and in common with the Cairns Group of agripowers vis-a-vis the US and the European Union. Our position, therefore, has to be nuanced.

Seventh, we must sign the CTBT linking the signature to withdrawal of curbs on some of our research institutions and linking our ratification to ratification by the US and China. This will unclog the flow of some $2-3 billion and bolster our global standing. The dialogue with Pakistan to negotiate the details of the Lahore MoU on verifiable confidence-building measures has to be resumed. A debate on autonomy to Jammu and Kashmir has to be initiated.

Eighth, investment has to be revived. For this, real interest rates have to start moving downwards with a 4-5 per cent destination. To do this, the government has simply to reduce the guaranteed 12 per cent return to 10 per cent on small savings, postal and other special deposits and on provident funds and transfer all the small savings collections to states. Freeing consumer industries from the clutches of small-scale reservation will boost exports. A collaborative National Manufacturing Competitiveness Council should be set up—we cannot survive by being just a service economy. A new textiles policy should be announced.

Ninth, the nuclear doctrine needs to be discussed in Parliament, and the nature, size and cost of the minimum, credible deterrent worked out. Kargil has thrown up the need to modernise our armed forces, even as we engage in diplomacy and dialogue. How the defence (plus nuclear) budget should be made to stabilise at 3 per cent of GDP is an issue that needs very careful and urgent analysis.

Finally, the new prime minister has to signal a desire for consensus by, for example, setting up two "wise-men" groups, one of former prime ministers and another of former finance ministers to guide the government. A meeting of the National Development Council in a state capital will not only reflect changes in the polity but also be a step in making economic management participative. A National Population Commission should be established to provide a political impetus to faster demographic transition in north India. Planning must be focused on the backward regions and on the expansion of social infrastructure.

09/10/1999

◆──────◆

CRY NOT FOR ULCRA
After seven years prospects for the repeal of a bad law brighten

Never judge a policy by its intent but always assess it by its consequences. Nothing could illustrate this more vividly than the Urban Land (Ceiling & Regulation) Act of 1976. The objectives of ULCRA, as it is usually referred to, were laudable. It was to prevent the concentration of urban land and to promote housing for the poor in cities. But in actual practice ULCRA has reduced the supply of land, inflated land prices, served as a dampener on housing and construction activities and impeded the timely closure of sick companies in places like Mumbai, Calcutta, Ahmedabad and Kanpur in a manner that would protect the interests of labour and generate new economic activity. Clearly, ULCRA is bad law and worse economics.

Under the Act, applications amounting to about 10 lakh acres have been received. After "scrutiny" and "disposal", phrases associated with discretionary powers that fuel corruption, the amount of vacant land in excess of ULCRA's ceilings has been whittled down to five lakh acres. The grease-intensity of UL-CRA has been further increased by "ex-empting" about one-fourth of the five lakh acres on various grounds. Less than nine per cent of the 5.5 lakh acres—about 38,000 acres—has physically been acquired. Housing schemes have been initiated on 2,000 acres. Theoretically, over 40 million houses could be built on the five lakh acres of excess vacant land.

In October 1992 , P.V. Narasimha Rao's cabinet first considered liberalisation of ULCRA. It buried the amendments by referring them to a group of ministers. In July 1995, Rao's cabinet considered the matter once again but this time it went one better in delay tactics and said that the matter must be discussed by all political parties. Then came H.D. Deve Gowda, who as chief minister had actually got the Karnataka Assembly to pass a resolution asking the Centre to repeal ULCRA. But as prime minister, he set up another committee to suggest amendments to ULCRA. The committee submitted its report in April 1997 by which time Deve Gowda had fallen.

I.K. Gujral's cabinet considered ULCRA changes in July 1997 and decided to refer it to a group of ministers headed by Murasoli Maran. Maran suggested a large number of amendments which were considered by Gujral's cabinet in October 1997, only to see yet another postponement. A frustrated Kautilya recalls reminding Gujral that he had piloted ULCRA in Parliament in 1976 as minister for works and housing and that he now had a historic opportunity of proving Mark Antony ("The evil that men do lives after them") wrong. Gujral was vastly amused and promised to get it done. His cabinet met once again on November 13, 1997, but for some reason Gujral lost his nerve at the crucial moment. It was left to Maran, P. Chidambaram and S. Jaipal Reddy to push through the repeal. But Gujral's government fell before a repeal bill could be introduced in Parliament.

Mercifully, the BJP appointed an iconoclast as its minister for urban development. In June 1998, Ram Jethmalani introduced a bill in the Lok Sabha for ULCRA's repeal. It subsequently went to the Standing Committee on Urban and Rural Development for examination. The 45-member committee submitted its report on December 21, 1998, recommending repeal. There were only two dissenters. One of them, Shabana Azmi, wrote that the committee was right in concluding ULCRA had been a failure but wrong in asking for its repeal. Jethmalani's ordinance to repeal ULCRA has to be converted into a bill and approved by Parliament. Even if Parliament repeals it, some state governments like the one in Mumbai are planning to have their own ULCRAs for "obvious" reasons. Jethmalani has to spearhead a campaign to combat this. He must also canvass for a tax on vacant land to encourage its use.

In Parliament itself, the argument will inevitably be made that it would be unfair to do away with ceilings on urban land while keeping ceilings on farm land. This is a shibboleth. Urban land and farm land are fundamentally different. In the language of economics, the supply of farm land is " inelastic", while the supply of urban land is "elastic". Ceilings on farm land have a strong redistributive element. Even though farm-ceiling laws have been circumvented, some 53 lakh acres have been distributed to about 54 lakh rural families. This is not an insignificant achievement. The capacity utilisation of land has not reduced in this process, unlike ULCRA's impact. The supply of farm land is fixed, while that of urban land is flexible in addition to having a vertical dimension.

Given the acute pressure on land in rural India and the lack of unambiguous evidence to suggest that productivity in large farms is higher than in small farms, it is more equitable and efficient to create a market in rural land. As a first step, the lease market for farm land should be freed. But this has to be accompanied by a system of up-to-date land records, something in which modern information technology (IT) can be of great value.

18/01/1999

◆———◆

SINHA DOES A JAYASURIYA
Sinha rediscovers himself with a bang after 10 years.
But let us not go overboard.

How the wheel of time turns. Exactly a decade ago, Yashwant Sinha was set to go down in India's economic history as the only finance minister not to have presented a regular budget. It was the time when his prime minister, Chandra Shekhar, had run foul of the Congress which withdrew its support from the outside, thereby forcing Sinha to seek a vote-on-account.

Sinha had prepared a reformist budget then and had initiated steps to seek the safety of the IMF to rescue India from an unprecedented financial crisis that was staring it in the face of a burgeoning current account deficit—our version of a currency crisis that was to strike east Asia six years later. But that was not to be. It was left to the P.V. Narasimha Rao-Manmohan Singh duo to rescue India from complete collapse in

June-July 1991 and subsequently put it onthe path to economic recovery and expansion. Sinha moved to more saffron pastures but even he would not have imagined that a decade later he would be presenting his fourth budget in his new avatar, a budget that has greatly boosted sentiment, given him and his Government a whole new image among investors, usiness-menand the media but whose impact on fundamentals will unfold only with time and is based on a wide array of assumptions.

The period 1991-2001 has been remarkable for the consensus that has emerged on the direction of economic policy. Compulsion triggered the 1991 economic reforms but gradually conviction has taken over. Whatever the rhetoric of political parties when they are out of power, the fact remains that the United Front (UF) boldly carried forward what the Congress had started and then the BJP stepped in where theUF left off. The essential validity of the Rao-Manmohan-P. Chidambaramline hasnowbeenwell and truly established. Moreover, there is not one state government today which is not following that line of economic thinking and practice. West Bengal and Kerala may think they are different but in reality they are not.

There is, thus, a fundamental agreement among those in power in the country on how economic policy should be conducted. There is no difference between a Vilasrao Deshmukh, an N. Chandrababu Naidu, a Keshubhai Patel, an O.P. Chautala, a Digivijay Singh, a Rajnath Singh or an M. Karunanidhi. Even Buddhadev Bhattacharya is talking the language of these chief ministers. Some are better managers thanothers. But all chief ministers today are on the same wavelength and that wavelength is the same as that of theCentral Government. Of course, there is aproblem of posturing. The Congress opposes power reforms in Andhra Pradesh where it is outof power but pursues them vigorously in Karnataka where it is in power. The BJP is aggressively reformist in Uttar Pradesh where it rules but opposes the same reforms in Rajasthan where it is in the Opposition. In a sharply polarised parliamenta·y democracysuchas ours, where youstand onanissue dependson where you sit. But that should not detract from the robustness of the consensus that exists, cutting across the political spectrum among those in power. What this shows, however, is the need now to craft a consensus among leaders of the Opposition in various state assemblies by, for example, coopting them as special invitees to the National Development Council.

While a consensus has emerged, sadly successive governments at the Centre have not leveraged it proactively. No government sees it fit to consult opposition parties except when there is a crisis. Sinha's budget contains many worthwhile ideas the future of which depends onParliament approving new legislation. But if the past is any guide, what will happen is that the new legislation will be introduced, set positions will be taken and no effort will be made by the government of the day to reach out to the other side. US President George Bush is building a pressure group of governors of different states in support of his economic policy. Nothing but sheer lethargy has prevented a critical mass of chief ministers being built up in support of sensible economic policies. Reforms have long ceased to be merely technocratic solutions. They have now entered an intensely political phase. Indeed, the second-generation reforms that Sinha has talked about depend crucially on legislative backing and action by the states. But the state budgets, in which the real action has to take place, do not attract the same attention that the Central budget does.

Sinha's fourth budget has been widely applauded and rightly so even if he missed opportunities for new initiatives like a food-for-work programme. But economic management is more than a one-day match. Growth deceleration and investment famine, the twin challenges confronting the macro-economy, have to be dealt with resolutely, collectively and on a sustained basis. The budget only provides the enabling framework.

12/03/2001

GET UP MR ABV

Unsolicited tips from the enemy to a beleaguered PM

Whether the results of the recent assembly elections write the epitaph for his Government is entirely dependent on Atal Bihari Vajpayee himself. Local factors did play an important role in the rout of the BJP in Rajasthan, Madhya Pradesh and Delhi. But underpinning them was the inflation issue—the unprecedented increase in the prices of many essential commodities since the BJP came to power at the Centre in mid-March, the absolute lethargy with which the Union Government responded to this astronomical price hike and the insensitive ridiculing of spiralling prices by various BJP leaders during the election campaign.

The seeds of disaster were sown in early May itself with the statement by the finance minister that he did not believe in controlling inflation at the cost of growth. This betrayed a certain mindset that was to prove extremely costly. Yashwant Sinha's lacklustre budget was not just a gigantic let-down. Worse, it implicitly assumed an inflation rate of 8-8.5 per cent in 1998-99, a doubling of the 1997-98 figure. Here was a finance minister who was sending out a signal that he would not be an anti-inflation hawk like his predecessors. Till mid-November, money supply was increasing at a disastrously high annualised rate of over 20 per cent. The Government announced an anti-inflation package of sorts in the third week of October. Why it did not do so earlier, say in July when the inflationary trends were clear, is a mystery.

The prime minister has never shown any interest in economics. To compound the problem, his top bureaucratic adviser is a foreign service officer busier in managing the global fallout of Pokhran than in troubleshooting on economic policy. To make matters worse, Vajpayee has little confidence in his finance minister. In any administration, the finance minister is the sutradhar of economic policy. Manmohan Singh and P. Chidambaram enjoyed the fullest support of their prime ministers. But the Vajpayee-Sinha relationship is different. The reform-oriented finance minister has not done a bad job. But he is hamstrung because of his lack of chemistry with the prime minister and his advisers.

If Vajpayee wants to restore confidence in his economic agenda, he must immediately find an honourable exit policy for his finance minister who could, more usefully, be a shadow chief minister of Bihar. Vajpayee might be tempted to appoint his old favourite Jaswant Singh. This will certainly improve style if not substance, English if not economics in North Block. But to make a deeper impact the prime minister must take a leaf out of P.V. Narasimha Rao's book and appoint a non-political person of the highest intellectual calibre—like C. Rangarajan—as Sinha's successor. He should also make his principal secretary a full-time national security adviser and find another incumbent more adept in economic and administrative matters.

Vajpayee must personally craft a legislative consensus on many key economic issues. A large number of bills are pending in Parliament which the Congress cannot, in its right mind, object to. But it is all a matter of ego massaging and consultations. In spite of the electoral debacle, Vajpayee enjoys personal appeal and the office of the prime minister is, after all, the office of the prime minister. He must reach out to build support for economic reforms that depend on Parliament's nod—like the opening of the insurance industry, the repeal of the Urban Land Ceiling Act, the passage of the new Companies Bill and so on.

Similarly, while Vajpayee does not need Parliament's approval for bringing a finality to the Jaswant Singh-Strobe Talbott talks, he must take political parties into confidence and push ahead on CTBT and FMCT. Sentiment on India will improve considerably if this happens. The prime minister must also push ahead with privatisation. The BJP remains the only political party not ideologically hung-up on a public sector. The recent disinvestment in the Container Corporation of India was a qualified success. It would have been better if the retail investor had been given an option. But no matter, there is still time. It is not only public-sector shares that must be offered to the public. Now is the time to disinvest the Government's equity in private-sector companies and banks as well.

The prime minister must put his full weight behind initiatives to ac-celerate reforms in infrastructure. The power minister has performed well. But there are major issues in petroleum, telecom, coal and surface transport that need to be addressed. He should also put an end to his penchant for announcing "packages". He must find people with an obsession for detail, as much as a flair for generating headlines. Finally, Vajpayee must reincarnate himself as a communicator, a role in which he has few peers, appealing directly to the people extempore in Hindi on the need to push reforms faster. The prime minister can either retreat into a shell or join the battle. As a political functionary opposed to the BJP, Kautilya hopes for the former. As somebody concerned with the pace of reforms, however, Kautilya prays for the latter.

Vajpayee's problems on economic policy have arisen not out of the compulsions of coalition politics but due to his laziness and timidity. General elections appear imminent in 1999. Before they come Vajpayee still has a chance, however slim, of leaving his imprint on India's economic history.

14/12/1998

VAJPAYEE'S THIRD WAVE

In his Varaha avatar he has to become a statesman

Atal Bihari Vajpayee is back in his thirdinnings. Tough decisions await him as Kautilya had detailed two weeks ago. He has already fired the first salvo by increasing the price of diesel. But whether he will stick out remains to be seen. He demonstrated boldness by giving the green signal for Pokhran-II in May 1998. Then he went into a deep slumber and woke up only when skyrocketing onion prices caused a debacle for his party in the November 1998 assembly elections. It was only then that he embarked on his reformist zeal. He allowed Kargil to develop but during the war he showed unusual clarity by laying down the bottom line—no crossing of the LoC. His relationship with his ministers was curious, to say the least. He allowed Ram Jethmalani to boldly push the repeal of the Urban Land Ceiling Regulation Act but refused to deal with a recalcitrant Jagmohan. He allowed his office to engage in shadow-boxing with the finance minister.

All in all, while his first 13-day stint was too short, his second 13-month tenure presented a very mixed picture. Perhaps, this is being unfair to Vajpayee who has never had a reputation for hard work, for interest in economic policy or for attention to detail. Vajpayee likes to think of himself as a Nehruvian but is really more in the Ronald Reagan mould. This need not be a disadvantage since Reagan actually turned out to be one of America's greatest presidents. But to emulate him, Vajpayee needs a change in style.

First, Vajpayee must not misread his 1999 victory. His success contains the seeds of the problems for his party. True, the V-factor worked to an extent in urban India and in states like Madhya Pradesh, Rajasthan and Andhra Pradesh but failed to deliver in other states like Punjab, Karnataka and Uttar Pradesh. Electoral arithmetic played a crucial role. He can very easily fall prey to hubris unless he recognises the complex nature of the national mandate which is, in many ways, a concatenation of a series of local verdicts. This does point to the regionalisation of the polity—in itself, a very desirable trend but which requires to be handled with consummate skill and finesse. Striking alliances to win elections is one thing. But governing effectively with a disparate coalition is quite another. Federalism cannot degenerate into parochialism.

Second, Vajpayee is by instinct a non-confrontationist, non-divisive personality. But of late, this instinct has not been in evidence. Much of the political bitterness over Kargil could well have been avoided had he agreed to a special Rajya Sabha session. If on May 11, 1998 he had assembled all former prime ministers next to him on the lawns of his house as he announced India's nuclear tests, it would have reflected the reality of India's nuclear policy. If he had not reacted in the bizarre way he did to violence against tribals in Gujarat—by saying insensitively that we should have a national debate on conversions—he would not have lost personal goodwill. Consensus seeking, however, cannot become a substitute for proactive executive action. More than consensus, the key is consultations. On many issues, he has just to push ahead. The NDA's manifesto had 10 photographs of Vajpayee which Kautilya likened to Vishnu's Dashavatar. Lord Yama will not allow all 10 incarnations but in his final sojourn Vajpayee could usefully recall that the third was Varaha—the boar—who rescued Lakshmi by doggedness and tenacity.

Third, even though the old fire and sting is missing, Vajpayee is a peerless communicator in Hindi. Half the battle is public education as the fates of Kalyan Singh and Chandrababu Naidu demonstrate. Kalyan has been no less a tough reformer as Naidu but the Andhra leader's projection and packaging has been superb and superior. Vajpayee has to travel relentlessly across the country explaining to people why our economic mindsets need to change. This education is needed most in north India. Sadly, Vajpayee has not firmly supported the Naidus of the north—Bansi Lal and Kalyan. Perhaps, caste considerations have come in the way. But it is time for him to focus on north India almost exclusively. Vajpayee is not a TV natural but he must utilise this medium in a more homely manner to speak to people without a tele-prompter on the issues of the day.

Fourth, Vajpayee has to avoid the temptation of building an all-powerful prime minister's office (PMO), what to speak of a prime minister's household (PMH), foster or otherwise. Under Vajpayee, the PMO has become more politicised and certainly more intrusive. Never before have so many party functionaries and personal loyalists packed the PMO as they have under Vajpayee. This is not healthy for Indian democracy. That you can have a low-key PMO and yet have decisions taken at a furious pace was shown during the brief tenures of H.D. Deve Gowda and I.K. Gujral. In his second innings, Vajpayee did allow an impression to gain ground that there was a PMH as well that orchestrated policies and personalities. He has to learn from that experience and make V.P. Singh his role model at least in this regard. Transparency is the key. He would not lose anything if he came out with white papers on Kargil and the sugar scandal.

25/10/1999

LAME DUCK DAME LUCK

Increasingly, the Vajpayee regime is becoming a farce to be reckoned with

The last few weeks has seen the emasculation of the Vajpayee administration. The bruised prime minister himself sits in splendid isolation. His finance minister has been badly mauled. His commerce minister is caught up in local politics. Neither of these two gentlemen have been able to provide leadership of any kind. His feisty minister for disinvestment has been undercut from within. Other economic ministers, like in power and petroleum, although well-meaning, have been unable to impart a new momentum. Vajpayee may well survive and pull the occasional rabbit out of the hat as he did a few days ago by introducing the Lok Pal Bill in Parliament. But the sparkle and zest has vanished and even industry, a most ardent supporter, is becoming impatient and disillusioned.

Vajpayee has never been known to be a man for details. He is a man for the grand gesture, for the theatrical flourish. And his tenure has proved this conclusively whether it be Lahore and Agra, whether it be his innovatively bold insaaniyat formulation to kick-start a political dialogue in the Kashmir Valley or whether it be his directive to the armed forces to evict the Pakistanis from Kargil without crossing the Line of Control or even his courageous decision to make India go overtly nuclear. Vajpayee also deserves credit for allowing his foreign minister to deepen India's relationship with the US. For the economy, his singular contribution has been to bury obscurantist swadeshi and RSS economics and embrace Manmohanomics. The fact that there have been no U-turns or reversals is all the more remarkable given that the BJP and many of its allies had opposed the economic policies of the Congress and the United Front in the 1990s.

So where and how did Vajpayee falter? Ironically, for somebody who had an awesome reputation as an orator, Vajpayee's single-most important failing has been in not being able to communicate. But that should not come as a complete surprise, since he is not the most gregarious or outgoing of men—spell-binding oratory is not a substitute for interactive communication. He has become a prisoner of bland speech writers. When Vajpayee has spoken extempore, he has shown flashes of his brilliance but these occasions have been few and far between. Worse, although he has national appeal, he finds himself a prisoner in the capital.

His second major failure has been his extreme reluctance and inability to assert prime ministerial authority. Contrary to popular belief, the Indian prime minister wields enormous powers, much more than even an American President. Vajpayee has much in common with Ronald Reagan. But Reagan built a formidable team. On November 20, 1957, while speaking in the Lok Sabha, Vajpayee admonished Jawaharlal Nehru thus: our prime minister is a dreamer but he does not have around him people who can translate those dreams into reality. Forty four years later, the wheel has turned full circle and it can truly be said—physician, heal thyself. The job of the chief executive is to proactively craft a consensus on national issues, not simply to bemoan the lack of one. And where a consensus is not possible because of the myopia of the Opposition, then the job of the chief executive is to just do it. Strong executive action automatically creates a consensus as we saw in 1991. On both these fronts, Vajpayee has failed from day one.

Third, Vajpayee has not networked with chief ministers to advance the nation's developmental agenda. On the occasions he has done so, the results have been dramatic. On June 3, he called a meeting of chief ministers on power-sector reforms. The stars of this meeting were Congress chief ministers who put partisan politics aside and supported what the Vajpayee Government was attempting to do. When the finance minister called a meeting of chief ministers last year on tax reforms, it was a Congress chief minister who saved the day for the Centre. Individual ministers interacting with states is one thing but the prime minister himself reaching out is quite another and sends a wholly different type of signal. Curiously, for somebody who belongs to a party that makes a fetish of nationalism, Vajpayee has never embarked on the task of reinventing the Centre without which decentralisation can easily degenerate into parochialism.

Vajpayee had tremendous goodwill and rightly so. Even his political opponents conceded his essential liberalism, his great decency and his record of transcending partisan politics. But that goodwill is evaporating. He is now a forlorn figure—in office but not in power, in the seat but not in control, heading a coalition that has no coherence, no discipline and no sense of national purpose. Cricketer Vijay Merchant when asked why he retired when he did replied: "Better to go when people ask 'why is he' instead of 'why isn't he'." The longer Vajpayee stays, more people will echo the second sentiment. Only a policy and a problem-solving blitz can save him.

27/08/2001

◄──────►

TEN DAYS OF ACTIVE STUPOR
Vajpayee raises great expectations, but will he and can he deliver?

The first ten days of september have been extraordinarily busy for Prime Minister A.B. Vajpayee and his economic team. Never before in his 40-month tenure has there been such a concentrated focus on the economy. Never before has the prime minister so frankly admitted that the economy is in a slow-down mode. Never before has the prime minister talked so tough on pushing reforms further. Never before has the prime minister accumulated so many ideas and so many reports on what is to be done to get the economy moving again.

- On September 1, the National Development Council (NDC), comprising the prime minister, key Union ministers and all the chief ministers, met. The approach to the Tenth Five-Year Plan was approved and the prime minister un-veiled a 14-point plan to steer the economy forward.

- On September 4, Vajpayee announced the formation of a new Cabinet Committee on Economic Strategy and direced major economic ministries to speed up the implementation of projects worth Rs 75,000 crore to invigorate a flagging economy.

- On September 6, the prime minister personally received a 13-point agenda for India's economic regeneration prepared by the Washington-based McKinsey Global Institute. Separately, the finance minister called the chieftains of the housing, cement and the automobile sectors and heads of financial institutions for a brainstorming.

• September 7 saw the prime minister's reconstituted Trade and Industry Council meet and call for speeding up the privatisation process and for greater government spending, specially on railways and roads. Vajpayee used the occasion to release another 25-point agenda.

• On September 10, the prime minister met with a group of economists comprising his Economic Advisory Council who, while supporting faster privatisation, bolder liberalisation of labour laws and increased private investment, expressed reservations on the wisdom of greater public spending when the fiscal and revenue deficit is already out of control, a view that contradicts what the industrialists told the prime minister.

Of all these, it was the NDC meeting that came up with the most interesting idea to manage the politics of econo-mic reforms which is really what is lacking. At long last, the prime minister is to use the NDC to build a coalition of the 30 chief ministers—11 of whom belong to the Cong-ress, 11 to regional parties, six to the BJP and two to the Left Front—to ensure that an environment is created to sustain the reform efforts of states in crucial areas like power, agriculture and public administration. The first such interaction is scheduled to take place next month near Bangalore, and from what the prime minister said at the NDC meet, it appeared that he wanted to institutionalise such interactions in between Parliament sessions. Clearly, he is hoping that the pragmatism of the Congress XI will influence the thinking of its "national" team when it comes to legislation that has to be passed by Parliament. He also appears to be aiming to bring about some consistency in the positions taken by national parties. For instance, the Congress in Andhra Pradesh is opposing what it is doing in Karnataka. Similarly, the BJP in Rajasthan is resisting what it is implementing in Uttar Pradesh. If this hypocrisy has to be tackled, Vajpayee has to be talking not just with the chief ministers but also with the national and state-level opposition leaders. And what will he do with his Punjab ally that is engaged in a financially disastrous race of competitive populism with the Congress?

Vajpayee's standing has taken such a severe beating that there is a great deal of scepticism and cynicism on whether the flurry of meetings will deliver anything substantial. His bizarre interview to The Indian Express has certainly not helped matters. On the contrary, his admission that Jagmohan was shifted because of Delhi's municipal elections calls into question his famed judgement. The question being asked is how exactly is Vajpayee going to implement what he has promised? Having a labour minister who is opposed to changes in labour laws to make them more employment-friendly does not help. Setting up a committee to examine the recommendations of a task force on employment just because George Fernandes is spewing fire and venom at those perfectly sensible recommendations makes a mockery of a stated commitment to moving purposefully ahead.

India is facing its gravest economic crisis in a decade. Unlike 1991 which was an external collapse, this time the catastrophe is internal. There is increasing growth hunger and spreading investment famine. The need of the hour is for a decisive government that uses the enormous powers that are at the disposal of the executive and an enlightened Congress that recognises the imperatives of governance instead of always succumbing to the compulsions of opposition. Sadly, neither is in sight.

24/09/2001

————◆————◆————

ATAL BETRAYAL VAJPAYEE
A Bhishmapitamah who became a Dhritharashtra

For decades he was the most endearing face of Indian politics. For decades, he was the most riveting of orators. For decades, he epitomised magnanimity towards rivals. For decades, while his contemporaries earned notoriety for deviousness, he maintained a reputation for goodness. But today, it is sad to see A.B. Vajpayee write his epitaph in such a cruel manner, a political coward unable to tame the social bigots masquerading as economic liberalisers. It is sad that Vajpayee's long innings is winding up in such a slow bleed.

The general view is that Vajpayee is all style and little substance. Not true. His tenure as foreign minister during the Janata regime in 1977-79 was marked by path-breaking initiatives in relation to Pakistan and China. His prime ministerial term was characterised by many bold moves starting with Pokhran II. It was Vajpayee who allowed Jaswant

Singh to redefine the Indo-US relationship. Again, it was Vajpayee who launched the Lahore peace process and earned great credibility for India during the Kargil war by not allowing our armed forces to cross the Line of Control in Jammu and Kashmir. It was Vajpayee who provided a glimmer of hope to Jammu and Kashmir with his insaaniyat formulation. It was Vajpayee who backed Arun Shourie to launch India's long-overdue privatisation programme. It was Vajpayee who allowed Pramod Mahajan to give a great boost to the country's IT and telecom industries. It was Vajpayee who personally mas-terminded the promising national highway development programme. It was Vajpayee who allowed Ram Jethmalani to have the Urban Land Ceiling Act repealed and who supported Yashwant Sinha in many crucial initiatives. Unlike many of his predecessors, he was willing to talk publicly about the need for unpopular change as, for instance, in the case of labour laws. By carrying forward reforms initiated by the Congress and taken further by the United Front, Vajpayee demonstrated great pragmatism, much to the chagrin of his own party.

Alas, all this will be forgotten. The laidback approach, designed to give colleagues functional autonomy, worked to an extent in foreign policy and in economics—but failed the larger social test. What Vajpayee will be remembered for is the supine manner in which he allowed the rabid M.M. Joshi to run amok. What he will be remembered for is his cynical response to the shame of Gujarat caused by the swaggering Narendra Modi and his patrons in Delhi. At a time when the nation expected action, Vajpayee delivered sermons. At a time when the nation wanted to see the exercise of prime ministerial authority, Vajpayee recited poetry. At a time when many—including an anguished liberal forced to take a break from economics this week—were willing to give the prime minister the benefit of the doubt, he simply could not bestir himself to ensure that basic con-stitutional responsibilities were fulfilled. And when he be-stirred, he sent confusing signals. To a Muslim audience he spoke feelingly. To a Hindutva audience, he became aggressively unrepentant. To a cosmopolitan audience in New York, he spoke about India's plurality. But to an NRI assembly in Staten Island, he prided himself on his RSS lineage.

There are many who believe that Vajpayee's image of a liberal was carefully cultivated and false. Certainly, he himself has provided enough evidence for this view to gain ground. But Vajpayee is fundamentally a decent man. His problem is that he is weak and aloof.

Claiming to be an admirer of Jawaharlal Nehru, when it came to the crunch Vajpayee just could not muster the political courage to protect the secular legacy of Panditji. India will survive Gujarat. Contrary to the elegies being written by BJP ideologues, secularism is not dead and will not die in India. Hinduism will survive the VHP and the Bajrang Dal and the overwhelming majority of Hindus will continue to be secular. But Gujarat has delivered a grievous blow while the prime minister remained a passive spectator. Even his most ardent admirers and well-wishers were critical of his inertia as governance collapsed. The disappointment is greater since the expectations were very high.

Vajpayee's greatest failure was to protect Hinduism from pseudo Hindus, to save the glory of cultural Hinduism from the fanatics of political Hinduism. Kautilya is proud to be a cultural Hindu in spite of its mixed legacy, a legacy of magnificent achievement as well as of institutionalised repression, a legacy of the greatest external tolerance as well as of internal violence. Parliamentary democracy is liberating Hinduism from much of its traditional obscurantism. But a new hatred is being propagated by the RSS and its cohorts that Vajpayee could have confronted. He did not, thereby damaging the very essence of the world's most liberal faith.

What remains now is the script of a dignified exit policy. It is time to recall Cromwell: you have sat here long enough to do good; in the name of God, go. But before you do so, please do tell us—those who were enamoured of you—who you really are, what you actually stand for.

BUDDHA IS NOT SMILING
West Bengal and Kerala finally have chief ministers who must succeed

To signal the successful completion of India's first nuclear test at Pokhran on May 18,1974, the then Atomic Energy Commission chairman Homi Sethna is supposed to have sent a message to Indira Gandhi: "The Buddha is smiling." This is a fine but apocryphal story. How, for West Bengal's sake, were it to be true today. Alas, it is not so and Buddha's flame in Kolkata flickers unsteadily. Last weekend, while the nation awaited the election results to the four state assemblies, a historic meeting took place in Kolkata. This was the 20th conference of the West Bengal CPI(M) held as a precursor to the 17th triennial national CPI(M) Party Congress to be held in Hyderabad on March 22. Over 100 delegates among the 532 assembled discussed a most unusual document titled The Left Front and Our Tasks, which has been authored primarily by Chief Minister Buddhadeb Bhattacharya and Industry Minister Nirupam Sen and enjoys the backing of Anil Biswas, ostensibly the most powerful CPI(M) leader in the state. Sen introduced the document with the usual quotes from Mao but interestingly also quoted Deng Xiaoping and Zhu Rongji and Bhattacharya responded to the debate.

The document is a roadmap for economic and political governance and seeks to wrest autonomy for the CPI(M) Government in the state from the party, its cadres and its trade unions. This is the first time such an attempt has been made. It is by no means revolutionary. By Chinese standards or even by standards of some other progressive states in peninsular India, its recom-mended reform doses are homoeopathic. For example, it talks only of privatisation of loss-making state enterprises. But its significance lies in the clear recognition of the need to shed ideological shibboleths and for Bengal to do things differently if it is to move forward and fulfil the aspirations of the younger generation. Predictably, the delegates objected vociferously. Over 60 amendments were made. Basically, the carte blanche the chief minister was seeking from his party for carrying out far-reaching reforms was denied to him.

Bhattacharya's initiative comes close on the heels of a series of four articles written in the local media by Bengali "navratnas", nine outstanding economists, all social democrats, who earned their laurels outside their home state. They include Abhijit Banerjee (MIT), Pranab Bardhan (University of California, Berkeley), Kaushik Basu (Cornell and MIT), Mrinal Datta-Chaudhuri (Delhi School of Economics), Maitreesh Ghatak (University of Chicago), Ashok Sanjay Guha (JNU), Mukul Majumdar (Cornell), Dilip Mookherjee (Boston University) and Debraj Ray (Boston University). They laid out a blueprint for the in-dustrial revival of Bengal based on the Chinese model of "people's capitalism". The blueprint has been criticised but it has also been hailed by none other than D. Bandyopadhyay, one of Bengal's most distinguished civil servants who played a key role in the Left Front's agrarian reforms. What the economists should have pointed out is that India's small-scale, fiscal and labour policies are killing labour-intensive industrialisation of the Chinese type here—and Bengal has been an enthusiastic accomplice in this national harakiri.

Undoubtedly, there has been a rural metamorphosis in West Bengal over the past three decades starting with the implementation of land ceiling laws by the two United Front governments during 1967-70, the empowerment of panchayats beginning 1978 and thereafter radical land reforms. These triggered very impressive agricultural growth; for example, Bengal is now the nation's top rice producer and second largest producer of potatoes. But all these achievements are contradicted by urban decay and industrial decline, largely the consequences of the CPI(M)'s own policies. Education has been thoroughly politicised and is drowning in mediocrity while students flock to other states. Since the mid-1970s, Bengal has been overtaken by Tamil Nadu, Karnataka and Andhra Pradesh.

For the time being, Bhattacharya has compromised and accepted a diluted ver-sion of his agenda. This could well be a political tactic designed to expand the canvas of consensus and give his colleagues a sense of participation. He may have settled for a small window of opportunity for now. But soon he will have to take on his opponents frontally. This is what his Congress counterpart in Kerala, A.K. Antony, is doing courageously. Bhattacharya and Antony share many characteristics. They are two of India's most honest politicians. They were both prisoners of the past till they became chief ministers. It is then that from being dogmatic they became pragmatic. Both are becoming zealous modernisers of decrepit systems they preside over. Both are facing formidable resistance, from within and without. And both represent the last chance for their states, states that have done India proud in the past but which now desperately need the duo to succeed.

———◆——◆———

STILL GOING STRONG
Pachmarhi reinforced Manmohanomics

For 24 consecutive weeks, Kautilya has tried to be impersonal and avoided being partisan. This week, its self-discipline has been broken so it can debunk the false notion that following Pachmarhi the Congress has abandoned its commitment to liberalisation and disavowed the legacy of Manmohan Singh. He is very much the guru but the Congress is rightly searching for a larger political and social strategy within which reforms and liberalisation can be embedded.

Pachmarhi started with the most forceful articulation yet of the Congress' view of economic reforms by its president. Sonia Gandhi said the essence of economic reforms was the redefinition of the role of government at all levels to make it a more effective instrument of economic change and social transformation. While exhorting the Congress to constantly reinterpret its economic philosophy in the light of changing circumstances, she made two significant (to the Congress mindset) observations. One, poverty can be abolished only through higher economic growth and more effective management of anti-poverty programmes. wo, we cannot spend our way to prosperity. The pattern of public expenditure must undergo a fundamental reorientation at both the Centre and in states so as to enable us to invest more in poverty alleviation and social development programmes.

This speech, not the resolution, is the authoritative statement of Congress policy. Following Sonia's speech, a group of 20-25 Congress leaders got down to discussing economic issues. There was all-round agreement on a number of points.

- Reforms had become essential in 1991. They had strengthened the Indian economy. Liberalisation had accelerated growth, exports and investments. Further liberalisation was required but this must be sequenced carefully.
- The Congress lost the elections in 1996 not because of eco-nomic reforms but because of political mismanagement.
- The Centre's expenditure on rural development and social sectors increased from 19 per cent of total Plan expenditure in 1990-91 to 31 per cent in 1995-96. Even so, the perception gained ground that liberalisation was anti-poor.

There were serious differences of opinion on a few issues. Some participants rejected the idea of an across-the-board privatisation of the public sector. Some said all loss-making public-sector units should be privatised. But there were some who felt that without the government reducing its equity to below 50 per cent, the public sector, including banks, could not be made autonomous and profitable. Some called for this bold approach selectively. The majority view was that both fertiliser and food subsidies must not be tampered with. It was but natural that Kerala Congressmen expressed opposition to the restructuring of food subsidies—with 3 per cent of India's poor, Kerala draws 10 per cent of the food subsidy, while Uttar Pradesh with 18 per cent of the poor draws 8 per cent of the subsidy. It is the vociferous airing of these differences and some aggressive posturing by a couple of Congressmen wanting to assert their relevance that gave journalists the mirch masala to report that the Congress is anti-reforms.

India's vibrant agricultural economy, vast manufacturing base and extensive scientific and technological infrastructure are undoubted strengths that give us the capability to engage the world in a self-confident manner. Pachmarhi justifiably felt proud of what had been accomplished in the pre-1991 era. But these days it is not fashionable to recall our achievements of the Nehru-Indira period. The media misinterpreted this recall as a defeat for the reformers. The Congress is not exactly bursting with liberalisers. No political party is. But Kautilya's estimate is that no more than seven out of the 275 who attended the Pachmarhi conclave had fundamental objections to the very idea of liberalisation. The Congress chief ministers were gung-ho on liberalisation, demonstrating that reforms have stronger proponents outside Delhi in all political parties.

Kautilya also suspects that the use of the word "socialism" dealt a body blow to the Congress's pro-reform image. But liberalisation and socialism are not mutually exclusive. The Chinese call their model a socialist market economy. At Pachmarhi, socialism was defined in terms of a commitment to egalitarianism, full equality of opportunity, greater redistributive justice in an expanding economy and in-creased access of the poor to the basics of education, health and nutrition. Defined this way, Kautilya believes the only true socialist society in the world is the United States. Pachmarhi should have taken place in 1991 or in 1992 itself. The packaging of reforms, the articulation of the linkages between liberalisation and social needs and an honest discussion of concerns and fears would have served the cause of reforms greatly. Sustained public education and communication in a simple idiom have been lacking. Most politicians are extraordinarily illiterate on economics, finance, trade and technology. The media too has done great damage by its simplistic either/or approach. It is possible to believe in purposeful state intervention and planning and champion faster liberalisation, as Kautilya does. But these nuances are lost in today's binary world. Despite the confusion it seems to have caused in the outside world, the Congress is more reassured about reforms after Pachmarhi—signal left, turn right and veer to the Centre.

21/09/1998

◆——————◆

RAO DOESN'T DESERVE THIS
A sherpa's reminiscences of those momentous days of June and July 1991

As perhaps the first "victim" of P.V. Narasimha Rao's manipulations, I should also be gloating at his plight. But I am genuinely sad at his indictment. Here is one of the most erudite and scholarly of prime ministers in the world found guilty of "fixing" a no-confidence motion in Parliament. Here is an unusually multi-lingual prime minister who changed our mindset on economic and foreign policy being subjected to public ridicule.

I was Rao's sherpa for exactly 100 days between June and September 1991. One morning, he asked me to shift to the Planning Commission. Thereafter, for five years he would use me for various assignments, both official and political. But things were never the same and I was summarily ejected from his A-team.

I came into contact with Rao only after the assassination of Rajiv Gandhi. On becoming Congress president, he called Pranab Mukherjee and me and said, "You both will have to brief me on economics." Thereafter, the three of us would meet regularly at 11 Safdarjang Road and go over various briefs. My main objective in these briefs was to show that the external crisis that had engulfed us had its roots in domestic profligacy. Both saw the point. On his first evening as prime minister, Rao sent for me. He said he had just been told by his finance minister that the country was facing an unprecedented crisis and that something immediate had to be done. I told him that we had basically four options.

First, we could declare a default on our external payment obligations. That would, however, be disastrous. Second, we could mobilise NRI funds. But at a time when NRIs were withdrawing money from India, this would not succeed. Third, we could issue gold bonds. But previous such attempts had failed and in any case this would not give us ready cash. Fourth, we could go to the IMF and the World Bank and work out a quick disbursing financial package. But there would be conditionalities. However, these conditionalities were policies that Indian economists and planners themselves had been advocating for a long time. We left the discussion at that although I could see that he was enamoured of the NRI option.

On the second night as prime minister, he asked me to come to Hyderabad House. We talked about how to approach the IMF. I had taken with me a one-page policy statement highlighting immediate initiatives that the government would take in the next seven-ten days and other initiatives that would be taken in the mid-July budget and thereafter. In the immediate steps were included reforms like the new trade policy, new industrial policy, new oil and power policy as well as foreign investment while the budget initiatives focused on fiscal restructuring. I told him that the IMF would insist on fiscal adjustments but we must proactively tell them that such fiscal measures would be part of a broader agenda of economic reforms, an agenda that had been worked out most recently in the Planning Commission during 1985-87.

Rao saw the one pager and asked me to fax it right away to our executive director in the IMF, Gopi Arora. He wanted Arora to take the note informally to the IMF managing director to show that we had embarked on a course of major reforms and request the IMF to come to our support quickly without insisting on too many tough steps to be taken in the first few days itself. The note was faxed and Arora reverted in a matter of hours to convey that the IMF would stand by us.

On a parallel course, Manmohan Singh, whose appointment itself had enhanced our credibility, was already moving to restore confidence in the rupee. To ensure that his personal rupee balance born out of modest dollar savings did not swell from the devaluation, Manmohan wrote to Rao, depositing the windfall gains into the Prime Minister's Relief Fund. Rao was bemused by this act of rare integrity. With the IMF support as-sured, Rao pressed ahead. Trade policy reforms were spearheaded by his commerce minister P. Chidambaram and did not raise protests. Industrial policy reforms, in the formulation of which Rakesh Mohan had played a key role, proved more controversial. Many cabinet members objected. Rao then asked Manmohan, Chidambaram and me to brief them. We produced a document showing how the 1991 policies marked a "change with continuity". The substance remained the same but the packaging was different! The Cabinet approved the very document it had rejected.

I hold no brief for the corruption that flourished during the Rao regime. But, on balance, considering Rao's manifold contributions, I do believe that just as Gerald Ford pardoned Richard Nixon in 1974, Prime Minister A.B. Vajpayee must display statesmanship and allow his good friend to live out his remaining years in tranquillity. But at the very minimum, this would require an apology of sorts from Rao himself.

16/10/2000

◆━━◆

PRAYER TO A JOGI
While wooing investment, the chief minister lands
Chhattisgarh in the smelter

Edmund Burke's opening salvo against Warren Hastings was memorable: "It is difficult to speak but impossible to remain silent." I am some what in the same predicament on the BALCO controversy but ultimately the need to preserve professional integrity even while serving as a political apparatchik has won out—perhaps foolhardily.

The privatisation of BALCO was first proposed by the United Front government in February 1997, although at that time the cabinet decided to sell only 40 per cent of the company's equity to a private investor. Subsequently, the NDA Government decided to sell 51 per cent to a private investor onthe ground that aluminiumis neither astrategic norcore sector, that there are many private companies who are more efficient and that the government would never be able to put in money year after year into running aluminium plants. The decision to sell 51 per cent made eminent economic sense.

Four years after the initial decision to privatise, the transaction has actually taken place and the Centre has sold 51 per cent of BALCO for Rs 551crore to Sterlite Industries, an Indian private company. The bidding process was gone through and Sterlite's offer was higher than 51 per cent of BALCO's market value as assessed by the govern-ment's adviser, Jardine Fleming. But the bidding process has been called into question. The only way this issue can be resolved is when the Department of Disinvestment hands over all the papers relating to the sale to the

Comptroller and Auditor-General (CAG) and CAG scrutinises these papers and submits its findings. Hopefully, CAG's evaluation report should be ready in three months at the most.

My esteemed colleague, the engineer-administrator-politician Ajit Jogi, is resisting the privatisation vociferously. He is personally spearheading an agitation against Sterlite, perfectly justifiable for a political activist but inadvisable for a chief minister of a new state desperate for fresh investment. BALCO is virtually under lock-out. The impasse lingers and the Supreme Court will hear the case again on April 9 by which time BALCO would have become a ghost facility. Is there a way out?

Jogi has categorically told Sterlite that it must agree to operate with 49 per cent equity. This is unacceptable to both Sterlite and the Centre. Jogi has also offered Rs 552 crore to the Centre to top Sterlite's offer. The Centre is not interested and for a valid reason. The bid has been closed and the deal finalised. Moreover, a 51:49 per cent arrangement between a state government and the Centre at log gerheads with each other is a recipe for continued conflict.

Jogi's other option is to offer Rs 1,100 crore and buy out the entire BALCO plant from the Centre. The Centre could agree to this but whether this can actually be done without Sterlite taking the Central Government to court for breach of contract is very doubtful. But assuming for a moment that Sterlite can be persuaded to withdraw amicably, where will Jogi find Rs 1,100 crore? Chhattisgarh's total revenues in 2001-02 will be around Rs 2,400 crore and its share of Central taxes will come to about Rs 1,479 crore. Let us say Jogi diverts his share of Central taxes to buying over BALCO. But what will this do to the finances of a state whose deficit, after payment of interest, salaries and pensions, will total Rs 664 crore this year? Clearly, the only option for Jogi is to borrow this money. But from where? And assuming that this can indeed be done, the legitimate question is—should not these resources be used for more essential physical and social infrastructure that Chhattisgarh so very desperately needs? Moreover, the state Government will need to set aside hefty sums of money, in addition to the down payment for buying the plant, for the next two years at least to keep BALCO going and bring it to a condition for a privatisation offer once again.

Successive governments have conclusively demonstrated their

incapability to run the public sector professionally and commercially. Autonomy in our political and bureaucratic system is a myth. The money that governments invest in the public sector is money taken away from irrigation, primary education, public health and nutrition. There is, however, still a role for the public sector as a venture capitalist in crucial areas like energy. But with bankruptcy staring us in the face, privatisation has become an economic imperative. Even Jogi knows that. He is preparing to privatise power distribution in the state.

Twenty-seven Central PSU privatisations are on the anvil. The BALCO episode is not without its lessons for the Centre. Privatisation must bring in foreign investment. State governments must be fully involved. Transparency should be seen and felt. Arun Shourie's words alone are not sufficient. And while privatisation must remain an executive decision, nothing would be lost if White Papers are introduced in Parliament on each privatisation deal, before it takes place and after it is concluded.

26/03/2001

MERCIES OF THE PAST
Why India is not facing an economic crisis despite political and stock market turmoil

Atal Bihari Vajpayee's government is facing a slow bleed. His NDA allies are uneasy. The Opposition has smelt blood. The swadeshi lobby within the Sangh Parivar, which had been lying low for some time, has got a fresh lease of life. How all this impacts on economic policy time alone will tell. The Government is dependent on Parliament to introduce and pass legislation. However, privatisation does not depend on Parliament and will be driven wholly by the tenacity of Vajpayee and his colleagues. WTO deadlines will be met. In other areas like power, progress will depend on how proactively Vajpayee reaches out and cements alliances with reforms-oriented chief ministers, something that he hasn't adequately done during his tenure.

But how is is that despite political turmoil and stock market shenanigans, India doesn't face a first-rate economic crisis? As, say, Turkey, Brazil and Argentina? These countries, more aggressive reformers than India, have collapsed in recent months and have approached the

IMF for emergency bail-outs because of domestic convulsions that have caused interest rates to soar, capital to fly out and investor confidence to beeroded. India has escaped lightly. Its relative security for the time being comes from four factors—all a valuable legacy of Manmohanomics. In some ways, we have become victims of our own success. If these factors were not present, perhaps we would have been confronted with a 1990-91 type crisis and that, in turn, would have precipitated another round of big-bang reforms, of the type introduced by the P.V. Narasimha Rao government in June-July 1991. But for now we must thank ourselves for what Manmohan Singh accomplished.

First, short-term debt (debt that normally has an original maturity of less than a year) as a proportion of foreign exchange reserves, that, for instance, destroyed East Asia in 1997, has been reduced dramatically from about 146 per cent in 1990-91 to about 12 per cent now. Short-term debt as a-proportion of external debt has also been slashed to less than 5 per cent now. Second, while foreign institutional investors (FIIs) have broughtin close to $13.4 billion in the past seven years, over 96 per cent of these funds have gone into equities. Therefore, these FIIs are not speculative investors or carriers of "hot" money but investors who take a medium and long-term view of investment prospects in both sectors and companies. Third, the current-account deficit in the country is hovering around 1 per cent of the GDP, half the safe level. The current-account deficit is in the secure zone, because the economy continues to be sluggish and there has been a phenomenal increase in dollar earnings from "invisibles" like software exports and remittances. Fourth, the Indian rupee is not freely convertible on the capital account for domestic residents. Experience from Mexico indicates that in times of crisis, domestic residents take their money out first before the much-maligned foreign investors. Convertibility on the capital account means that we as ordinary citizens cannot exchange rupees for dollars and take that out, for instance, to buy property and shares.

India is different in other ways. Unlike in Brazil where the threat of default by the state of Minas Gerais was enough to momentarily bury the country, Indian states are not allowed to borrow abroad. Unlike in Turkey, we have not started taking tough decisions with regard to public- sector banks whose performance conceals more than it reveals. However, the absence of a visible crisis should not become a recipe for complacency. Once confidence takes a knock, the deterioration can be very rapid. Fundamentals may be looking good but if the sentiment turns negative, then it is downhill all the way. India's external vulnerability is not all that great at the moment but if policy paralysis persists then we may well see the onset of disenchantment. We may not worry too much about an external crisis but we are already in the throes of a grave internal cri-sis. Two-thirds to three-fourths of government expenditure is being con-sumed by interest payments, salaries and pensions of government employees, subsidies and public-sector losses. It is this completely distorted structure of public expenditure that is causing aninvestment famine in the country. In turn, this famine is contributing to the deceleration in economic growth.

Political arithmetic will probably ensure Vajpayee's continuance. But the chemistry has dissipated itself sub-stantially. He has to rebuild and change his style of functioning. So far, he has cast himself in the Ronald Reagan mould, but only partially. Reagan may not have been a details manbuthewas asuperbcommunicator. Vajpayee has failed to cash in on his greatest asset and has reduced himself to reading anodyne speeches written in the worst possible bureaucratic English. If he becomes himself, there is hope for his administration. Otherwise, it will continue to be in intensive care. That will not be good for the economy.

02/04/2001

◆—◆

CONSTITUTION NEEDS NO REVIEW
The noise of politics is the music of democracy—don't kill it

Nothing has given rise to more misgivings among those opposed to the BJP and its cohorts than the proposed review of the Constitution. During the debate on the confidence vote in the Lok Sabha, Prime Minister Atal Bihari Vajpayee tried to assuage these fears and quoted a list of "distinguished" personalities like R. Venkataraman, B.K. Nehru, Nani Palkhivala, V.R. Krishna Iyer and others who want the nearly 50-year-old Constitution to be reviewed.

The prime minister was being economical with the truth. He did not reveal that the main motivation of most of the patricians, other than Krishna Iyer, is a disillusionment and frustration with representative parliamentary democracy. Once you cross a certain age, you tend to become wistful and want to return to the good old days. The good old days for these geriatric upper-caste, upper-class gentlemen are the days of benevolent elitism, when "people like us" (PLUs) were in politics and when the system did not have to deal with the Mulayams, the Laloos, the Mayawatis and their ilk.

B.K. Nehru speaks well for this class. He wants a separation of legislative and executive functions. He wants an elected chief executive with the freedom to appoint the brightest-read, upper-caste and upper-class professionals who know all and who know best as cabinet ministers. He speaks for a group who would want the Constitution amended to bring "professionals" into politics. What is being suggested is an American or a French system to replace this "messy" one we have—no matter that the American and the French systems have problems of their own. In the United States, for example, a gridlock between the executive and the legislature a year ago actually resulted in the closure of the federal government for a few weeks.

In India, electoral politics remains the only vehicle for social advancement. It remains the only instrument for empowering communities which have been subject to the worst forms of discrimination for centuries. It remains the only public arena for asserting group identities so essential for self-respect and self-confidence. Representative parliamentary democracy is the only system that can mirror and celebrate India's diversity. The makers of our Constitution knew this. What makes this even more remarkable is that, other than B.R. Ambedkar, they belonged to the "privilegentsia". Yet, they did not allow this to cloud their judgement. Another view holds that since elections are throwing up fractured mandates, the Constitution should be reviewed to provide for political stability. But why blame the Constitution? Mandates are fractured because society itself, particularly in north India, is in a state of flux and ferment. Society is undergoing a churning as the old social order is giving way to new alignments. This is a phase that we must, and should, go through. Any attempt at sabotaging this process will be a betrayal of the hopes and aspirations of millions.

There is a third motivation for a review: dissatisfaction with specific provisions like Article 356 or the Tenth Schedule, which deals with splits in political parties, or Article 200 that concerns governors. Amendments to specific articles may well be needed, although in some cases changes in the Representation of the Peoples' Act will suffice. But for the most part, it is the executive's abuse of the Constitution that has created problems.

There can be no excuse for the way in which governors have been appointed. Both Congress and non-Congress governments have erred. If reports are to be believed, the BJP-led Government is all set to follow the tradition of treating the Raj Bhavan as a party pensioner's paradise. This is the real problem, not the Constitution.

Reviews of the Constitution reflect the times. That is why reviews can sometimes throw up the desirable—and sometimes the undesirable. Jawaharlal Nehru had the Constitution reviewed in 1951, when the judiciary was thwarting the Congress' efforts at abolishing zamindari and promoting land reforms. This review led to the Ninth Schedule. But the 1975 review by the Swaran Singh Committee, was more controversial. Apart from other things, it led to the notorious 42nd Amendment. The '90s have seen disenchantment with the political system among the educated and the intelligentsia. No doubt, they will be on the BJP's review committee. This is what leads to fears. There is nothing that amendments cannot solve; reviews are the thin end of the wedge. The BJP should give up the review idea. Such a flip-flop would not be out of character. Till some years ago, L.K. Advani used to go on about the need to have a "states reorganisation commission". Now, he says there is no need.

Finally, this is what Granville Austin, one of the world's preeminent authorities on the Constitution of India, had to say in a 1994 monograph published by the Rajiv Gandhi Institute of Contemporary Studies: "The Constitution has shown no serious weaknesses since 1950. When change has been seen as necessary, the Constitution has been amended effectively. To think that by altering the Constitution radically, human character—citizen's or politician's— would be reformed would be a greater mistake. Institutions may shape human conduct, they do not change character."

20/04/1998

◆——◆

HALF A CENTURY AND GOING

Now is the time to celebrate, not derogate India's Constitution

November 26 marks the 50th anniversary of the adoption of our Constitution, a magnificent document conceived and finalised by some of the finest minds and noblest hearts assembled at any time at any place. Sadly, the President's address to the opening session of the 13th Lok Sabha on October 25 contained no mention of this momentous occasion. All it had was the reference to the Government's intention to set up a commission to review the Constitution. In any other country, such a golden jubilee would have been celebrated with greater gusto.

Granville Austin's *The Indian Constitution* and B. Shiva Rao's *The Making of the Indian Constitution are evergreen* classics. Everytime Kautilya reads these books there is a new thrill, a renewed excitement, a fresh sense of pride at what our founding fathers bequeathed to us, a feeling of awe at the sheer intellectual brilliance that was on display. These books describe in vivid detail how our Constitution came into being, the debates that took place, the disagreements that surfaced, the clashes that occurred, the compromises that were negotiated, but above all the pervading spirit of give and take that animated all discussions. On December 9, 1949 when it first met, the Constituent Assembly comprised 296 members elected by allegedly upper caste and upper class in character, even though Muslims accounted for about 13 per cent and Scheduled Castes about 14 per cent of those elected from the provinces. It was, Austin and Rao remind us, indirectly elected but highly representative. In just three years, it prepared the framework for a quiet social revolution based on universal adult franchise and representative parliamentary democracy. If at all there was an elite with a burning social conscience and an irrevocable commitment to egalitarianism, this was it. Austin admits that most of the Constitution is plainly non-Indian but that this is different from being un-Indian. In many ways, the Constitution epitomises the quintessential syncretic character of our culture.

The drafting committee of the Constitution was chaired by Dr Babasaheb Ambedkar that led him to later remark that the three works that define India—the Ramayana, the Mahabharata and the Constitution—had the Dalit imprimatur. He also piloted the Constitution through the assembly. The choice was that of Jawaharlal Nehru and Vallabhbhai Patel who were mindful of the fact that Babasaheb had a background in law and economics but had also been the law member in the viceroy's executive council. The committee had such luminaries as K.M. Munshi, Alladi Krishnaswamy Aiyyar, N. Gopalaswamy Ayyangar and T.T. Krishnamachari. The adviser to the assembly was B.N. Rau, a distinguished civil servant who along with two others, S.N. Mukerjee and D.D. Basu, prepared the first drafts. The drafting committee was supported by the oligarchs, as Austin calls them—Nehru, Patel, Rajendra Prasad and Abul Kalam Azad, with Govind Ballabh Pant championing the cause of the provinces. According to Austin, the oligarchy's influence was nearly irresistible, yet the assembly decided issues democratically after genuine debate.

And what a spirit of bipartisanship existed. M.R. Jayakar, former president of the Hindu Mahasabha, came into the assembly on a Congress ticket and Syama Prasad Mookerjee, the founder of the Jan Sangh, became a member when he was appointed as industry minister in Nehru's first cabinet. Indeed, the way it formed the Constituent Assembly, the way it conducted the proceedings of the assembly, the way in which it coordinated the government's functioning with that of the assembly reflected the Congress at its accommodative zenith. Ambedkar was to later reflect that without the Congress there would have been no Constitution. This was a Congress that, mindful of the need to bring in the best talent from the widest crosssection, ensured that such notables as S. Radhakrishnan, H.N. Kunzru, K. Santhanam, apart from Alladi and Munshi, came into the assembly. It is also forgotten that after Partition cost him his Bengal seat, Ambedkar was re-elected as a Congress member thanks to the Mahatma and S.K. Patil.

Our problems are the outcome more of the abuse of the Constitution than its use. The Constitution has been criticised for being conservative. But the failure to carry through land reforms is exclusively that of the executive. The Constitution has been criticised for being too long. But its length is understandable given the lack of democratic traditions and conventions in India. In an oral culture, the written word brings transparency and accountability. The Constitution has been criticised for not leading to political stability in Delhi. Political instability at the Centre reflects the transition from a unicentric to a polycentric polity and the profound social churning that is taking place across the country. The Constitution has been criticised for being too rigid. Actually it has proved to be flexible and whenever change has been needed, it has been amended. More amendments may well be required. But the disenchantment which seems to be behind the "review" is unwarranted. The least we owe these intellectual giants is that the review be done by the "best, the brightest and the noblest", as was assembled 50 years ago.

08/11/1999

A LEVEL PAYING FIELD

Financing the democracy surplus is as important
as reducing the fiscal deficit

There are two things important in politics, said American politician Mark Hanna in 1896, "the first is money and I can't remember what the second is". Across the world, whether it is the US, Germany, France, Japan or England, the issue of political financing is nowoccupying centrestage. In India too, the Tehelka tapes episode has brought this issue into sharp focus. While the Tehelka expose does establish a "level p(l)aying field" for political corruption, it also offers a opportunity for cleaning up the non-transparent way in which our democracy is financed.

India is the only major democracy in the world where there is no mechanism for the public exchequer supporting elections. State funding will not eliminate, onlyreduce corruption. In the US, where federal funds are used in presidential campaigns since 1976, there is now a big debate taking place on how to curb the influence of "soft" money—that is, funds which go from corporations, unions, foundations and wealthy individuals to political parties—as opposed to "hard" money which flows to individual candidates. And although Germany has strict laws for state financing, Helmut Kohl, the man who single-handedly redrew European geography and rewrote European history during his tenure, has had his reputation shattered by illegal contributions he received on behalf of his party.

In India, the idea of state funding of elections has impeccable political and intellectual lineage. The idea was first mooted way back in January 1972 by the Joint Committee of Parliament on Amendments to Election Law that had amongits members none other than Atal Bihari Vajpayee and L.K. Advani. Thereafter, in 1990, a committee set upby the V.P. Singh governmentunder the chairmanship of Dinesh Goswami, then the Union law minister, reiterated the idea.

Next, in September 1998, a committee of MPs chaired by Indrajit Gupta and having, among others, ManmohanSingh and Somnath Chatterjee as members, worked out some details of such state funding. Finally, the Law Commission under the chairmanship of B.P. Jeevan Reddy backed the Gupta Committee's recommendations fully in its 170th Report on Reform of Electoral Laws submitted to the government in May 1999. But it said that state funding must be preceded by incorporation of legislative provisions in the Representation of the People Act, 1951 to ensure (i) innerparty democracy; (ii) regular maintenance, auditing, submission and publication of accounts by political parties; and (iii) deletion of the present provision that excludes expenditures incurred on behalf of a candidate by the party or anybody else while calculating the expense of the candidate in elections.

Assuming Rs 10 a voter, the Gupta Committee suggested that a separate election fund be created with Rs 600 crore contribution coming annually from the Central government and another Rs 600 crore from the state governments.Thecommittee emphasised that state funding should be in kind—facilities like accommodation, communications, fuel, postage, publicity material and electoral rolls—and not in the form of cash. But where was this money to come from?

The Gupta panel mentioned that an election cess could be levied on profit-making companies, or funds now being provided for the MP Local Area Development Scheme (MPLADS) could be diverted to create a corpus. Of the two, the second option is preferable. In 2001-02, the allocation for the scheme, under which Rs 2 crore is given to every MPfor work in his or her constituency, is Rs 1,580 crore. Ever since MPLADS was most ill-advisedly introduced in 1993, Manmohan Singh has been advocating that either the whole or half of it should be used to set up a corpus for state funding of elections. Arun Shourie, the minister in charge of MPLADS, calls the scheme "organised loot". Even if half the existing MPLADS allocation is diverted, we can start with a sizeable election fund of about Rs 800 crore. But given their awful fiscal position, states will find it impossible to chip in. Parties can also finance their annual non-election year requirements from such a fund—for the Congress this sum works out to around Rs 10crore. To augment the corpus, individuals and companies could be allowed to contribute to this fund on a tax-deductible basis and contributions could also be welcomed from overseas Indians. In the 1998 and 1999 Lok Sabha polls, the Election Commission allotted free time on Doordarshan to all political parties but only for speeches. This is a form of state funding. To salvage his image, and in the larger national interest, Vajpayee should now spearhead the creation of a separate election fund that will finance normal political activities as well as elections. Nobody can dare oppose him now.

09/04/2001

VII

Foreign Relations :
Not For the Birds

This chapter begins with the United States and much of what I have written here has been expanded into a larger publication *Yankee Go Home, But Take Me With You: A Perspective on Indo-US Relations*, that was published by the Asia Society in the run-up to President Clinton's visit to India in March 2000. India's ties with the US are undergoing a sea-change and these articles capture that changing flavour. China is a country that has fascinated me for long and although I do not speak Mandarin Chinese, I have been lucky to have been afforded many opportunities for building up some expertise on our Himalayan neighbour. I was pleasantly surprised that when I met some Chinese economists in international conferences, they had read some of these articles. There are seven articles on Pakistan, a country that we have to learn to live with. My friend Rohit Saran of India Today whose father-in-law is a former High Commissioner to Pakistan told me once that Kautilya had a following in Pakistan. I am happy and one of my continuing regrets is that I have never been to that country. I take consolation in the fact that some of the greatest works on India—Max Mueller, for example—, are by those who never come here! I wish I had written more on South Asia; just three pieces on Nepal, Bangladesh and Sri Lanka is simply inexcusable.

Americas

BILL IN THE CHINA SHOP

Why Uncle Sam offers Beijing a warm heart and Delhi a cold shoulder

President Bill Clinton came to China. He saw; whether he conquered or concurred time alone will tell. But one thing is clear. Human rights notwithstanding, the special Sino-American relationship goes on. Indians are just not able to understand why. Why not India? After all, it is a democracy and also a big market. True, we are more of a democracy than China. But there are some dimensions of democracy that China has in greater measure. Provinces in China have far greater economic powers than states in India. For example, 60 per cent of all revenues goes to the provinces in China. The provinces also account for 60 per cent of all expenditure. In India, the states get 50 per cent of all revenues collected but share just a third of all expenditure.

The Communist Party of China is able to publicly acknowledge mistakes. Some years ago, it declared Mao was 60 per cent right and 40 per cent wrong. In India, we deify our leaders and are unable to shake off their troublesome legacies. Recall Deng Xiaoping's aphorism: "What does it matter if the cat is black or white as long as it catches mice." In India, there would be endless debate on the attributes of the cat while the rodent population multiplied.

Americans have always felt a moral guardianship for China. In the late 19th and early 20th centuries, over 13,000 missionaries helped create an image of China in America that, in Barbara Tuchman's words, "carries an accom-panying sense of obligation towards the subject of one's beneficence". The children of some of these missionaries became pillars of the American establishment. An example is Henry Luce, who founded Time magazine.

America's future history, thundered President Ted Roosevelt in 1905, "will be more determined by our position in the Pacific facing China than by our position in the Atlantic facing Europe". China has been a major issue in almost all US presidential campaigns since 1920.

American interest in India began in the '50s. Even then, it was seen largely in relation to China. India was the great experiment in democracy that caught America's fancy, just as its prodigal pupil embraced communism. Gradually, this fancy gave way to disenchantment with India's slow economic growth, inward-looking policies and niggardliness in publicly acknowledging American assistance. This coincided with the rediscovery of a "lost" China by the US.

Thus, history and emotion provide the foundation for the growing Sino-American commercial relationship. China's imports from the US are eight times India's. This is what gives Beijing greater leverage in Washington and even in some state capitals. Contracted American equity investment in China since 1991 amounts to some $28 billion. The figure for India is $9billion—$4 billion equity and $5 billion of FII investment in our stock market. China is a make or break market for some key American companies in a way India is not. Fourteen per cent of Boeing's sales are to China. Proctor and Gamble sells more soap in China than in the US. It is a multibillion dollar market for Microsoft. McDonald's opens a new franchise there every week. Ten per cent of Motorola's revenues come from China.

An economy growing at 10 per cent year after year—and at 7 to 8 per cent in a "bad" year—just can't be ignored. True, China runs a $50 billion trade surplus annually with the US. But cheap exports brings not just dollars to China but also new friends. Among the most aggressive US lobbyists for China are consumer organisations like the National Association of Retailers. India could also be a major exporter but its policies are choking exports of many consumer products. This is the major area of growth. Eight per cent of US imports are from China; India's share is a minuscule 0.8 per cent. But trade alone cannot explain China's clout. After all, America exports more to Belgium than to China. One key "extra" for China is that apart from the US, Russia and France it is the only country which launches satellites commercially. In the next 10 years, one satellite will be launched every two days. China's satellite launches are a third the price of America's. This gives it enormous leverage with politically influential US hi-tech companies.

China scores heavily over India where it counts for the morrow—on American university campuses. After being the flavour for a brief while in the '50s, India has dropped out of favour. The rich Indian diaspora is doing precious little to help. One of the richest donors to Princeton University is Gordon Wu, the Hong Kong magnate. He contributed $100 million some years back. With the imminent drying up of the PL 480 funds, whatever little intellectual interaction is taking place between India and the US will end.

The Indian scientific, political and military establishment thinks China has influence because of its nuclear arsenal. This is a profound misreading of reality. Its pragmatic policies, economic performance and manner of conduct give China a decisive edge over India. The sooner we understand this the better.

13/07/1998

US AND WE

India's war cry: Yankee go home. Take me with you.

Whatever its short-term impact, the Washington Statement of July 4 is a significant development. We have interpreted this in our usual conspiratorial way. The Washington Statement actually reflects a changing American approach to the subcontinent and not "evenhandedness". The question is whether we will draw the right lessons and consolidate to our long-term advantage. That we will be called upon to launch a meaningful, bilateral dialogue after the status quo has been restored in Kargil is abundantly clear. At the same time, we will be forced to fashion a new and mature approach to the United States.

Indians are working themselves into an apoplectic fit over the possibility of American mediation. Kautilya does not subscribe to the fear that an initiative on the lines of Camp David—which brought Israel's Menachem Begin and Egypt's Anwar Sadat to this presidential retreat near Washington to finalise a peace agree-ment— is on the cards. Even so it is useful to recall that the most enduring monument to India-Pakistan amity, the Indus Waters Treaty, would not have materialised in 1960 without international mediation.

Americans are concerned with Israel because of the Jewish factor in American life. For similar reasons they have been worried about Northern Ireland as well. Kashmir bothers the American establishment largely because it is in a nuclear cockpit. Three nuclear powers own property in Jammu and Kashmir and this ownership is disputed by all three. Two of these nuclear powers have seen it fit in their wisdom, misguided in Kautilya's view, to remain outside the mainstream of global nuclear non-proliferation regimes.

J.N. Dixit, the distinguished former foreign secretary, once told Kautilya that the problem with India's approach to the US is that it is based on panga, not pragmatism. Panga is one of those Hindi words that convey the meaning beautifully, a meaning that gets lost in its translation into the English "prickly confrontation". How very true, although parenthetically and respectfully Kautilya has to point out that the redoubtable gentleman was himself seen to be a great practitioner of this art while in service.

We certainly do not have to become lackeys but we could do without hypocrisy. Kautilya is amused whenever there is a whiff of the US imposing visa restrictions and the outcry that results in this country from people who otherwise rave and rant against American hegemony. Kneejerk anti-Americanism and the failure to engage the Americans constructively across a wide spectrum has cost this country dearly. Kautilya will incur the wrath of his party colleagues but it has to be admitted that the eight rounds of Strobe Talbott-Jaswant Singh talks have been an exception. It is true that the US still looks at us largely through the prism of nuclear non-proliferation but there are ways of balancing that out by engaging in a wider dialogue more frequently at the highest levels. A bilateral commission of the type that the US has with Mexico is a good model for us to propose.

Since 1945, no nation has become an economic powerhouse without exploiting American markets, investments and technologies. China runs a $50 billion trade surplus with the US even while it indulges in sharply critical rhetoric on the political level. Its volume of trade with the US is over seven times that of India's and it draws almost 10 times the investment we attract from the US. Even though our economic ties with the US have expanded significantly since 1991, old mindsets linger. Today India and Pakistan are the only two countries opposing a new Millennium Round of trade negotiations under the WTO. It is a sign of how immature our reactions are that in 1998 we berated the Americans for attacking Osama Bin Laden's sites in Afghanistan but now we are seeing convergence between our own and US interests to rein in the Saudi millionaire's terrorists.

A recent study by Anne Lee Saxenian shows that 7 per cent of Silicon Valley's 11,443 high-technology firms started since 1980 are run by Indians. This understates Indian influence since it does not include those firms started by Indians that have non-Indian CEOs. Many top US companies like United Airlines, US Air, Arthur Andersen and McKinsey have India-born CEOs. Interestingly, Worth magazine has just put out a list of 50 top American CEOs in which Kashmir-born M. Farooq, the CEO of Ethan Allan, is the only Indian to figure. Top academics and Wall Street figures are ethnic Indians. Indians are gradually becoming active in American politics as well. How we leverage this diaspora and sustain the networks will be critical. But this has to be accompanied by a second, big-bang liberalisation wave at home.

India's record in narcotics control has been exemplary and we must cash in on this. Cooperation in science and technology, especially in agriculture and health, is another promising area for mutual benefit. PL-480 funds have sustained such cooperation. But these funds are drying up and have to be replenished. Interest in India on American campuses has to be revived. This will require a new mindset on visas and research project clearances. A most promising MIT India programme has just been launched but it is running on individual initiative. Long-term sources of funding from industry and government have to be found.

19/07/1999

◆━━◆━━◆

LAST TANGO IN BUENOS AIRES
Orthopraxy on an unorthodoxy has killed Argentina for the moment

The land of evita, CHE, borges and Maradona, the land of the Pampas and Patagonia, the land deriving its name from the Latin for silver is in anarchy. Three presidents in the past month. A default on its $155 billion external debt. Total collapse of investor confidence. Run on bank deposits. Violent rioting. All this and more in a country that had European standards of living in 1900 but then went on a steep downward spiral, a country blessed with a variety of riches and whose appalling performance must rank as one of history's greatest puzzles.

The only mitigating circumstance is that the latest Argentinian crisis has not resulted in contagion. The debt default has not destabilised world markets. What explains this unusual phenomenon? Three factors. First, the Argentinian crisis was a slowbleed and the tragic drama was playing itself out for the past six months at least. In the language of finance, markets had "discounted" what was happening in Argentina. Second, markets are getting better informed and countries are being distinguished according to their special features, unlike in the past when a crisis spread like a virus. Third, this time the international creditor response has been tepid. High-profile interventions impart a global dimension and their absence heighten the localised flavour of the crisis. In the past, Argentina has been bailed out by the International Monetary Fund (IMF) with American support—$40 billion in December 2000 and $8 billion in August 2001.

Why did Argentina collapse? It was after all a country that averaged an economic growth of 5.7 per cent during 1991-98, a country that privatised aggressively and attracted about $90 billion of foreign investment in the 1990s largely from the US and Spain. Paradoxically, Argentina became a victim of its own success. In the 1980s, it was torn apart by hyperinflation. In 1989, the annual inflation rate crossed an astronomical 3,000 per cent. It was then that it adopted an unorthodox system called the currency board. The peso:dollar parity was fixed at 1:1 with full convertibility. Peso supply could not expand without a corresponding increase in the supply of dollars. With this move, Argentina abandoned monetary independence in trying to assure exchange rate stability and free capital mobility.

The effect was astounding. Hyperinflation was licked by the mid-1990s itself. Argentina weathered the Mexican crisis of 1994-95 and the East Asian and Russian shocks of 1997-98 relatively well. But beginning January 1999 with the currency devaluation in Brazil, Argentina's main trading partner, the adverse effects of the currency board began to be felt. The peso started appreciating, exports became uncompetitive and current account deficits mounted. The currency board depended on external borrowing and as a result the debt burden accumulated rapidly. With fiscal indiscipline, interest rates zoomed. The net result was a recession and growing unemployment. Argentina's fiscal abandon during 1995-99 destroyed any possibility of using fiscal stimulus to revive growth. The absence of growth magnified the debt and deficit burden. It is the combination that proved lethal.

The obvious response to the growing crisis would have been an abandonment of the currency board. That did not happen since the Argentines felt that such a move would threaten a return to high in-flation. Devaluation has also been anathema to foreign investors and local companies and families holding dollar debts. As things turned out, it was only on January 7 this year that a devaluation took place but recovery will be a long and painful process. Undoubtedly, there are other factors responsible for Argentina's predicament. Over half of its exports are food and farm commodities, prices of which have been depressed in the past few years and trade in which continues to be strangulated by huge subsidies in the US, Japan and Europe. Its unions wield enormous power and prevent restructuring, making labour markets inflexible. The IMF may also not have been tough enough when it approved the August 2001 bailout and should have insisted on a devaluation then. Then there is Argentine politics—venal, populist, particularly in provinces, and deeply divisive.

The fundamental lesson from Argentina is that a country cannot make its currency freely convertible and be fiscally reckless at the same time. With a fiscal deficit close to 11 per cent of GDP, as compared to around 4 per cent in Argentina, India could be disaster-bound. What has saved us is that we still retain controls on both inflows and outflows of capital. Prudence has paid off but is it really such a good thing? In our case, the closed capital account and public ownership of banks act like aspirin—it keeps the fever down while the bacteria of fiscal profligacy keep eating away at our innards. Argentina exploded into an external crisis. India is imploding into a growth crisis—somewhat like Japan.

21/01/2002

◆——◆

WHAT WILL BUSH PUSH?

Bush will continue where Clinton left off but there will be some changes

Generally, Indians believe that democrats in the US are to be preferred to Republicans. In actual fact, we have got along famously with Republicans (barring the Nixon regime) in America. However, with the growing political clout and economic strength of the Indian diaspora in the US and the progress of economic reforms in India, there would hardly be any difference between a Republican or a Democratic president. Moreover, the real power of the American president tends to get vastly exaggerated, circumscribed as he is by the equally powerful American Senate and the House of Representatives. Even so, while the legislative branch can certainly have its own agenda, the US president's policies do set the trend, particularly where America's relationship with the rest of the world is concerned. How would George Bush's election as President influence Indo-US ties?

First, the Comprehensive Test Ban Treaty (CTBT), which prohibits nuclear tests, will finally be junked. During the election campaign, Bush came out strongly against the CTBT. Some of his advisers want him to go in for a whole new national missile defence system while some others have argued for non-proliferation. Whatever Bush ends up doing, it is clear that the CTBT as it exists today is dead and the pressure on India and Pakistan to come on board will definitely ease. Giving up the CTBT does not mean that non-proliferation will cease to be an American concern. It will continue to be so although what form a new CTBT will take remains to be seen. However, the death of the CTBT does in no way diminish our responsibility to be part of any inter-nationally accepted regime of nuclear control and to arrive at an agreement to avert nuclear clashes with both Pakistan and China. The pressure on the Indian Government from our own scientists and nuclear strategists to resume testing will, undoubtedly, manifest itself. It will call for extraordinary statesmanship to resist this pressure.

Second, Bush will certainly try and explore new ave-nues of military cooperation with Pakistan. There are many influential advisers in the Republican camp who still recall the Pakistani contribution to ridding Afghanistan of the USSR's presence, a key trigger for the ultimate demise of the communist regime in Moscow. It will be in our interest that any new US-Pakistan military tie-up is linked to getting Pakistan back to the Lahore spirit and for Pakistan to work with India to translate the fine-sounding MoU signed in February 1999 at Lahore into a set of demonstrable, verifiable and monitorable confidence-building measures to manage the risks of nuclear conflicts in our region.

Third, Bush's position on China may not be wholly unwelcome to us as we strive to settle borders with our Himalayan neighbour. No American president can afford to take a very hard line on China. The Chinese have simply swamped the American consumer market with cheap but high-quality goods. They are also large importers of American goods even though they run a huge annual trade surplus of about $50 billion. China's trade with the US has given it enormous leverage. Bush supported the Clinton initiative to establish permanent normal trading relations with China a few months back. But it is the nuance that counts.

The Republicans see China as a strategic competitor and not necessarily as a strategic partner which was the language of Clinton.

Fourth, American pressure on human rights, environment and other social issues as part of trade links will ease considerably. Al-ready Bush has announced his opposition to the Kyoto agreement on climate control which would have limited India's greater use of coal. The Democrats are linked more closely to trade unions and NGOs who were primarily responsible for the fracas at the ministerial meeting of the WTO in Seattle a year ago which quashed the prospects of a new round of global trade negotiations. Bush's commitment to the WTO may not be as strong as his commitment to bilateral free trade agreement along the lines of NAFTA—the North American Free Trade Agreement that covers the US, Canada and Mexico—with South and Central American countries. Free trade agreements with Jordan and Singapore are also on the anvil. It is really up to India to engage the Bush administration proactively and constructively on WTO-related matters. In agriculture, information technology and services, Indian and American interests converge.

Republican strategists have called for America to take India more seriously. That sentiment is certainly to be welcomed. But what will give us our legitimate due is sustained economic growth, continued liberalisation and faster translation of the intentions behind the reforms into actual practice. If we focus on the internals with a single-minded purpose and a greater sense of urgency, the externals will fall into place.

01/01/2001

——◆——◆——

A COMMON HERITAGE?
The idea of a US-India free trade agreement gets new and influential support

The heritage foundation in washington is one of the pre-eminent think tanks of the American conservative establishment and has close links with the Bush regime. Very recently, after a visit to India, Dana Dillon, a policy analyst at the foundation, has produced a report, "Time for Expanded Trade Relations with India", in which he advocates a free trade agreement (FTA) between the US and India.

The idea is not new. Last year, just before Bill Clinton's yatra to this country, two Washington-based Indian economists, Aaditya Mattoo and Arvind Subramanian, had put forward the idea of USINTA, a US-India Free Trade Area. Writing in the January-February 2000 issue of Foreign Affairs, Robert Zoellick, now Bush's top trade negotiator, had said the US should propose trade and investment liberalisation to India.

In a free-trade area, countries maintain their own import duties against outsiders while scrapping duties among themselves. This is different from a customs union where countries have common tariff nomenclatures and identical tariff rates. In a common market all restrictions on the movement of labour and capital are removed while in an economic union national economic policies are harmonised. Worldwide, there are 130 FTAs in force and India itself is committed to a South Asian FTA (SAFTA) by 2003.

The US has had an FTAwith Israel for some time. The North American Free Trade Agreement (NAFTA) involving the US, Canada and Mexico came into force seven years ago. Currently, the US is negotiating FTAs with Chile, Singapore and Jordan and an FTAA—the Free Trade Agreement for the Americas—involving 34 countries of South, Central and North Americas. The three bilateral FTAs could be con-cluded in the next few months while the FTAA is slated to come into force by January 2005.

How will India gain from an FTA with the US? As Mattoo and Subramanian and Dillon explain:
- textiles and clothing exports will face lower import duties, as indeed will our exports of labour-intensive manufactured goods;
- highly skilled Indian technical personnel will have greater employment opportunities in the US;
- inflows of US investment in key sectors like telecommunications, IT, financial services and infrastructure will get a boost;
- broader strategic engagement between the world's largest and richest democracies will be strengthened;
- the European Union will be encouraged to seek a similar agreement with India.

Of course, an FTA does not automatically guarantee market share. That would depend on how competitive our exports are and this, in turn, will be influenced largely by domestic economic policies. Are there any costs to an FTA? Decidedly so, on at least two counts.

First, the US could insist on including non-trade issues like labour and environment in the FTA. The US-Jordan FTA follows this approach. But on the other hand, labour and environment do not form part of the main NAFTA but are the subjects of two side agreements which commit members to enforce their own standards and to only engage in consultations. The Jordan template is bad but we could live with NAFTA.

Second, there is a real danger that bilateralism will undermine the multilateral process and the WTO. The guru of trade economics, Jagdish Bhagwati, has called FTAs not "building blocks" of free trade but actually "stumbling blocks" to the goal of free and fair trade since they constitute preferential, discriminatory trade liberalisation. His fear that the world's trading system could be damaged in the name of free trade rather than in the name of protection is genuine. But with multilateral negotiations, to use Dillon's term, "ensnared" by a whole host of issues and with the US committed to a three-pronged global, re-gional and bilateral strategy for trade negotiations on the grounds that by moving on multiple points, competition in liberalisation is created, India cannot afford to reject the FTA route. However, we cannot wish away Bhagwati.

India should proactively engage the US in talks about a bilateral FTA even as it works with the US and others to launch a new round of multilateral trade negotiations in Qatar in November 2001. Great progress between the two countries in the field of security has been made by the so-called Track-II diplomacy where non-officials from both sides exchange views to facilitate convergence of official positions and a consensus. Non-officials are not hamstrung in discussions as officials are. A similar Track-II effort is now needed in the trade area as well. Running with the multilateral hare while hunting with the bilateral hound will do India no harm, keeping in view global realities.

04/06/2001

◆——◆

STOP WHINING, START DOING
Petulance and pique will get us nowhere with the US—performance will

India and the US have been described as estranged democracies that have since become engaged democracies. However, after September

11, the atmosphere has changed. Embittered democracies may be too strong a phrase to describe this new phase in the bilateral relationship. but it certainly captures the present mood in India, which feels that Pakistan has scored over it.

Pakistan's media strategy has been, as usual, far superior to ours. But the truth is we are behaving petulantly, viewing September 11 and its fallout exclusively from the prism of cross-border terrorism in Kashmir. Pique is preventing us from thinking clearly.

- Is not the decimation of Pakistan's Afghan strategy and extermination of terrorist camps in Afghanistan in India's national interest?
- Is not the destruction of Osama bin Laden's extensive global network and the neutralisation of his perversion of Islam in India's national interest?
- Is not the replacement of the fundamentalist Taliban regime in Afghanistan by a genuinely multiethnic and secular government in India's national interest?
- Is not America's greater leverage in Pakistan going to moderate China's influence and strengthen the forces seeking peaceful accommodation with India?
- Is not the increased American and world involvement in fighting global terrorism in India's national interest?
- Is not the changing geopolitics of Central Asia with its long-term impact on energy markets in India's national interest?
- Is not this a moment of historic opportunity for India to work out a new relationship with Pakistan without which we can never fulfil our global destiny?

The short answer to these questions is a loud and un-qualified "yes". Of course, the Americans did have the option of telling Pakistan that, look, we know your specialisation in export-oriented terrorism, we know that you aborted an earlier US plan to capture bin Laden in 1998 and we know that the Taliban has been created by you, so cooperate or else.

Instead, the Americans have indulged the Pakistanis. But why not? Does it not make eminent tactical and strategic sense? Unlike India, Pakistan shares a border with Afghanistan which is about 1,800 km long. Pakistan has built up the Taliban and was one of the three countries that had diplomatic relations with it. On the other hand, India had no contact whatsoever with the Taliban as it supports the Northern Alliance along with Russia and Iran. Pakistan is also not without its friends in the US conservative establishment and in the US military from the 1980s, although our fears of a parallel between America's current ardour for Pakistan and its alliance of two decades ago are vastly exaggerated.

Given the presence of religious fanatics in such large numbers in Pakistan and knowing fully well the under-current of antipathy to it in that country, America had to sugarcoat its approach to President Pervez Musharraf who may well be perfidious but at least draws inspiration from the father of Turkey's modernisation Mustafa Kemal Ataturk, incidentally also a great favourite of pre-1947 Jawaharlal Nehru. Pakistan is now poised to get a fresh IMF loan of about $ 1.5 billion over and above the $600 million it has received since November 2000. Why should we grudge this since a bankrupt Pakistan is simply not in our national interest?

For the moment, quite naturally the Americans are fixated exclusively on two objectives—get bin Laden and force the Taliban out. Everything else is secondary. And why shouldn't it be? But we want the Americans and the world to also focus on Jammu and Kashmir. Is this the moment to thrust ourselves in such a childish manner knowing fully well that the US tend to be unifocal in its approach? On the one hand, we shout that Jammu and Kashmir is a bilateral issue to be sorted out by India and Pakistan. Then why are we disappointed when Tony Blair does not read from our script? We bemoan the US media's anti-India bias. But it is this very media that is exposing Pakistan's links to terrorism and is urging President George W. Bush to be cautious in cozying up to Pakistan. It is wrong to assume that the Americans would allow its rapprochement with Pakistan endanger Indo-US ties. However, the moment the US realises that India has become a NATO—No Action, Talk Only—economy and that diminishing returns to incentives for engagement with India have set in, then we are in serious trouble. Sadly, that moment of reckoning is fast approaching as our political parties are unable to transcend partisan positions and agree on a national agenda for the acceleration of economic growth, preservation of social harmony and resumption of the regional peace process.

22/10/2001

A SOLDIER'S JOURNEY
Powell came, Powell saw, Powell concurred—but with whom?

US Secretary of state colin powell has just completed a whirlwind visit to the subcontinent. It is now abundantly clear that the Americans have decided to put all their Pakistani eggs into the Pervez Musharraf basket. Whatever the Indians may say about the General's duplicitous nature and lack of trustworthiness, Washington has gambled and decided to back him to the hilt.

Such a strategy is not without its risks. In the past, unstinted support to an individual has cost the US dear as its experience with the Shah of Iran demonstrated. American backing of repressive, non-democratic regimes in many West Asian countries has also fuelled great resentment. Thus, the US will have to think of engaging Pakistan across a broad front over a period of time in as comprehensive a manner as possible. Musharraf himself is probably a marked man. Hence, a commitment to him should be accompanied by some thought to fallback positions.

But for the moment, Musharraf appears to be holding firm and has certainly impressed the Americans by taking on the fundamentalist forces in his country. That he may have done so out of compulsion and only because of American arm-twisting is besides the point. The fact is that the entire international community now sees Musharraf as a reasonable-sounding man with whom India must do business. Agra may have been a bitter experience but do we have any alternative other than to resume the peace process? A quiet American role may help structure the peace process better and not hold everything hostage to a settlement on Jammu and Kashmir. The war in Afghanistan is grinding on. The US is groping for a quick solution. The military window of opportunity is open for just about a month before the onset of both Ramzan and the winter. This lends greater urgency to military operations, in the success of which India has a stake. Richard Haas, director of policy planning in the US State Department, has just been appointed to coordinate the political strategy. Although he is a West Asia expert, for the past few years Haas has been actively involved with the subcontinent as well. Zalmay Khalilzad, an Afghan-American scholar of distinction, is also playing a key role out of the White House. India has to work closely with them to ensure that a non-Taliban regime is installed in Kabul.

The primary requirement in the political strategy should be to look after Afghanistan's interests first and foremost and not be overly worried about what Pakistan thinks. However, we cannot deny Pakistan's legitimate security concerns in Afghanistan, although it may well be the case that Pakistan is deliberately overplaying the demographic dominance of Pashtoons in Afghanistan. Russia and Iran also have vital interests in Afghanistan, as do Uzbekistan and Tajikistan. Iran has made statements both supportive and critical of the US action in Afghanistan. But American suspicion of Iran runs deep. Uzbekistan has embraced America warmly and it looks as if the Americans will use it as a base for expanding their sphere of influence in Central Asia. The key resource-rich countries in the region, however, are Turkmenistan and Kazakhstan which are not directly embroiled in the Afghan conflict. It will help the US as well as all other countries if the UN were to orchestrate the political strategy and reconstruction.

Powell's visit has brought Kashmir back into sharp focus, more so because it was preceded by India's attack on terrorist-training camps across the Line of Control in Jammu and Kashmir. This was in keeping with the penchant of te two subcontinental adversaries for using high profile visits to make their respective points in a dramatic manner. Kashmir may not quite be a "core" issue as Musharraf makes it out to be, but Powell and the rest of the world believe that it is a "central" issue between the two nuclear countries. At some stage surely we have to recognise this reality.

And at some stage surely we have to admit to ourselves that Jammu and Kashmir's continuing tragedy is not just the creation and consequence of cross-border terrorism masterminded by Pakistan. To be sure, in recent years the nature of militancy in the Valley has changed and we have been brutally exposed to export-oriented terrorism from Pakistan and Afghanistan. But this cannot be and is not the whole picture. There are strong domestic roots to our predicament in the Valley. Military options are extremely limited. Elections to the state Assembly are due in about a year. The next few months, therefore, are going to be crucial for broad-basing and sustaining the political process in that state and for taking steps to show to the world the great resilience and absorptive capacity of representative Indian democracy. The US can play a key role in reining in Pakistan so that the electoral process is conducted in a peaceful manner, but the primary responsibility to ensure that the elections are perceived as free and fair is ours.

29/10/2001

13/12 AND THE US
India and Pakistan will come together only with US prodding

September 11, pr 9/11 in the way American juxtapose day and month, has been a defining moment for the US and indeed for the world at large. 13/12 is a watershed for India. Anger and outrage at what happened at Parliament House is perfectly justifiable. However, it is equally important to keep a sense of balance, the sort that A.B. Vajpayee kept during Kargil and earned India international support. What-ever India's short-term response, military or otherwise, the events nevertheless underscore the urgent need for the US to have a long-term strategy in South Asia given its influence with both the nuclear adversaries. This may not be the best of times in this country to even think of a US role. But for the sake of peace and prosperity in this troubled region we must look beyond the immediate.

Between a policy of benign neglect that the US has followed in the past and a policy of active "intervention" sought by Pakistan along the lines of the American involvement in the Middle East and Northern Ireland peace process but unacceptable to India, there is a middle ground that the US can occupy to the advantage of India, Pakistan and itself. It is time for the US to formulate a minimalist agenda based on realistic milestones that are achievable. This would not be third-party intervention but certainly third-party cajoling, persuading, catalysing, nudging and all other such verbs that convey a more friendly image than pressurising and intervening. The sad reality is that without such US prodding, India and Pakistan just will not engage each other meaningfully.

First, the US must take an active interest in pushing India and Pakistan to enter into a confidence-building agreement on nuclear and missile matters. In February 1999 the two nuclear adversaries had signed a memorandum of understanding (MoU) to enhance peace and security between themselves but unfortunately the Kargil conflict intervened and it was forgotten. It is this MoU that needs to be converted into an enforceable, monitorable and verifiable nuclear and missile management treaty.

Second, the US must get India and Pakistan to enhance economic ties between themselves. It was largely with American and World Bank support that India and Pakistan signed the landmark Indus Waters Treaty in 1960 after eight years of negotiations. An Iran-Pakistan-India or a

Turkmenistan-Afghanistan-Pakistan-India natural gas pipeline could have great political symbolism apart from its economic benefits. On trade, the US must prevail upon Pakistan to give up its resistance to extending MFN (most favoured nation) status to India which is India's legitimate due under international trade agreements. This means duties imposed by Pakistan on Indian imports will be no different from those imposed on imports from other countries and India will not be discriminated against. As for India, it already grants MFN status to Pakistan.

Third, the US must ensure that Pakistan and its proxies do not vitiate the atmosphere in the run-up to the elections to the Jammu and Kashmir Assembly that are due before October 2002. It must also gently tell India to enhance the credibility of the electoral process in Jammu and Kashmir. One way to do so would be for India to invite an international group of observers comprising people like Nelson Mandela and Bill Clinton. India will also have to think seriously about broad-basing the political process in Jammu and Kashmir. The US could also get India and Pakistan to appoint high-level political envoys to start talking about longer-term options in Jammu and Kashmir.

Fourth, the US must move India and Pakistan to start serious talks to resolve non-Kashmir-related disputes. Twice, in 1989 and 1992, a deal on the Siachen glacier had almost been clinched at the official level but was killed by political pusillanimity on both sides. Similarly, the elements of how to solve the land and maritime boundary problems in the Sir Creek area in the Rann of Kutch had been agreed to by both sides over eight years ago but no agreement has materialised.

Fifth, given the influential role played by the subcontinental diaspora, American think tanks must take the lead in starting what could be a Track-III in addition to the official Track-I and non-official Track-II, both of which, sadly, are themselves stalled presently. Recently, two American foundations supported a study that resulted in a remarkable book India and Pakistan: The Costs of Conflict, the Benefits of Peace by a distinguished Pakistani militaryman Major-General Mahmud Ali Durrani. Indian and Pakistani scientists working in the US, like M.V. Ramana and Zia Mian, have co-authored blueprints for nuclear peace.

Patience and low-profile are words not normally associated with American diplomacy. But that is exactly what is needed in our region where a historic opportu-nity has opened up. It is up to the Americans to grasp it.

24/12/2001

◆   ◆

B. China

SINO-INDIAN THAWING

The background to the Chinese response to Kargil

In 1970 the british journalist academic Neville Maxwell first published his scholarly book India's China War. The book was a searing indictment of the way India handled the border dispute with China in the 1950s. Maxwell's thesis was that India provoked the 1962 Sino-Indian war by deeply flawed political, military and historical judgement. However, despite his formidable mastery over detail, Maxwell's remains a minority view. But one of our former foreign secretaries whose dealings with China go back to 1961 tells Kautilya that Maxwell was 60 per cent right. Another foreign service officer, widely acknowledged to being one of our foremost experts on China, feels that Maxwell was 75 per cent right!

Now 29 years later, Maxwell has revisited the Sino-Indian border dispute and published another exhaustive piece in a recent issue of the Economic and Political Weekly. One of his conclusions is that had India done in the 1950s what prime minister P.V. Narasimha Rao did in September 1993 in signing the Agreement on Peace and Tranquillity along the Line of Actual Control (LoAC) in the India-China border areas, history would have been different. There is an irony here which escapes Maxwell. As external affairs minister, Rao was a voice of doubt on any major initiative towards China in the '80s.

Rao was, of course, building upon years of efforts. In 1976, realising that China was changing and that the Soviets and Americans were making up with it, Indira Gandhi decided to resume ambassador-level relations by sending our current President as envoy. In 1979, foreign minister A.B. Vajpayee visited China when Deng Xiaoping, who was in the midst of launching the "Four Modernisations" drive, told him that China was prepared to negotiate the border dispute with India. In 1981, the Chinese foreign minister Huang Hua returned the visit.

The even keel of the evolving relationship was suddenly disturbed by the little-analysed Operation Chequerboard launched by General K. Sundarji on the Chinese border at Sumdurong Chu in March-April

1987. Maxwell quotes Sundarji as having told him that "the challenge that India had mounted and China's passive response to it had restored the morale the Indian Army had lost in 1962". This may well have been the case but other assessments are that it was another explosive military action taken by a flamboyant military mind without regard to broader consequences.

To reassure the Chinese about India's peaceful intentions, prime minister Rajiv Gandhi then sent the venerable P.N. Haksar as his special envoy to Beijing in May 1987. Haksar's brief was to tell the Chinese that the Indian prime minister would not be averse to accepting their invitation for a visit. Then followed a succession of visits by mandarins, politicians and journalists from India, finally culminating in the historic December 1988 visit of Rajiv himself. The Deng-Rajiv meeting was an unprecedented success. One key participant told Kautilya that it appeared as if Deng was compensating for 1962. It was this visit and that of Chinese premier Li Peng in December 1991 to India that laid the foundations for Rao's achievement of 1993.

The September 1993 agreement was signed, at India's insistence, in Beijing to increase, in the words of one key player "China's stake in honouring it". The agreement commits both sides not to use or even threaten to use force, to strictly observe the LoAC and to reducing their troop strengths along this line. In the past four years, over 20,000 Indian troops have been deployed away from the Chinese border to more critical areas. The 1993 agreement was followed up by a more operational Agreement on Confidence-building Measures in the military field along the LoAC signed during President Ziang Zemin's visit to India in November-December 1996. Incidentally, following this, the Chinese President went to Pakistan and startled his hosts by suggesting the Kashmir dispute be set aside for the time being so that Indo-Pak relations could improve.

It is this background that explains China's restrained reaction to Kargil. The two agreements worked to India's advantage. If they had not existed, all that the Chinese had to do was leak news of some troop movements near Arunachal Pradesh for India to go into a tizzy. That did not happen. The Chinese mindset on India has changed partly because they know they have simply outstripped us as an economic power. But our mindset on China is frozen. Wisdom lies in recognising realities, in taking advantage of the openings the 1993 and 1996 agreements provide and in adopting a flexible approach on the border question. One option would be to convert the LoAC into the international boundary. That mutual compromises have to be made, keeping in mind each other's strategic interests, is inevitable. The Chinese appear to be ready. But we are not. A symbolic beginning could be made, as J.N. Dixit has suggested in his memoirs Across Borders, by redesignating the McMahon Line. Perhaps, this could be called the Deng-Rajiv Line in recognition of their long and emotional handshake of 1988 that transformed the Sino-Indian relationship. Delineation of the boundary using modern technology and other steps could then follow.

02/08/1999

◆━━━◆

GREAT MALL OF CHINA
Indian industry is clamouring for protection against dumping by China. Why?

Just over two years ago, the Atal Bihari Vajpayee Government demonised China saying our going nuclear was prompted by the threat from across the Himalayas. Now, it is the turn of Indian industry. We are being told that Chinese products and goods are being dumped in Indian markets. Dumping is said to take place when the export price is lower than the price normally charged in the home market. Countries impose anti-dumping duties but only after a prescribed process of investigation is gone through and "material" injury to domestic producers is proven. In the past three years, of about 70 petitions put forward by Indian companies to the Union Commerce Ministry for imposition of anti-dumping duty, 32 have been triggered by Chinese imports.

Figures with the Union Finance Ministry give some idea of the Chinese penetra-tion. In a dry cell battery market of about Rs 1,000 crore, imports from China are about Rs 35 crore; in a writing instruments industry of about Rs 1,200 crore, Chinese imports are around Rs 50 crore; in an umbrella market of about Rs 100 crore, Chinese imports are about Rs 4 crore; and in a locks market of around Rs 100 crore, Chinese imports are placed at about Rs 4 crore. Thus, judged from a national market perspective, it is difficult to support the contention that Chinese imports are swamping the country.

Moreover, in some cases, Chinese imports do not compete directly with their Indian counterparts. Take raw silk, for example. India produces around 15,000 tonnes of silk a year but this is of an inferior variety called multivoltine silk. Our imports from China of about 7,000 tonnes a year are of the vastly superior bivoltine variety which we do not produce. No wonder silk weavers are happy with imports—which illustrates a more general point that while dumping may be bad from a local producer's point of view, it may well offer benefits to local consumers and users.

Garments, toys, sports goods, plastic goods and a slew of household appliances are all areas where Chinese goods have simply swamped world markets. Indian industry cannot be blamed for lack of competitiveness in such sectors where small-scale reservation has held us back. If this reservation is removed, as it must, production will still take place in small units, but not small as defined by us. The Chinese may well be dumping. China is not yet a member of the WTO and therefore can get away with pretty much what it does specially since its companies are not subject to the type of financial transparency as companies elsewhere in the world, including in India, are. In a number of cases, Chinese selling prices do not even cover raw material costs. Indian industry does deserve a break on this score.

Anti-dumping duty investigation and imposition procedures are long and cumbersome and the minimum time taken is around six months. That is one reason why P. Chidambaram introduced the concept of "safeguard" duty in his July 1996 budget. This is a duty imposed to deal with a sudden surge in imports and to give timely but temporary relief to Indian companies who are facing "serious" injury. But while anti-dumping duty can be country-specific, safeguard duty is not. In any case, like the anti-dumping duty, a quasi-judicial procedure has also to be gone through. This means that even the safeguard duty will take a minimum four to five months for imposition.

Indian industry has called for faster completion of anti-dumping investigations and reliefs. That call is justified but no process can take less than 90 days. But the real problem is that we can be hurt more by the use of anti-dumping duties by other countries on our exports than we can benefit by imposing anti-dumping duties on imports. We, therefore, stand to gain by the abolition of the very system of anti-dumping duties. India should play a leading role in the WTO in this regard.

Since anti-dumping duty takes time and is counter-productive, what can be done immediately is to insist on goods coming into India conforming to Indian standards specifications and displaying the maximum retail price in rupees. These are called "non-tariff" measures to provide relief to local producers facing unfair competition. And to deal with Chinese goods being smuggled in from Nepal,we could renegotiate the 1996 bilateral treaty and insist that India will allow duty-free imports from Nepal only if there is, say, 30 per cent value-addition in that country itself.

However, the broader point is that the Chinese manufacturing industry is more efficient than India's. That is because the government there has engineered a competitive advantage specially for labour-intensive manufacturing. This is an area where, unfortunately, the Government's small-scale and fiscal policy and poor infrastructure have denied and are still denying India the opportunity of emerging as a world power.

11/12/2000

❖ ❖ ❖

MAO TO MURTHY
Li Peng's visit to Infosys shows our software strength but we should not be smug

Li Peng's visit to infosys in Bangalore on January 16 is the first public show of Chinese respect for India's contemporary achievements. India's software exports in 2000-01 will be around $6.2 billion with Infosys accounting for about 5-6 per cent of this amount. Here, we are miles ahead of China whose software exports annually are just about double that of Infosys. But in other segments of the "new" econ-omy—Internet, telecom and PCs—we are way behind by a factor of between three and five and in mobile telephony by a factor of over twenty. The star of the new economy is Cisco—China accounts for about 5 per cent of Cisco's business as compared to our share of about 0.3 per cent. If we don't watch out, China may soon surpass us in software as well. An example of the Chinese push is the plan to set up 100 IIT-type institutes.

Actually, on almost every indicator China's performance is vastly superior to that of India—and the gap is widening. Only in Kerala have we done better than China in social development. Only in Gujarat and Maharashtra have we had Chinese-type economic growth rates in the past decade, but neither in Mumbai nor Ahmedabad are there visible signs of renewal or progress as in Shanghai.

True, we are a democracy. True, China is socially more homogeneous and less stratified. But Chinese provinces enjoy greater economic freedom than Indian states. American political scientist Susan Shirk has written of how policymaking in China is a pluralistic process. Also, Pranab Bardhan, one of India's most eminent economists, has pointed out that countries like South Korea and Taiwan have more local-level democracy than India reflected in the way irrigation systems have been managed. One of India's top Sinologists, C.V. Ranganathan, once posed a troubling question: would any political party in India emulate the National Peoples' Congress that passed a resolution saying Mao was 60 per cent right and 40 per cent wrong?

Between 1950 and the mid-1970s, China's economic record was only marginally better. But since 1975, China's GDP has grown at an annual average compound rate of over 9.5 per cent as compared to India's 5.3 per cent. In 1975, China's exports were about twice that of India; now they are six times higher. Chinese import duties are half that of India. Industry accounts for close to 50 per cent of the GDP in China as compared to India's 25 per cent, showing that India is becoming a service economy without reaping the benefits of the intervening stage of broad-based industrialisation.

Chinese agricultural yields are two to three times higher than in India. Around 45-50 per cent of area under rice cultivation grows hybrid rice. Silk production is of the vastly superior bivoltine variety. Arable land in China on a per person basis is about half of that in India. This makes its agrarian record even more noteworthy. We have outperformed China only in milk production—perhaps only because the Chinese don't drink milk. China simply invests more: gross domestic investment rate has always exceeded 35-40 per cent of the GDP whereas our rates have hovered around 25 per cent. Foreign investment is only a part of the story. Yes, foreign direct investment into China in the 1990s has totalled close to $300 billion as compared to about $15 billion in India. More basically, domestic resource mobilisation itself has been greater and that is the key.

The Chinese have excelled in labour-intensive mass manufacturing—textiles, electrical and electronic goods, sports goods, toys, plastic goods, leather goods and consumer items. Chinese exports of this basket are almost eight times that of India while they were on a par with each other just about a decade and a half ago. We have been handicapped by the Gandhian legacy that devalued mass production and hamstrung by our extraordinary emphasis on heavy industry. Indian civilisation has been more knowledge-based but our social system has prevented the diffusion of knowledge. On the other hand, the Chinese have been more application-oriented and gave the world the magnetic compass, gun-powder, printing press, paper, cast iron, the harness, the suspension bridge and numerous other inventions.

China has gained immeasurably more from its diaspora, particularly in Hong Kong and Taiwan, which to-gether account for three-fourths of the foreign investment flowing into the mainland. The diaspora has also boosted exports. On the other hand, hapless Indian workers in the Middle East do more for India by way of remittances than their vastly more privileged counterparts elsewhere. Ultimately, where the Chinese have scored over us is in their pragmatism, exemplified in Deng Xiaoping's aphorism, "What does it matter if the colour of the cat is black or white as long as it catches mice?" In India, we get stuck in wholly useless debates on the nature of the cat while the population of mice proliferates.

29/01/2001

———◆———

THE DRAGON AND THE COW
Zhu Rongji's visit draws attention to the India-China issue again

India and China have finally signed an agreement on civil aviation. The Beijing-Delhi air link will start on March 28. There is a depressing history to this as the recently released Volume 27 of the Selected Works of Jawaharlal Nehru reveals. This volume contains detailed accounts of Nehru's meetings with Mao, Zhou and other Chinese leaders during his only visit to China.

On October 21, 1954, Zhou told Nehru: "We desire that Indian Airlines should come into Canton via Hong Kong so that they can be connected with China ... Similarly, on the basis of equality our airlines should extend to Calcutta. Of course, we will not be having any airlines to India immediately while India may be able to start airlines to China immediately. But since we are friendly countries Indian extension can start and we are giving it as a gesture to a friendly country." Nehru replied, "The question of airlines requires careful consideration."

Well, the matter took 47 years to be resolved and the roles are reversed. Then, India would have started the service first. Today, China will be first off the block. This episode reflects the India-China economic story of the past five decades, a tale of missed opportunities for us, opportunities that continue to get lost entirely because of poor infrastructure, rigid labour laws, small-scale reservation and other policy bottlenecks .

In the 1950s and '60s the two countries were roughly on a par and in many areas India was even visibly ahead of China. But from the mid-1970s, China raced ahead and the gap increased spectacularly in the 1990s largely because of China's stunning performance in exports and in investment. Barring software exports, there is no area where India's performance is superior. China is the second-largest economy in the world and India is the fourth largest, measured in terms of purchasing power parity. On present reckoning, by 2010, India could overtake Japan to occupy third place while China could overtake the US by 2030. But the India-China gap would remain. The extraordinary success of China in labour-in-tensive mass manufacturing has given it the big edge over India, an edge that cannot be compensated for by our current leadership in knowledge-based industries. In any case, this leadership is itself under threat, reflected in Premier Zhu Rongji's recent pilgrimage to Bangalore, following a trip there by Li Peng last year.

India scores over China in its commitment to political democracy and in its celebration of social diversity. But that is no excuse for being left behind in economic development where China has outstripped India thanks to vastly superior political leadership. As an example, no political party in India has seen it fit to do what the Chinese Communist Party (CCP) has done: set up a training institute. For the past five years, this school was run like any American graduate school by Hu Jintao who soon takes over from Ziang Zemin as general secretary of the CCP.

Are India and China natural adversaries? A new book by the noted American Sinologist John Garver, Protracted Contest: Sino-Indian Rivalry in the Twentieth Century, thinks so. It is a work of formidable scholarship and is unusual for the use of primary Chinese source material. Garver's thesis is that India and China have a fundamentally conflicting relationship. Their political and military strategies are such that their interests clash—in relation to the western and eastern borders, Tibet, Nepal, Bhutan, Pakistan, Myanmar and the Indian Ocean. Garver's conclusion is that "unless India is able to alter its lacklustre development record and to work out a skilful and confident programme employing Indian national capabilities in the South Asian region, India could well conclude that the prudent way to enhance its security is to assume a role as junior partner to an emerging Chinese superpower".

Of course, Garver's thesis has its critics. India and China, written by C. V. Ranganathan, India's foremost Sinologist, and Vinod Khanna, appeared last year. The duo recognised the deep differences between India and China but had argued for India's engagement with the Chinese across a broad spectrum of areas. But are we ready for it? Since August 1999, Ranganathan has been spearheading a non-official "Kunming Initiative" that seeks to build economic linkages between India's north-east, China's south-west, Myanmar and Bangladesh. But nothing concrete has materialised so far.

The pace of implementation of the two historic Sino-Indian agreements on the border in September 1993 and November 1996 has been disappointing and we have to share a good part of the blame for this. V. V. Paranjpe, who was the interpreter and note taker during Nehru's trip, wrote last week in the Hindustan Times that India is befogged with prejudice and misunderstanding about China. What India needs is the boldness of a Rajiv Gandhi who, ignoring many of his advisers, radically redefined our relationship with China with his revolutionary trip to Beijing 34 years after his grandfather's journey.

28/01/2002

<hr>

MAO MEETS MOHAMMED
Few associate Islam with China but there is a strong connection

September 11, 2001 revived global interest in Islam but because 90-91 per cent of its population belongs to the Han ethnic group we do not read much about China in this context. China has been facing

"Muslim" unrest in the strategically important, resource-rich north-west province of Xinjiang for a long time. Beijing witnessed major protests in May 1989 against Salman Rushdie's book Satanic Verses and the Tiananmen Square pro-democracy revolt of June 1989 was spearheaded by a Uyghur. China's long and durable relationship with Pakistan, seen by us solely in anti-Indian terms, actually has a distinct Muslim and West Asia perspective as well, as pointed out by John W. Garver in his very recent Protracted Contest in which he also points out that China's diplomatic and deterrent support for Pakistan has weakened just as its military assistance has not diminished.

There are differing estimates on the size of China's Muslim community since the Chinese census canvasses ethnicity and not religion. Official figures are about 20 million, which is slightly less than 2 per cent of the total population. The Indian scholar Rafiq Zakaria in his The Struggle for Islam places the proportion at at 10 per cent. Dru Gladney of the University of Hawaii, an acknowledged authority, in his Muslim Chinese gives a range of 2-4 per cent.

Around half of the Muslim Chinese belong to the Hui nationality who have their own autonomous region of Ningxia. The Uyghurs are the second-most populous Muslim nationality and dominate Xinjiang. Han migration promoted by Beijing has radically altered the demographic mix in Xinjiang as it has in Xizang (Tibet). Other provinces with significant Muslim population include Gansu, Qinghai, Yunnan, Guizhou and Beijing itself. Guizhou is China's poorest province, followed by Xizang, Gansu, Shaanxi, Ningxia, Sichuan, Yunnan, Qinghai, Chongqing and Xinjiang. The gap between these provinces and Shanghai and Guangdong has increased in the past two decades. That is why the focus of China's Tenth Five Year Plan (2001-05) is the massive development of its western region that covers these provinces. India's own growth plans for its eastern and north-eastern regions can be linked to China's "remake the west" campaign.

Muslims have played a crucial role in Chinese history. The most colourful of them is perhaps the eunuch admiral Zheng He, the subject of Louise Levathes' fascinating When China Ruled the Seas. Between 1405 and 1433, Zheng He's fleet made seven epic voyages reaching all the way up to the east African coast. It was a stunning achievement. The first two expeditions brought Zheng He to Calicut. The Chinese wanted cardamom, cinnamon, ginger, turmeric and pepper, while they offered silk, porcelain and lacquerware. Calicut is described in glowing terms in the chronicles of the admiral's colleague, another Muslim, Ma Huan. Zheng He was to die in Calicut itself in 1433 but was buried in Nanjing. Incidentally, the Kerala-China link has an even more ancient history—according to legend Damo, among the most revered Buddhist figures in China, was originally a Namboodiri. In contemporary times as well, distinguished Keralites have moulded our China policy—K.M. Panikkar, Krishna Menon and the K.P.S. Menon clan, with the grandfather serving as our envoy in Beijing during 1947-48, the son during 1985-87 and the grandson now in his third stint in Beijing as ambassador.

In June 2001, presidents of six countries—China, Russia, Turkmenistan, Uzbekistan, Kazakhstan and Kyrgyzstan—formally launched the Shanghai Cooperation Organisation (SCO). This is basically a Chinese initiative in order to build bilateral relations, promote regional cooperation to China's advantage specially with reference to central Asian hydrocarbon resources and counter America's influence in world and regional affairs. This assumes special importance given that China's net oil imports now account for about a sixth of consumption and are growing. The SCO's main objective is to fight a war against the three evils of international terrorism, religious extremism and ethnic separatism.

Following September 11, which has led to an increased US military presence in Pakistan, Afghanistan, Uzbekistan and Kyrgyzstan, and with the growing bonhomie between America and Russia, the SCO faces an identity crisis. China's designs on resource-rich Siberia are a flashpoint in its relationship with Russia and Japan is very much part of this equation. There also are question marks over China's relationship with Pakistan. What will happen, for instance, to the Chinese project to develop the strategic Gwadar port on the Baluchistan coast near the Iranian border? The SCO is obviously of interest to India but we must not be ensnared into any arrangement that has anti-American overtones, just as we have to resist American efforts to build us up as a bulwark or counter-weight to China as well as the efforts of our own Sino-phobes to match China's military buildup.

04/02/2002

GEOECONOMY, NOT GEOMETRY

The idea of a Delhi-Moscow-Beijing strategic
triangle surfaces once again

The Russian Deputy Prime Minster Ilya Klebanov and Foreign Minister Ivan Ivanov have just visited Delhi. Defence collaboration is all set to expand hugely, perhaps a bit too hugely. These visits have also revived talk of an India-China-Russia relationship. It was the then Russian premier E. Primakov who first floated the idea of such a "strategic triangle" during his trip to India in December 1998.

The Russians are very keen on teaming up on the triangle as a counterweight to America, a feeling shared by the Chinese as well who are worried by the growing US presence in South and Central Asia. The Chinese also feel that they could use the Russians to "soften" India in relation to Sino-Indian differences. There are many in this country too who instinctively warm up to a triangular alliance to make the world less dependent on Washington.

Before 1980, both India and China aligned their economies closely with that of the USSR. The remnants of that dependence are still very much there. Sixty per cent of Russia's military sales are to India and China. And, of course, the three countries are in close geographical proximity with each other. All this makes for a cozy threesome. But realities have changed and the three countries are basically competitive, not complementary economies.

China's growth has been stunning since 1980 and this was achieved by abandoning Mao-era policies completely. India too has moved steadily forward. But Russia has been decimated. If real (inflation-adjusted) GDP in 1990 was set at 100, Russia's real GDP in 1999 was down steeply to around 60, whereas China's zoomed to about 244 and India's to around 164. In 2000 and 2001, Russia's growth recovered but that was almost entirely due to increased oil prices and the 1999 devaluation. Sharp regional disparities have emerged in all three countries and this is an important area where the trio could have a dialogue.

Russia is also in demographic decline. Its population is estimated to fall by some 10 million to about 135 million by 2015. The trend will continue thereafter. China and India, on the other hand, will see their numbers swell even further. This has strategic implications, particularly in resource-rich Siberia in Russia's far east. Russian anxieties are deepening with Chinese influx into the region, something that has also got the Japanese worried. Russia too is worried about China's growing influence in Mongolia and in Central Asia.

Islamist terrorism is a prime area for a coordinated strategy. The six-nation Shanghai Cooperation Organisation (SCO) comprising Russia, China, Kazakhstan, Tajikistan, Kyrgyzstan and Uzbekistan was formally launched in July 2001. It has decided to set up a counterterrorism centre in Bishkek, the capital of Kyrgyzstan. Pakistan has been keen to join the group but this has been vetoed by Russia and other Central Asian members since it is seen as the main champion of religious extremism. China remains silent on the issue. India has not taken the SCO seriously so far. How the SCO will evolve now that the US also has a long-term presence in the region remains to be seen.

Energy could be a second area of three-way cooperation. Central Asia, particularly Kazakhstan and Turkmenistan, is rich in oil and gas. China has already made major investments in Kazakhstan and some years ago there was talk of a Turkmenistan-India gas pipeline. With growing bonhomie between Russia and the US following the cataclysmic events of September 11 last year, Russian and American cooperation in the exploitation of Central Asian energy resources is bound to increase.

Noted foreign policy scholar Kanti Bajpai of Delhi's Jawaharlal Nehru University feels that as pivotal states, India, China and Russia can also combine to develop a security system spanning the entire Asian continent. The radical rethinking on missile defence in the US also forces the three nations to act in close concert with each other not to counter the US but to ensure that the responses of each does not have adverse reactions on the others.

Pursuing areas of common interest is worthwhile. But a triangle to take on America is just not in our national interest. We have to be careful that the triangle is not perceived as and does not become an "axis". More than trilateralism, what is needed is deepening bilateralism. We have major differences with China but that should not deter us from forging closer political, economic and cultural Sino-Indian links. For most of the 1990s, India and Russia ignored each other. Fortunately, both realise closer ties with each other and closer ties individually with the West are not mutually exclusive.

Foreign policy is all about geoeconomics and geopolitics, not of geometry. It is also not about geology, given the prime minister's idea of India and the US as "natural allies". Hopefully, this will shape our worldview as we construct new partnerships with America, Russia and China.

18/02/2002

HOT FUDGE IN BEIJING
All of a sudden, China is accused of Enron-type manipulations

Is Jaswant Singh having the last laugh? On January 21 this year he created a stir while addressing an international audience in the capital when he said that China was "fudging" its growth numbers. Now, along come *The Economist* of the UK and *Newsweek* of the US with long articles that question China's national output, or GDP, statistics in particular.

It has generally been recognised that Chinese growth is exaggerated by at most 2 percentage points: that is, when the Chinese claim a 9 per cent rate of economic growth during 1978-97, it could well be 7 per cent, a great feat nevertheless considering that it is an annual compound rate of increase. But now there are far more serious accusations and the man to first give international respectability to these charges is an eminent American economist and China scholar, Thomas Rawski of the University of Pittsburgh. Since early 2000, Rawski has been writing extensively on the dubiousness of recent Chinese growth figures. He believes that the problems started in 1998 after the East Asian crisis, when, faced with the prospect of declining growth in exports and foreign investment, Chinese Prime Minister Zhu Rongji launched a personal crusade for an 8 per cent rate of economic growth terming it a "great political responsibility".

Shorn of all technical detail, what Rawski says is that China's reported GDP growth during 1998-2001:

- implies a drop in energy use and an increase in energy efficiency which is simply inconceivable;
- is based on an increase in farm output that could not have been realised given the extensive natural disasters that hit China in recent years;

- is not consistent with the sharp fall in investment spending and with the indifferent growth in retail sales.

Rawski's own estimates are that in 1998 and 1999, the Chinese economy may well have had a negative growth rate of around 2 per cent. In 2000, as against the official figure of 8 per cent, Rawski estimates a 2-3 per cent growth and in 2001, as against the 7.9 per cent claim, the alternative "realistic" estimate is 3-4 per cent. Interestingly, Rawski's doubts are based extensively on Chinese official, academic and media sources of criticism. The major culprit seems to be the data being generated by local and provincial governments. Chinese scholars have been writing about a "wave of deliberate falsification and embellishment", comparable to the harvest data during the disastrous Great Leap Forward in the late 1950s which hid 25-35 million famine deaths from the public for almost three decades.

However, in an e-mail to Kautilya a few days back, Nicolas Lardy, a distinguished American economist on China currently at Washington's Brookings Institution and author of the just released Integrating China into the World Economy, points out that:

- China's import growth in the past four years does not support the contention that the economy is contracting or sharply decelerating. This import data is consistent with export figures in trading partner countries like the US.
- Monetary growth has been substantial and if real output is falling as Rawski claims, this should have resulted in increasing inflation. This has not happened.
- If GDP growth is falling then family incomes should also be declining. But household savings have been growing, a sign of an expanding, not collapsing economy.

The debate will go on. Doomsday books like Gordon Chang's recent The Coming Collapse of China will continue to hit the stands. But what should not be missed is the tangible nature of Chinese growth. Poverty and backwardness still prevail widely but the spectacular pace of change is visibly evident. Visually, China's performance is simply awesome. Even our 8 per cent growth regions of Gujarat and Maharashtra or the Bangalores and Hyderabads do not come anywhere close to what can be seen in China. That is primarily because growth is being accompanied by massive urban renewal and frenzied construction activity, unlike in India. Further, China continues to extend its dominance in labour-intensive mass manufacturing like consumer goods, toys, personal appliances and gadgets and textiles. It has also, with the help of Taiwanese firms, become the world's third largest power in IT hardware. "Made in China" is ubiquitous. The debate on GDP numbers cannot gloss over this achievement which has been denied to India because of its policy stupidities. Our own statistical system, once the envy of the world, is in a shambles as brought out vividly in the voluminous report of a high-level National Statistical Commission chaired by noted economist C. Rangarajan, now the governor of Andhra Pradesh. Worse, the Government has done nothing so far about its recommendations that were submitted over seven months ago. Meanwhile, the credibility of our own growth numbers continues to take a severe knock.

15/04/2002

C. East Asia

LET'S NOT KID OURSELVES

One visit to east Asia is enough to show just where India is

Last week over 50 economists, political scientists, diplomats, lawyers, investment bankers, government officials, journalists and public personalities from China, Japan, South Korea, Thailand, Hong Kong, Indonesia, Philippines, Taiwan, Malaysia, Singapore, Australia, New Zealand, Canada, the US, Pakistan and India spent four days in South Korea discussing the present economic, political and social scene in the Asia-Pacific region. It was for Kautilya a most depressing experience. The growing disconnect between India and the rest of Asia came into sharp focus and the world's frustrations and increasing disenchantment with India became painfully evident.

Indian politics is diminishing our credibility and standing. The only thing we can feel very proud of is Buddha who, along with Confucius, shaped society in this region. We can feel proud of our democracy as well. But only up to a point. How long can we justify the virtues of our democracy as an instrument of identity, empowerment and representation when it is failing in its most basic duty—that of purposeful governance. And we should not carry this democracy argument too far. After all, provinces in communist China have more autonomy than states in democratic India. Further, economists like Robert Wade and Pranab Bardhan have shown that local-level institutions in authoritarian South Korea enjoy greater freedoms than in democratic India. The substance of democracy is more fundamental than its form. Kautilya has himself in these columns defended the noise of Indian politics as the music of its democracy and championed it as the only arena where genuine equality of opportunity exists. But this defence is beginning to wear thin. What people abroad are unable to understand is why the goals of social justice and good administration should be incompatible with each other.

Countries like South Korea are now restructuring their economies with a vengeance. They are using the crisis of 1997-98 as an opportunity for bringing about a profound transformation in their economic policies and programmes. China and Taiwan desperately want to join WTO. Thailand is making major moves in privatisation and in reforming its financial sector. There is a fierce sense of determination and firm sense of purpose in east Asia today. The crisis has hit the region hard but it has hit it after over two decades of a sustained 8 per cent rate of growth that has brought unprecedented prosperity. While we are still patting ourselves on the back for having escaped the ravages of the Asian contagion, the unmistakable signs of a recovery have manifested themselves in the region in lower interest rates, current account surpluses, stabilising currencies and modest GDP growth rates. When they come out of this phase in four to five years time, these tiger economies will be leaner, meaner and fitter, making life for us even more difficult and tough in the global and regional marketplace. The current buoyancy in our stockmarkets should not blind us to the deep distress that manufacturing is in because of lack of new investments and technology.

We do not have many friends and well-wishers in east Asia. Goh Chok Tong, Singapore's prime minister, is a rarity but even he is getting embittered. In the past, we have behaved sanctimoniously. After all, do not Singapore and Cambodia derive their names from Sanskrit? J.N. Dixit, former foreign secretary, writes in his recent *Across Borders* that between 1965 and 1967 the south-east Asian countries wanted India to be a full member of ASEAN but India rebuffed these overtures. Today, we are trying desperately to become a member of APEC but it is unlikely that we can make it if we continue to opt out of CTBT and other such regimes for nuclear non-proliferation.

In the past we dismissed these countries as lackeys of America. But these lackeys used access to American markets to build their textiles, electronics and consumer goods industries, generating wealth and employment for themselves—something we are loath to do even today because of some romantic fixation on small-scale industry that defies economic and technological logic. The government that encourages students to stone the American Embassy is the same government that has been pragmatic in building up an annual $50 billion trade surplus with the "imperialist pigs".

Kautilya was also struck by another remarkable feature of public life in east Asia exemplified by China, where the first two generations of political leaders were dominated by those who participated in the Long March and those who were trained in the USSR. But now increasingly public affairs is being influenced by those who have been educated in the best American universities. The academic institutions in the region are comparable to the best in the West. But in this country institutions of intellectual activity are in a pathetic state and can be regenerated only with massive infusion of new talent from the outside. But for this to happen the conscience of those who educate themselves with huge subsidies and flee to the West has to begin to prick to give back to a poor society what that society has given them.

24/05/1999

◆——◆

LAND OF THE SETTING SUN
After a decade of growth recession, is Japan headed for growth depression also?

Given its spectacular growth performance in the past, it appears blasphemous to even contemplate the title of a new book by Michael Porter of the Harvard Business School Can Japan Compete? Or of Murray Sayle's recent piece in the London Reviewof Books, "Japan Goes Dutch". But it is a sign of howsteep the recent decline of the Land of the Rising Sun has been that the unthinkable has now become commonplace with Porter and Sayle being the latest entrants to a growing list of those trying to understand why and how the world's biggest savings and creditor economy has collapsed.

There was, of course, a time when Japan could do nothing wrong. The 1970s and 1980s saw scholarly encomiums like Ezra Vogel's Japan as Number One (1979) and Chalmers Johnson's MITI and the Japanese Miracle (1982). Japan, we were told, had invented a vastly superior form of state-managed capitalism. Or so it seemed from its record. Between 1950 and 1973, Japan's national income or gross domestic product (GDP) grew at a fantastic real (inflation-adjusted) annual average compound growth rate of 9.3 per cent. In less than three decades, Japan had become the world's second-largest economy.

But the Japanese growth engine sputtered in the 1980s when real GDP growth averaged just about 4per cent annually. The 1990s were even worse when real GDP growth averaged around 1.2 per cent annually. The unemployment rate is now knocking at 5 per cent and bankruptcies are surfacing. Successive governments have tried everything by way of remedies. Short-terminterest rates are close to zero but there has been little effect on investment. Almost $1,500 billion worth of public spending programmes, tax cuts, bank bailouts and governmentloans have failed to have any effect. These have only succeeded in boosting the government's gross debt which now stands at a whopping 140 per cent of GDP, the highest in the world and over twice America's level.

What went wrong? Paul Krugman in his The Return of Depression Economics (1999) and now Porter identify three main reasons for Japan's continuing misery.

- The speculative bubble of 1985-1990, which saw the trebling of land and stock prices and whose bursting caused a decline in investment and consumption;
  Asick banking sector which nowholds almost $600 billion of problem loans on its books and that, as a result, has caused a "liquidity trap"—that is, no credit;
  Over-regulation, overprotection and lack of competition in a number of domestic sectors like agriculture, construction, housing, retailing, wholeselling, financial services, health care, energy, telecommunications and logistics.

Sayle likens Japan's affliction to the success and failure of the modern world's first miracle economy—that of the Dutch Republic between 1588 and 1/95—saying that all economic booms contain the seeds of stagnation. Krugman calls Japan's condition one of "growth recession" giving way to "growth depression". There is growth all right, but not enough of it. Since it is mired in long-termdeflation—that is, when all inflation-adjusted prices are tumbling—Krugman wants Japan to print more money to generate ex-pectations of a mild inflation that would make savings less attractive and borrowing moreso. It would also weaken the yen and make Japanese goods more competitive. But giventhe deficit of around 10 per cent of GDP and its huge debt stock, Japan has been reluctant to follow this route.

While Krugman seeks salvation in macroeconomic policy, Porter's focus is on microeconomics. Hedebunks the conventional wisdom on the role of government in Japan's competitive success by studying areas where that country failed to acquire global pre-eminence.. He calls for redesigning the role of government and sees the emergence of a newJapanese company radically different from the earlier generation of Toyotas, Hitachis and Mitsubishis. From among that generation, Sony and Honda fit the Porter paradigm of competitiveness in the changing context of Japan. New names like Nidec, Rohm, Kyoden, Shimono, Orix, Soft-bank, Pasona, Rakuten and NetAge represent the new breed that can bail Japan out.

To compound its economic woes, Japan faces a severe demographic shock. Its population is expected to decline from 127million nowto around a 100million in the next 50 years. With half of Japan's women under 30 now single, Sayle points out that greenfield household for-mation, once the engine of Japan's miraculous growth has practically ceased. Quite clearly, the chrysanthemum has begun to wilt in more respects than one. This will not be without its impact on the rest of the world. HowJapan responds to this social challenge will be more critical than mere economic policy changes.

14/05/2001

MAHATHIR'S MANTRA
Malaysia's politics is messy but its economic
performance has many lessons

Atal Bihari Vajpayee is in Malaysia for four days beginning May 13. The south-east Asian country has a population the size of Haryana, of which roughly 8 per cent is of Indian origin. Although he hates it being mentioned, Malaysian Prime Minister Mahathir Mohamad's grandfather came from Kerala. Mahathir is a great champion of indigenous Malay interests. The word used to describe his strong pro-Malay policies is bhumiputra—pure Sanskrit for sons of the soil.

Malaysia played an important role in triggering anew economic thinking in India in 1990. In the first week of June that year, our then prime minister V.P. Singh went to Kuala Lumpur for a Commonwealth Heads of Government meeting. After this visit, Singh confessed to his aides that he had been stunned by the progress in Malaysia since his previous trip there in 1974 as deputy minister of commerce. Malaysia has generally been known mainly as a commodities producer with a global presence in tin and palm oil. What impressed Singh apart from the urban renewal in Kuala Lumpur was how Malaysia became a major exporter of electronics, emerged as a major producer of crude oil and natural gas and attracted huge foreign investment in manufacturing.

Singh asked his economic adviser Montek Singh Ahluwalia to prepare a paper on economic policies that would help India emulate Malaysia's spectacular success. Singh did not know this but along with Suresh Tendulkar, another distinguished Indian economist, Ahluwalia had advised the Malaysian government in the early 1970s as part of a World Bank team. Ahluwalia's paper, prepared in June 1990 and later referred to in the press as the "M" document, was a comprehensive blueprint for liberalisation. It was discussed extensively but political instability prevented its implementation. The 1991 economic reforms derived much inspiration from it.

Malaysia is of significant interest to economists for another reason. In mid-1997, when after almost two decades of over 7 per cent growth in per capita income east Asia began collapsing, Thailand, Indonesia and South Korea went to the International Monetary Fund (IMF) for emergency bail-out packages in quick succession— Thailand in July-August 1997, Indonesia in October-November and South Korea in November-December. However, Malaysia did not go to the IMF.

But under the then deputy prime minister Anwar Ibrahim, elements of the orthodox IMF prescription were intro-duced—the IMF package without the IMF as it came to be called. Interest rates were raised to stem the depreciation of the ringgit. Drastic cuts in government spending and on imports were announced and tight measures to regulate Malaysia's banks were introduced. But all this failed to control capital flight, reduce interest rates and bolster investor confidence.

It was against this background that on September 1, 1998, Mahathir abandoned Ibrahim's IMF-style policies and announced sweeping controls onboth capital inflows and outflows to end speculation against the ringgit. He also moved swiftly to fix the exchange rate, cut interest rates and restore government spending. There is an "im-possible trinity" in macro-economics which states that a country cannot simultane-ously achieve independence of monetary policy, exchange-rate stability and full capital mobility. At most, a country can achieve any two of these objectives. By giving up capital mobility, Malaysia sought to achieve exchange-rate stability and monetary independence. Mahathir also had non-economic reasons for his new economic policies: by then he was at war with his one-time protege Ibrahim and also because of his nexus with Malaysian companies.

Mahathir's package caused a furore. The only mainstream economist who supported him was Paul Krugman of MIT, who lauded his policies in an article published in Fortune magazine in September 1998. After a disastrous 1998, the east Asian economies have recovered. A recent research paper, "Did the Malaysian Capital Controls Work?", by two Harvard economists Ethan Kaplan and Dani Rodrik *and published* by the National Bureau of Economic Research concludes that compared to the performance of Thailand, South Korea and Indonesia while they were undergoing IMF programmes, Malaysia's non-IMF policies produced faster economic recovery, lower inflation, smaller declines in employment and inflation-adjusted wages and a more rapid turnaround in the stock market.

The wheel has turned full circle. On July 1, Ahluwalia will take over as the IMF's first independent evaluator, reporting to the organisation's board directly. And among his first tasks will be to pronounce on how effective the IMF was in east Asia and what lessons the Malaysian experience with capital controls has for the future.

21/05/2001

D. Europe

ONE FLYING EMU
Europe's single currency, the Euro, is finally launched

For almost two millennia what we know as Europe has been bound together by Christianity. But from New Year's day this week, a part of it will have an-other unifier—a single currency called the Euro. On January 1, 1999, 11 countries—Germany, France, Italy, Spain, Portugal, Ireland, Belgium, the Netherlands, Austria, Finland and Luxembourg—will switch to the Euro. Denmark, Sweden and the UK have, for the time being, post-poned a decision on joining, while Greece which wanted to join has failed to do so since it does not meet the economic criteria. After over three decades, the European Monetary Union (EMU) has finally come of age. For the next 43 months, both the Euro and E-11 currencies will co-exist. By July 1, 2002, however, the Euro will be the only legal tender.

In economics there is a concept called an "optimal currency area", an area in which the currency is the same. For a group of countries to have the same currency, two conditions must be met—there must be complete labour mobility among them and they must all be impacted in a similar manner by external shocks. E-11 and indeed all of Europe is far from an optimal currency area. Yet economics has been set aside and monetary union has been tirelessly pursued more as a political objective. The corporate and financial sectors have been great champions of the Euro. Exchange rate crises, most recently in 1992-93, have further fuelled the desire for currency stability through a Euro-type instrument.

The E-11 is already a formidable economic grouping. Its population of 290 million is more than the 268 million of the US. It accounts for almost exactly the same share of world GDP—around 20 per cent—as the US. It trades more with the world—23 per cent of GDP—as compared with the US where the share of exports and imports is around 19 per cent of GDP. The dollar's dominance arises from America's economic might, political clout and cultural influence, all of which are unlikely to diminish in the next decade. Thus the Euro is no serious threat to the dollar. What it will do, however, is provide an element of choice as a reserve currency.

E-11 faces a high unemployment rate of close to 12 per cent. With the advent of socialist governments in countries like Germany and France, the temptation to follow expansionary fiscal policies in the face of such unemployment is great. Some conflict might then arise between the individual E-11 governments and the Frankfurt-based European Central Bank (ECB). It is not just that unemployment is high. Unlike the US, Europe suffers from the twin maladies of what economists call "wage rigidity" and "labour market inflexibility". In simple English, this means that wages do not fall as easily when unemployment is high so that more people can seek jobs and labour does not migrate easily from depressed to prospering regions. It is this coupled with the reluctance of European governments to reform their bloated welfare states that has led to doubts on the Euro's future.

While its macroeconomic impact is open to question, the Euro will bring microeconomic benefits. It will reduce "transaction costs" or the costs of doing business in Europe. This can be seen from a simple example—a tourist starting out with $1,000 and just going through E-11 not doing anything but converting into local currencies will have $500 at the end of the trip! Consumers will gain; a Coke in Germany now costs twice as much in Spain. Corporate treasury management will become less complex. Jurgen Schrempp, CEO of Daimler Chrysler, estimates that for his company 50 per cent of revenues will be in Euros with 80 per cent of the costs incurred in the same currency unlike the present situation where there is a wide gap between the Deutsch Mark costs and revenues. Mergers and acquisition activity will get a boost and the face of European industry is most likely to change significantly.

Europe is India's main trading partner accounting for about 27 per cent of our exports and 30 per cent of our imports. However, just about 7 per cent of our trade is invoiced in E-11 currencies. The Euro by itself will have little direct effect on our trade although we have to adjust to Europe gradually moving over to the settlement of traders in Euros. The Euro will also provide Indian companies with one large unified market for experts and distribution. Indian companies will also now have another deep and liquid retail capital market from where they can raise funds. Indian banks and financial institutions will bear the brunt of the initial impact and they will be called upon to effect major changes in their accounting systems and practices. New interest rate benchmarks will emerge.

A little over half of the world's official foreign currency reserves is now held in dollars and around one-fifth in E-11 currencies. In managing reserves, any central bank has three objectives in descending order of priority—liquidity, safety and returns. Whether Reserve Bank of India increases its Euro holdings at the expense of its dollars remains to be seen, although the Chinese and the Japanese have announced their plans to switch a part of their reserves to the Euro. Thirteen per cent of our external debt of about $94 billion is denominated in E-11 currencies plus the pound. If the Euro is strong vis-a-vis the dollar, our ex-ternal debt in dollar terms will increase and if it is weak, then our external debt in dollars will decline. All depends on how effective the ECB will turn out to be.

04/01/1999

◆━━━◆

VASCO TO VAJPAYEE
The prime minister's Lisbon sojourn evokes Lusitanian memories

The Indian Prime Minister has just been to Lisbon to attend the first-ever European Union (EU)-India Summit. India is the sixth country with which the 15-nation EU now holds such annual meets. If we had a sense of history, this summit might well have taken place in the Portuguese capital in May 1998 to mark the 500th anniversary of Vasco Da Gama's historic sea journey around the Cape of Good Hope to Calicut in search of pepper, spices and Christians.

The Portuguese were the first of the Europeans to arrive in India and the last to depart. Historians have generally been unkind to them. We have been taught that Catholic Portugal left behind no traces of modern civilisation in its colonies unlike the more refined and enlight-ened Dutch, French and the English. This is unfair. Just think—the word that defines the very essence of Indian civilisation, namely caste, comes from the Portuguese word *castas* meaning species or breeds or tribes or races or clans or lineages. We are today among the world's leading producers of potatoes; the tuber came here from the Andes courtesy the Portuguese. Tomato, cashew, tobacco, papaya, guava, pineapple and chillies are some other Portuguese gifts to India, along with grafting techniques.

Vasco Da Gama is dwarfed in western history by Magellan, Cabral and, of course, the Genoese Christopher Columbus who might well have won the Americas for the Portuguese emperor but who was forced to seek the patronage of Castille and Aragon. Da Gama who died in Cochin has been applauded as an intrepid explorer just as he has been condemned as a barbaric marauder. It was left to India's most gifted and multilingual economic historian Sanjay Subrahmanyam to produce a tour de force on the Portuguese nobleman-admiral in 1997. Subrahmanyam, who now teaches in Paris, places the captain of the *Sao Gabriel* in a larger cultural, social and historical perspective. His *The Career and Legend of Vasco Da Gama* is a brilliant piece of biographical history and is the most recent addition to his distinguished line of works on the Portuguese empire in Asia.

Many myths surround Da Gama. The most celebrated of these is the one linked to the role played in his voyage by the greatest non-European navigator of the 15th century, Ahmed Ibn Majid. History records that the ruler of Malindi, a port city close to Mombasa in modern-day Kenya, lent the services of a pilot to Da Gama both as a hostage and to enable him to know the precise location of Calicut. The general belief is that this pilot was Ibn Majid himself. Richard Hall, for instance, in his hugely captivating *Empires of the Monsoon* has a whole chapter on this great Arab from Oman. Ibn Majid has come to symbolise in the words of Subrahmanyam "non-western knowledge incorporated and crushed by the hegemonic expansion of western culture". Subrahmanyam delves into hitherto unpublished sources in Italian and Portuguese and concludes that Ibn Majid just could not have guided Da Gama to Calicut. The pilot, incidentally, was a Gujarati Muslim. Noted historian Sardar K.M. Panikkar has written about the "da Gama epoch". But the honour of founding the Portuguese empire in India belongs to Afonso de Albuquerque. Other than Genevieve Bouchon's 1992 book in French, Albuquerque has not been subject to biographical analysis. Perhaps Subrahmanyam will now devote his prodigious talents to fill this gap.

And what of Albuquerque's greatest legacy? A little known feature of Goa, which is 65 per cent Hindu, 30 per cent Christian and 5 per cent Muslim, is that the Portuguese civil code still operates there. This code derived from the Napoleonic Code and has long been repealed in both France and Portugal. With a highly literate population of just 1.2 million, with infant mortality rates on par with that of Kerala's, with the third lowest population growth rate after Kerala and Tamil Nadu and blessed by nature in diverse ways, Goa could well have been an economic engine. But alas, its politics is *feni*-shing it. Its non-development expenditure as a proportion of aggregate disbursement at over 43 per cent is the second highest in the country, just below Punjab's 44 per cent. In the 13 years that it has been a full-fledged state, Goa has seen eight chief ministers and 14 governments. There was a time just two years ago when in an assembly of 40 there were about 20 ministers. It was this that led the Congress president in her election campaign last year to publicly commit to a Congress cabinet not exceeding 15 per cent of the size of the Assembly—meaning no more than six ministers. The Congress won the elections, kept that pledge—and soon fell victim to Goa-itis!

10/07/2000

◆━━◆

NEW CZAR SHEIKHS OIL
Russia re-emerges as a major oil power and the Saudis don't like it

Oil price have begun to do what they do best—swing wildly. After the September 11 terrorist attacks in New York and Washington DC, oil prices fell surprisingly by over $5 to as low as $18 a barrel. But in recent weeks, they have spurted and the benchmark price is now already at around $27 a barrel. Why did oil prices fall so steeply in the first place when they could have been normally expected to rise following fears of the "West vs Islam" in the wake of 9/11? It was Russia's decision to keep increased supplies going that led to a decline in oil prices in the last quarter of 2001. Why then have oil prices climbed again?

The escalating war between the Israelis and the Palestinians, fears of an American attack on Baghdad and Iran's call for an oil boycott of the West are obvious causes. But there are other factors also. Iraq has just an-nounced a 30-day embargo on oil exports as a gesture of solidarity with the embattled Yasser Arafat and Venezuelan refineries are facing major strikes. Venezuela is the US' third largest crude oil supplier and the most important source of gasoline imports. And even though it raves and rants against Saddam Hussein, the US still buys a substantial amount of oil from Iraq under the UN's oil-for- food programme. In 2001, for instance, the US imported close to 0.8 million barrels a day or mbpd (1 mbpd equals 50 million tonnes annually) of crude oil from Iraq which accounted for about 9 per cent of its total imports. America is key to oil since it accounts for close to a fourth of world oil consumption, imports slightly over half its annual crude requirement and picks up around 30 per cent of the crude that is traded internationally.

The erstwhile USSR was the world's largest oil producer but after its dissolution in 1991, the Russian oil industry suffered a setback. From 1996 onwards, however, Russia has made a striking recovery and become the world's second largest oil producer and exporter after Saudi Arabia. Beginning 1999, Russia has increased its oil output by 0.5 mbpd, something no other oil producer has been able to do. In 2001, Russia's oil production was slightly over 7 mbpd, only about 1 mbpd lower than that of Saudi Arabia. The OPEC has been pressing Russia to cut supplies. But Russia has obliged only half-heartedly. The aggressive Russian oil industry that has been privatised is in no mood to listen.

In an incisive article in the March/April 2002 issue of Foreign Affairs, Edward Morse and James Richard discuss the growing contest for dominance between Saudi Arabia and Russia in oil. They conclude that Russia right now holds the upper hand because of the dynamism being shown by its companies even though the desert kingdom is sitting on about one-fifth of the world's reserves and is among the lowest-cost producers. Following September 11, there has been growing bonhomie between Presidents George W. Bush and Vladimir Putin. This might reflect in the growing convergence of interests between the Americans and Russians to develop the oil resources of Central Asia. The duo could take on China which is a major investor in Kazakhstan. China's annual oil output has been stagnating at a little over 3 mbpd and it now buys about 1.5 mbpd from outside. The Sakhalin region of Siberia in Russia's far east is oil-rich and many countries like China and Japan are looking at it as a possible source. Uncharacteristically, but for-tunately, India has stolen a march with a massive $1.7 billion investment there. This ONGC venture will probably be among the largest foreign investments in Russia ever. Oil could flow from 2005, resuming Indo-Russian oil links after a long hiatus. This project must succeed.

Saudi Arabia is central to OPEC. It is what is called the "swing" producer in the 11- member cartel. This means that it can bring in or take out substantial amounts of oil quickly from world markets to influence prices. The conservative monarchy is not averse to imposing discipline on its compatriots as evidenced by the way it reacted to Venezuela's breach of its production quota during 1996-98. It was Saudi Arabia that took the lead to institute the $22-28 a barrel price band for OPEC that is now in force; if prices fall below the lower limit, OPEC production would be cut to push up prices and if prices crossed the upper limit output would be increased in order to cut prices.

Saudi Arabia and the US have had a mutually reinforcing relationship that has become closer after the September 11 events, given the heightened insecurity in the ruling monarchy. The Americans have a substantial military presence in the desert kingdom, while the Saudis charge the US (and Europe) about a dollar less for every barrel of oil sold as compared to India and other Asian countries east of Saudi Arabia. Saudi Arabia is also the largest supplier of crude oil to the US. Clearly, as Morse and Richard point out, the trilateral Washington-Moscow-Riyadh relationship is key to the evolution of world oil markets, in which India too has a vital stake.

22/04/2002

◆――――◆

E. Pakistan

FIRE THE REAL ICBMS
Proactive 'Indian Confidence Building Measures' can revolutionise south Asia

Inter-continental ballistic misiles (ICBMs) are an integral part of a nuclear superpower's arsenal. But what the country needs is an entirely different class of ICBMs—Indian Confidence Building Measures, to bring enduring peace and trigger tangible development in south Asia. These ICBMs must be offered in a comprehensive and authoritative manner and not in a piecemeal fashion in press interviews by the prime minister and his peripatetic aides. ICBMs must be offered proactively since the worldwide perception is that we are intransigent in bilateral and regional matters.

ICBMs will not be a panacea for peace. If two sides are determined to destroy each other, there is nothing that confidence-building measures can do. But by improving the atmospherics, by providing transparency in military activities and by serving as a channel for mutual consultations, confidence-building measures lessen tensions.

Both Rajiv Gandhi and P.V. Narasimha Rao understood this. In December 1988, Rajiv and Benazir Bhutto signed a historic agreement that pledged the two countries not to attack each other's nuclear installations. Later, in August 1992, India and Pakistan agreed to ban the use of chemical weapons. In September 1993, India and China entered into a whole range of confidence-building agreements. Atal Bihari Vajpayee must consolidate on all these. The existing Sino-Indian agreements must go full speed ahead in spite of the current chill.

The first new ICBM in relation to Pakistan could well be the extension of the Rajiv-Benazir nuclear accord to cover no attack on irrigation dams, oil and gas fields, chemical factories and population centres as well. Strategic gurus have also suggested India unilaterally offer a pact that pledges both countries to the "no first use" of nuclear weapons. To be really meaningful, the offer of such a pact must be accompanied by one to scale down conventional weaponry as well.

Rajiv and Benazir also came tantalisingly close to settling the dispute over the Siachen Glacier. It costs each country at least a million dollars a day in addition to the heavy human price. A second set of ICBMs could, therefore, aim at resuming negotiations over Siachen. Talks could also reopen on two other major outstanding issues. One, delineation of the maritime boundary and resolution of the land boundary in the Sir Creek area. Two, construction by India of the Wular Barrage on the Jhelum river.

A third set of ICBMs could revolve around proposals made by various scholars: deepening military-to-military contacts, expanding communications facilities, an agreement to curb the spread of small arms and minor weapons, and cooperation in narcotics control. In the past, Pakistan has also proposed its version of confidence-building measures. It has, for example, suggested a nuclear weapons-free zone in south Asia, a bilateral treaty banning all nuclear tests, a regional non-proliferation conference, simultaneous accession by India and Pakistan to the Non-Proliferation Treaty (NPT) and acceptance by both countries of international safeguards on all nuclear facilities. All along, we have rejected such proposals outright and lost considerable propaganda advantage. This attitude must change. In any case, following the nuclear tests by the two countries, the past is no longer relevant.

A fourth ICBM could be to renegotiate the timetable for the South Asian Free Trade Agreement (SAFTA) and advance its launch to

January 1, 2000. That would be a good way to enter the new millennium. We have had two rounds of the South Asian Preferential Trading Arrangement (SAPTA), in which each country offered commodities that would attract lower import duties. In SAFTA, import duties will come down to zero.

The problem with SAPTA I and SAPTA II, as economists Rajesh Mehta and Swapan Bhatacharya have shown in a recent study, is that the gains to trade are minuscule and the offers themselves are meaningless. Under SAPTA II, for example, they estimate that the total imports of the 902 goods and commodities offered for preferential tariffs by India amount to just Rs 40 crore. SAFTA, on the other hand, will confer substantial benefits. Pakistan's exports to India alone will go up by 17 per cent. That will create economic vested interests in Pakistan for peace with India.

ICBMs are needed not just with Pakistan and China. For the past two decades, B.G. Verghese has been a voice in the wilderness calling for an integrated effort by India, Bangladesh and Nepal to develop the Ganga-Brahmaputra-Barak basin. The number of people mired in poverty and backwardness in this region will shortly touch a billion. The economic and social problems of states like Uttar Pradesh, Bihar, West Bengal and the entire North-east cannot be resolved without collectively addressing basic issues of land and water management in this basin. Thus, an important regional ICBM could be the offer to set up a Himalayan rivers commission. It could make plans for the prosperity of India's richly endowed but still backward regions—and also confer great benefits on our indigent neighbours.

29/06/1998

ENTERING THE VALLEY OF TALKS
Very soon India will have to start a real dialogue on J&K

India's restraint so far in not crossing the Line of Control (LoC) with Pakistan has been widely appreciated. But once some sort of status quo is restored in Kargil we will undoubtedly come under great pressure on Kashmir itself, an issue that has domestic, regional and international dimensions.

Bilateral efforts have been made in the past to arrive at an amicable settlement. Between June and August 1953, the Indian and Pakistani prime ministers negotiated directly. It was agreed to appoint a plebiscite administrator by April 1954. But in November 1953 the US and Pakistan announced a security pact. This, along with agitations in India by the Praja Parishad, a protege of the Jan Sangh, vitiated the atmosphere and the talks broke down. Then between December 1962 and May 1963 Sardar Swaran Singh and Zulfiqar Ali Bhutto had six rounds of detailed talks. These have been delightfully analysed by diplomat Yezdi Gundevia in his memoirs Outside the Archives. Just before his death, Sardar saheb himself was to tell Kautilya that his brief was just to keep the Pakistanis engaged in discussion to ward off American and British pressures.

A second track of negotiations involved the UN between 1948 and 1958. In January 1948 a five-member UN Commission for India and Pakistan was set up. India's nominee on this commission was Josef Korbel, a Czech diplomat whose daughter Madeleine Albright is the US secretary of state. Later Korbel was to write Danger in Kashmir, an indictment of the Indian claim. In March 1949, Admiral Chester Nimitz was appointed the plebiscite administrator. In December 1949, proposals for demilitarisation and a plebiscite were prepared by General MacNaughton, president of the Security Council. In April 1950, Sir Owen Dixon was appointed the UN repre-sentative for India and Pakistan. Then in April 1951, Frank Graham was appointed to succeed Dixon. Between April 1951 and February 1953, Graham submitted five detailed reports to the UN and after a long gap made one last effort at mediation between February 1957 and March 1958. Half a century of negotiations and thinking on Kashmir all over the world have thrown up 10 options.

- Plebiscite under UN auspices for the entire state of Jammu and Kashmir as it existed on August 15, 1947.
- Integration of Jammu and Ladakh into India and POK into Pakistan and a plebiscite only in the Valley.
- Conversion of the Kashmir Valley into a UN trust territory for 10 years and plebiscite thereafter.
- Independence for the state of J&K as it existed on August 15, 1947, with its territorial integrity guaranteed.
- Integration of Jammu and Ladakh into India and POK into Pakistan and independence for the Valley.
- Integration of Jammu and Ladakh into India and independence

for a united Valley.

- Condominium or joint sovereignty of India and Pakistan over J&K as it existed on August 15, 1947, with the maximum possible autonomy for the state.
- A confederation of India, Pakistan and J&K as it existed on August 15, 1947.
- Partition of the state with the Valley and large parts of Jammu in Pakistan and with Ladakh and the districts of Jammu and Kathua in India.
- Recognition of the existing LoC as the international boundary, either sealed or "porous".

Clearly, independence or partition should never be agreed to by India. India's best bet is to negotiate to have the LoC declared the international border. The same applies to the Line of Actual Control. It must become the India-China border, particularly since China occupies part of Jammu and Kashmir. Pakistan won't agree but we can get the international community to put pressure on it. However, this will yield results only if we improve our own image.

We are not given credit for not doing in Kashmir what the Chinese have done in Tibet or what the Israelis have done in the West Bank. On the contrary, India is seen as the "oppressor". The propaganda has been fuelled by the influential overseas Kashmiris. But not all is propaganda. There is alienation in the hearts and minds of the young in the Valley. But our own experience has shown that alienation is not a permanent condition and with creative power-sharing agreements and regional autonomy as recently suggested by the Balraj Puri Committee, in Jammu and Kashmir itself, the divide can be bridged.

What needs to be done following the end of the Kargil crisis is for India and Pakistan to appoint two political personalities each to carry forward the dialogue on Kashmir. On the Indian side, the two must be acceptable to the BJP and the Congress and on the Pakistani side to the military and the political class. This dialogue can take months or years. But in a world where optics is as important as reality, this move will serve as a signal that new beginnings are being willed in south Asia as they have been elsewhere in the world like in the Middle East and Northern Ireland, where people have been long-suffering victims of a Kashmir-like cocktail of religion, geography, history and politics.

12/07/1999

NOT FOR THE BIRDS
Realpolitik, not ornithology, should guide our Pak policy

In December 1988 the erudite diplomat-politician K. Natwar Singh was accosted by a journalist in Islamabad and accused of being a hawk. Kanwar Sahib's response was classic, especially for someone coming from Bharatpur, the winter destination of the Siberian crane. He said, "I run a foreign policy establishment, not a bird sanctuary." For the record, this bibliophile is a rare species—a dove when it comes to Pakistan and China but a hawk vis-a-vis the US, quite the opposite of current thinking in the government.

That our bilateral relations with Pakistan are based on ornithological perceptions and not realpolitik has been painfully driven home in recent days. Pervez Musharraf, the villain of Kargil as we see him, is a super-hawk. His foreign minister, *Abdus Sattar*, who has served for six years in New Delhi in the '80s is portrayed as a hawk. So we are backing off. Track-I, that is contact at the official level, is dead. Track-II, that is interaction between non-official "experts", is sputtering along, although just a few days back a conclave took place in Lahore. The larger problem of Track-II is that it involves rounding up the usual suspects. The constituency on both sides has to expand to include, for instance, political leaders. In the context of Track-II, Khalid Ahmed, a noted Pakistani journalist, wrote re-cently in Lahore's The Friday Times that hawks on both sides develop a chemistry between themselves, isolating the doves on either side.

It is time to break out of this avian syndrome. South Asia is the only hotspot in the world that does not have a serious, ongoing peace process—the word "process" is key, for Lahore in February 1999 was an event, full of atmospherics, even though a crucial MoU on nuclear risk reduction to be detailed through further negotiations did get signed. Then Kargil and the coup intervened. This has further frozen Indian attitudes, exemplified by the wholly ill-advised initiative we took to get the SAARC summit postponed and the hamhanded efforts we are making to isolate Pakistan in the Commonwealth. Our position following the recent Srinagar killings is that we cannot talk to someone who masterminded Kargil, subverted democracy and is supporting cross-border terrorism. Incidentally, the peace process with China seems to be stalled too with hardly any follow-up to the historic pacts India signed with China in 1993 and 1996.

Under the circumstances, it might appear unpatriotic to even suggest that India must engage Musharraf and his cohorts proactively in both Track-I and Track-II diplomacy and that India must, while fighting cross-border terrorism, announce that is willing to sustain a peace offensive. But that is exactly what is needed. We have always maintained contact at different levels with Pakistan in the past even as militancy has continued. So such a simultaneous iron fist and velvet glove policy is not anything new. It could well be argued that just as only Nixon could have opened China to the US, only the Pakistan Army (and a right-wing Hindu nationalist party in India?) can keep a peace process going without inviting domestic suspicion. However, conventional wisdom here is that the Pakistan Army does not want real peace with India, particularly after it has been "Islamised" in the past two decades. The most independent assessment is that by Stephen Cohen in the 1998 edition of his classic The Pakistan Army where he speculates that perhaps 20-40 per cent of the officer corps want to "bleed" India. The hands of the moderates will be strengthened if we also seriously examine autonomy, governance and representation issues in Jammu and Kashmir. This is something we must do anyway.

It is also in our interests that the US has some leverage in Pakistan. Over the past few years that clout has been lost, which is evident from the dwindling number of Pakistan Army officers going to the US for training. While hardware sales by America in any significant measure to Pakistan would be a cause for concern, there is no reason to lose sleep over intensified military training programmes and frequent visits of military personnel between our neighbour and the world's superpower. President Clinton will, most probably, not be visiting Pakistan when he comes to India sometime in February 2000. But this is no cause for exultation. Over time it is possible that some high-level political contact between the US and Pakistan might well be resumed. India should, in fact, be facilitating this and along with other countries like Iran and Turkey working to keep Pakistan on an Ataturkist path. There is no need for us to be patronising or sanctimonious, as is our wont. We must do so out of sheer self-interest. We might also encourage some American think tanks to launch a Track-III comprising diaspora Indians and Pakistanis, who by replicating subcontinental rivalries and tensions in the US and UK are greatly complicating matters.

Some of our hawks believe that we should jack up our defence spending to at least double of the present levels. India, it is argued, can afford to do so. Pakistan would then try to match this and since its economy is highly vulnerable and weak, it would soon meet the fate of the Soviet Union. From our point of view, this scenario has highly dubious economic logic and dangerous political consequences. Worryingly, the draft nuclear doctrine prepared by members of the Govern-ment's National Security Advisory Board admits of such a scenario. That is why it is imperative that there be an informed debate in Parliament soon on the draft doctrine.

22/11/1999

LIFTING THE VEIL OVER PAK
Unravelling why Kargil became neighbour's envy, owner's pride

Now that the Kargil crisis is winding down, it is time to ask a most basic question, a question that got lost in the perfectly understandable jingoistic fervour that swept this country over the past six weeks. It is now clear that the Kargil intrusions started way back in November 1998 and by March 1999 critical heights had been captured. But why did Pakistan do what it did?

Four broad motivations emerge. The first is psychological. Army chief General Pervez Musharraf is the man, along with Chief of General Staff Lt-General Mohammed Aziz, widely credited with having masterminded the operation. Indeed, India believes that Musharraf 's immediate predecessor, the more cerebral Jehangir Karamat, refused to go along with a Kargil-type operation and that was one of the reasons why he was replaced in October 1998. Musharraf is Allahabad-born and is in the language of Pakistani society a mohajir, a refugee from India. This argument was also used earlier to explain the tough position that one of Musharraf 's predecessors, Azamgarh-born Mirza Aslam Beg, took in regard to India. Why is a mohajir supposed to be more anti-Indian than most? Perhaps because his loyalty is always under test and perhaps because the Uttar Pradesh-born immigrant to Pakistan is more conscious than anybody else that it was his ancestors who fought for Pakistan, much more than the Punjabi Muslim. The mohajir argument, however, places far too much importance on an individual's likes and dislikes. In any case, for a definitive analysis of its direct impact we have to await a detailed Bruce Mazlish-type psycho-histories. More persuasive than Musharraf 's origins as far as psy-chological factors go, is the argument that the current leadership of the Pakistani Army comprises those who were majors and captains during the 1971 war, which ended humiliatingly for Pakistan. Lt-General Satish Nambiar has written that the desire to avenge the trauma of 1971 has led to Kargil. Later, Pakistanis themselves put out the argument that Kargil was revenge for India's 1984 Siachen operation. But this was clearly an afterthought even though it could well be argued, as J.N. Dixit has done, that by dominating Turtok, Batalik, Drass, Kargil and Mashkoh, Pakistan aimed at neutralising our strategic position on the Siachen heights.

A second explanation is sociological. The Pakistani Army is no longer western-influenced. The number of Pakistani Army officers going to the US over the past decade has dwindled. The army has changed its character and is being gradually dominated by a non-secular class educated in traditional madarsas. In other words, the army is becoming increasingly "Islamised". It has an instinctive empathy with and admiration for the Osama Bin Laden-types. The prism through which this army sees the world is religion. Its top hierarchy comprises those who ran the mujahideen and more recently the Taliban operations and, therefore, are prone to look to a wider applicability of the "Afghan" model in India. The zealots and training camps are already in place in Pakistan.

A third explanation is military. Pakistan's doctrine is now to engage India in the heights where we are at a comparative disadvantage. This doctrine evolved after Operation Brasstacks in 1987, when India showcased its full military might and it became obvious to Pakistan that it could not win a conventional war in the plains. Hence was born the strategy of incursions where India would bleed most and where her positions were weakly held—like Kargil. This assumed special significance after the May 1998 nuclear tests. Pakistan may well have thought that since it had the nuclear deterrent, India would not risk a full-fledged confrontation. To Pakistan, this is lowcost nuclear brinkmanship to disturb the status quo. Challenging the LoC is the easiest first step.

A fourth explanation is political, that Pakistan wanted somehow to raise the pitch and bring Kashmir back to centrestage. The Pak Army is deeply suspicious of the Lahore spirit. Indeed, service chiefs broke protocol and did not receive Atal Bihari Vajpayee at Wagah in February 1999. Pakistan may well have figured the Lahore bonhomie, the return of tourists to and the whittling down of militant activity in the Valley are not conducive to its interests. This is not the first time that Pakistan's military has been proved hopelessly wrong. It totally miscalculated the Indian response and resolve and overestimated its clout with China and the US—China because it is keen on consolidating the historic 1993 Sino-Indian border agreement and the Americans because they possess clinching satellite evidence about movements of the Northern Light Infantry. But what Pakistan has been able to do is to convert Kargil into a Siachen for us to defend at considerable extra cost and revive world interest in Kashmir. However, this has been only a qualified success since—more than ever before—the idea of converting the LoC into the international border has gained global respectability. India can actually convert Kargil into an opportunity for settling Kashmir. If this is accompanied by big-bang economic reforms, then it would be what the Americans call a double whammy.

26/07/1999

<hr>

MAKE MOU A TREATY

A conflict management agreement is a must for nuclear South Asia

While American Newpapers *specilate* on Al Qaida's nuclear weapons arsenal, atomic South Asia has just made the cover of two leading American publications. *The New Yorker* has a piece "The Iran Game" by Seymour Hersh on how Pakistan has helped in the making of Iran's bomb. According to Hersh, Russia has played a key role in building Iran's nuclear capabilities but the ubiquitous Dr A.Q. Khan has also made his contribution. The other article, "India, Pakistan and the Bomb" in the monthly *Scientific American*, is of direct relevance to the subcontinent. It is also unusual in its authorship, having been written jointly by two noted physicists and peace activists—M.V. Ramana, an Indian working at Princeton University in the US, and A.H. Nayyar, a Pakistani now at the Quaid-e-Azam University in Islamabad.

Ramana and Nayyar are clear in their conclusion: the Indian subcontinent is the place where a nuclear war is most likely. According to them, even before the watershed events of September 11, South Asia had all the ingredients of a nuclear war: "possession and continued development of bombs and missiles, imminent deployment of nuclear weapons, inadequate preparations to avoid unauthorised use of these weapons, geographical proximity, ongoing conflict in Kashmir, militaristic religious extremist movements and leaders who seem sanguine about the dangers of nuclear war". Even if we accept the fact that the subcontinental nuclear arsenal is only "strategically active but operationally dormant", this is a chilling message.

In the past 24 months, two masterly books on India's nuclear policy have emerged from the American intellectual establishment. George Perkovich's *India's Nuclear Bomb* and Ashley Tellis' India's *Emerging Nuclear Posture* are authoritative works that have become essential reading. Unlike these academic tomes, Ramana and Nayyar's account is cast in the popular mould and summarises pithily the current state of nuclear play in the subcontinent. After providing a detailed description of the nuclear and missile establishment of both India and Pakistan, Ramana and Nayyar estimate that India has plutonium for between 55 and 110 bombs whereas Pakistan has an inventory of enriched uranium equivalent to 20-40 bombs. Of course, since India's nuclear pro-gramme is directed as much against China as Pakistan, India's arsenal needs to be compared with that of China. Ramana and Nayyar write that in spite of India's missile capability, it is unlikely to achieve nuclear parity with China. What they don't talk about is the debilitating con-sequences for the Indian economy if ever the Indian government made nuclear parity with China its objective, as many experts in this country advocate.

The reality is that India and Pakistan are two nuclear adversaries whose missiles can reach the other's territory in a matter of seconds, not minutes as was the case with the US and the USSR. They are also nuclear antagonists without the type of official and non-official confidence- building contacts that the US and the USSR had during the height of the Cold War. At the February 1999 Lahore Summit India and Pakistan did sign a Memorandum of Understanding (MoU) to "adopt measures for promoting a stable environment of peace, stability and security between the two countries". Unfortunately, the Kargil conflict intervened soon after and this fine declaration of intent could not be translated into a concrete conflict avoidance and confidence-building agreement.

It is not as if India and Pakistan do not have confidence-building agreements in the nuclear arena. For example, Rajiv Gandhi and Benazir Bhutto signed the Agreement on the Prohibition of Attack Against Nuclear Installations and Facilities in December 1988. Agreements have also been signed on advance notification of military exercises, prevention of airspace violations and prohibition of chemical weapons. But the conversion of the Lahore MoU into a treaty containing communication, constraint, transparency and verification measures would be an even more gigantic step forward.

Pakistani President Pervez Musharraf has been making some encouraging noises in this regard and India must seize the initiative to ensure that such a treaty for nuclear and missile conflict management does get signed soon. This must not be linked to discussions on Jammu and Kashmir, something that Musharraf has insisted upon in the past but on which he might well relent with some gentle but firm nudging by the US. The world's fears about a nuclear South Asia would be assuaged to a great deal if such a treaty were to be put in place in the next few months and if the two nuclear adversaries agree to a cooperative monitoring regime to enhance stability along their border. The finalisation of such a treaty must be America's top priority in its diplomacy in our region.

PIPEDREAMS TO PIPELINES

Iran and Pakistan are keen on an Iran-India gas pipeline—but we are sceptical

India and Iran *Sharemany Civilisational* affinities. Now, the Iranians are pushing a project that will bind the two countries closer together. A few weeks ago, an Indian team of officials was in Teheran where the idea of a natural gas pipeline from Iran to India came up for discussion. But we are very reluctant since such a pipeline will have to come through Pakistan. Iran has almost 15 per cent of the world's gas reserves, next only to those of Russia, and is also uniquely situated to act as a transit point for the abundant Caspian and central Asian gas.

The Iranians are worried about the growing Talibanisation of Pakistan and the impact that could have on their country. As it is, they are very concerned with Afghanistan. Their belief is that if there are projects like the pipeline venture, Pakistan will be forced to be moderate and sensitive to world opinion. They see greater economic interaction with neighbours as the only way to keep religious extremists at bay in Pakistan. This is a profound transformation in Iran's own thinking and reflects its growing desire to rejoin the mainstream. Of course, a financially strapped Iran could do with the extra cash from gas exports.

The pipeline will be approximately 2,000 km long and will originate in the South Pars field in the Persian Gulf, go through about 700-800 km of Pakistani territory all the way to Multan to join Pakistan's gas grid and then deliver gas at the northern or southern Rajasthan border. This gas can be used to generate power, as boiler fuel in industry, as cooking fuel in cities and for producing petrochemicals. The pipeline would cost about $2-3 billion (Rs 9,000-13,500 crore) and would deliver anywhere between 60 and 100 million cubic metres of gas per day (mcmd) to India and one-third that amount to Pakistan. The current consumption of gas in India is around 60 mcmd.

Our main concern is that Pakistan will disrupt supplies at will and hold us to ransom. This fear is legitimate. Pakistan will earn about $500-700 million per year as transit fees. This is a considerable amount for a bankrupt economy. But even assuming that it would be willing to forego this for the nobler cause of squeezing India, there are other ways of keeping Pakistan in check. A tripartite contract could, for example, provide for explicit penalties to be paid by Pakistan in case of disruption of supplies. R.K. Pachauri of the Delhi-based Tata Energy Research Institute has formulated a detailed securities package to safeguard India's interests. What is as noteworthy as Iran's enthusiasm for the project is the interest shown by General Pervez Musharraf himself and the readiness with which Pakistan has talked about "guarantees" with the Iranians without linking the pipeline to Kashmir.

There is an earlier model for the gas pipeline—the historic Indus Waters Treaty that was signed in September 1960 by Ayub Khan and Jawaharlal Nehru. Since then, that treaty has survived two major wars and numerous smaller conflicts. The treaty was undoubtedly amenable to a neat technical solution but it was made possible because of American support and because of the World Bank's sustained involvement between 1952 and 1960. The presence of the World Bank and American companies would be essential to make the Iran-Pakistan-India gas pipeline a reality.

The overland pipeline from Iran would serve the energy needs of north India. For peninsular India, LNG (liquified natural gas) is the preferred option. Here, gas is liquified at source, transported via cryogenic tankers and regassified at the point of delivery. LNG terminals are now coming up at Dahej, Pipavav, Jamnagar, Dabhol and Kochi on the west coast and at Ennore and Kakinada on the east coast. We could sustain an LNG supply of about 10-12 million tonnes per year (40-48 mcmd) which, if used entirely for power, would generate 10,000-12,000 MW annually. The other way to transport gas across countries is through deepsea pipelines. In the early 1990s we were starry-eyed about a mega-project to bring gas from Oman. Mercifully, that proposal is now dead.

Noted Pakistani journalist Ahmed Rashid, in his vastly engrossing book *Taliban* published very recently, has described both the promise of and pitfalls in pipeline diplomacy in our region. Today, India's participation in this new "Great Game", as Rashid calls it, appears highly unlikely. But given a new and bold strategic vision, we can emerge as a major player as well. What we need to do is push for a trilateral group of non-official experts to work out operational details for the pipeline project fully realising that the project would be as much an exercise in politics as in economics. The non-official dimension is important to kickstart the process because officials very often have frozen mindsets.

18/09/2000

◆━━◆━━◆

DAWN OF A NEW HOPE
A Pakistani economist says that Pakistan could be
India's Mexico or its Canada

India and Pakistan are both testimonies to the proposition that the growth rate of an economy is inversely proportional to the brilliance of its economists. One of the most distinguished of this tribe has been the Shimla-born, Washington-based investment banker Shahid Javed Burki who topped off a glittering international career by serving as finance minister in Islamabad between November 1996 and February 1997.

Burki has just written a series of five fascinating articles in the daily *Dawn*. He analyses the future of the world economy as it is likely to evolve in the next few decades and the options before Pakistan. He calculates that by 2025 China and India will be the second and third largest economies of the world respectively and together account for about 40 per cent of world output—a throwback to the pre-18th century as it were. Burki says Pakistan faces a choice. If it continues on its present low growth path, it will place itself in reference to India in the same position that Mexico currently has to the US. If its growth recovers, Pakistan could be to India what Canada is to the US. In Burki's picturesque words, Pakistan can either be India's Mexico or Canada.

Burki's calculations are based on what are called purchasing power parity (PPP) rates. When its national income or gross domestic product (GDP) is converted into dollars at the present exchange rate, India is the 11th largest economy in the world. But a dollar can fetch more in India than in developed countries. The prices of most services, for instance, are lower in developing countries. The PPP rate derived from price surveys converts GDP figures into international dollars. On this basis, India becomes the fourth largest economy and China sees its position go up from seventh to second. India is poised to overtake Japan and become the world's third largest economy based on GDP (PPP) by 2010.

Burki's vision is magnificent but makes two big assumptions. First, that the current phase of growth fatigue in India will end and we will soon return, at the very minimum, to the 7 per cent growth trajectory witnessed during 1993-97. Second, that Pakistan will want to anchor itself with south Asia. Presently, both assumptions appear heroic. The Indian economy cannot grow at 7 per cent with things as they are in Delhi and in the states. Prime Minister A.B. Vajpayee means well but his administration is in a deep coma. National political parties are unable to come together on economic essentials. State chief ministers are talking reforms alright but actual action is disproportionately low. As far as Pakistan is concerned, its commitment to south Asia is suspect. It sees itself more as part of the Middle East and Central Asia. In spite of tangible benefits that will accrue to it, Pakistan resists the idea of a South Asian Free Trade Area (SAFTA) and continues to deny MFN status to India.

MFN stands for "Most Favoured Nation" and is a pillar of the global trading system. When country A extends MFN status to country B, it means that A will not discriminate against B and B's exports to A will face import duties no higher than the lowest level set by A. Pakistan fears that extending MFN status to India will destroy its industry; actually the fear is more that greater trade will open a window to normalisation that will endanger Pakistani society. Some Karachi-based businessmen favour greater trade with India but that is not being permitted by Islamabad. Officially recorded bilateral trade is now around $800 million, although trade through third places like Dubai could be many times more. Burki's vision also calls for open borders, greatei trade, investment, cultural and educational contacts. The 1980s saw Pakistan's GDP growth still at an impressive 1950-1980 average of 6 per cent per year. This was the decade in which India broke out of its pre-1980 Hindu rate of growth of 3.5 per cent per year and recorded almost a 5.5 per cent growth rate. However, the 1990s were dramatically different when India increased its GDP growth rate to about 6.5 per cent while Pakistan's growth rate plummeted to about 3.8 per cent. Pakistan is now classified as a severely indebted country (India is lowly indebted) and is in the middle of a $600-million IMF borrowing programme with tough conditionalities that started in November 2000 and runs till September 2001. Burki feels that Pakistan is on the mend and that the worst is over but is perplexed why the press and the public in his country think otherwise.

If General Musharraf is savvy, as he surely is, he should propose a joint panel of experts that includes the Indo-Pak community in the US to prepare a blueprint for greater economic ties between the country he rules and the country of his birth. To hold everything hostage to Kashmir is to ensure that south Asia remains the last bastion of poverty and obscurantism—economic and religious.

11/06/2001

F. South Asia

WATER IS THE KEY

An eastern Himalayan rivers initiative is waiting
for an Indian vision and effort

We were all so mesmerised by Bill Clinton's trip to India that his visit to neighbouring Bangladesh was almost completely ignored in our media. In his meeting with Prime Minister Sheikh Hasina on March 20, President Clinton is believed to have urged Bangladesh to develop its natural-gas reserves keeping in view India as a market and, of course, with the assistance of American companies. Bangladesh's reserves of high-quality natural gas are substantial and are now estimated at about

350 billion cubic metres, roughly half that of India. Some experts feel that the reserves could increase five fold given the extraordinarily high success rate in drilling, a rate that obtains in our North-east as well. A number of American companies like Unocal and Occidental and other majors like Shell are developing Bangladesh's gas reserves.

One specific proposal that has been mooted is a pipeline from the fields in eastern Bangladesh that would bring the gas to its more populous western part for domestic use and then extend into India. Its length would not exceed 400 km. Another proposal is to pipe the gas from the Sangu offshore field into West Bengal. Many Bangladeshis have reacted apoplectically, saying that they would rather send blood than gas to India! India's approach also has been less than fair. If we discourage the export of raw materials and encourage the export of manufactured goods and commodities, why shouldn't Bangladesh also want to do so? For example, instead of importing gas, we might import urea specifically from a dedicated facility in Bangladesh—last year our total imports of urea were over half a million tonnes. Moreover, generating more power in the east does not alleviate our misery since the missing link is a stable national grid.

More than gas, however, what is of greater importance is cooperation in developing the Ganga-Brahmaputra-Barak/Meghna basin or the eastern Himalayan rivers that are part of a single, integrated drainage system. This enormously resource-rich basin has, alas, also the largest single concentration of abject poverty in the world. This is where we could certainly do with American and international assistance. The 1960 Indus Waters Treaty between India and Pakistan that has survived two wars and numerous skirmishes was, after all, made possible because of the untiring efforts of Americans like David Lillienthal and because of the perseverence of the World Bank. From a purely domestic point of view, India itself has to take the lead since there is no long-term solution to the floods that ravage eastern Uttar Pradesh, northern Bihar and the Assam valley year after year without controlling the erosion in the upper catchment area that lies outside India.

Mutual suspicion has characterised Indo-Nepalese and Indo-Bangladesh relations on water. But in February 1996, India and Nepal signed the Mahakali Treaty largely because of the indefatigable efforts of our High Commissioner K.V. Rajan and the sagacious leadership of prime minister P.V. Narasimha Rao. Following this, in December 1998, the Ganga Treaty was signed between India and Bangladesh, thanks largely to the vision of prime minister Inder Gujral and West Bengal Chief Minister Jyoti Basu and to the spadework done by the Delhi-based Centre for Policy Research and its water expert Ramaswamy Iyer. But such is the state of politics in the subcontinent that none of the countries have been able to build on these two momentous events. And there is so much that needs to be done. For instance, there are, as Iyer has noted in an analysis of the treaties published in the *Economic and Political Weekly* in June last year, 54 rivers that cross the Indo-Bangladesh border whose water can be shared.

For over two decades, noted journalist and academic B.G. Verghese has been crusading for a comprehensive, multi-sectoral eastern Himalayan rivers initiative. His 1990 classic *Waters of Hope* contains a detailed agenda for action that retains contemporary relevance. The most crucial recommendation is to establish an Eastern Himalayan Rivers Commission, along the lines of those set up for developing the Mekong, Zambezi and the Amazon basins. Bhutan and China will also have a stake in such a commission. However, practical politics demands that bilateralism and multilateralism go hand-in-hand. India feels that others prefer to deal on a river-by-river basis but the truth is that India itself would be more comfortable bilaterally. To overcome the Big Brother syndrome, we might consider the participation of Indian states—Uttar Pradesh, Bihar, West Bengal and Assam—rather than the behemoth called India. It is now up to us to display statesmanship.

10/04/2000

DISCORD OVER WATERS OF HOPE
The economic future of India and Nepal depends crucially on water agreements

Poor Nepal. Just five weeks back, it appeared to have won the archaeological race to lay claim to Kapilavastu, the ancient Sakya capital where Gautama Siddhartha was brought up in his father's palace. Indian archaeologists have claimed that Piprahawa in Siddharthnagar district of Uttar Pradesh was Kapilavastu. Now a team from UK's University of Bradford working under a UNESCO project has reinforced Nepal's case for Tilaurakot, 6 km across the border from Piprahawa, being Kapilavastu.

But when it should have been exulting in these findings, Nepal has been plunged into grief. The royal slayings will enhance instability in Nepal's politics which, as it is, is very volatile. Our relations have been very prickly. Nepal considers the 1950 Treaty of Peace and Friendship with India an anachronism and has often accused India of denying it rightful trade and transit facilities. India has been very concerned that Nepal has allowed itself to be used as a haven for Pakistan-sponsored anti-India activities. India has also been worried that Nepal needlessly plays China off against it. Strangely, two countries who share cultural legacies and whose economic destinies are intertwined are far apart. Indian myopia, which sees any expression of legitimate Nepalese sovereignty through the "anti-India" lens, has combined with Nepalese paranoia, which wants to have its cake and eat it too, to produce this result.

Water epitomises best the shared heritage of the two countries, reflecting both the promise and the pitfalls. All of Nepal's major rivers flow into India. Nepal's hydro-electric power potential has been assessed at about 43,000 MW of which it has exploited a measly 8 per cent. Its hydel resources just cannot be developed without India as a partner. No permanent solution to the endemic floods that devastate eastern Uttar Pradesh and northern Bihar year after year is possible without afforestation in the upper catchment areas of the wayward Kosi and Gandak rivers in Nepal.

Based on various studies, three specific Indo-Nepal irrigation-cum-flood control projects with a total installed power generation capacity of around 20,000 MW have been identified. These are the Chisapani project on the Karnali and the Pancheshwar project on the Mahakali in western Nepal and the Barakshetra project on the Saptkosi in eastern Nepal. There is also a 600-MW Burhi Gandak project and the Nepalese want us to purchase electricity from their eastern Arun project. Nepal, however, is sore that the earlier Indo-Nepal projects on the Kosi and the Gandak, implemented in India in 1950s and 1960s, have not yielded the desired benefits for them and there are other irritants as well.

That statesmanship is indeed possible on both sides is demonstrated by the breakthrough that materialised in February 1996 in the form of the Mahakali Treaty. Indeed, 1996 was the golden year for bilateral relations, for apart from the Mahakali Treaty, the Nepal-

India Trade Agreement also got signed in December of that year. But progress on implementation of the Mahakali Treaty has been very slow. It is our bureaucracy that has stymied the establishment of the binational Mahakali River Commission. Also, India has been critical of the trade agreement from which Nepal has gained substantially (the pact is up for renewal in December 2001). No doubt, there are still some vital unre-solved technical and economic issues but after the departure of P.V. Narasimha Rao and I.K. Gujral, India is being very lethargic in its approach.

Mega projects apart, other avenues of ecological collaboration like soil conservation, social, farm and agro-forestry and grassland and watershed management have to be pursued by us. Environmental degradation and poverty go hand-in-hand in both our countries. One innovative suggestion made by B.G. Verghese in his Waters of Hope (1990) is that a joint Indo-Nepal eco-development programme should be taken up by NGOs and ex-servicemen's cooperatives. The political resistance to this in Nepal will be lower and might even appeal to King Gyanendra who is known to be an avid environmentalist. A number of such government-funded but NGO-implemented projects can proliferate very quickly and less expensively, while having tangible impact.

When things cool down in Kathmandu, we must demonstrate some leadership in water resource management and actively solicit international involvement. To be sure, Nepal does have a psychological small country hang-up vis-a-vis India but as Ramaswamy Iyer, one of India's leading water resource experts, puts it, "(Nepal's) Fears may be exaggerated but they are not absurd." The real problem is that Nepal comes on India's radar screen only when there is a crisis. We treat it as a quaint outpost of Hinduism. The onus is really on India to change both the atmospherics and substance of the bilateral relationship. In the process, we may well have to give more than we get. Greatness does not come cheap.

18/06/2001

THE KILLING OF BUDDHA
Why Sri Lankan Buddhism is different from the image
of Buddhism that we have

The *Agony* of Sri Lanka continues. What appears paradoxical is the role played by Buddhism in fuelling what has been essentially a linguistic conflict. Paradoxical simply because we have all been taught how the Buddha was the apostle of peace, compassion, harmony and non-violence. The powerfully positive role of Buddhism in creating a highly educated and egalitarian society in Sri Lanka as compared to other South Asian countries like India and Pakistan has been recognised by economists like Amartya Sen. But how and when did Buddhism acquire a destructively negative dimension?

H.L. Seneviratne, an anthropologist at the University of Virginia in the US, has just published a stunningly brilliant book *The Work of Kings: The New Buddhism in Sri Lanka* in which he discusses Buddhist social and political ideology that has given Buddhism a distinct flavour in the island country. Seneviratne builds on two other all-time classics— *Buddhism Betrayed?* by Harvard anthropologist Stanley Tambiah that came out in 1992 and *Buddhism Transformed* by the Princeton anthropologists Richard Gombrich and Gananath Obeyesekere that came out in 1988. Historian K.M. De Silva's *Reaping the Whirlwind* published in 1998 is essential reading to understand how Sri Lanka got to where it has and to appreciate Buddhism in its larger setting.

Seneviratne argues that neither in the Ashokan nor the Ambedkarite versions is Buddhism an "establishment". But in Sri Lanka, Myanmar and Thailand, Buddhism became an establishment in religious and economic terms. It is this that explains the difference between Buddhism as we Indians think of it and Theravada Buddhism as it has evolved in other settings—a case of an Indian export being adapted to local circumstances! Of course, what complicates matters in Sri Lanka is the interplay of religion and language in a social environment of multiple diversities and adversarial parliamentary politics.

Buddhist revivalism goes back to the last decades of the 19th century. 1879 saw the publication of Edwin Arnold's tribute to the *Buddha, Light of Asia,* one of history's most influential books, that incidentally also had a profound impact on Jawaharlal Nehru. It was in the very next year that Madame Blavatsky and Colonel Henry Olcott, founders of the Theosophical Society that was to be headquartered later at Adyar in Chennai, began a campaign to educate the Sri Lankans about their precious heritage.

But the first really great local champion who saw in Buddhism the only way to take on British imperialism and Christian proselytisation was Anagarika Dharmapala, born in 1864. Although he was the father of Buddhist revivalism, he was no obscurantist xenophobe. He believed in westernisation but on a strong foundation of Buddhist values and traditions. Dharmapala viewed Buddhism as the only route to a cultural renaissance as also to economic regeneration in a land that had been under colonial domination for almost five centuries.

Dharmapala is almost forgotten in India although he spent many years here and derived inspiration from Indian sources. It was in this country that he started the Maha Bodhi Society in 1891. This society spearheaded the struggle to regain for the Buddhists control of the historic Bodhi tree and Bodh Gaya Temple in Bihar. He died in April 1933 at Sarnath, where the Sakyamuni had preached his first sermon. Next only to Dharmapala is Walpola Rahula whose *Bhiksuvage Urumaya* (The Heritage of the Bhikku) is considered as having the greatest influence on recent Sri Lankan Buddhism. Rahula's manifesto published in 1946 draws on many sources including Indian nationalism and the philosophy of the Ramakrishna Mission. Tambiah writes that Calcutta, where Rahula spent two years in the mid-1940s, had the same kind of stimulating effect on him as it did on Dharmapala earlier.

Both Dharmapala and Rahula saw in Buddhism an instrument for social emancipation and political change. They envisaged an aggressively active role for the monks. It is no wonder that an Indian monk who was influenced most by them and who had studied for a while in Sri Lanka, Rahula Sankrityayan, was among the most relentless crusaders for peasant rights in Bihar in the 1930s. But while Dharmapala and Walpola remain charismatically noble figures, it is the use of an activist brotherhood by successive generations of politicians starting with S.W.R.D. Bandaranaike and the brotherhood's succumbing to the lure of wealth, power and status that has led to a subversion of the duo's ideals. Seneviratne terms this "from regeneration to degeneration". What has happened is that economic Buddhism, cultural Buddhism and social Buddhism as originally conceived by Dharmapala and Walpola to modernise Sri Lanka has become a political Buddhism with horrific consequences for managing a multi-ethnic, multireligious and multilinguistic society. Surely, there is a lesson in this for us also. The propaganda of Hinduism in Peril is really no different from the cry of Betrayal of Buddhism, the title of the 1956 official inquiry report that set Sri Lanka on the path to chaos.

26/06/2000

VIII

International Disagreements :
An India That is Out of Step

Here, the focus is very much on the WTO and what it means for India. Unlike China which is using the WTO to carry out fundamental, India's attitude towards the WTO has generally been hostile. Unfortunately, successive governments in Delhi have not seen it fit to mount a vigourous education and awareness campaign on the WTO and how India stands to benefit from an active and constructive participation in its affairs. NGOs, social activists and anti-globalisers (some of whom are prominent women!) perennially in search of a cause have not helped matters by their strident and ill-informed comments and criticisms. CTBT is another issue that has aroused passions in this country and I have taken a strong position in favour of signing it, even though that is not the dominant view here. Recent events in the subcontinent have highlighted the urgent need for denuclearisation in this region.

Old mindsets change slowly as our stance at the Doha Ministerial Meeting of the WTO held in November 2001 revealed. India is a leader in search of followers. We cling to old shibboleths while other countries strive to maximise their national interests. The articles in this section are based on this premise that a country seeking global recognition must also be alive to its global responsibilities and that instinctive and aggressive third world-ism that comes naturally to us no longer serves any useful purpose. The last article in this section got me into serious trouble with religious leaders and I had to tender an apology for the title and the accompanying illustration as well.

SIGN CTBT, IT SUITS US

The Talbott-Jaswant talks could lead
to a great strategic future

Four rounds of Indo-US talks have been held in the past threemonths. Quite rightly, the Jaswant Singh-Strobe Talbott meetings have been kept away from the media's gaze. Five issues have figured in the talks which look like being wrapped up in the next few weeks. These are:

- India signing the Comprehensive Test Ban Treaty (CTBT);
- India joining the discussions and negotiations on the Fissile Material Cutoff Treaty (FMCT);
- India legislating export controls on the transfer of nuclear and missile technology to other countries;
- India's plans for deployment of nuclear weapons;
- Confidence-building measures (CBMs) to minimise the risk of nuclear confrontation in south Asia.

While there are no serious differences on any of these issues—except our weaponisation plans—the CTBT is the most contentious domestically. Fortunately, there is now growing recognition both in the Government and among security and foreign policy experts that after Pokhran II, signing the CTBT will be in India's interests.

The very commentators who spearheaded India's opposition to the CTBT in the past two years—K. Subrahmanyam, Muchkund Dubey, J.N. Dixit, Brahma Chellaney, Jasjit Singh and Raja Mohan—have changed their stance. They now believe that the May 11 and May 13 nuclear tests have made India's objections to the CTBT irrelevant. But the CTBT remains an emotive issue to many sections of our political class, which react on emotion and dogma, not facts. There will be an orchestrated outcry if the Government signs the CTBT. It should just ignore these protests.

The world could never understand why India opposed the CTBT in the first place. After all, it was Jawaharlal Nehru who initially proposed such a treaty way back in 1954. It was Nehru again who got India into the Partial Test Ban Treaty in 1963. In 1988, India presented to the UN an action plan for total nuclear disarmament. It included a CTBT. In 1993, India co-sponsored, along with the US, the CTBT at the UN.

Given this anti-nuclear commitment—unmatched by any country, including Japan—India's aggressive opposition to the CTBT when it came up for finalisation at Geneva in 1996 was baffling. In a forthcoming article in *World Affairs*, Subrahmanyam, India's leading security expert, has tried to explain this paradox. His argument is that what changed between 1993 and 1996 was the extension of the 1968 Nuclear Non-Proliferation Treaty (NPT).

The NPT sees the world in two categories. First, the five nuclear haves, those countries (the US, the UK, Russia, China, France) which had nuclear weapons before January 1, 1967. Second, the nuclear have-nots, among them India. In 1995, the NPT was indefinitely extended. This made India a permanent non-nuclear power. If India had signed the CTBT in 1996, then it would have forever foreclosed its nuclear option—whereas our policy had been to keep this option open. As it turned out, after an attempt in 1995 by P.V. Narasimha Rao and another in 1997 by Inder Kumar Gujral, we finally exercised the option in 1998. The basic scenario has, therefore, changed.

Going by Atal Bihari Vajpayee's statement in the Lok Sabha, it is apparent that the Indian nuclear establishment believes no further tests are necessary to build and deploy a minimum, credible deterrent. The prime minister has announced India's unilateral moratorium on further nuclear explosions, thus accepting the spirit of the CTBT. This statement could have been made either to calm an anxious world or to signal that no further tests are, in fact, required by India. Both explanations are probably true. Thus, signing the CTBT will not harm India. We could stipulate conditions while signing—like the US has done. Pakistan has already announced its intention to sign. We may well be the only country left outside the CTBT. This is a document the world takes as a test of commitment to nuclear non-proliferation.

Many in India still believe the CTBT, like the NPT, is discriminatory. This is not true. The CTBT does not differentiate between haves and have-nots. Neither does it preclude computer-aided design and testing and laboratory experiments. India has strong capability in these. Further, it is likely that all sanctions on India will be lifted if we sign the CTBT. It is also possible that curbs on technology transfer and collaboration in the defence, nuclear and space industries will get eliminated progressively. But for this we have to keep the US engaged in constructive dialogue and be serious about CBMs with Pakistan and China.

The ball is in Vajpayee's court. He should have had all living former prime ministers standing next to him on May 11, as he announced India's tests. This would have acknowledged the continuity and consensus in our nuclear policy. Uncharacteristically, Vajpayee behaved in a partisan manner. He can make amends by taking other political parties into confidence on the fallout of the Singh-Talbott talks. He should also look beyond his Government and put together a panel of experts to prepare a blueprint for nuclear policy, strategy and diplomacy. The CTBT is just the beginning.

14/09/1998

◆———◆

IT'S CTBT TIME ONCE AGAIN
Understanding the real options in the CTBT debate

In a previous article ("Sign CTBT, It Suits Us) Kautilya had advocated that India sign the CTBT for a number of reasons—mainly because the compulsion for not signing had significantly reduced with the nuclear tests of May 1998. This had landed him in political difficulty but intellectual honesty demands that risk be taken again. The CTBT's text says that "if the treaty has not entered into force three years after the date of the anniversary of its opening for signature, the secretary-general of the UN could, at the request of a majority of states that had ratified, convene a conference to examine the situation and to decide by consensus what measures consistent with international law may be undertaken to accelerate the ratification process". That date fell on September 24.

The CTBT issue bristles with scientific, technological, political and strategic complexities of the highest order. But three questions are fundamental:

- Are the five tests conducted in May 1998 at Pokhran sufficient in terms of sheer numbers to develop the nuclear arsenal we have in mind?
- Are those tests of sufficient yield so as to deter those who have to be deterred?
- Is there anything be gained by India signing the CTBT now instead of waiting for its ratification by the US and China?

Answers to these questions, not emotion and arguments like "CTBT is a son of NPT", should guide our stance. The US has conducted 1,036 explosions and China has probably conducted 45 tests. If our intention is to match the Americans and the Chinese quantitatively, then we should not be signing the CTBT. The quest for quantitative parity is suicidal—and also unnecessary. Five tests are enough, say our top scientists. If our scientific assessment is that qualitatively the five tests are not enough, then too we should not be signing the CTBT. That, according to India's nuclear and defence science establishment, is not the case. However, all this presupposes that the government has a clear idea of the nature and size of our "minimum credible deterrent". This, however, may be a heroic assumption to make at this stage.

Acceding to an international treaty is a three-stage process—signature, ratification and deposit of the instruments of ratification. 153 countries have already signed the CTBT. 44 countries, including India and Pakistan, have to sign and ratify it before it comes into force. 21 countries, including China, Russia and the US, have signed but not ratified. All eyes are on the US. What the US does will determine the fate of the treaty. The CTBT has actually been lying with the US Senate Foreign Relations Committee for two years and has got caught up with domestic politics. Just a few days ago, Democrat Senator Byron Dorgan and Republican Senator Arlen Specter made a bipartisan plea for the US Senate to ratify the CTBT quickly. They argued that the US must lead by example and ratify the CTBT in order to persuade India and Pakistan to also do so.

In India, Parliament does not have to ratify a treaty. It is the government that has the exclusive right to do so. Many people in this country think that since the same body signs, ratifies and deposits, the three are simultaneous processes. This is false. India signed the Chemicals Weapons Convention in January, 1993, ratified it in October 1995 and deposited the instruments of ratification in September 1996. Thus India signing the CTBT does not mean that it has ratified it. It could very well link ratification to ratification by China. But signature now could afford us a leverage in our bilateral relationship and also help us to pursue our goal of universal nuclear disarmament.

What India has to ask itself is whether it should sign the CTBTnow or allow the pressure to build up after the US ratification which may be by March-April 2000. We may well decide to wait for the US Senate to ratify the CTBT before deciding to sign but the question we should be asking ourselves is whether we gain in our vital relationship with the US by coming on board on our own in a proactive manner. Of course, India can keep out. But if it does so and if the US, China and Russia also ratify, then India could be in for UN sanctions.

Paradoxically, the anti-nuke lobby in India says no weaponisation but also no CTBT. This is because CTBT is seen as an American ploy, which is far from the truth. On the Internet, the CTBT pays tribute to Jawaharlal Nehru for first proposing it in 1954. The memoirs of Dean Rusk and Mani Dixit reveal that Pandit Nehru refused American blandishments to develop nuclear weapons during 1962-64. India and the US co-sponsored the CTBT in the UN in 1993. Actually, whatever the public rhetoric, all political parties support a moratorium on further nuclear tests by India. This is perhaps what has prompted the Washington-based Economic Strategy Institute to suggest that pending India's formal signing of the CTBT, our Parliament legislate export controls and also pass a resolution, citing the key provisions of CTBT and explicitly pledging that India will comply with these provisions. This could then take the form of an undertaking to the UN. What the world wants us to do is convert a de facto situation into a de jure position. This could be a signal that a country aspiring for global leadership is fully conscious of the responsibilities that such aspirations impose.

04/10/1999

USE WTO, DON'T ABUSE IT
Those who want India to walk out of the WTO simply don't know their economics

It must be something in the food we eat, the water we drink, the air we breathe. The world moves in one direction, India in another. For decades, we held that international trade would not grow. It did. For decades, we have indulged in Brahminical sophistry and kept away from global regimes of nuclear non-proliferation. Somehow, India is an exception to all international trends. The latest example is the outrageous statement attributed to the respected Kushabhau Thakre, BJP president, that India must walk out of the World Trade Organisation (WTO).

The statement has been contradicted but it betrays a mindset that is widely prevalent. The anti-WTO lobby has many supporters, some vocal and some suppressed, in all political parties and many academic establishments. But mercifully these views have not got reflected in policy—showing that there is indeed a God somewhere, protecting us from ourselves. It would be a disaster for India to even contemplate withdrawal from the WTO, which today has 132 countries as members. China and Russia have been lobbying to join.

Thakre and his ilk allege the WTO is an American stooge. Actually, the only other country with an anti-WTO clamour is the US. Many Yankee politicians believe the WTO erodes the powers of the US. In fact, a WTO was to be set up way back in 1948 but President Harry S. Truman was forced into sabotaging it. Instead, we got the ad hoc GATT, the General Agreement on Tariffs and Trade, which got stuck with the label of the General Agreement on Talk and Talk. GATT, of which India was a founder member, managed to do a lot of useful work. Finally, a more comprehensive and legally-backed WTO came into being on January 1, 1995.

India's membership of the WTO saved it from trade sanctions post-Pokhran II. There were some sections in the US calling for withdrawal of India's "Most Favoured Nation" (MFN) status. India has been spared this ignominy because it is a WTO member. On the other hand, China is made to go through the exercise of MFN renewal year after year. MFN really means a member country has to treat all other members equally and follow a policy of non-discrimination.

For a country like India, a multilateral, negotiated system of transparent rules and regulations—like WTO—is preferable. The alternative is a bilateral system of agreements, where the powerful partner calls the shots. At the heart of the WTO is the dispute settlement mechanism. Countries take trade disputes to the WTO. It hears all sides and gives a judgement. Countries abide by the judgement. The US has been at the receiving end so far, which is why the WTO is not liked by America's Thakre- types. Since its inception, the WTO has settled 11 disputes. The US was a respondent in three; it lost all three. It was a complainant in one—and lost again.

India has taken three disputes to the WTO. In May 1998, the WTO upheld its complaint against US curbs on import of shrimps. In April 1996, India won a case against US curbs on import of woollen coats for women. In November 1996, India won another case against the US on its curbs on import of woven, woollen shirts and blouses. In

May 1998, India complained against the European Union's curbs on rice import. A decision is awaited.

In turn, India has had two complaints against it. One is on quantitative restrictions (QRs) on the import of some 2,700 items. We have agreed to phase out the QRs by 2003. The other is on our intellectual property protection system. Here we have agreed to amend the law to allow for product patents and make other changes in pharmaceuticals and chemicals. In both cases, the WTO is telling us to do something which is in our interest but which we are loath to do.

WTO agreements are opening new markets for our textile and agro-products. Our share of world trade in these is minuscule, although our potential is enormous. M.S. Swaminathan, the noted agroscientist, has written that India could corner 25 per cent of the world trade in seeds and planting materials during the next decade. All textile import quotas imposed by the developed world will go on January 1, 2005. We have criticised this agreement without realising that quotas have actually saved us and compensated for our inefficiencies. That we have been unable to take advantage of the WTO is due to continuing domestic policy distor-tions—small-scale reservations, quotas and bans—and lack of world-class quality, safety and health standards.

Thakre's party talks about making India a super-power in information technology; and rightly so. But obviously nobody has briefed him on the WTO-sponsored Information Technology Agreement (ITA) which covers computers, semiconductors, telecom equipment software and scientific instruments. As usual, India got on late but we got on nevertheless. Now we are one of the 43 countries which are members of the ITA. If we walk out of the WTO, the cyber-plans of the BJP and of N. Chandrababu Naidu will remain a pipe dream. The challenge now is to use the WTO, not abuse it. If only there was a way of injecting the pragmatism virus into our DNA.

06/07/1998

OFF TO SEATTLE
A menu for Maran as he prepares for the WTO meet

On November 30, trade ministers from 134 member countries of the World Trade Organisation (WTO) will assemble for their third meeting at Seattle in the US. The declaration they will issue on December 3 will set the stage for the launch of a new round of trade negotiations. The Europeans are very keen to start what they call a Millennium Round. The Americans are not very keen on a whole new round and all they really want is to link trade with labour standards. The East Asians and the Latins will go with the wind. India, as usual, is singing a different tune from all other major countries.

Murasoli Maran is an extremely pragmatic minister. It is upto him to give India's position at Seattle and beyond a forward-looking and professional perspective. He must now send a clear signal that India has buried its reputation for being obstructionist and argumentative. Cold economic self-interest should guide our stance. Our approach has to be highly nuanced and flexible. It must also be proactive so that our own specific concerns are reflected in the negotiating mandate from Seattle. A comprehensive approach to the US encompassing issues in security, defence, trade, investment, environment, technology, energ and agriculture will help identify trade-offs—what India can give and what it can get. Jagdish Bhagwati, the guru of global trade, has suggested a two track approach—track I comprising negotiations on the built-in agenda and track II involving discussions on contentious issues.

Kautilya has seen a copy of the draft declaration prepared on October 8 by the WTO secretariat. India must put industrial tariffs back on the agenda. In a detailed paper prepared for a seminar to be held at Harvard very shortly, an eminent India-born, US-based economist Arvind Panagariya shows that in areas like textiles and clothing, leather and footwear, import duties in developed countries are still very high. For instance, over half of US imports of textiles and clothing attract an import duty between 15 and 35 per cent. Of course, this would mean that we too will have to continue to cut import duties to at least Asian levels by 2002, which means a halving in the next three years.

Negotiations on liberalisation of agricultural trade are bound to commence. We must participate proactively since it will open up new markets, provided we get our domestic policies right which is true for textiles as well. In agriculture, we have absurdly high levels of binding duties going up to 300 per cent. The highest rate of duty should not exceed 40-50 per cent in farm commodities. India must forcefully state that it wants new provisions to be included in the agreement on intellectual property rights so as to protect its biological and genetic resources like neem and turmeric. This is mentioned in the draft declaration. But we have to the past two years.

Maran must continue to resist US pressure to bring in labour standards and environment into the WTO. The West believes that imports from lowwage countries cause them economic distress. This is wrong. Labour in these countries is hurting because of rapid technological change and ageing.

The Europeans will call for a new multilateral agreement on investment and for a competition policy. The Americans are not keen on this. We should make common cause with them. However, we must have a competition policy of our own to combat monopolies and oligopolies and to ensure that consumers benefit. Transparency in government procurement is another issue dear to the Americans and the Europeans. India is resisting it and inexplicably so. Our procurement procedures are corruption-intensive and involve huge delays. It is in our interest to follow the best global practice. We must play a leading role in negotiating an agreement on labour-intensive, technology-intensive and skill-intensive services that will open up more visas for our engineers and scientists. Here, while we strive for a global agreement, we have to take a number of decisions irrespective of the WTO. For example, 51 per cent foreign equity in telecom. We must bring e-commerce into trade in services at zero-duty. India must argue that preferences granted to partners in any regional trade agreement should be extended to all WTO members. And we must push for the abolition of antidumping laws altogether even though we are among the world's most frequent users of anti-dumping clauses and their re-placement by safeguards actions.

Maran is taking an industry delegation to Seattle. This is welcome but what he really needs to do is upgrade our technical capability. To start with, he should immediately set up a special WTO strategy group comprising top economists, lawyers and diplomats to make our approach more research-based. Apart from Pangariya, names of economists like Jagdish Bhagwati, T.N. Srinivasan, Arvind Subramaniam, Ashok Gulati, Omkar Goswami, Harshvardhan Singh and Bibek Debroy, of lawyers like Suhail Nathani, Lakshmi Kumaran, Praveen Anand, Krishnan Venugopal and Pallavi Shroff and of diplomats like A.V. Ganesan and Hardeep Puri come to Kautilya's mind as people who have the *analytical* skills to contribute to India's negotiating stance on an ongoing basis. Maran could also include in this group his former political ally who has been a commerce and finance minister and knows the WTO intimately.

01/11/1999

◆━━◆

GRAIN TRADE WILL YIELD GAIN
The WTO negotiations on agriculture will restart soon

After the recent seattle fiasco, the US and the European Union have just reached an agreement to resume negotiations on liberalisation of agricultural trade presumably from January 1, 2000. The Agreement on Agriculture that was finalised as part of the Uruguay Round and came into force on January 1, 1995 has three main components. First, all countries are mandated to convert all quantitative restrictions to tariffs and indicate maximum tariffs. Second, all developed countries are mandated to reduce aggregate subsidies to 5 per cent of the value of production and all developing countries to 10 per cent of the value of production, with subsidies to small and marginal farmers out of the purview of these cuts. Third, direct export subsidies have to be phased out. These commitments were to be fulfilled over a six-year period. But that has not happened. India should be complaining but it is not since we are deeply ambivalent ourselves on liberalisation of agricultural trade.

India is committed to removing quantitative restrictions on all imports by March 31, 2003. This means that anybody can import anything after paying the applicable duty. But on maximum tariffs or on "bound rates" we have gone overboard. We have indicated that the maximum import duty would be anywhere between 100 per cent and 300 per cent. Rice and skimmed milk powder, for historical reasons, have been bound at zero per cent. However, in practice, wheat and pulses are imported at zero duty and edible oils at 15 per cent. Considering that it is in our interests that developed countries reduce their tariffs on farm imports sharply so as to create new markets for our farmers, we should abandon this approach and say that the import of all agricultural commodities and products into India would attract a duty of 50 per cent as has also been suggested by Ashok Gulati, India's top agrieconomist. This is adequate protection and would give us the necessary moral authority to press the richer countries to follow suit.

On subsidies or on what the World Trade Organisation (WTO) calls the "Aggregate Measure of Support", India is actually comfortably placed. The method of calculating these subsidies is complicated. But WTO's own calculations and those made by Gulati reveal that for the reference period 1986-88, total farm subsidies in India were a negative 30-32 per cent, the negative sign indicating in the aggregate, Indian farmers receive prices lower than their international counterparts. In the '90s, world prices have come down and Indian prices have increased but even if 1996-98 is used as the base, the subsidy is still around a negative 10 per cent. Thus, we would not be called upon to reduce subsidies by the WTO. We have to do so simply because we are bankrupt.

Under another WTO agreement on intellectual property rights, all countries have to institute a sui generis system of protection of plant varieties. Sui generis means unique. Thus, a country is free to choose the system it wants. Just a few days ago, after four years of debate, the Government introduced a Plant Varieties Protection Bill in the Lok Sabha. This Bill protects the rights of researchers and breeders as also that of farmers to save and exchange seed. What is prohibited is commercial sale of registered seed from farmer to farmer. The Bill does not provide for patents but only for a system of registration. The global regime for plant protection is the Union for the Protection of Plant Varieties (UPOV) that operates under the World Intellectual Property Organisation. There are two UPOVs—UPOV1978 and UPOV1991. The former gives governments total freedom and allows farmers to save and exchange seed, whereas, UPOV 1991 does not. Luckily, membership of UPOV 1978 that had closed on December 31, 1995 has now been re-opened for a year. India must use this opportunity to become a member at the earliest so there is no conflict between its domestic legislation and global obligations. Agricultural scientist M.S. Swaminathan estimates India could have a 25 per cent share of world trade in seed.Cultivation of one acre of wheat seed gives five times more income than an acre of grain.

The developed countries have pushed India hard to lower industrial tariffs. This has been in India's own interests but global pressure cannot be denied. Now we have an opportunity of "taking our revenge". The US, Japan and the European countries are the heaviest subsidisers in agriculture and the worst distorters of world trade in farm products. But gains will not accrue to us automatically. Global standards of different types will have to be met. Export policy must be stable and long-term. Public investment in agriculture, particularly in irrigation, research and seeds has to be stepped up but this can happen only if the money is diverted from subsidies to infrastructure. Domestic distortions themselves also will need to be removed. For example, the minimum support price for wheat is Rs 550 a quintal but the economic cost at the consumer end is Rs 808 per quintal—no wonder then that it is cheaper to import wheat into the south than haul it all the way from Punjab. We could be exporting sugar but import it instead only because of our own stupid policies. Of course, food security must remain the overriding goal. But what we must realise soon is that agricultural trade can contribute substantially to fulfilling this objective.

03/01/2000

◆━━━◆

AN INDIA THAT IS OUT OF STEP
Ten years after reforms, the country is still groping
for a proper global role

What is it about India that even after a decade of economic reforms and major changes in foreign policy, we still cling to shibboleths of the past? We crave global recognition. We desperately want to take on a leadership role on the world stage. But while we are more than ready to assert and demand our rights, we are less than enthusiastic in taking on responsibilities. On many important international issues, India stands isolated and quite frankly, our credibility is taking a knock day by day.

The most recent example of our solitariness comes from the recently concluded UN General Assembly session on HIV/AIDS. Every country facing an epidemic came out strongly in favour of large scale use of antiretroviral drugs. While these drugs are not curatives, they control the spread of the infection and prolong lives. India was the sole exception and struck a discordant note arguing that we just could not afford the large-scale use of these drugs in our anti-AIDS programme. True, at a cost of about $1 (Rs 47) per person per day, the annual bill for the use of the anti-retrovirals if they were to be distributed free, as they are in countries like Botswana and Brazil, would be over a billion dollars. But our position was not nuanced and what others could not understand was how India could come out against anti-retrovirals when Indian companies are revolutionising the supply of these drugs elsewhere in the world.

The Kyoto Protocol is a second example of how mis-aligned we are with the rest of the world. Signed in 1997, the protocol sets targets for reductions in emissions of greenhouse gases which are warming the earth. It imposes no quantitative targets on developing countries like India and it is actually a very good deal for us, a deal that we will definitely not get in the future. Yet we are not signatories to the protocol. But that does not prevent us from being sanctimonious. We went into apoplectic fits when US President George Bush announced America's rejection of the protocol.

The Comprehensive Test Ban Treaty (CTBT) is a third instance of our being different. First, the argument was that there is no national consensus on India ratifying it. This is actually a nice way of saying that we do not have the courage to do what needs to be done and what the world recognises as the right thing to do. Then, the argument veered to why India should sign the CTBT when the US Senate had rejected it. A further twist was given by the argument that India had already declared a moratorium on further nuclear tests and that this brought India into the CTBT regime on a de facto, if not a de jure, basis. But then why not sign the CTBT and signal that India wishes to be in the international mainstream of nuclear non-proliferation?

Or take the issue of a new round of global trade negotiations under the aegis of the WTO. Such a round is inevitable and may be kick-started at the next WTO ministerial meeting in November this year at Qatar. India is perhaps one of the few countries which have expressed reservations, if not opposition. The point is that India stands to gain from a new round that focuses on issues like tariff reductions in advanced countries for imports of labour-intensive manufactures, reduction of agricultural subsidies in the developed world, liberalising trade in services and abolition of the antidumping mechanism where our ability to hurt is dwarfed by our probability of getting hurt. Our approach to the WTO stands out in sharp contrast with how the Chinese are negotiating their entry on terms which are less favourable than what India has been able to get away with.

Intellectual property rights or the matter of patents have acquired a whole new dimension in the wake of the AIDS crisis. Countries like Brazil and South Africa have tough patent laws that give them flexibility to reduce prices of essential drugs. The Americans have chosen not to challenge these laws realising that it would be a public relations disaster if they are seen to be putting the profits of a few multinationals ahead of the needs of millions of poor and suffering patients. But India figures nowhere in this debate since our patent laws have yet to be in full accordance with the WTO agreement called TRIPs (Trade-Related Intellectual Property Rights). What other countries are demonstrating is that you can be in TRIPs and protect consumers while we in India are still engaged on theological debates on the matter.

The problem with us is we think that as the world's second-most populous country and the world's fourth-largest economy based on purchasing power parity, we have an automatic right on the world's head table. The sad truth is that the world is increasingly getting cynical about India. We have never been known to say what we mean and mean what we say. However, in the 1990s, we had succeeded in convincing the world that we were changing. But it is clear that the more things change, the more they remain the same.

09/07/2001

———◆◆———

AS USUAL, INDIA IS AN OUTLIER
The WTO summit in Qatar is just three months away but India is ill-prepared

The fourth ministerial meeting of the WTO is being held in Qatar from November 9 to13 this year. The main agenda item is bound to be the launch of a new round of global trade negotiations. India is the only major country to have publicly opposed a new round. Privately, we may well tell US Trade Representative Robert Zoellick when he visits Delhi shortly that India will ultimately come on board. But this two-faced approach does India no good. What is also ironic is that while we express opposition, much of the cutting-edge work on the WTO is being done by Indian scholars like Jagdish Bhagwati, T.N. Srinivasan, Ashok Gulati, Arvind Panagariya, Arvind Subramanian, Aaditya Mattoo and Jayashree Watal.

First, all important countries have come out in support of a new round. On July 16, 2001, in an unprecedented move, Zoellick and Pascal

Lamy, his EU counterpart, wrote a joint article in The Washington Post arguing strongly for a new round. This is significant because the US and the EU have been engaged in a number of trade disputes. Earlier, on July 4, Chinese vice-minister of foreign trade had unequivocally stated that China (which is likely to join the WTO at Doha) supports a new round. Latin American and east Asian countries have also expressed their support.

Second, India has stated that its main concern is the implementation of the commitments made during the earlier Uruguay Round. Assuming that our position is legitimate, the question is how best it is addressed. Discussions have commenced in the WTO on agriculture and services. The review of the agreement on trade-related aspects of intellectual property rights (TRIPS) has also started. These discussions will meander along. But if these issues are taken up as part of a new round—and a round is a politically mandated, intensive period of negotiations on a basket of issues which involve give and take—then the chances of reaching a resolution are significantly enhanced. That single-subject negotiations do not offer scope for bargaining is borne out by the Information Technology Agreement in which India did not participate to begin with but had to finally accept without any quid pro quo.

Third, although it does not form part of the "built in" Uruguay Round agenda for review, we have a great interest in bringing the issue of industrial tariffs to the negotiating table. The general perception is that with their tariffs averaging 3-5 per cent, more cannot be extracted from the developed countries on this score. This is wrong and in areas like textiles, plastics, leather, footwear and fisheries, tariffs of 5-35 per cent still persist. To be sure, domestic policies constrain India's emergence as a global leader in labour-intensive mass manufacturing but high tariffs in importing countries could emerge as a bottleneck.

Fourth, India has rightly raised its voice against growing protectionism in the West. India has also stood for the strengthening of the multilateral process. But of late bilateral and regional trading agreements have proliferated. In the memorable words of Bhagwati, regional trade blocs are not building blocks of free trade world-wide, rather stumbling blocks. Only the launch of a new global round can curb the growth of protectionism and push the process of globalisation of preferential tariffs.

Fifth, a new round is inevitable. The exact agenda has yet to be worked out and undoubtedly the process of finalising it will prove acrimonious. India's interest is best served by its being in a position to influence the agenda, if not actually determine it. That position of being able to influence the agenda to reflect our concerns will accrue to us only if we take a proactive approach of support to the very idea of a new round.

On the substance of the new round, India should take a broad three-track approach fully realising that the WTO is as much about trade as it is about trade law—which means the involvement of not just civil servants and economists but also of lawyers. Track-I would be issues on which we want to see negotiations and commitments quickly. These include agriculture, services, industrial tariffs, anti-dumping, TRIPS, e-commerce and globalisation of preferential tariffs. Track-II would be issues that we are prepared to discuss, where we need to bring forward domestic legislation but where negotiations and commitments need to be made later. These are investment, pro-curement and competition policy. Track-III would be issues that we reject for linkage with trade negotiations but on which we are prepared to talk in the appropriate forums. Labour standards are best dealt with in the International Labour Organisation. There is already a Committee on Trade and Environment in the WTO and our position should be one of no negotiations but a commitment to implement our own environmental standards and regulations strictly.

06/08/2001

◆━━◆

BASMATI GETS STEAMING AGAIN

India wins the Basmati patent case but the trademark issue remains

Ill-informed MPS, scare-mongering NGOs and a sensationalist media have raked up the Basmati rice patent controversy yet again. It is being claimed that the US has granted a patent for Basmati to American company RiceTec and that this would hit our exports of this long-grain, high-premium, aromatic rice variety that is grown by around three lakh farmers in Haryana, western Uttar Pradesh and Punjab. Unfortunately, facts are at a deep discount.

To begin with, the problem is just in the US. There is no dispute in Europe and West Asia. About 10 per cent of our Basmati rice exports go to the US. In 2000-1, the total Basmati rice exports were around 0.85 million tonnes valued at about Rs 2,200 crore. Two specific aspects of the US patent law are relevant here. First, anything under the sun is patentable provided there is novelty, inventiveness and industrial application. This was enunciated in the landmark US Supreme Court decision of 1980 while allowing the patenting of a genetically engineered bacteria developed by Dr Ananda Chakraborty of the University of Illinois. Second, under the US law, it is only after a patent is granted that aggrieved parties approach the US Patent Office for a "re-examination" that is based wholly on a written brief.

RiceTec has been selling Basmati rice grown in the US under the trademark Texmati and Kasmati for almost two decades. Texmati carries the description "American-style Basmati rice", while the superior Kasmati is described as "Indian-style Basmati rice". In December 1995, at the initiative of the then Union commerce minister P. Chidambaram, a Basmati Development Fund was set up to, among other things, protect the Basmati trademark. Battles have been won by the Agricultural Products Export Development Authority (APEDA) and its lawyers, the Delhi firm of Kumaran and Sagar in countries like the UK, Greece, Colombia, Brazil and Spain.

RiceTec, which used a number of Indian scientific publications in its support, was granted a US patent on September 2, 1997. India submitted a detailed re-examination brief on April 28, 2000. On September 11, 2000 RiceTec withdrew four key claims from the original 20 that it had made to get the patent and which had been challenged in the Indian brief. Three of these claims sought to define Basmati in a way that would have allowed RiceTec to keep out Indian-grown Basmati. On August 14, 2001, the final decision was handed down changing the title of the invention from Basmati Rice and Grains to Rice Lines Bas 867, RT 117 and RT 121. This is a victory for India. A patent has been granted for only these three lines which, incidentally, are derived from Pakistani Basmati varieties.

We cannot tell the world not to have intellectual property protection for its research. And research cannot be stopped. India's famous Pusa Basmati variety, for instance, is derived from a dwarf gene from a Taiwanese variety introduced into a local variety. The difference is that we do not patent plant varieties while the US does. It is only now that we are also thinking about protect-ing our own research in agriculture. But legislation is still pending. We are also yet to put in place a system to scientifically inventorise our genetic wealth and to use our biodiversity in a sustainable manner.

How do we get RiceTec to stop using the word Basmati? Since Basmati is used pre-dominantly by NRIs and Indian restaurants abroad, a mass e-mail boycott campaign could be started. Another more serious option suggested by Jayashree Watal, one of the world's leading scholars on intellectual property rights and now at the WTO, is to approach US courts on the allegedly deceptive use of the name Basmati or similar sounding trade-marks by RiceTec. But our case may have taken a beating with the May 9, 2001 ruling by the US Federal Trade Commission on a petition filed by the activist Vandana Shiva, that "there is no specific statutory or regulatory limitation on references to US-grown rice as Basmati".

The WTO affords protection for what is called a "geographical indication", that is, a product that is associated with a region. But at present, only wines and spirits like Champagne and Burgundy are covered. Basmati may well be a geographical indication but it is cultivated heavily in Pakistan as well. Thus, joint action is necessary. And we cannot hope to have the world recognise Basmati as a geographical indication if we ourselves do not do so quickly. Our national law to protect products like Basmati and Darjeeling tea was passed in December 1999 but has yet to come into effect. Moreover, the law and the rules appear very cumbersome. The immediate option is to pursue a bilateral approach based on some reciprocity with the Americans to protect our geographical indications while pursuing the WTO route as well.

03/09/2001

◆━━━━◆

MARAN'S HARANGUES

The commerce minister has not done himself
or India good by his outburst

What a depressing spectacle! Here are the Chinese all set to join the WTO after 15 years of tortuous negotiations and on vastly tougher terms than the price India had to pay for membership. Here are the Russians and the Iranians wanting their entry to be expedited. Here is the 21-country Asia-Pacific Economic Cooperation (APEC) forum meeting in Shanghai and declaring its support for a new round of global trade negotiations. And what does India do? Our Commerce Minister Murasoli Maran declares that the WTO is a "necessary evil". And to compound Maran's fulminations, another NDA ally, Punjab Chief Minister Parkash Singh Badal, moves the Supreme Court against the WTO agreements.

Obviously, a beleaguered Badal has the forthcoming state elections in mind. But it is ironic that Maran, among the most well-read, competent and reforms-friendly of politicians, should be talking like this. Maran should be asked: if the WTO is an evil, how has India managed to win some trade disputes against the US and Europe even as it has lost some others? If the WTO is an ogre, how is it that the Brazilians have used their patent laws to successfully challenge American drug companies to supply anti-AIDS drugs cheaply? If the WTO is merely a cabal of the powerful, what about disputes between the US and Japan and between the US and Europe?

Maran should be educating and preparing India for the WTO. He should be building a consensus for increasing India's engagement with the world economy. Instead, he is orchestrating a collective harakiri. What explains his attack? It is possible that he is doing so because of domestic political imperatives. Indian politicians never like to do anything proactively but they will accept something as an international obligation or compulsion. Thus, Maran could be telling his compatriots across the political spectrum—look, I tried to uphold India's national interest but what could I do, the world is stacked against us and we have no option but to go along.

India has a very strong case when it says that the developed countries have not fulfilled the commitments they made to the WTO to cut their agricultural subsidies, remove barriers to agricultural imports and to liberalise entry of skilled manpower from the developing countries. The WTO itself is saying so. Other organisations like the Paris-based club of rich countries, the OECD (Organisation of Economic Cooperation and Development), are also saying so. There are no doubts about the correctness of India's position that implementation of liberalisation commitments already made by the advanced nations should be given top priority in any further liberalisation of global trade. The question is how best our objective is achieved. The reality is that it can be achieved only through a new round of negotiations. India just does not have the economic muscle to change this reality. And it lacks this muscle entirely on account of its own policies.

The issue is also of negotiating style, of keeping bilateral channels of communications and negotiations open and active particularly with the US even as we marshal support for our arguments. The issue is not of "developing country versus developed country" as Maran makes it out to be. After all, two developing countries, South Africa and India, are engaged in a bitter dispute over anti-dumping duties imposed by the former on imports of pharmaceuticals. The issue is one of India see-ing where its interests lie. In this new round, paradoxical as it may appear, India's interests and those of developed countries like the US and Australia converge.

India does command influence disproportionate to its share of global trade. But the problem is that other developing countries want us to lead the charge and keep fighting even as they quietly strike deals with the US and other developed countries. This happened during the Uruguay Round of negotiations on patent laws and this is happening even today. Recently, Egypt, Indonesia and Pakistan have broken ranks with India and are supporting a new round of global trade negotiations. There is nothing wrong with this. These countries have decided that it is in their national interest to change their position. If only we could also be pragmatic and realistic and not be hung-up on assuming the leadership of the poor nations with such alacrity.

Going into the crucial WTO meeting in Qatar between November 9-13, India stands isolated. However, that should not come as a surprise. Maran and his senior bu-reaucrats have worked hard to ensure this outcome. Now damage control is of the essence. We can either obstruct a consensus at Doha—something we could safely be expected to do. Or we can change our approach so as to be able to influence the agenda and conduct of the new round of global trade negotiations— and move forward to prepare ourselves better for the inevitable.

05/11/2001

◆——◆

TIME TO MOVE ON

Substantively, Doha was not a disaster for an India committed to reforms

The biannual meeting of trade minsters of the WTO member countries held at Doha is over. The WTO will launch a new round of global trade negotiations. This round is to be completed by January 1, 2005. As far as India is concerned, there are five major benefits to be had from the broad negotiating agenda agreed upon. How much we will actually gain, of course, depends on the negotiations themselves and, more importantly, on domestic policy reforms.

- The protectionist anti-dumping laws and rules which Europe and America use liberally to stop imports from developing countries are to be liberalised;
- Europe, Japan and America are to phase out their huge farm subsidies;
- In case of an emergency involving public health, the interests of consumers could override the patent rights of pharmaceutical companies;
- America and Europe will reduce the duties they levy on imports of textiles and other labour-intensive manu-factured goods from developing countries;
- Movement of skilled manpower from developing countries to rich countries will be facilitated further.

The main setback to India is that the linkage between environment and trade figures explicitly in the negotiating agenda, although negotiations are to begin after two years and only with the explicit consent of all WTO members.

Union Commerce Minister Murasoli Maran is claiming victory. His trumpeting makes for smart politics at home but the reality is that the outcome is contrary to his shrill pre-Doha rhetoric and his stance at the conference. India was isolated at Doha with all developing countries deserting it. The Americans were completely exasperated with us. India lobbied for the wrong issues. For instance, it sought faster dismantling of the textile import quotas by the developed countries, which would not serve India's interests given our domestic policy distortions. On patents, Brazil and South Africa achieved the breakthrough and on agriculture, it was pressure from countries like Australia, New Zealand and Canada, with support from the US, that persuaded the Europeans to come around. India's opposition to transparency in government procurement, a global competition law and simplification of customs procedures was simply unjustified. Its harping on "implementation issues" though justifiable to some extent, was overdone, unrealistic and, at times, misleading.

However, Maran should not be criticised too much. He was,

after all, reflecting a solid domestic consensus with Indian industry, media and political parties supporting him in his aggressively confrontationist posture before and at Doha. But it is now time to look ahead and prepare ourselves for the difficult task of actual negotiations that lie ahead.

First, our negotiating style has to change. Whatever case we may have is lost because of this style and approach. The Brazilians are also tough like us but not as disliked as we are.

Then, the Government needs to appoint a high-level political personality to function as a minister for WTO affairs exclusively and that person must not be disturbed till the negotiations are over. This is a public and proactive role that cannot be played by a bureaucrat. Moreover, the commerce minister has other equally important responsibilities to be able to do justice to the demanding WTO assignment.

We also need to put in place a genuinely multi-disciplinary team of sectoral experts, economists, trade administrators and lawyers who will provide sustained intellectual support to both the strategy and specifics of India's negotiations. There are a number of Indian experts like Jagdish Bhag-wati, T.N. Srinivasan, Arvind Panagariya, Aaditya Mattoo, Arvind Subramanian, Ashok Gulati, Hardeep Puri and Jayashree Watal working abroad who are consulted by all but by their home country. Stronger research capabilities in trade policy and law also need to be built up.

While we negotiate in the WTO in Geneva, we must keep bilateral windows open and humming, especially with the US. That bilateral window has been damaged in recent weeks by India's provocative approach in the run-up to and at Doha. Bilateral channels at both the official and non-official levels need to be established.

Finally, we must realise that Indian tariffs are now the highest in the world and they dilute our bargaining advantage. We must also ensure that domestic legislation is in place soon in areas like competition policy, government procurement, biodiversity protection, patents, etc. On contentious issues like environment, investment, competition and labour standards, we need to think more positively on what constructive position we can take without jeopardising national interests.

03/12/2001

◆━━◆

LONG MARCH TO GENEVA

After 14 years of negotiations, China's WTO entry is facing
the last mile problem

In July 1986, China started negotiating its re-entry into the
General Agreement on Tariffs and Trade (GATT). China and India were
among the 23 founder-members of GATT whenit was formedin 1948.
From January1995,the country has been negotiating its membership
of the WTO which replaced GATT.It was expected that China will finally
become a member by November 2001 when trade ministers of WTO
member countries meet next in Qatar, although it now looks that this
deadline may well slip. Hong Kong and Macau will continue as members
even after China's accession and Taiwan will join immediately after
China's entry. Thus, after China's final accession, among the major
trading nations only Russia and Saudi Arabia will not be in the WTO.

China is following a two-track approach. On the bilateral track,
following the Sino-US pact signed in November 1999, it has signed
market-access agreements with 35 other trading partners including India.
Nine more bilateral agreements remain to be finalised, including one
with Mexico which is proving to be especially sticky on the issue of
anti-dumping. Simultaneously, it is negotiating multilaterally in the
WTO. The bilaterally agreed com-mitments become part of the treaty
terms of China's membership in the WTO.

Five issues are proving contentious in the multilateral
negotiations. First, China wants to be treated as a developing country
for determining the extent to which agricultural subsidies are permitted;
the Americans contend that China is an advanced country. Second, China
wants to be treated as a developing country in industry also so that it
can invoke the developing country provisions of the WTO Agreement
on Subsidies and Countervailing Measures. This is being opposed by
the US and Europe. Third, there are differences over commitments
that China is prepared to make to liberalise some of its services industries
like retailing, franchising, insurance and brokerage. Fourth, China's
conformity to the WTO Agreement on Technical Barriers to Trade is in
dispute. The argument given by the Americans and the Japanese is that
China uses inspection standards and quality and safety licences to
discriminate against imports. The procedures it uses to implement
technical regulations and standards is also very discretionary. Fifth, China's
trading partners want that foreign companies be granted greater access

to the local distribution system through free imports and exports—the so-called trading rights issue.

Twice before the negotiations have been derailed over Sino-American spats. The first was in June 1989 when the Tiananmen Square firings took place. The second was in May 1999 when the Chinese Embassy in Belgrade was bombed. Now with the recent spy plane incident, some influential Americans are calling for further delaying of China's entry into the WTO. In September 2000, the US Congress approved what is called permanent normal trading relations (PNTR) agreement with China which freed China from the obligation of seeking MFN status year after year through protracted wranglings. But this PNTR depends upon certification by the US President before June 3, 2001 that the final accession package agreed to between China and the WTO is as favourable to the US as the Sino-US bilateral deal. This deadline may not be met and China will then have to revert to the conditional MFN regime which it finds very embarrassing.

The WTO Agreement is as much about law as it is about trade, something we too are yet to fully come to grips with. Ontrade, China has done outstandingly well. In the 1990s, exports andimports averaged about a third of its GDP. China is now the world's 10th largest trading nation based on dollar values. Chinese exports and imports are nowalmost six times that of India's whereas it was just about twice just two decades ago. But it is on law that serious questions remain. Qingjiang Kong, a Chinese trade scholar, argues that ina society that is based on the Confucian rule by virtue—something that goes beyond mere rule through law or legal instrumentalism—the notion of rule of law is still somewhat alien. The Chinese will also face serious problems on transparency obligations arising from various WTO agreements.

There are fears within China that the foundations of its spectacular prosperity will be endangered if it joins the WTO. There are powerful forces in the Chinese power structure that would not be unhappy if China's entry is delayed. But Prime Minister Zhu Rongji clearly thinks otherwise and sees the entry vital not just for consolidating the gains from growth but also for making a major political statement. It is in India's interests that China's entry materialises at the very earliest. A leadership role in this regard will not be out of place, especially given that China's absence from the WTO hurts us more than it does the developed countries.

07/05/2001

THE DRAGON STRIKES AGAIN
China bags the 2008 Olympics and also puts the seal on a 2001 WTO entry

You have to hand it to the Chinese. They pursue their objectives with a single-minded sense of national purpose. For the past decade, they have been lobbying hard for hosting the Summer Olympics. That effort has finally paid off and the 2008 Games will be held in Beijing. But what is even more significant is the manner in which China has moved swiftly in the past few weeks to resolve all outstanding issues to facilitate its entry into the WTO, probably in November this year, completing a tortuous 15 years of hard bargaining and tough negotiations. Immediately following China's accession, Taiwan will also become a member. This is very much what the Chinese also want since Taiwan is critical to their plans of becoming an IT superpower.

China has had to make major compromises but it has not baulked at doing so. For example, the WTO stipulates a ceiling of 10 per cent (of the value of production) on agri-cultural subsidies for developing countries and 5 per cent for developed countries. China's level of subsidies is currently around 2 per cent of the value of production. It wanted to be treated as a developing country while the Americans wanted it to be in the developed category. Ultimately, the ceiling for China has been fixed at 8.5 per cent. On almost all pending issues like trading rights, technical barriers to trade and intellectual property rights, China has yielded to the demands of its trading partners. We should thank our stars that we got in at a vastly lower entry price.

China has stood firm and rejected the demand to reduce average tariff levels to that of developed countries. But even here, China is ahead of India. World Bank data reveals that the average tariff levels in China for all products are in the range of 17-19 per cent as compared to 28-33 per cent in India. Again in contrast to India, by deciding to forego the transitional period allowed to developing countries, China has obtained the capability for implementing Trade Related Aspects of Intellectual Property Rights (TRIPS) Agreement fully.

In the past year, the "atmospherics" surrounding TRIPS had changed dramatically with countries like Brazil and South Africa asserting their sovereignty to ensure cheap anti-AIDS drugs. The Americans have not retaliated knowing that it would be a public-relations disaster to fight on behalf of multinationals and be seen to be insensitive to the needs of poor and suffering patients. The WTO itself has taken the lead in looking at TRIPS from the angle of consumers. Undoubtedly, China will assume a leadership role on TRIPS, a role that we could be playing if only our Government is bold and our Parliament can pass laws on time. Ironically, it is an Indian company, Cipla, and an Indian scholar, Jayashree Watal, who have played prominent roles in redefining TRIPS.

China has also come out publicly and unequivocally in favour of a new round of multilateral trade negotiations. On the other hand, India's public stance has been one of opposition and, as usual, it stands virtually alone. Our stated position so far has been that no new round is required and that the priority is for implementation of commitments made during the earlier Uruguay Round. To be sure, implementation is important but the question is how best to address it.

The WTO has already started negotiations on agriculture and services, two areas in which we stand to gain from liberalisation. The TRIPS review has also begun. But these discussions will meander along. It is only in the framework of a "round", which is a politically mandated process of intensive negotiations in a focused manner, that India can even hope to have its legitimate concerns on implementation addressed meaningfully. It is only in a round encompassing various issues like agriculture, services, industrial tariffs, anti-dumping and TRIPS that countries can indulge in give and take which is what negotiations are all about. Industrial tariffs are particularly important since we face high import duties for labour-intensive manufactured goods, an area in which we can take on the Chinese provided we get our domestic policy right as well. Further, only a new global round can help counter protec-tionism in the West and also mitigate the adverse impacts of mushrooming bilateral and regional free trade agreements and preferential trading arrangements.

A new round is inevitable and will, in all probability, be given shape when the WTO meets in Qatar in three months' time. We can either hope to influence its agenda proactively or be dragged into it reluctantly. It is possible that the Government, for reasons of domestic politics, wants to follow the latter route, while privately giving assurances to the Americans that India will come on board eventually. This two-faced approach would be entirely consistent with our penchant for hypocrisy but will do our rapidly shrinking international standing no good.

30/07/2001

FORTY AND GOING STRONG
India and Pakistan fight when they should be
marking a historic anniversary

How ironical that just as the petulant India-Pakistan war of words at the United Nations completes its course, the 40th anniversary of the Indus Waters Treaty falls on September 19. Alas, this occasion will pass unsung. The treaty took eight long years to negotiate. It was finally signed in Karachi in 1960 between Ayub Khan and Jawaharlal Nehru. Broadly, it gave the western rivers—Indus, Jhelum and Chenab—to Pakistan and the eastern rivers—Ravi, Beas and Sutlej—to India. The definitive account of how this treaty came into being is contained in N.D. Gulhati's *The Indus Waters Treaty* (1973) and in Edward Mason and Robert Asher's *The World Bank Since Bretton Woods* (1973).

Partition immediately spawned the Indus dispute. Pakistan's fear was that since all its rivers originated in India, it would be held to ransom. An initial agreement, bilaterally negotiated, had been reached on May 4, 1948. But soon a stalemate ensued with Pakistan claiming that it had been forced to sign under duress and that India was interfering with water supplies to its canals. In February 1951, David Lillienthal, a former chairman of the Tennessee Valley Authority (TVA) and of the US Atomic Energy Commission visited the subcontinent to study how the Indus waters problem could be resolved. Nehru and Lillienthal were great admirers of each other. The TVA was the model for one of Nehru's "temples of modern India", namely the Damodar Valley Corporation (DVC) launched in May 1948. While in New York in October 1949, Nehru had met with Lillienthal who had emerged as an ardent champion of democratic India then seen to be in fierce competition with communist China and in danger of losing.

Lillienthal wrote a highly influential article entitled "Another Korea in the Making" in the journal *Colliers* in August 1951. He drew attention to the potentially explosive Indus dispute and called for American and World Bank involvement to arrive at a solution. For good measure he added that "unless a better answer on water is forthcoming, even if the Kashmir plebiscite could be held, peace would not come". To cut a long story short, Lillienthal's enormous clout led the World Bank to take a hands-on role as a mediator with full US backing. However, his idea of a TVA-like Indus Engineering Corporation to be operated by India and Pakistan together to develop the Indus system in an integrated fashion was rejected as being impractical. The bank's president Eugene Black tenaciously pursued an alternative agreement. His day-to-day team included a British civil servant, Sir William Iliff, and a US army engineer, Lt-General Raymond Wheeler. This team doggedly kept the negotiations going, mostly in Washington DC, providing technical inputs and dangling the promise of project aid. What is more, even as the treaty was being pursued, annual agreements kept getting signed. This helped to maintain a fragile peace and kept the talks on course.

The treaty was drafted primarily by Iliff but the key insight was Wheeler's who looked at the map in 1952 and came up with the simple solution of partition that formed the basis of the final agreement. That the arbitration clause has never been invoked is a testimony to the treaty's durability.

For four decades, the Indus Commission has continued meeting each year unmindful of wars and other conflicts. Pakistan has gained immensely by the Tarbela dam on the Indus and the Mangla dam on the Jhelum, by numerous barrages and link canals, by remodelling of pre-Partition river works and by substantial hydroelectric capacity. In India, the Bhakra Nangal project that made the Green Revolution possible was facilitated. The Rajasthan Canal, that has transformed a desert even though it has not yet been fully com-pleted, came into being. But we have not made full use of the treaty. Projects like the Thein Dam on the Ravi await completion. Only about 60 per cent of the permissible limit has been brought under irrigation from the Indus, Chenab and Jhelum. Just about 15 per cent of the 8,825 MW of hydro-electric power potential on these three rivers has been harnessed. Optimal utilisation of the Ravi river and effective drainage in the command areas of Bhakra-Pong and the Rajasthan Canal, will require cooperation with Pakistan.

The treaty has served the subcontinent very well although it could be argued that it was excessively Punjab-centric and did not provide adequately for Kashmir. That both countries face serious challenges of salinity and waterlogging in the Indus basin has less to do with the treaty itself and more an outcome of how agriculture and water resources have been managed. An Indus Treaty-II focused on these ecological concerns and founded on Lillienthal's vision of joint action would be a natural sequel.

25/09/2000

BUSHFIRES OVER KYOTO PROTOCOL
In another display of aggressive unilateralism,
son Bush junks father Bush

On June 11, President George W. Bush announced that the US had rejected the Kyoto Protocol, an international treaty which had been finalised on December 11, 1997 in Kyoto, Japan. This treaty requires 39 industrialised and excommunist nations to reduce, according to specific targets and timetables, their emissions of greenhouse gases that contribute to global warming.

Energy from the sun heats the earth's surface. A part of that energy is radiated back into space by the earth. Some of this outgoing energy is trapped by clouds and by atmospheric gases that retain heat like a greenhouse, an enclosure of glass panels in which plants are grown. This is why the gases that trap the earth's outgoing radiation are called greenhouse gases (GHGs). These GHGs act as a blanket and if they did not exist, temperatures would be much lower than they are now. But when the atmospheric concentration of GHGs increases beyond a level, temperatures begin to rise. Over the past century, the average land surface temperature appears to have risen by 0.45-0.6 degrees Celsius. Worldwide sea levels have risen by about 15-20 cm. Rainfall patterns have also changed.

Water vapour is the most abundant greenhouse gas. Six others are covered by the Kyoto Protocol. Three are naturally occurring—carbon dioxide, methane and nitrous oxide, all of which are released into the atmosphere by the burning of solid waste and fossil fuels like coal, oil and natural gas. Methane emissions also result from the decomposition of organic wastes, rice cultivation and the raising of livestock. The other three, ironically, are the synthetic substitutes for the chlorofluorocarbons that deplete the protective ozone layer around the earth. Ozone is also a greenhouse gas.

The US has about 5 per cent of the world's population but accounts for about a quarter of the world's man-made GHGs. China with about 16 per cent of the world's population emits about 14 per cent of the GHGs while India with about 15 per cent of the world's population contributes about 4 per cent of emissions. While junking Kyoto, President Bush made a pointed reference to the fact that two of the world's top emitters, China and India, are exempted. The Kyoto Protocol indeed imposes no obligations on developing countries whereas during the commitment period 2008-2012 Europe has to reduce emissions by 7 per cent below the 1990 level, the US also by 7 per cent and Japan by 6 per cent. Developing countries get in through the Clean Development Mechanism (CDM), which allows developed countries to enter into cooperative ventures to reduce emissions in the developing countries. These investments could include environmentally-clean power plants, renewable energy and forestry projects and improved industrial processes. The developed countries can claim "credit" against these projects which would go towards calculating their own emission reductions. The CDM has proved controversial and India has been arguing that it helps the developed countries to escape direct responsibility for emission reductions. In fact, India is the only major country yet to sign the Kyoto Protocol. This will hurt us.

The reason why developing countries are not called upon to have quantitative targets for reductions is simply because global warming so far is the outcome of what has happened in the developed countries. That is why the UN Framework Convention on Climate Change signed in May 1992 by, among others, the US under President George Bush, talks about sharing sacrifices fairly among countries in accordance with their "common but differentiated responsibilities and respective capabilities".

The protocol cannot come into force unless it is ratified by enough countries that account for at least 55 per cent of the industrialised world's carbon dioxide emissions. With the US out, this means that Europe, Japan, Russia and a few others like Ukraine will necessarily have to ratify. There is no formal deadline but if the ratification is not completed before September 2002 when the next global ecomeet will be held in Johannesburg, South Africa, the protocol is as good as dead. For the time being, brave noises are emanating from Europe about its commitment to Kyoto.

While lending support to Europe to rescue Kyoto, India better get prepared for a new round of negotiations and this time it will not escape without making quantitative commitments. In the 1990s, India's GHG output grew by about 5.4 per cent annually, which is about five times the American rate. Before long we will also be called upon to sustain economic growth with a lower rate of growth of greenhouse gases. Two developing countries, Argentina and Kazakhstan, have already announced their intention to take on emission reduction targets during 2008-2012. We cannot hide behind moral posturing.

25/06/2001

◆──◆

EAST ASIAN ALPHABET SOUP
World Bank says U. IMF says V. It may actually be W.

Two of the world's most powerful and influential organisations, the World Bank and the International Monetary Fund (IMF), face each other in Washington DC. Broadly, the World Bank lends for development projects while the IMF bails out countries that face balance of payments problems. The common perception is that they work in tandem. But now for the first time since their birth these two agencies are locked in mortal intellectual combat. The dispute has become public.

The issue is East Asia. The World Bank now says the IMF was plain wrong in its diagnosis and in its prescription and is equally wrong in its prognosis. The IMF says its medicine was bitter but desirable. The World Bank champions the U view—the crisis will prolong, economies will be flat for quite some time before looking up. The IMF is for the V view—once the economy hits rock bottom, turn-around can be pretty fast even though problems may well remain. It might well be that the recovery is actually W shaped, that is economies would fall and recover in one cycle and then repeat that pattern. But that is another story.

This is a battle among some of the most brilliant economists of our times involving the best and the brightest. Leading the IMF's brigade is Stanley Fisher, one-time professor at MIT, author of a bestselling textbook and for long a friend of India. Leading the World Bank's attack is Joseph Stiglitz, formerly President Bill Clinton's chief economic aide, academic at top US universities, author of many influential tracts and also, incidentally, a great India-wallah.

Fisher is supported by Lawrence Summers, nephew of two Nobel laureates, widely acknowledged as being among the most outstanding economists in the world and now the No. 2 man in the US Treasury. Joining the attack on the IMF are Martin Feldstein and Jeffrey Sachs, two famous Harvard dons. Plus there's Jagdish Bhagwati himself, the guru of free trade and the next Indian economist in line to emulate Amartya Sen.

What Stiglitz and company are saying, and this is factually correct, is that unlike previous debt crises as in Latin America in the '80s, the 1997 East Asian crisis was not caused by excessive borrowings by governments or by high fiscal deficits. The IMF, however, did not recognise this difference and applied its standard mantra—less government spending, higher taxes, lower subsidies, credit tightening—which resulted in increased suffering and misery in east Asia. On the other hand, the IMF says the monetary tightening was inevitable given the alarmingly massive depreciation of east Asian currencies. Michael Mussa of the IMF likens this to a cancer patient undergoing chemotherapy, which doesn't make you feel better in the short-term, but may nevertheless be essential for a successful cure.

This has indeed happened. The Indonesian rupiah, which had touched a nadir of 12,000 to the dollar, is now trading at around 7,500. The baht and the won have also appreciated substantially. East Asia minus Singapore had a combined current account deficit of $40 billion in 1997. It will actually post a current account surplus of about $60 billion in 1998, a dramatic turn-about although brought about largely by a huge fall in imports.

The Bhagwati attack on the IMF is based on his contention that trade in goods is fundamentally different from trade in capital. While arguing for continuing liberalisation of trade in goods and financial and other services at the World Trade Organisation (WTO), Bhagwati is suspicious of free capital mobility and advocates a more careful approach to capital account convertibility. The learned professor is being a little too harsh. No country allows unregulated cross-border flows of capital. And it is the east Asians themselves who opened their land to foreign capital.

The IMF is also under criticism on the grounds that it enhances the risks of what economists call "moral hazard". Good behaviour is deterred when you know that you will not be penalised for bad behaviour. In the financial world, this means that you take excessive risks fully aware that you will get bailed out in case of failure. The IMF was indeed caught napping when the East Asian crisis struck. But if it had not in-tervened when it did, East Asia's recession would quickly have deepened into a depression. True, a currency crisis was used to force structural and institutional changes. But few can deny that these changes were not needed. A crisis is a rare window of opportunity that must be grasped.

Many in this country will be gleeful at the IMF's discomfiture. But India's economic malaise remains both the quantity and quality of its fiscal deficit. This, more than anything else, is what is choking investment and growth. The health of India's financial system continues to be very fragile and its structure is a drag on growth. Policy barriers to faster exports, most notably reservations for small-scale industry, persist. The way to keep the IMF at bay is to sustain the reforms momentum and maintain fiscal discipline on our own steam. As things stand now, we are IMF bound. What will be hailed as "reforms" now will then be criticised as "conditionalities".

11/01/1999

◆——◆

GURDWARA IMF-SAHIB
While our economy may not be globally competitive,
some Indian economists are

After over eight years of discussion, the International Monetary Fund's (IMF) independent Evaluation Office (EVO) will finally become operational from July this year. This is a move to make its governance more effective and transparent. The first incumbent of this crucial post will be the distinguished Indian economist, Montek Ahluwalia, now member of the Planning Commission.

Ahluwalia assumes charge when the organisation is in transition and turmoil. Its deputy managing director for the past seven years and a great economist in his own right, Stanley Fischer, has just decided to call it quits. So have the IMF's Chief Economist Michael Mussa and Jack Boorman, who heads its powerful policy review department. A commission set up by the US Senate and House of Representatives under the chairmanship of Allen Meltzer two years ago had recommended radical changes in the way the IMF functioned. The Meltzer Commission favoured a smaller IMF. It was highly critical of the IMF's role in putting together bail-out packages for different countries, saying that the knowledge that such bail-outs will always be available encouraged wrong economic policies—what economists call the "moral hazard". The Clinton administration had opposed these proposals but there is much support for them in the Republican camp. Academic economists of great repute like Jagdish Bhagwati, Martin Feldstein, Joseph Stiglitz and Jeffrey Sachs have been very critical of the IMF. With globalisation under siege in the western world, the heat has been stepped up against the IMF (and the WTO) among NGOs and in the media.

Technically, Ahluwalia is not joining the IMF. He will not be an IMF staff member nor can he hope to become one after his tenure at the EVO. While operating at an arm's length from it, he is answerable only to the IMF's 24-member Executive Board that represents 183 member countries. What makes his appointment all the more prestigious is that it is the Executive Board that sought him out after a global search exercise.

There were three specific factors that went in Ahluwalia's favour. First, he has been a well-known figure internationally for over two decades, both as a pragmatic policy-maker and as an academic whose research on poverty is standard reference. Second, he has been closely associated with two of the more successful IMF programmes—in India in the early 1980s and then in the early 1990s. Third, he has made outstanding scholarly contributions to the ongoing debate on the global economy. In September 1999 he produced a brilliant piece for the Commonwealth finance ministers' conclave in the Cayman Islands which was publicly released in April 2000 under the title "Reforming the Global Financial Architecture". Earlier in February 1999, he had written another classic "The IMF and World Bank in the New Financial Architecture" for the G-24 group of developing countries.

Argentina and Turkey are now going through IMF programmes. Mexico, Brazil and east Asia are considered by the IMF to be successes, although some economists have argued that in Malaysia, which did not go to the IMF, the recovery has been less painful than it has been in Thailand, Indonesia and South Korea which sought the fund's help. Russia is seen to be a failure although there is evidence to suggest that the IMF was pressurised into continuing with the programme by the Clinton administration, calling into serious question the role of the IMF's board, Ahluwalia's bosses. On Turkey, a contrary view is that the fund's intervention is a mistake and that the Turkish lira should have been allowed to depreciate. Ahluwalia's post mortem of all such programmes will have major repercussions.

IMF also has a surveillance role. But it clearly failed to fulfil this role in Thailand in 1997. How this can be improved to prevent crises is something that will be on Ahluwalia's agenda. He will also have to grapple with the basic issue of conditionalities. Conditionality is the link between IMF financing and specific actions by borrowing countries. Some believe that the IMF's conditionalities are wrong. In east Asia, for example, the argument is that the IMF insisted on a tight fiscal policy and caused a recession, an admission made by Fischer himself recently. Others think that the conditionalities should be based on actual outcomes rather than on promises made by borrower governments which are not fulfilled, as in the case of Russia. The IMF's foray into political issues like governance and corruption has also become controversial. In Turkey, it has insisted that all coalition partners in the government sign the IMF agreement.

At a time when the IMF is going through convulsions and when the debate on a new global financial system is likely to intensify, Ahluwalia will be strategically positioned to exercise decisive influence. India's loss—hopefully, only temporarily—will be the world's gain.

28/05/2001

IX

Social Issues :
The Way to Go

This is a relatively small section. Every once in a while, I would take a break from dry economic subjects and write on social issues that have a vital bearing on the economy. Here, there are a number of pieces on population and one of them on Andhra Pradesh spawned a number of follow-up articles in other newspapers and magazines. The article on AIDS was picked up internationally by organisations like the Gates Foundation and the International Aids Vaccine Initiative. There is also a piece on Gujarat that elicited considerable hate mail from many NRIs. The events of September 11, 2001 and its aftermath spawned a number of pieces on the Hindu-Muslim encounter in India over the past thousand years and more. These articles similarly received both bouquets and brickbats. Needless to say, the Hindu-Muslim issue will continue to dominate the public agenda in this country.

WAY TO GO, INDIA

Economy globalises, polity regionalises,
society localises

India is going thruogh three fundamental transitions. One, economic liberalisation. Two, political decentralisation. Three, social empowerment.

The movement from an inward-looking, state-controlled, public sector-dominated economy to an outward-looking, market-oriented and private investment-influenced economy constitutes the economic transition. The rise of regional parties and the devolution of power to the people—from the Centre to the states and from the states to local self-government bodies—forms the political transition. The empowerment of traditionally disadvantaged and discriminated groups is the social transition. Each depends on and reinforces the other. Economic reforms have been facilitated by social changes which are also transforming the political landscape. Changes in the polity are creating new pressure points for changes in economic policy. In turn, economic growth is leading new social groups into the mainstream.

Liberalisation was triggered by economic compulsions in 1991. But conviction, not compulsion, has sustained reforms—albeit sometimes at a homeopathic pace. Where is this conviction coming from? Very simply, pro-change dynamics within society.

- A profound demographic shift has taken place. Two of every three Indians are under 40 years. This generation has come of age in the growth era of the '80s and '90s—at a time when ideology has been at a discount and the pursuit of wealth has lost its guilt edge.
- The acceleration of urbanisation is creating new economic opportunities and new mindsets impatient with the status quo.
- The spread of agricultural prosperity to new regions and the multiplier effects of farm growth on the rest of the rural and semi-urban economy are creating a whole new class of consumers.
- The rapid proliferation of communication technology is changing the face of India.
- The growth and influence of the new Indian diaspora is ensuring reforms are on track.

From a situation where the Centre virtually ruled the states, the states are now calling the shots in Delhi. Even the so-called national parties are, in essence, regional powerhouses. One of every two BJP MPs is from Uttar Pradesh or Madhya Pradesh. Maharashtra, Andhra Pradesh and Rajasthan account for 50 per cent of the Congress' MPs. The CPI(M) is really a force only in West Bengal, Kerala and Tripura.

Of course, India has a long way to go before it becomes a China. There, paradoxically, the provinces have far greater financial and administrative powers than Indian states. But gradually states are demanding and wresting autonomy from the Centre. Transfer of all centrally sponsored schemes, the creation of a single divisible pool of taxes and total freedom to attract foreign investment will further enhance the powers of state governments.

The Centre-state issue is just one dimension of decentralisation. Far more significant is the role of local bodies, rural and urban. But our view of these bodies must change. Traditionally, they have been looked upon as the third tier of development. Local institutions, instead, should be viewed as the first tier of democracy. They must be guaranteed powers to raise resources and spend according to their needs and priorities. The development of a municipal bond market, for example, can transform the finances of urban self-government institutions. Similarly the direct transfer of funds from the Centre to, say, zilla parishads will transform panchayats.

States like Kerala, Tamil Nadu, Karnataka and Maharashtra have already gone through a social revolution. Political power has passed peacefully from narrow upper caste elites to long-oppressed and more populous communities. The process has taken the good part of this century. Social reform movements, the spread of education and enlightened political leadership have all played their part. Now comes the next phase in these states—transition from a creamy layer of the disadvantaged to the truly disadvantaged.

But it is in the great Hindi heartland—home to over 200 million of the poorest Indians—that new battles are being waged and a million mutinies, to use Naipaul's evocative phrase, are taking place. The old social order in the north is dead. New alignments are being forged. Parity, not charity, is the demand of communities that have been kept outside the political and social mainstream for centuries.

This aggressiveness has been fuelled in part by the birth of a new agricultural class following the abolition of zamindari and the spread of new farm technology. But the great paradox in north India is that the markedly higher degree of political consciousness has not resulted in a clam-our for better governance.

Globalisation of the economy. Regionalisation of the polity. Localisation of society. These should not be seen as the Three Horsemen of the Apocalypse. Instead, they should be viewed as the trishul of a new India—of a civilisation which is entering its sixth millennium with the prospect of faster growth and greater equity. It is something India has not experienced in the five millennia it has existed. It is something to celebrate.

07/09/1999

CASTE VOTE YOUR CASTE
Competitive politics is transforming the nature and role of caste

Caste is the DNA of Inidan civilisation. It effloresces most during election time. The air is thick with Reddys, Kammas and Kapus, with Lingayats, Vokkaligas and Kurubas, with Nadars, Thevars and Vanniyars, with Nairs and Ezhavas, with Marathas, Malis and Dhangars, with Patidars and Kolis, with Rajputs and Jats, with Brahmins, Thakurs, Yadavs, Lodhas and Chamars. Within Dalit castes, we talk about Malas and Madigas, about Chamars, Valmikis and Pasis. Within OBCs, we talk about Yadavs, Kurmis, Koeris and Gujjars. Muslim society too is not caste-free and has to be seen, as the eminent sociologist Imtiaz Ahmed has been pointing out, in the OBC/non-OBC perspective to gain any meaningful insights. Sikh politics is a matter of Jats and Mazhabis. And if you think that literacy has made any difference, try understanding the intricacies of Kerala's Christian politics without a knowledge of Syrians, Latin Catholics, the Christians and the Southists. West Bengal is an exception of sorts but this has less to do with the CPI(M) and more to do with the nature of bhadralok society and the fact that the bulk of the lower castes converted to Islam, thereby converting caste fissures into a Hindu-Muslim divide.

That caste resurfaces with competitive politics was first pointed out way back in 1957 by the doyen of Indian sociologists, M.N. Srinivas. But he did not foresee its metamorphosis. New insights had to await the seminal contribution in 1970 of India's guru of political theory,

Rajni Kothari, who wrote that casteism in politics was just the politicisation of caste. Since then, because of rapid urbanisation, the spread of literacy, rising aspirations, the impact of reservations, the growth of mass communications and the diffusion of economic growth, caste has been further transformed.

Instead of being the instrument of hierarchy and stratification, caste is becoming a means of ameliorating social conditions. Instead of being a tool of oppression, it has become the main vehicle for identity assertion, social mobilisation and political co-optation. Caste as a vertical divisive concept has been supplanted by its use as a device for horizontal alignments in a multi-ethnic society—leading to a colourful vocabulary like AJGAR (Ahir, Jat, Gujjar and Rajput), KHAM (Kshatriya, Harijan, Adivasi, Muslim), MAJGAR (muslim+AJGAR), DYM (Dalit, Muslim, Yadav), MY (Muslim, Yadav) and MAMULI (Marwaris, Muslims, Lingayats). Caste as a means of exclusion is becoming a means of inclusion. In short, paradoxical as it may sound, caste is no longer a symbol of institutionalised inequality—it is, instead, a catalyst for institutionalising egalitarianism. But equality of dignity is all very well—it must now yield better governance specially in north India.

That caste fundamentalism and caste domination does not yield political dividends on a sustained basis has become amply clear. The lesson is simple—you cannot be seen to be ignoring an influential caste but you cannot be perceived to be dominated by it. The Congress in Karnataka and Andhra Pradesh suffers on both counts. So does Laloo. But see how the BSP has grasped this truth going by the way it has distributed tickets. And in probably his last scholarly work, shared with Kautilya just before his demise three months ago, Myron Weiner argued that by strengthening the tendency towards regionalism and federalism, caste-based politics is reinforcing the historic tendency towards decentralised authority in India. That itself, is the key for keeping this land of multitudinous diversity together.

There has been significant academic revival in caste in its new avatar. Kautilya can recall at least 12 significant books that have been published in the '90s, all exploring the theme of caste's transformation and its relationship with contemporary parliamentary politics. To add to this list, Susan Bayly's majestic treatise on caste, society and politics since the 18th century has just come out as part of the New Cambridge History of India. And Dhirubhai Sheth has published in Economic and Political Weekly a perceptive analysis of what he calls the secularisation of caste which is also leading to the rapid entry of new castes into the middle class.

After almost a decade of painstaking field research, the Anthropological Survey of India has identified 4,635 communities that make up the sum of Indian society. These jatis continue to thrive as endogamous groups—a brief glance at the matrimonial columns in any Indian newspaper is proof of this. Also, caste oppression survives not just in Bihar but also in states which have witnessed a social revolution, like Tamil Nadu. But caste wars no longer reflect just the inequities of the old social order. They symbolise the decay of that order, the growing Dalit assertiveness and the competition between upwardly mobile lower and middle castes and Dalits. It is this changing nature of economic relationships that aborted the unique BSP-SP subaltern alliance in 1995 after less than two years of cohabitation. Still, as a result of the crusade of caste-based parties, sensitivity to caste issues is slowly being internalised in the Congress and the BJP. But in north India particularly these parties are still uneasy with the politics of parity, used as they are to charity politics.

27/09/1999

THREE BUNDLES OF JOY

Kerala, Tamil Nadu, Andhra Pradesh: India's population revolution

Kerala is now part of development folklore. Its social indicators are world class. It has a female literacy rate of well above 90 per cent, even male life expectancy of over 70 years and an infant mortality rate of around 13 per 1,000 live births. Its population growth rate is about 1.2 per cent per year. While Kerala is admired, it has been considered un-replicable because of its unique social history, matriarchal traditions and political culture. But now Tamil Nadu has emulated Kerala in family planning.

The key milestone in demographic behaviour is the replacement level of fertility. This is called the total fertility rate (TFR) and is defined as the average number of children a woman will have if she experiences the current fertility pattern throughout her reproductive span. The magic number for the TFR is 2.1. After about 20-25 years of reaching this level, the population growth rate becomes zero. Kerala reached replacement levels of fertility in 1988. Tamil Nadu achieved this in 1993. Its population growth rate is now around 1.3 per cent per year.

At first sight, Tamil Nadu's success is intriguing. Its female literacy rate is now 56 per cent, roughly on a par with Punjab. Its infant mortality rate in 1996 was 54 per 1,000, compared to Punjab's 52. Punjab's per capita expenditure on family welfare is about 60 per cent more than Tamil Nadu's. Punjab is a smaller state and has the same level of son-fixation as Tamil Nadu. Yet, Tamil Nadu has reduced its birth rate dramatically since 1980. Punjab, on current reckoning, will not reach replacement levels of fertility till 2019.

Way back in the '20s, leading citizens of Madras set up an organisation called the Malthusian League. "Periyar" Ramaswamy Naicker, the great social reformer, advocated family planning. Independent India's first census commissioner was an ICS officer of the Tamil Nadu cadre, R.A. Gopalaswamy. He incurred the permanent wrath of Jawaharlal Nehru by suggesting the result of the 1951 census—which put India's population at 350 million, vastly more than commonly ex-pected—was the outcome of "improvident maternity".

Gopalaswamy recommended terminal methods to control India's population. He was banished to his state for heresy. Thereafter, there were other outstanding family planning missionaries in the IAS. Most notably, T.V. Antony, who retired as Tamil Nadu's chief secretary and was nicknamed Tubectomy Vasectomy Antony. But fundamentally, it was the political leadership of Kamaraj and Soundaram Ramachandran—and later from the DMK and AIADMK—which established an effective family planning programme. NGOs too have helped.

The experience of American academic Myron Weiner is revealing here. Some years ago, he wrote *The Child and State in India*, in which he suggested making primary education truly compulsory. He sent copies of his book to various political leaders. The only enthusiastic response he got was from J. Jayalalitha, then Tamil Nadu's chief minister. Her record in backing social programmes was impressive, like had been that of her mentor, M.G. Ramachandran.

It was MGR who launched the midday meal programme that now reaches six to seven million children. Tamil Nadu has also pioneered a number of special nutrition programmes and schemes to provide social security to those in the unorganised sector. In 1995, Manmohan Singh replicated these nationally. The hallmarks of Tamil Nadu's success have been a better health service and an innovative communications campaign. Extensive primary health infrastructure has facilitated this. Like Kerala, Tamil Nadu has used sterilisation as the most common contraceptive method. The approach was targeted at younger couples in early stages of fertility.

Next, Andhra Pradesh will reach a TFR of 2.1 in 2001 or 2002. This state's achievement too flies in the face of conventional wisdom. It has a low female literacy rate (36 per cent), high infant mortality (66 per 1,000 live births) and a low mean age of marriage for women (17.8 years). Further, unlike Tamil Nadu, it has no tradition of family planning advocacy. Yet, Andhra Pradesh's fertility rates are falling rapidly. Perhaps N.T. Rama Rao's social welfare programmes empowered people. An active women's movement has taken root. Food security through fair price shops has been extensive and effective. Expenditure on social welfare programmes—at 3.3 per cent of the state's GDP—leaves other states trailing.

Tamil Nadu and Andhra Pradesh show what is possible given sensitive political leadership, a proactive development administration and an overall ethos conducive to social welfare. The two states exemplify what political scientist James Manor has called the power of "regional progressives". They also show that theories are useless. Each state has its own dynamics. What works is people's desire for family planning. Even today, in Uttar Pradesh there is a 30 per cent unmet demand. The failure of the Government to meet this demand for family planning is the real tragedy, not just poverty or illiteracy.

10/08/1998

———◆———

INDIA STEPS INTO THE BC ERA
Our demographic karma reflects both success and failure

According to the venerable New York Times, just as India will be celebrating its 52nd Independence Day, its population will be entering the billion club (BC)—19 years after China. But M. Vijayanunny, our census commissioner, has calculated that India's B-date will actually be May 11, 2000. Ironically, this will be the second anniversary of our nuclear bomb!

India's demographic journey does not stop there. We keep moving up and up reaching about 1.3 billion by 2016 and about 1.5 billion in 2040 when we overtake China for the dubious distinction of being the world's most populous country. We keep growing, touching probably around 1.7- 1.8 billion and could well enter the 22nd century closer to the two billion mark. For a country whose population actually shrank between 1911 and 1921, this is some achievement. It is also a qualitative powder-keg we are sitting on—three out of every five infants in India are born underweight and malnourished.

The transition point in population growth is when the total fertility rate (TFR) drops to 2.1. This is called the replacement level of fertility. A layperson would probably ask why not two, which means parents will replace themselvesexactly. But to take care of things like unmarried men and women and infertile couples, demographers use 2.1. Kerala reached this milestone in 1988. Tamil Nadu followed in 1993 and shortly thereafter Goa, Manipur, Mizoram, Nagaland and Tripura also reached the transition point. Andhra Pradesh is poised to follow in 2002. Then come four states—Karnataka, Maharashtra, West Bengal and Orissa—which reach this goal in 2009-10. Gujarat comes next in 2014, followed by Assam the next year, by Punjab five years later and by Haryana in 2025. The laggards will be Bihar which is projected to reach the transition point in 2039, Rajasthan in 2048, Madhya Pradesh beyond 2060 and Uttar Pradesh beyond 2100.

For India TFR=2.1 will be in 2026. Normally, a population should stop growing after about a generation of around 25 years after achieving TFR=2.1. But it will not happen that fast in India because of the age distribution of our population. In 1991, 36 per cent of India was below the age of 15. In 2001, this proportion would be around 34 per cent and in 2016 would still be over 28 per cent. It is this that gives an already large base the extra momentum of continued growth. Instead of one generation after TFR=2.1, population growth will be zero after perhaps two generations. Thus, Kerala's population will stop growing only around 2045. Then other states will follow but because of Uttar Pradesh, Madhya Pradesh, Rajasthan and Bihar, India's population will keep growing inexorably. And around 2060 or thereabouts, this Gang of Four will constitute over 60 per cent of India's population, as compared to about 40 per cent now.

These are all projections. Once fertility declines set in, they have a dynamic of their own. Urbanisation is a powerful stimulus. Fifteen years ago, nobody predicted what is now happening in Tamil Nadu and Andhra Pradesh. Even in the north, there are a few districts like Jhansi, Garhwal, Purbi Singhbhum, Sahibganj, Indore, Raigarh, Churu and Ganganagar where the TFR has declined appreciably. Although round 280 districts have a TFR greater than four and need sharper focus, India's hardcore of laggards comprises of about 125 districts, 100 of which are in the Hindi-belt. These are districts where performance is well below the corresponding state average itself. These require even more special investment, mobilisational and managerial concentration.

What does all this mean for the two critical areas of employment and food? We have to be creating at least 10 million new jobs every year across the country. In the '80s, our annual rate of job creation was 5-5.5 million and in the '90s, around 6.5-7 million. Without sustained economic and investment growth, which will require a radical restructuring of all public expenditures at the Centre and in the states, particularly in Uttar Pradesh and Bihar, this rate of job creation cannot accelerate.

One of India's most distinguished agri-economists, G.S. Bhalla, estimates that we will need to produce around 370 million tonnes of cereals by 2020. In 1996-97, cereal production peaked at about 185 million tonnes, which means that cereal output has to double in the next 20 years. It is not impossible—in the past it has doubled in roughly 25 years. But Bhalla adds a crucial caveat and says that rapid economic growth will lead to escalating demand for milk, eggs and meat which will, in turn, mean greater use of cereals for livestock feed. This will jack up cereal needs in 2020 by a third.

India's demographic destiny is not just the result of its failure to take population issues seriously. It is also a reflection of its success in increasing life expectancy and -reducing mortality in significant measure. That very progress, desirable in itself, is now extracting a heavy price. This is no reason to slacken efforts to prolong life expectancy and push mortality down even further. What is needed at the same time is a national commitment to ensure that TFR=2.1 is reached for India by

2015 and for Uttar Pradesh and Madhya Pradesh no later than 2050 at the outside. It can and must be done.

23/08/1999

◆━━◆

PAYING FOR A GREY FUTURE
They have old-age problems. We have age-old concerns.

The Council of Foreign Relations is a pillar of the American intellectual establishment. Its publication, Foreign Affairs, is arguably the most influential journal of its kind. In the latest issue, Peter Peterson, distinguished Wall Street personality and now president of the council, draws attention to what he calls the transcendent economic and political challenge for the developed world in the 21st century—namely, the ageing of its population.

By 2010, 30 per cent of Japan, 25 per cent of Italy and Germany, 23 per cent of the UK and France and 20 per cent of the US, Canada and Russia will be over the age of 60. The dollar cost of the age wave, according to Peterson, works out to a minimum of $64 trillion (that is, 12 zeros), a mind-boggling number that could destroy the finances of many governments and trigger an economic crisis that will make the current slow-down look like a picnic.

Where does India figure? In the year 2010, 9 per cent of India's population is expected to be over the age of 60. Our main challenge is that of a population that is getting younger; by 2010, 60 per cent of India will be below the age of 29. In its simplest terms, a younger popu-lation means faster job creation. That much should be clear. We have to generate something like 10 million jobs every year. Over the past decade, we have achieved six-seven million jobs annually on an aggregate basis.

What is, however, less understood is that social security is also becoming a major issue here simply because of the absolute numbers, not proportions. It is therefore timely that the Government has just issued the first report of the expert committee of Project OASIS (Old Age Social and Income Security), chaired by Surendra Dave, former chairman of UTI and SEBI.

Around 23 million Indians are covered by contributory provident fund (PF) and another 11 million by non-contri-butory pension schemes. This means roughly one in six Indian families has this form of social insurance, although in terms of workers the proportion is about one in 10. Coverage under various pension plans of the LIC is around seven lakh. There has been no marketing of pensions as a product perhaps because the commission to LIC agents is just 2 per cent.

If the objective is income security in old age, then the existing PF schemes will have to be radically restructured. Coverage itself cannot expand without such reforms. As noted economist Ashok Desai has written, in none of the existing pensions and savings funds does the income stream cover the costs of future pensions, a fundamental requirement of actuarial balance. In technical language, these funds are pay-as-you-go schemes, that is, the current year's contributions do not cover the same year's pensions. So there is an in-built fiscal time bomb that ticks away as life expectancy goes up.

The OASIS committee has done well to debunk the commonly held perception that the Indian PF system has low contribution rates. Instead, the weaknesses are, one, low rates of return brought about by the mandatory investment guidelines that allow the government to take away 80 per cent of the PF's money and, two, poor accumulation resulting from liberal withdrawal rules.

The committee reveals that PF earnings are 2.5 per cent above inflation, while the average lump sum accumulation that is available to a PF member at age 60 is just about Rs 25,000. The committee has recommended incentives and disincentives to encourage accumulation and has suggested professional management of the PF system.

Future reports hopefully will deal with reforms of the non-contributory government pension system, which has become a huge fiscal burden. In the railways, for example, for every 10 employees there are six pensioners. In 1998-99, state governments will fork out almost Rs 20,000 crore as pensions—around half of their expenditure on education. The Centre's pensions liability will be over Rs 10,000 crore. All of this is unfunded.

But what about India's core problem—that of the vast unorganised sector? Very recently, the International Labour Organisation came out with an extremely valuable study called Social Security for All Indians. It has contributions from noted scholars, especially a classic by the late S. Guhan. Manmohan Singh introduced the National Social Assistance Programme in 1995-96 based largely on Guhan's intellectual inputs, which has also provided the inspiration for many of the DMK's social welfare schemes in Tamil Nadu.

Guhan's estimate for a modest, nationwide minimum social assistance package is about 0.2 per cent of GDP. In 1998-99, this would have amounted to about Rs 3,000 crore, whereas the actual budgetary allocation was Rs 700 crore. The only way to find the funds is to cut fiscal deficit, trim the government, target subsidies and privatise faster.

But more important than mere outlays is the delivery mechanism that has, inevitably, revolved around local bodies. Thus while the organised sector could do with privatisation and professionalisation, the unorganised sector will demand more public investment. But this won't happen unless we recognise India's organised sector has become a parasite, an oasis of relative prosperity in a desert of destitution.

08/03/1999

◆━━◆

COUNTING US IN CENSUS

Two million enumerators are out there collecting data on over a billion people

The world's largest enumeration exercise will go on till February 28, with about two million field workers criss-crossing the country to figure out the basic economic and social characteristics of over a billion people. By the end of the year, the results will be public. This is modern India's 14th census which is held every 10 years, the first dating way back to 1871. Successive censuses, particularly those before Independence, have played a key role in, to use the words of the great American anthropologist Bernard Cohn, classifying and making objective to the Indians themselves their culture and society.

Regrettably, the census has got mired in controversy even as it has started. Some Christian organisations, for example, have objected to Scheduled Castes (SCs) being categorised only as Hindu, Sikh and Buddhist SCs. These organisations quite obviously are not aware of our Constitution. One leading national newspaper blared in its front page that this would be free India's first caste-based census. This is not a caste-based census. Attempts were made to make it one but the idea was dropped. Like in all censuses since 1951, the only caste data that will get collected relates to SCs and Scheduled Tribes (STs). The last census which collected, analysed and published detailed caste data was in 1931. And about the President's sub-caste, on which editorials castigating the Census Commissioner, who is an IAS officer soon to get a doctorate in demography from the London School of Economics, were written, the simple point is that there is no national list of SCs and STs. There are only state-specific lists. And less than 3 per cent of the people are enumerated outside their state by place of birth or place of residence. Thus, the census will, in fact, cover 97 per cent of the population, an impressive achievement.

Controversy over caste and the census is not new. The doyen of Indian anthropologists G.S. Ghurye wrote way back in 1932 in his classic Caste and Race in India that the caste-spirit has been livened up in India by the treatment given to caste in each successive census. M.N. Srinivas, India's greatest sociologist, in his Social Change in Modern India published in 1966, described howcensus operations stimulated a widespread desire for caste mobility right from the first census itself. Further, a number of castes claimed different status in different censuses. The census operations of 1901 under the leadership of H.H. Risley popularised caste sabhas. Cohn points out that it is no coincidence that most of the basic treatises of the Indian caste system were written by men who had served as census commissioners—the more famous of them, apart from Risley, being E.A.H. Blunt, J.H. Hutton, Denzil Ibbetson and L.S.S. O'Malley.

Censuses had far-reaching impact also on religion. Kenneth Jones in his noted book Arya Dharm, which came out in 1976, has shown how Hindu consciousness and Hindu politics was shaped in the early 1900s by data thrown up by censuses. Lala Lajpat Rai himself acknowledged that orthodox Hinduism became sensitive to the issue of untouchability largely due to fears generated by the census data on the religious status of Indians.

By contrast, independent India's censuses have been staid but solid affairs. However, the 1951 census did get off with a big bang. The then census commissioner R.A. Gopalaswami, an ICS officer, wrote in his report of "improvident maternity" as a "form of antisocial self-indulgence" that if not controlled would destroy India. Gopalaswami defined improvident maternity as the child birth occurring to a mother who has already given birth to three or more children, of whom at least one was alive. Incidentally, its incidence is still around 45 per cent. His passionate language, combining superb English and precise mathematics pointing to the need to control population growth vigorously, was an anathema to Delhi's rulers who believed that population was a resource and not a problem. He was denied promotion at the Centre. But India's loss was Tamil Nadu's gain because Gopalaswami was to combine with K. Kamaraj to lay the foundations of a successful family planning programme which was continued with remarkable results by later chief ministers and administrators like T.V. Antony.

Risley bequeathed to us the Anthropological Survey of India. This organisation mounted a massive exercise between 1985 and 1992 called the People of India Project. The project identified 4,635 communities/castes that inhabit our country out of which 16 per cent were SCs, 14 per cent were STs and 23 per cent were OBCs. Forty-three volumesof this project were to bepublished of which, alas, only 29 are out. It is the most exhaustive study of who we claim we are. The truly remarkable conclusion, as noted by K.S. Singh under whose leadership the study was done, is that every one of us in India is an immigrant.

05/03/2001

◆━━◆

LIGHT FROM THE CENSUS
Census 2001's first report raises many questions—some pleasant, some disturbing

The first results of census 2001 are out. There is both good news and bad news. Performance on literacy has been truly extraordinary. Some states are doing extremely well in reducing the rate of population growth. But the sex ratio in the 0-6 age-group, that is the number of girls per 1,000 boys in that age range, is worsening.

The male literacy rate is about 76per cent, while that of females is about 54 per cent. The female literacy rate (age seven and above) increased by about 10 percentage points during 1981-91 but by almost 15 percentage points during 1991-2001. The most outstanding increases in female literacy rates during 1991-2001 were recorded in (i)

Chhattisgarh from 27.5 per cent to 52.4 per cent; (ii) Rajasthan from 20.4 per cent to 44.3 per cent; (iii) Madhya Pradesh from 29.4 per cent to 50.3 per cent; and (iv) Orissa from 34.7 per cent to 51 per cent. Andhra Pradesh and Uttar Pradesh have also shown a significant increase in female literacy.

In limiting population growth, the 1990s clearly belonged to Andhra Pradesh just as the 1970s belonged to Kerala and the 1980s to Tamil Nadu. Going by present trends, Kerala's population may stop growing by 2010-15, Tamil Nadu's by 2015-2020 and Andhra's by 2020-25. What is even more remarkable about Andhra's performance is that it has taken place at comparatively lower levels of female literacy. However, counter-balancing this is the increase in population growth rates in Uttar Pradesh, Bihar, Haryana and Gujarat and the extremely sluggish reduction in population growth rates recorded in Punjab, Jharkhand and Rajasthan.

What explains Andhra's success? Could it be NTR's Rs 2-a-kilo rice scheme that provided almost universal food security cheaply between 1983 and 1996? Could it be due to the successful implementation of social development schemes and empowerment of women? Could it be due to Andhra accounting for 30-40 per cent of all vasectomies and about 15 per cent of all tubectomies done in India? Has the mass media contributed to raising anawareness? Or could it be due to rapid agricultural growth and positive changes in the rural labour market?

The conventional wisdom is that India's north-east is facing a demographic invasion. Population growth rates in Assam and Tripura have fallen sharply and they are now lower than that of many northern and western states. But Nagaland and Manipur have seen increasing growth rates.

The overall sex ratio for India has risen from 927 females per 1,000 males in 1991 to 933 in 2001. In-migration of male workers does explain in part why the overall sex ratio in Punjab, Haryana and Gujarat has dipped, just as out-migration would explain partly why Kerala, Uttaranchal, Chhattisgarh and the Azamgarh area of eastern Uttar Pradesh have high sex ratios. Incidentally, tribal India has a much higher sex ratio and this explains Chhattisgarh's sex ratio of 990 in 2001.

But the migration factor does not operate when we look at the

0-6 sex ratio. This ratio for the country has been falling steadily—from 976 in 1961 to 945 in 2001. The standard sex ratio at birth is in the 943-952 range. What is shocking is that in India's most prosperous state Punjab, the 0-6 sex ratio—which actually went up from 894 in 1961 to 908 in 1981—fell to 875 in 1991 and further to 793 in 2001. Haryana too has shown a similar trend with its 0-6 sex ratio falling from 902 in 1981 to 820 in 2001. In 2001,Chandigarh's 0-6 sex ratio is 845, Delhi's is 865 and Himachal Pradesh's is 897. Could rich Punjab-Haryana-Chandigarh-Delhi-Himachal be the sex-selective abortion zone of India?

All 17 districts of Punjab have low 0-6 sex ratios, with Gurdaspur, Kapurthala, Fatehgarh Saheb, Patiala, Bhatinda, Mansa and Amritsar being particularly bad. Punjab is a paradox. Female life expectancy at birth has gone up sharply from 56.8 years during 1970-75 to 68.6 years in 1992-96 whereas that for males has increased from 59 years to66.4years over the sameperiod. In fact, at age 50, female life expectancy in Punjab is around 28.8 years, almost on a par with that in Kerala. Does it mean that Punjab's society dislikes baby girls but when these infants do survive they survive well?

The Census Commissioner deserves kudos for serving a rich sociological menu so soon after the headcount two months ago. The real issue is what lessons the states draw from the data and what action they will take.

23/04/2001

◆————◆

WE NEED MORE AID FOR AIDS
As the UN meet opens, the world thinks AIDS is a
time bomb ticking in India

For the first time the UN General Assembly begins a special session on June 25 devoted to a public health issue—AIDS. Estimates are that over 35 million people are currently infected with HIV, the virus that causes AIDS. Over 16 million people have already died, with more than three-fourths of the deaths in Africa alone.

For some years, smug in our moral superiority, we believed that

India would be immune to the AIDS epidemic. But that has proved to be hopelessly wrong. Currently, according to official figures, 3.8-4 million Indians carry the HIV virus. If we go by the official figures, about 0.4 per cent of Indians have the virus. If the infection level crosses 1 per cent, we have an epidemic on our hands. In six states, the epidemic level has already been reached. These are Manipur, Nagaland, Maharashtra, Andhra Pradesh, Karnataka and Tamil Nadu. On account of their proximity to Thailand and Myanmar, Manipur and Nagaland are suffering because of rampant intravenous drug use. But what about the other four economically advanced states? It would be tempting to say that these are sexually more promiscuous states and that people in north India are more conservative and have greater fidelity to their sexual partners. There is actually no evidence to suggest this. The high-incidence states are more urbanised, have higher literacy and better reporting systems, and have a more active network of NGOs. More crucially, migration both within and to and from these states is higher. This is what could well be driving the epidemic. Gujarat and Pondicherry may soon be joining the epidemic states.

If the experience of the past two-three years is any guide, the number of Indians infected with the HIV virus could increase to about 4.5-5 million in the next couple of years, stabilise and then start declining. This, of course, assumes that the current low rates of infection in north India are contained. Any increase here would trigger an epidemic of gigantic proportions. Many international experts and Indian NGOs doubt the official numbers. But only the Government has the mechanism to collect the data through 230 sentinel centres spread across the country. Those who claim that India's official numbers are fudged really do not have an independent source to base their claims on.

In 2001-2, India will be spending about $43 million on AIDS control, 85 per cent of which comes from foreign donors. This is more than what we spend on malaria, tuberculosis (TB) and other public health programmes. Judged internationally, India is certainly under-spending on AIDS. The only way our expenditure can go up is if more international funds come in. Private philanthropic foundations are one source waiting to be tapped. The $21 billion Gates Foundation is not only supporting anti-AIDS programmes but is also stepping up its support for anti-malaria and anti-TB research and projects. TB and the TB-AIDS nexus is of particular relevance to us.

The other issue we need to face relates to the anti-retroviral drugs that stop the replication of the virus. Right now, India does not support the treatment by these drugs in its AIDS-control programme on the grounds that it is prohibitively expensive (anywhere between $1-3 per person per day). Brazil, for example, probably spends around $300 million a year on its free anti-AIDS drugs programme alone. But just two weeks back, US multinational Pfizer announced that it would be offering an unlimited free supply of its drug Diflucan to combat fungal infections that strike AIDS patients in 50 of the world's poorest and most badly affected countries. Earlier in April, 39 pharmaceutical companies withdrew their case against a 1997 law of the South African government that allows it to obtain cheaper versions of expensive branded drugs like those that combat AIDS from sources other than those who hold the patent. Ironically, the man who has completely destabilised the world's pharmaceutical industry and single-handedly induced a change in the approach to the prices of and patents on anti-AIDS drugs is an Indian—Dr Yusuf Hamied, the London-based chairman of Cipla, India's third largest drug company. With the involvement of people like him and by participating in the New York-based Seth Barkley's International AIDS Vaccine Initiative (IAVI) that was launched in 1996, India can give its anti-AIDS programme a whole new dimension.

The anti-AIDS campaign has been taken up in great earnest in Tamil Nadu and Andhra Pradesh. Sonagachi, Kolkata's red-light district, has controlled HIV infection rates. The national blood safety programme has also been quite successful. In the past, whether it was small-pox or polio, India has shown it can achieve remarkable results. The world thinks that India is waiting to go Africa's way. We can and must prove these fears wrong, sooner rather than later.

22/07/2001

———◆—◆———

SEPTEMBER 11 AND AFTER
The three Ds—democracy, diversity and
development—assume new significance

By the Admission of the new US Ambassador in Delhi, the scholarly Harvard don Robert Blackwill, George W. Bush is fascinated by India, by how a billion people rooted in democracy are trying to improve their standard of living.

But September 11, 2001 will undoubtedly cast a long shadow. There is understandable nervousness in this country that the US will once again revive its special relationship with Pakistan and that this would be at the cost of closer ties with India. Blackwill has denied that the US will let India down. He has, in fact, rejected suggestions that the US has given a sympathetic hearing to Pakistan's "conditions" for cooperation. But not everybody is convinced and there is widespread worry here at the prospects of some secret deal between Pakistan and the US that would result in greater American pressure on India on Jammu and Kashmir.

The US cannot absolve itself of its responsibility for the awesome militarisation of Afghanistan. Its role in making the Taliban possible has been detailed in the noted Pakistani journalist Ahmed Rashid's classic Taliban which was published last year. In October 1996, I recall meeting a very senior State Department official in Washington who was making the case that the Taliban would bring stability to Afghanistan and make possible vast supplies of natural gas from Turkmenistan to India for which an American company, Unocal, had prepared a detailed proposal. The US has also been very insensitive to Indian cries about terrorism being supported by Pakistan, first in Punjab in the 1980s and subsequently in Jammu and Kashmir over the past decade and more. But this is not the time to remind the Americans about the present-day consequences of their past policies and deeds both in South Asia and West Asia. This is also not the time for India to adopt the high moral ground with a "I-told-you-so" attitude for we too are guilty of having fostered Frankensteins like Bhindranwale and Prabhakaran as deliberate instruments of state policy. India has to understand that September 11 has decisively changed the world and we just cannot afford to be non-aligned as we were during the Cold War.

To be sure, India's predicament is acute and there are no soft options. On the one hand, it can't allow the solid gains made in Indo-US ties over the past decade to dissipate. It cannot be insensitive to the fact that we have over 1.7 million Indians in America, a highly distinguished and accomplished community that has acquired great economic and political clout. On the other hand, we also cannot wish away the fact that we are the world's second-largest Muslim nation with a Muslim population now at about 125 million, quite apart from the two million or so Indians working in the Middle East who are remitting $6-7 billion of their savings back home every year.

We must certainly not succumb to the blackmailing fulminations of obscurantist Muslim religious leaders and organisations and must vigorously combat the activities of Pakistan's ISI in India. Yossef Bodansky, an American expert on terrorism, has described these activities and how they derive support from Osama bin Laden's own network in his 1999 book Bin Laden which is now enjoying renewed sales. Yet, at the same time, we cannot ignore mass Muslim sentiment altogether. Bodansky, incidentally, is perhaps the only analyst who uses the term "Islamist" instead of "Islamic" to make the distinction between the majority of Muslims and a minority comprising terrorists, a dis-tinction of special significance in this country.

What then is the way out of this dilemma? How do we ensure that the US does not abandon India and how do we guarantee that whatever we do in its support—as indeed we must, both now and later—will not hurt social harmony in our society? The answers to these questions lie in returning to basics and focusing on the three Ds—democracy, diversity and development. India has only one truly sustainable mantra—strengthen democracy, celebrate diversity and accelerate development.

Indian democracy faces its stiffest international challenge in the matter of Jammu and Kashmir. September 11 does not, in any way, diminish the importance of reinvigorating and broad-basing the political process in the state and vastly improving basic governance. India is a civilisation-state that has been defined by diversity. It is the respect of this diversity—actually of multiple diversities—that has kept us united and made us unique in the world. In recent years, nothing has hurt India's image more than premeditated attacks on innocent Christians by Hindu zealots who are as much enemies of the very idea of India as Muslim, Christian or Sikh fundamentalists. And nobody can ignore a country that records a broad based 7-8 per cent annual rate of economic growth consistently and intensifies its engagement with the global economy constructively.

01/10/2001

THE RENEWAL OF INDIA

Since 712 A.D., an immovable object has been meeting
an irresistible force

These are extraordinarily turbulent times for religious amity in
the country, made doubly difficult by the Sangh Parivar's cynical communalisation of the post-September 11 situation with the help of its
Muslim counterparts. How do we regenerate the well-springs of
harmony in our society?

We can turn to medieval history and salute remarkable
personalities like Shaikh Moinuddin Chishti, Amir Khusrau, Akbar,
Ramanand, Kabir and Dara Shikoh. We could go back even earlier and
applaud the Arabs and Central Asians like the great Al-Khwarizmi who
were the first to make Hindu mathematics, astronomy and medicine a
world heritage. We could remember the great historians Al-Biruni and
Ibn Batuta who enhanced our understanding of ourselves.

We could also recall the magnificent legacy of Sufism influenced
both by Buddhism and Hinduism and the Bhakti movement, that great
efflorescence of Dalit protest, on which Islam had a decisive impact.
We could re-read Eknath's unique Hindu-Turku Samvad and Shaikh
Mohammed Qadiri's unusual Yo-gasamgrama. We could invoke the
profound traditions of syncretism that are so visible in Indian music,
painting, architecture, poetry, language and films. Among today's figures,
we could herald Bismillah Khan and A.P.J. Abdul Kalam as epitomising
India at its noblest.

But there are some other unlikely candidates for inspiration. In
1904, Allama Iqbal wrote the most stirring lines in praise of Indian
civilisation; how can any Indian be failed to be moved by "Mazhab
nahin sikhata, aapas mein bair rakhna, Hindi hain hum, watan hai
Hindustan hamara"? Today's generation in the subcontinent would not
have heard of Maulana Muhammed Ali of Rampur, a key figure in the
unprecedented Hindu-Muslim unity movement of 1919-21. He is
famous for his declaration: "I belong to two circles of equal size but
which are not concentric. One is India and the other is the Muslim
world ... We as Indian Muslims belong to these two circles and we can
leave neither."

Muhammed Ali also delivered, what along with Maulana Abul

Kalam Azad's 1940 Ramgarh oration, is the most memorable Congress presidential speech. Speaking at the 1923 Kakinada session, he proclaimed, "For more than 20 years, I have dreamed the dream of a federation, grander, nobler and infinitely more spiritual than the United States of America and today when many of the political Cassandras prophesise a return to the bad old days of Hindu-Muslim dissensions, I still dream that old dream of a United Faiths of India." And who can forget the immortal words of Mohammed Ali Jinnah himself while addressing Pakistan's Constituent Assembly in August 1948: "... in the course of time, Hindus will cease to be Hindus and Muslims will cease to be Muslims, not in the religious sense because that is the personal faith of each individual, but in the political sense as citizens of the state."

The Hindu-Muslim encounter has been a struggle between two "imports" into India. It has been described as a face-off between a religiously tolerant but socially bigoted way of life (Hinduism) and a religiously intolerant but socially egalitarian faith (Islam). In the past 1,300 years— since Mohammed bin Qasim invaded Sindh in 712 A.D.— Islam could not obliterate Hinduism and Hinduism could not assimilate Islam. However, both destroyed Buddha in the land of his birth. Islam confronted Hinduism but in that process Hinduism acquired social identity and India got political unity.

Volumes have been written on this encounter. Some stressed the tensions and resentments. Some others emphasised the mutual accommodations, interactions and adaptations. A few writers like Aziz Ahmed, Rafiq Zakaria, Rajmohan Gandhi, Robert Eaton and Andre Wink have sought to maintain a fine and fair balance. New scholarship is also forcing a rethink. Yohanan Friedmann, for instance, has argued that Shaykh Ahmad Sirhindi, long considered as Aurangzeb's guru, was primarily a mystic. However, romanticising the encounter is as inaccurate as condemning it. Hinduism and Islam have enriched each other immensely just as they have opposed each other bitterly. As Maulana Azad's Ramgarh speech put it, "Both are an integral part of the indivisible unity of Indian nationality, both are indispensable to this noble edifice of India and without both of them this splendid structure of India is incomplete." The Deobandis distort this reality as does Bal Thackeray.

Secularism is India's destiny. When India's quintessence is under assault from fanatics of all hues, what is needed is inter-faith dialogue, communication and understanding between devout Hindus and equally devout Muslims who will see in their piety the seeds of a United Faiths of India. If the task of reconciliation is not taken up in right earnest, India's very existence is threatened.

12/11/2001

THE FUTURE IS PAST
A new scholarly book makes us understand our communities a little better

At the best of times, there is an uneasy calm in Hindu-Muslim relations in the country. The present is a very fragile period made even more turbulent by Murli Manohar Joshi's efforts to rewrite history textbooks. Thus, when there is a contribution to furthering a deeper understanding of our composite heritage, it is to be welcomed. Beyond Turk and Hindu, edited by David Gilmartin, a noted historian, and Bruce Lawrence, an eminent scholar of religions, and published recently by the University of Florida Press, falls into this category. In this fascinating and wide-ranging volume, 13 distinguished scholars challenge the popular presumption that Hindus and Muslims are irreconcilably different groups, inevitably clashing with each other.

Tony Stewart, who teaches at the North Carolina State University, writes about the little known Satya Pir who has immense following among Hindus and Muslims in West Bengal, Orissa and Bangladesh. His very name embodies his appeal to both religious traditions as an avatar of Vishnu and as a Sufi saint. Christopher Shackle of the University of London explores romantic poetry from the Punjab and demonstrates that religious divisions get tran-scended as epitomised in Bulle Shah's famous lines: "Neither Arab am I nor man of Lahore, nor Indian from the town of Nagpur? neither Hindu am I nor Turk of Peshawar."

Moving on to Tamil Nadu, where Muslims pride themselves on being among the oldest Islamic communities in the world, Vasudha Narayanan, a professor of religions at the University of Florida, focuses on Cirappuranam, a 17th century poem in praise of the Prophet composed by Umaru Pulavar. The poem positions Mohammed simultaneously in the wider world of Islam and in the world of India. Most Indians do not know that eminent Muslim scholars have written on Kamban's Ramayana. Narayanan rightly draws attention to M.M. Ismail, a former chief justice of the Madras High Court who has authored over 40 books on the Ramayana. One of the most moving passages in Narayanan's article is the one where she quotes a song from a Tamil cassette that goes thus: "India is our motherland; Islam is our way of life; only Tamil is our language."

Literary texts are not the only markers available to scholars to debunk the modern notion of clearly bounded Hindu and Muslim identities. Carl Ernst, a professor of religion at the University of North Carolina, examines how Indo-Muslim authors have written about the famous Ellora temples near Aurangabad. Ernst writes that attempts to describe Muslims as essentially prone to idol smashing are confounded by historical records, which indicate that Muslims who wrote about idol temples had complex reactions based as much on aesthetic and political considerations as on religion. Even Aurangzeb was a great admirer of Ellora and lies buried just a few miles down the road from the temples.

Richard Eaton, who teaches at the University of Arizona and is best known for his brilliantly innovative The Rise of Islam and the Bengal Frontier, analyses the question of temple desecration in Indo-Muslim states. Nobody has carried out such a meticulous investigation as Eaton has. Between 1192 and 1729, he concludes, there were 80 instances of temple desecration whose historicity appears reasonably certain, a figure completely different from the 60,000 peddled by the RSS and its cohorts.

Moreover, temple destruction was more a political and military act and had less to do with religious fanaticism. A point conveniently ignored by the RSS but brought up by Eaton is that Hindu rulers in the pre-Islamic period also destroyed places of worship owing allegiance to their rivals. Philip Wagoner, a professor at Wesleyan University, turns conventional wisdom about the Vijayanagar kingdom on its head and points out that its rulers saw themselves not so much as "saviours of the south" but as "sultans among Indian kings". Nothing else can explain the widespread use of Islamicate elements in Vijayanagar culture.

There are other seminal pieces like Stewart Gordon's discussion of Maratha patronage of Muslim institutions in Burhanpur and Khandesh, Muzaffar Alam's explanation of the relationship between the Shari'a and gover-nance in the Indo-Islamic context and Catherine

Asher's reconstruction of religious identities through the architecture of Shahjahanabad and Jaipur. The theme running through this extraordinary collection is the interplay and overlap between the larger Islamicate and specific Indic world views, rather than the Hindu-Muslim conflict, a perspective that has come to be deeply embedded in our thinking. We do not have to deny the presence of antagonism to derive inspiration from the enormous degree of syncretism that characterises Indian civilisa-tion. Illuminating our past as has been done in Beyond Turk and Hindu does show the way to the future.

10/12/2001

◆━━◆

THE ENIGMA OF GUJARAT
Is the Gujarati diaspora fuelling more than diasporadic communal tension?

This is the land that has seen the confluence of Hinduism, Buddhism, Jainism, Zoroas-trianism and Islam for centuries. This is the land where Hindu kings built mosques and where Muslims still follow many Hindu traditions. This is the land of the author of the haunting Vaishnava Janato ... and of that inspiring apostle of ahimsa and tireless crusader for communal harmony whom we call Father of the Nation.

This is also the land of boundless entrepreneurial energy, a state that is among India's most urbanised and industrialised. This is India's fourth richest state, which clocked Chinese-style economic growth rates in the 1990s. Yet something is very profoundly disturbing about Gujarat. The communalisation of Gujarati society predates the BJP's rise as a political force in 1990. In the 1980s, even somebody as distinguished as Ghulam Sheikh, the painter who was even married to a Hindu, could not obtain a professorial appointment in Vadodara's MS University in spite of its vice-chancellor Bhikhu Parikh championing his case. But the 1990s have been worse. Pravin Togadia, educated and a cancer surgeon to boot but a Hindu version of Mullah Omar, represents a widely prevalent obscurantist mindset as does the suave and slick Narenda Modi, now exposed as the cheerleader of genocidal goons. How do you explain this Gujarati cocktail of heady economic growth and sharp social retrogression?

Could it be due to the burdens of history? After all the historic Somnath temple ravaged by Mahmud Ghazni almost a thousand years ago and reconstructed in 1950 is located in the state. M.A. Jinnah himself hailed from Gujarat. A number of the erstwhile princely states, ministates and feudatories in the region that eventually became Gujarat had to be forced into the Indian Union by Sardar Vallabhbhai Patel, Junagadh being a prime example.

Second, have the traumatic September 1969 Ahmedabad riots grievously damaged the Gujarati psyche, both Hindu and Muslim? Ahmedabad had witnessed communal clashes earlier in 1941 and 1946 but 1969 was a bloodbath, taking place ironically in the birth centenary year of Sabarmati's saint. Over 600 lives were lost in the holocaust spread over four to five days. Gujarat's subsequent history has been one of religious clashes that have not spared even cities with a history of peace like Surat.

Third, has Muslim disenchantment and frustration, exploited by mischief-makers from outside, fuelled Hindu revivalism? Nine per cent of Gujarat's population is Muslim. Yet, in a Vidhan Sabha of 182, there are but four Muslim MLAs. Even at the peak of social engineering—the KHAM alliance between Kshatriyas, Harijans, Adivasis and Muslims which gave the Congress huge majorities in 1980 and 1985—the number of Muslim MLAs was seven. In states like Kerala, Karnataka, West Bengal and even Uttar Pradesh, Muslim representation in politics is substantial and not as marginal as it is in Gujarat.

Fourth, what social impact has the decline in the textile industry and the "casualisation" of the labour force had? In Ahmedabad alone, about one lakh workers, 20,000 of them Muslims, have been retrenched in the past two decades. A large number work in the vastly lower wage informal sector, other avenues of employment being closed to them. This is a readymade pool of the disaffected and the frustrated. The underworld has been able to spread its tentacles as well because of the counterproductive prohibition policy that is in force.

Fifth, how has the decline of civic institutions, of which Gujarat has a rich tradition, impacted on communal harmony? This is a thesis that has been analysed in scholarly detail in a very recent book, Ashutosh Varshney's Ethnic Conflict and Civic Life. The noted Indian-American academic at the University of Michigan looks at three pairs of cities, Calicut and Aligarh, Hyderabad and Lucknow and Ahmedabad and

Surat to understand communal violence and the wellsprings of communal harmony. His conclusion: the decline of the Congress as a civic force and of trade unions and labour movements in Ahmedabad specially has adversely affected communal amity.

Finally, could there be something in the nature of Gujarati urban capitalism in the 1970s and thereafter that engenders social chaos? Economic growth has created sharp regional disparities within the state and its human development indicators like infant mortality do not do it proud. Has a new, rugged class, different from the high-minded Sarabhais and the Lalbhais, taken over, a class that eminent journalist-academic Harish Khare has called "lumpen capitalists"? Along these lines, is religious fervour at home, both Hindu and Muslim, also being fuelled by long-distance nationalism, by the globalisation of the Gujarati middle class—at least one-third of the Indians in the UK and US have Gujarati origins. At this benumbing moment of darkness and despair, of shock and shame, this Indian's immediate catharsis can only take the form of such troubling questions.

18/03/2002

X

Notables :
Men & Matters

This is a section largely devoted to personalities who featured prominently in the news at the time the columns were being written. It also contains a couple of reviews of books by economists that I felt deserved a wider audience. I would get a number of requests from authors to review their books in the column, but I rarely did so unless I felt it absolutely necessary. The only time that I felt the wrath of Swapan Dasgupta, India Today's erudite Managing Editor, was when I was taken to task for using the entire column to comment on books. Not wishing to antagonise him any more than I had already done, I was careful in the future! Two pieces—the one on John Nash inspired by the release of the award-winning motion picture *A Beautiful Mind* and the other on Satyendranath Bose inspired by the Nobel Prizes of 2001—received highly favourable notice. I recall T.N. Ninan, the distinguished editor of *Business Standard* telling me that these two "offbeat" columns set Kautilya apart. I am thankful to him for his generosity. It is unfortunate that I did not write more often on issues relating to science and technology, particularly as I have a background in engineering and have spent years working with wonderful people such as Sam Pitroda. While I have done so elsewhere, it is nevertheless a lacuna in this collection, the Bose tribute notwithstanding.

SEN HIJACKED
Nobel Amartya's abduction by the anti-reform brigade

Amartya Sen is a most deserving winner of this year's Nobel Prize for economics. He is a rare polymath, an uncommonly inspiring teacher, a versatile intellectual colossus and an epitome of humility and accessibility. He has defied neat categorisations. But this has not stopped the anti-reforms lobby in India from appropriating him as its patron saint.

This is amusing to say the least. In the 80s, when Sen produced his book on the Bengal Famine of 1943, leading intellectuals of Calcutta derided him. They complained that he was stating the obvious—no money, no food; bad distribution, higher prices. At the time, the Indian leftists were incensed with Sen for his attack on Mao Zedong. Sen had compared India's record in successfully combating famine with China where, according to his estimate, more than 20 million perished without the world noticing in 1958-60.

To be honest, Sen himself has been ambivalent on liberalisation. But the great mind that he is, he has had the courage to admit where he may have got it wrong. Eight months ago, in a book called Indian Economic Reforms and Development—brought out by Oxford University Press on Manmohan Singh's 65th birthday and containing essays by 15 distinguished economists—Sen confessed he was wrong in propagating the view that India's exports could not increase (and, Kautilya adds, should not increase).

The only voice that argued empirically against export pessimism in the early 60s was Manmohan's, in his now-famous doctoral dissertation at Oxford. Sen candidly writes that he was wrong and his friend was right. The anti-export bias continues. Our average import tariff levels are about double east Asia's. We want to export what we produce but not what the world wants. The world has a voracious appetite for "low-tech" goods—garments, toys, household appliances, sportsware, components. China and India were on a par 13 years ago in the export of these goods. Today China's sales amount to $70 billion, five times India's. Our failure is entirely manmade and policy-induced, small-scale reservations being the main culprit. Sen's main contention is that for market reforms to succeed in abolishing poverty, we need mass literacy, universal public health, meaningful land reforms and an end to all forms of gender discrimination. No genuine liberaliser will disagree. Sen's concern is that since 1991 public discourse has come to be dominated by issues of efficiency. The more pressing concerns of equity have receded into the background. But Kautilya's question is simple: When were they ever paramount?

The key question that Sen ducks is whether we can continue to be inefficient, profligate and inward-looking and yet meet the objectives of social justice. We cannot. Sen has written volumes on the success of Kerala on the human development front, ignoring what Tamil Nadu has achieved, but has not highlighted the costs of the Kerala model. Kerala could not have sustained its human development strategy were it not part of a larger federal framework and had it not been rescued by remittances. Otherwise, Kerala may well have ended up as a Sri Lanka.

Sen was right in being among the first to point out that you can have equity without growth. But what he downplayed was without growth equity just can't be sustained. Sen makes much of the role of left parties in Kerala; the very parties have a less distinguished record on literacy and health in West Bengal. Sen repeatedly asserts that East Asia invests more in social infrastructure than India. But apart from cultural factors, it is the shape of public finances which is responsible. East Asia does not have a fiscal deficit of 10 per cent of GDP, half of which covers the revenue deficit. Sen is absolutely right: the Indian state is not a social investment state. It never has been. It will be one only when reforms move faster.

Are we more of a social investment state now than before? Only marginally. Reforms have upped public expenditure on education from 3.4 to 3.8 per cent of GDP, still short of the needed 6 per cent. More disturbingly the finances of states which account for 85 per cent of social development expenditure have deteriorated sharply. Social investment has been a casualty, declining from 5.4 per cent of GDP in 1990-91 to 5.2 per cent in 1996-97. Reforms in the sense of restructuring of public expenditures have a long, long way to go in India. But the "how" of social investment is as critical as the "how much". Sen's own figures reveal 60 per cent of the rural primary schools in Kerala are private and half the students enrolled in such schools get free primary education.

In the Manmohan birthday volume, Sen has criticised India's reforms on the grounds that they have concentrated on correcting government over-activity in industry and trade and have not done enough to correct government under-activity in social development. With respect, the great man is being unfair. At no time have the liberalisers advocated a retreat of the state from essential human development areas. The under-activity is both a reflection of the anti-egalitarian DNA of our society as well as a direct consequence of the over-activity Sen talks about.

The state as we know it is an enemy of both efficiency and equity. Its whole apparatus has to be redesigned if Sen's concerns are to be met. Sen's criticism is an indictment of the Indian elite's preoccupations—not of reforms.

02/11/1998

CASTE IN HIS OWN MOULD
An institution builder passes away but lives on in his contributions

The date : September 21, 1999. The venue : Delhi's India International Centre. The occasion: a public lecture by an 83-year-old doyen of Indian sociology who has devoted over 50 years to studying caste and social change in India. He comes with a prepared text and speaks, as usual, incisively. Age has not dimmed his formidable intellectual prowess one bit. He speaks of why anti-caste Bhakti movements in our history did not institutionalise egalitarianism. He talks about the paradox of individual castes thriving just as the caste system is dying. He expounds on how the diffusion of economic growth is breaking the caste-occupation link for good. He explains how the universal adult franchise and massive affirmative action are bringing about a welcome transformation of a deeply stratified society.

The scholar speaks non-stop for an hour. He patiently answers questions. He is asked about the future of caste. He replies that caste will now be conceived in terms of ethnicity and not in terms of hierarchy. He is accused by some to be an apologist for the upper castes to which the response is that he is only an academic. He is asked for his prescription to demolish the caste system faster. His answer—rebuild the architecture of Indian villages. Kautilya himself has many questions but asks just one—why is the course of social justice movements in south India so very different from that in the north. Views are exchanged—different impacts of Islam and Christianity, the zamindari-ryotwari and the rice-wheat dichotomy, the values of the upper castes, the rise of social reform movements, etc. But time is short and the shishya is invited to the guru's Bangalore abode for a fuller discussion. The great man also invites Kautilya to a seminar on IT that he is co-organising. Kautilya suggests that IT is fast becoming a revenge of the Brahmins and the upper classes. The great man merely smiles.

Fast forward to December 3, 1999. The venue: Indian Institute of Science, Bangalore. The occasion: a seminar on how information technology can become socially purposeful in India. The mood is sombre for just three days ago, one of the organisers of the seminar, the same active 83-year-old public intellectual, has suddenly passed away. The scholar: M.N. Srinivas, India's pre-eminent social anthropologist. He was the author of numerous classics, like Religion and Society Among the Coorgs of South India (1952), Caste in Modern India (1962), Social Change in Modern India (1966), The Remembered Village (1976), The Cohesive Role of Sanskritisation (1989) and Village, Caste, Gender and Method (1996). The Remembered Village made history not just for its content but for the way it came to be written. Srinivas was on sabbatical at Stanford in the US when anti-Vietnam war demonstrators burnt down the building where he was working on this book. He had then to "remember" almost two decades of field research. He was an ardent advocate of intensive field studies, his own areas being first Coorg and later Rampura village in Mysore district. He moulded successive generations of academics. And he was one of the key founding fathers of the Delhi School of Economics, a rare sociologist accepted by that most arrogant and clanish breed—the economists.

Srinivas made many contributions but two are seminal. The first, originally propounded in his Coorg book, was called "Sanskritisation", a process by which a "low" caste or tribe or other group takes over the customs, ritual, beliefs, ideology and style of life of a high and, in particular, a "twice-born" caste. Later other scholars were to point out that Sanskritisation is not just Brahmin-centric. In 1996 Srinivas wrote that Sanskritisation began as an emulatory phenomenon but has become a gesture of defiance. The second, put forward in 1955 and derived from his Rampura experiences, was that of "dominant caste" which

Srinivas defines as one that is numerically preponderant over others and wields preponderant economic and political power. In one of his last essays, Srinivas highlights the conflict between the old and the new dominants and suggests that the taming of dominant castes is a major task for Indian democracy, especially in the more backward regions.

Srinivas was also among the earliest to argue that the pan-Indian, fourfold categorisation of castes was not reflective of Indian social life. What constitutes our society are a myriad of jatis that, most distinctively, marry among themselves and have evolved as occupational groups. There are 4,635 such communities in India. Building on Louis Dumont's famous statement that whoever had power was a Kshatriya, Srinivas wrote elaborately, and now it is not politically fashionable to accept this, that there has always been fuzziness in the caste system, with medieval mobility coming from fission and modern mobility from fusion.

Srinivas was deeply critical of the Mandal Commission. It is also true that he glossed over the horrible inequities of the caste system. Even so, he epitomised Indian scholarship and intellectual pursuits at its shining best, an all-too-rare commodity these days.

20/12/1998

◆——◆

ONE GREAT INDIAN
Ambedkar as a market friendly economist

April 14 marked the birth anniversary of one of the most remarkable and inspiring Indians of all time, a man who fought prejudice and discrimination all his life but scaled the peaks of intellectual achievement as few have done anywhere. Bhim Rao Ambedkar was more than an icon who gave pride, dignity, self-respect and political power to one-sixth of India. He was the man who chaired the committee that drafted the Constitution which committed the world's most stratified and hierarchical civilisation to the ideals of equal opportunity. He was the man who piloted the revolutionary Hindu Code Bill in its initial phases. And he was the man who rediscovered for Indians, in an unusually original way, one of India's greatest gifts to the world—Buddhism.

But what few know is that Ambedkar was also among the earliest Indian scholars in economics. He was, in fact, a double PhD. His first was in 1916 from Columbia and was called "The Evolution of Provincial Finance in British India". In 1918, he wrote a brilliant paper in the Journal of the Indian Economic Society, drawing attention to the small size of farms in India and the tendency towards fragmentation and stressed that industrialisation must precede consolidation.

In 1922, he received a second doctorate from the University of London for "The Problem of the Rupee". This work has contemporary relevance as well. Ambedkar argued for devaluation since India's textile and other exports were being hurt by British policies. His evidence before the Hilton-Young Commission in 1926 is a masterly exposition on ex-change- rate management. Subsequently, Ambedkar did not write much on economics. He had little sympathy for the Gandhians, who he felt were anti-industry. He also had little time for Marxists, dismissing them as Brahmin boys not sufficiently committed to furthering the cause of parliamentary democracy, so essential for India's salvation. He also differed from the socialists, who he felt were wishing away caste, the basic Indian reality.

Ambedkar's early writings reveal his firm belief in state socialism largely because of his fears that private enterprise would accentuate social inequalities. At the same time, he pointed out that Lord Buddha praised the moral accumulation of wealth. He held that collectivisation of agri-culture along the Soviet model was the only way for securing Dalit welfare. As a member of the viceroy's executive council, Babasaheb made notable contributions to industrial relations and social security. One of his grouses against Pandit Jawaharlal Nehru was that the latter had reneged on a promise to give him charge of the Planning Commission, a job he very much wanted.

In recent years, there has been a renewal of interest in Ambedkar's economic philosophy. Many Dalit ideologues have lambasted the economic reforms saying they will hurt the Dalits. But there are others, like Narendra Jadhav, who believe Ambedkar would have supported a social-market economy. Nagesh Chaudhury, Divakar Bhoyar and Siddharth Kamble have written that participation in a global economy has been a part of Dalit heritage—unlike the upper castes, who prefer a closed economy.

Gail Omvedt, sociologist-activist and a student of Ambedkar for three decades, feels he would have been pragmatic and looked for the most effective combination of state, market and community roles. She created quite a stir a year ago with her thesis that the pre-1991 economic system was actually an upper-caste construct that had little for Dalits.

That globalisation can assist in the empowerment of Dalits can be seen from the socio-economic impact the growth of the leather industry has had in states like Tamil Nadu and Uttar Pradesh. Here is a fine example of how swadeshi can be married to globalisation. But opportunities are being missed. Over the past decade, India's share of the world market in leather and leather goods has declined from 8.5 per cent to around 3.5 per cent.

The main worry of many Dalit thinkers is that public sector employment, including in government, is shrinking. This is a legitimate concern, particularly since more than the income aspect such employment has great prestige value and has done a good deal to break down social inequities. It has created a Dalit middle class that is around two million strong. But the size of the government and of the public sector has to shrink if the country is to grow and create wealth faster. How we do this while safeguarding the social aspirations of Dalits is a big challenge. Private industry too must pay greater attention to affirmative action. Technical and professional education opportunities for Dalits must expand and this has to be done by the government.

To the extent that reforms will enhance the capability of the government to invest more in infrastructure like irrigation and education, Dalits will benefit. It is certainly in their interest that the government reorients the pattern of public spending, a fundamental tenet of liberalisation. The great paradox is that the so-called social justice parties of the north have not made land reforms, minimum wages, primary education, health, nutrition and gender equality part of their agenda. Unlike in the south and in the west, the Dalit struggle in the north is for political power. This is a worthwhile objective. But there has to be something more to social justice than political power and reser-vations in government jobs.

26/04/1999

NOT IN THE FAMILY WAY
Core inheritance is different from core competence

A remarkable development took place in corporate India on June 8. One leading owner-manager wrote out his own exit policy when the going was good and passed the baton to a professional, overlooking his two sons. Kautilya salutes Parvinder Singh who has blazed yet another new trail. From October 1, Ranbaxy, India's leading drug company, will have a CEO from outside the family, even though Singh will continue to hold about one-third of the company's shares. There are many who believe that this transition is because of Singh's serious illness. Kautilya disagrees and feels that this was something that had been planned for almost a decade because of Singh's idea of demarcating ownership from management in the teeth of severe family pressures.

Kautilya first met Parvinder Singh in 1984. At that time, Singh was a rabid foe of all multinationals. He was a crusader against foreign investment and launched a public campaign against India making changes in its patent laws to provide for product patents in pharmaceuticals and agro-chemicals. But then something strange happened. In the late '80s and early '90s, Ranbaxy started exporting pharmaceuticals. When it went abroad, naturally questions began to be raised about the sources of its technology and manufacturing practices. Singh found that the reputation of Ranbaxy being a patent pirate would hurt his plans of entry into world markets.

When Ranbaxy started international marketing, Singh sensed new investment opportunities as well. This also made sense because our own policies in the drug industry were strangulating profitability in the domestic market. Thus, in order to spread out risks, Ranbaxy began an overseas investment drive. It has invested close to $75 million in the US, Netherlands, UK, Ireland, South Africa, Nigeria, Egypt, Poland, Thailand, Malaysia and China. Exports are almost 48 per cent of turnover in India. Roughly 25 per cent of sales emanate from outside India, if all of Ranbaxy's operations are consolidated. One-sixth of its workforce is non-Indian. These are all telling indices of true globalisation.

When his horizons expanded, Singh realised if you want to be a global player you'd have to play by global rules and have global networks and alliances. The fact that he had a doctorate in pharmacy from the University of Michigan gave Singh an appreciation for science and technology that is unusual among Indian CEOs. It is not a coincidence that among his closest advisers are those two doyens of Indian medical science—V. Ramalingaswamy and Nityanand. Singh has pushed aggressively for collaborative research between private industry and CSIR laboratories and universities. He also conceived and lobbied actively for a government-industry joint venture for pharmaceutical education and research. This has since come up in Chandigarh.

Singh's commitment to science could get translated into reality only when Ranbaxy started generating profits in the early '90s. Today, Ranbaxy's R&D expenditure is around 3.5 per cent of sales, a ratio that will need to at least double in the next five years if it is to survive. Ranbaxy's world-class research centre outside Delhi became operational in 1994. The first drug to be discovered and developed fully by an Indian company will be in world markets sometime in 2003 and this will be for the treatment of enlarged prostate gland. In 2006, perhaps, two more drugs—one an anti-asthmatic and the other an anti-infective—may be unveiled.

Corporate governance has been a bee in Singh's turban. Kautilya recalls that during his tenure in the finance ministry, he would be badgered with notes on employee stock options from Singh and from N.R. Narayana Murthy, chairman of Infosys. That such options have now been introduced as part of policy is a tribute to these two persevering individuals. When the owners of a leading company on whose board Singh was a member gave themselves a huge Rs 5 crore commission when the company itself was struggling, Singh was tremendously agitated. He vowed to ensure his board would not be a rubber stamp. He sought advice from global gurus like C.K. Prahalad to make the transition to a board-managed company. Prahalad also reinforced Singh's own thinking on core competence, which is reflected in Ranbaxy's growth strategy.

Some years back Vikram Lal, the owner of Eicher, passed on the company's management to professionals. Ajay Piramal has a professional CEO for Nicolas Piramal. Dabur has recently hired a non-family man as its CEO. Companies like Marico, Wipro, Arvind Mills and SRF are others where professionals call the shots—and could well take over the company, Eicher-style. Of course, the advantage professionals have in these companies, including Ranbaxy, is that the heirs and heiresses are all still very young. It could well be that the professionals are stop-gaps. After all even in a company like Ford, after almost 40 years of professional management, the family has exercised its voting power to appoint

William Clayton Ford, the great-grandson of the founder, as the CEO. Ford's brother, incidentally, happens to be the president of the Hare Krishna movement.

21/06/1999

◆━━◆

TALE OF TWO CMs
The Digvijay-Naidu duo is changing political mindsets

In recent years, few politicians have captured the popular imagination and exude the "feel-good" aroma as Digvijay Singh of Madhya Pradesh and Chandrababu Naidu of Andhra Pradesh. Both are in their early 50s and have enthused the youth. Both have made developmental performance their ideology. Both are tremendously media-savvy and are skilful political managers. Both are men of indefatigable energy. Both harp incessantly on themes of good governance and of responsive administration. Both are peripatetic leaders. Both have escaped being embroiled in personal controversies, although not for want of trying by their adversaries. Both are exemplars of the type of "managerial" politicians India needs.

Digvijay became a hero only after he won the assembly elections in December 1998. It was after this that his painstaking initiatives in primary education, watershed development, drinking water and panchayati raj got prominence. Naidu is going to the polls already a celebrity. If he wins, he becomes a superstar. If he loses, he would still be the barometer against which his successors will be compared.

There are other crucial differences between the two, albeit largely in the matter of nuances and style. Digvijay speaks the NGO language, is a votary of Gandhian economics and has given primacy to social development. Naidu's emphasis has been more on growth, fiscal management and new investments. Digvijay is strengthening and transforming panchayats. Naidu has created a parallel delivery mechanism and instead of one village sarpanch, there are now five-six "coordinators" in every village owing allegiance to him and receiving government funds directly. Digvijay operates mostly in a government framework whereas Naidu stresses popular mobilisation and self-help. Each has a flagship—Digvijay's Education Guarantee Scheme and Naidu's Janmabhoomi.

Both are professionals. Digvijay's training is in engineering and Naidu's is in economics. This gives them a certain mental discipline and analytical outlook. Both are receptive to new ideas. The enthusiasm with which Naidu lobbied for the appointment of Dr C. Rangarajan, the eminent economist, as governor of his state reveals his mindset. Digvijay has positioned himself as an ecological crusader, while Naidu has positioned himself as the tireless champion of information technology (IT), although he has used IT so far more in the Orwellian sense as a tool for command, control and micro-management. In his commitment to IT, Naidu has leveraged a comparative advantage of the Telugus. President Clinton has just appointed Dr Raj Reddy as the co-chairman of his IT advisory group.

Of the two, Naidu has demonstrated far greater political courage and a reformist outlook partly on account of fiscal compulsions. He has reduced unsustainable food subsidies and abandoned prohibition. He has initiated radical reforms of the power sector and gone in for a tough $3-4 billion loan from the World Bank that enforces financial discipline on the state and demands a major reorientation of public expenditures and pri-vatisation. Too bad the two cannot swap jobs even for a while. Madhya Pradesh needs fiscal fundamentalism, just as Andhra Pradesh could do with some social sensitivity, given that it is among the six most educationally backward states in the country.

Of the two, Naidu's job is vastly easier. Andhra Pradesh's agriculture is prosperous. He is working in an environment which is conducive to a technocratic moderniser. His Congress opponent is a medical doctor who is equally dynamic and capable. Naidu is in a long distinguished line of development-oriented, investor-friendly chief ministers. The record of successive Andhra Pradesh governments in fostering entrepreneurs who have made a name for them-selves is outstanding. It was the idiosyncratic and populist NTR who carried out India's first privatisation by selling Allwyn's commercial vehicles unit to Mahindras way back in 1987. The state has excellent infrastructure. And in a remarkable testimony to what has been happening in Andhra at the grassroots, the state now stands poised to reach the replacement level of fertility in 2001, the third state to do so.

Digvijay, on the other hand, faces a far more serious development challenge. His initial conditions are far more daunting. The state is very poor and sprawling. Its infrastructure is woeful and politics is still very much in the mai-baap mould. There are no rich NRIs or big industrialists to help him as is happening in Andhra Pradesh. To make matters worse, the room to manoeuvre is circumscribed by his belonging to a "national" party that looks at regional satraps with suspicion. Digvijay's attempt to personally visit Naidu was stymied recently. Naidu, like NTR, is pretty much the master of all he surveys. National parties have had their regional bosses who have dramatically transformed their states. But such examples are rare. Devaraj Urs was one who changed the face of Karnataka in the '70s. Sharad Pawar is a latter-day instance. In the BJP perhaps Bhairon Singh Shekhawat comes close at least in mindset if not in actual achievement. Kalyan Singh is another regional shogun who surprisingly is proving to be a bold reformer. But since he is part of a national party he is not finding the going easy. The ability of the BJP and the Congress to accommodate such regional progressives will, to a large extent, determine how India's polity will evolve.

20/09/1999

◆━━━◆

IT'S OUR HAQ

Real poverty in South Asia is the poverty of governance

Mahbub-Ul-Haq was an outstanding Pakistani economist who first shot into fame in the late '60s when he exposed Pakistan's domination by 22 families. He went on to join the World Bank where he was one of the key aides of its then president Robert McNamara and was largely responsible for making that institution more poverty-oriented. He returned to Pakistan and was finance minister in the mid-'80s. Sadly he passed away last year. But before his death he had left behind a very valuable legacy in the form of a Human Development Centre in Islamabad that for the past three years has been bringing out annual reports on different aspects of development in South Asia. Incidentally, he had hit the headlines in India very much earlier in late 1971 when parts of one of his speeches dealing with the limitations of the Gross National Product (GNP) as a measure of development found their way without attribution into one of Indira Gandhi's speeches. There was a furore then but later Dr Haq was to look back amusedly on his contribution to Indian thought!

Dr Haq's wife, an economist in her own right, the Bangladesh-born Khadija Haq, was in India recently to release the latest report of his centre, Human Development in South Asia, 1999: The Crisis of Governance. Two eminent economists, Nobel laureate Amartya Sen and Lord Meghnad Desai of the London School of Economics, have been associated with this report. The report breaks new ground and puts forward the concept of humane governance—a package that integrates economic, political and civic governance. The exercise is quantitative and measures the extent of humane governance in our countries and compares them internationally. The report itself has not generated much debate here and that is a real pity. For we ignore its basic message at our own peril—not only are our countries the poorest but are also the most poorly governed and governance is worsening.

What stands out in the analysis is the total mismatch and growing disconnect between the pattern of public expenditure and investment in South Asia and the extent of human deprivation and the backlog of social needs that have to be met at a very basic level. Indeed, South Asia is, in many respects, worse than subSaharan Africa on critical social indicators. Sterile debates on state and market preoccupy us, whereas the harsh reality is that South Asian governments are simply bankrupt and their fiscal position will just not enable and be able to sustain human development in any tangible measure.

A second feature of South Asia that stares us in the face is the absurdly high level of military expenditures particularly in light of the vast backlog of unmet social needs. While elsewhere there is a downward pressure on such expenditures, in South Asia the reverse is happening, especially with nuclearisation. Worse, while there is a peace process under way in all hot spots across the world, South Asia alone is a depressing exception. Regional confidence-building measures are being attempted by erstwhile adversaries, barring those in this region. External hostilities apart, countries of South Asia are racked by internal sectarian strife that is tearing the social fabric apart. This again points to the absence of mechanisms that institutionalise the search for harmony and mutual tolerance.

Third, politics is at once both part of the problem and of the solution in South Asia. Its nature of adversarial and confrontational politics is almost unique and does not yield effective governance. Bipartisanship that goes beyond breaking bread at social occasions is an extremely rare commodity in the region. Democracy is a value in itself, more so when it gives representation and leads to assertion of social identities. But democracy is more than holding elections. And this is where South Asia and indeed even India is losing out. The report shows that many other countries have a higher rating on political governance than India. This is because while we have absorbed the form of democracy, we have a long way to go before mastering its substance. This has its economic implications as well. For example, South Asian countries have very low tax-GDP ratios. Not only do our governments spend on the wrong things but they are unable to mobilise revenue that is their legiti-mate due. It is one thing having an independent judiciary but quite an-other when over 20 million cases are pending in courts at various levels as they are in India.

Producing human development reports has now be-come a growth-industry. Perhaps this assuages our con-science. States like Madhya Pradesh and Karnataka have also produced such reports and Rajasthan's is on the way. But beyond documenting what is poignantly clear, there has to be follow-up. One reason why this is missing is that these reports remain confined to a narrow constituency of economists, administrators and NGOs. They are just not fed into the political process. For instance, Karnataka's excellent report shows that the north Karnataka districts have poor social indicators that we tend to forget about in our fascination with Bangalore as Silicon Valley. But whether this moves the state government to skew investments to these districts remains to be seen. The value of Dr Haq's reports themselves would be enhanced if we had a South Asian Parliament, like the European Commission, providing a forum for engagement on regional issues.

13/12/1999

◆——◆

BOOKS OF GNOMES

Two books that constitute the monetary and financial history
of India in the '90s

Central Bankers are supposed to preserve a mystique about themselves. It is commonly believed that they should neither be heard nor seen but their presence and influence should only be felt. Thankfully, two distinguished members of this fraternity have broken ranks and have spoken frequently on major issues of economic policy, in the process educating the government, the media and the public at large.

The first is C. Rangarajan, now hibernating in Hyderabad's Raj

Bhavan. He was the governor of the Reserve Bank of India during 1992-1997, a momentous period in which the essentials of our economic policy underwent a profound transformation. As a trusted colleague and confidant of Manmohan Singh first and P. Chidambaram later, Rangarajan played a key role in this transformation. Some of his important speeches and lectures have been published as a book *Indian Economy: Essays on Money and Finance* brought out a few months ago by UBS Publishers. Rangarajan has now been made chairman of a commission to revamp the country's statistical system which is in a hope-less mess. Hopefully, this will afford him an opportunity to resume speaking on economics as his combination of academic rigour and policy experience is most unusual.

Following his footsteps, his *shishya* in more respects than one, Y. Venugopal Reddy, deputy governor of the RBI for the past three years, has put together all his speeches in *Monetary and Financial Sector Reforms in India*, also brought out by UBS. Reddy has served in key positions in the Finance Ministry also, although bureaucratic machinations have denied him the top post in North Block in spite of his being the best qualified by education, training and temperament. These two books are more like a set and could well be called Volume I and II of the monetary and financial history of India in the '90s. Apart from the wealth of theoretical knowledge that is on display, which is a tribute not just to the duo but also to the intellectual pool available to them in the RBI, the books tackle arcane and complex issues in simple language. More than anything else, this is their most important contribution. Simplicity in language can come only from clarity of thought.

Rangarajan and Reddy demystify the intricacies of monetary policy, its links with fiscal policy and its impact on prices and output. Both make the point, based on econometric exercises, that the inflation rate should stabilise at around 5 to 6 per cent on an average for growth to sustain itself in the country. Incidentally, with openness, could this figure be on the higher side? They discuss the importance of bringing down interest rates to boost investment and dwell on how the fiscal deficits of the Centre and states is eroding the capacity of governments to increase investments in essential physical and social infrastructure. Without disrespect to Rangarajan, two papers by Reddy, one on interest rates and the other on inflation in the section on monetary policy are simply outstanding.

The second area tackled by the two is reforms of our banks and financial institutions, a process that was launched in 1992. There is still little understanding of why these reforms had become imperative. Rangarajan and Reddy go into great length on this topic and put into proper perspective the relationship between economic growth and financial development. Rangarajan has a brilliant chapter on rural credit and on what needs to be done to increase the flow of institutional funds into agriculture, an issue that is of pressing importance, given the slowdown of farm growth in recent years. Reddy pays special attention to the development of debt, money and forex markets.

Third, the spotlight is on external sector issues, on how we successfully weathered the balance of payments crisis of June 1991, on how India moved painlessly to a market-determined exchange rate system in 1993 and on how we have been successfully managing our external debt. Much of what we did on the external sector between 1992 and 1998 was based on a blueprint prepared by a committee chaired by Rangarajan, of which Reddy was the secretary. This gives their accounts definitive authority.

There are some non-overlapping themes as well. Rangarajan dwells upon larger issues of planning and the role of the state in the new economic policy. Reddy gets into issues related to state government finances and public debt. All in all, the publishers deserve our thanks for putting together these volumes that, unlike most collections of speeches, will stand the test of time and will serve as valuable reference material on a most exciting period of change in economic policy.

21/02/2000

◆——◆

UBIQUITOUS INDIANS
The Indian diaspora living in two worlds is an essential
feature of globalisation

Ujjal Dosanjh becomes premier of the Canadian province of British Columbia. Vijay Singh wins the prestigious Augusta Masters golf title. Jhumpa Lahiri bags the Pulitzer for her maiden novel. Gururaj Deshpande's start-up Sycamore takes American stock markets by storm. And Hamid Cassim emerges as a key player in the Hansie Cronje betting scandal!

These are all members of what is now being called the community of diaspora Indians. Diaspora is a Greek word and originally referred to the forced dispersion of Jews among the Gentiles between the 8th and 6th century B.C. Then it described Greek and Armenian dispersion. Now it is loosely used to describe a transnational community. Two weeks ago, the India International Centre (IIC) in Delhi organised a conclave on the Indian diaspora, a subject that is part of an on-going research study.

Prakash Jain of Delhi's Jawaharlal Nehru University has analysed major clusters of the Indian diaspora. There are approximately 15-20 million Indians across the globe. Other than Nepal, this population has emerged in five different ways. The first arose in the mid-19th and early 20th century when the British took Indian labour to raise sugar plantations in countries like South Africa, Mauritius, Trinidad, Jamaica, Guyana and Fiji. This numbers about 3.3 million. The second cluster of about 1.5 million in Sri Lanka, Malaysia and Myanmar has descended from *kingani/maistry* labour. The third category numbering over two lakh is made up of free passage emigrants, largely from Gujarat, who went to Kenya, Tanzania and Zambia. The fourth group comprises workers in Saudi Arabia, UAE, Oman, Kuwait, Bahrain, Qatar and other West Asian countries, now estimated at about three million. The final group comprises around four million emigrants to the US, UK, Canada, Australia and other western countries.

India's links with the first three clusters are mainly cultural and political. The West Asian cluster fares only marginally better. It is the fifth "knowledge-based" cluster based in North America that is the focus of all our attention. This cluster, particularly in the US, is largely drawn from the "privilegentsia" although at the seminar Bhikhu Parekh talked about the Dalit diaspora that controls the shoe industry in England.

The 55-million strong overseas Chinese bring in over $30 billion of investment capital a year into China, almost 60 per cent of which is from and through Hong Kong and another 15 per cent from Taiwan. The Indian diaspora's contribution comes in from three routes. The annual remittances are now running at about $10 billion (Rs 43,500 crore) a year. NRI deposits in our banks are presently around $23 billion. And NRI equity investments since 1991 amount to about $2.5 billion.

Given the largely professional nature of our diaspora these numbers are not disappointing, although it needs to be said that the trading networks of the diaspora have not been leveraged effectively by us—except perhaps in one or two cases like gems and jewellery. But the "informal" influence of the diaspora is very significant. When the history of N. Chandrababu Naidu is written, the role of the Telugu Association of North America (TANA) and US-based Telugu professionals will stand out as having shaped his ideas. The impetus to continue economic liberalisation in India has also come from the diasporabased progeny of many in the ruling elite. A swadeshi finance minister cannot be oblivious to sons in McKinsey and ING Barings and a daughter-in-law in Oppenheimer!

Diaspora nationalism has fuelled ethnic surges at home. In the '80s, the Khalistan movement was spear-headed by diaspora Sikhs and today the Kashmir azadi movement is led by non-resident Kashmiris. Stanley Tambiah, the Harvard anthropologist, estimates that today there are over 400 Hindu temples in the US. This, coupled with the growth of the Internet, has given birth to "hyperlink Hindu" nationalism— analysed in detail by Harvard's Anita Khandelwal—which has had a deep impact on Indian politics.

The IIC seminar attracted many scholarly contributions. But diaspora studies must now have a continuing institutional thrust and engage our attention more systematically and analytically with focus on the local level—for instance, Kerala and the Jullundur Doab have been transformed by the diaspora. Over time, we also need to expand our horizons and begin talking about the South Asian diaspora—the Mirpuris, the Tamils and the Sylhet Bangladeshis, too, are very much part of our transnational community and ethos.

01/05/2000

A CLASH OF THE DIVAS

An extraordinarily personal attack on the IMF by a former World Bank economist

It is a clash among friends, among the best and the brightest of economists. The first salvo has been fired by the Indophile, Joseph "Joe" Stiglitz who has taught at Yale, Stanford and MIT, has been chairman of President Bill Clinton's Council of Economic Advisers and who has just relinquished his position as chief economist at the World Bank.

Stiglitz has written a devastatingly critical piece in *The New Republic* in which he accuses the IMF of dismissing his advice during the East Asian financial crisis of 1997-98 and of imposing unwarranted misery on millions of East Asians.

Another brilliantly distinguished economist, Rudiger Dornbusch, now a professor at MIT, co-author of a classic text on macroeconomics, sometime adviser to the Mexican, Argentinian and Brazilian governments has counterattacked. He has acknowledged that Stiglitz is on the short list of the Nobel Prize for his work on the economics of information but has called into serious question his policy judgement. Dornbusch defends the IMF, arguing that in a panic situa-tion stabilisation starts with exchange rate and public finance and that investors will take confidence when they see fiscal conservatism and really high interest rates. Dornbusch ridicules Stiglitz for suggesting a devaluation of the Chinese yuan at the peak of the East Asian crisis.

This is actually a proxy war. Stiglitz's real target is not just the IMF, whose deputy managing director incidentally is Stanley Fischer, another top-flight MIT economist and Dornbusch's co-author. Stiglitz's bete noire is Lawrence "Larry" Summers, the US treasury secretary who is, genetically and intellectually, among the pantheon of the all-time greats. His father is a well-known economist. His paternal uncle is Paul Samuelson, Nobel laureate in 1970, and his maternal uncle is Kenneth Arrow, co-Nobel laureate in 1972. Summers became the youngest tenured professor at Harvard at the age of 28. After occupying the post that Stiglitz has just vacated in the World Bank, he joined the US Treasury in 1993. Stiglitz believes that the IMF passively dances to the US Treasury's tune.

Stiglitz is not the first to attack the IMF for it role in East Asia. Noted Harvard economists Martin Feldstein and Jeffrey Sachs have done so earlier. Jagdish Bhagwati has also castigated the IMF for being a prisoner of what he calls the "Wall Street-Treasury" complex, a mindset that pushes financial sector liberalisation at a dangerously unsustainable pace. Paul Krugman of MIT, another probable Nobel laureate, has supported Malaysian President Mahathir Mohamad's policy of imposing controls on "hot", short-term capital. But Stiglitz is the first "insider" to break ranks.

Stiglitz's point is that the East Asian collapse of 1997-98 was not caused by fiscal profligacy on the part of the governments. It was caused by the build-up in debt by the private sector. Financial markets extracted a punishment from East Asian governments that bore no relation to their crimes. Stiglitz writes that what these governments needed was instant liquidity. Instead, the IMF bamboozled the governments to sharply cut public expenditure and raise interest rates. This caused investment to fall and GDP to contract. The IMF medicine, according to Stiglitz, is meant for governments that are living beyond their means and where inflation is raging.

As it turns out, even though Japanese growth continues to be sluggish, the depression in East Asia has been remarkably short. Confounding all pundits including perhaps even Stiglitz and the IMF, East Asia has quickly and spectacularly re-bounded with robust GDP growth, accumulating current account surpluses, healthy reserve levels, falling interest rates, buoyant stock markets and strengthening currencies. South Korea, for instance, is poised for 8 per cent growth in GDP in 2000 on top of 11 per cent growth in 1999. Its foreign exchange reserves have zoomed from just $9 billion in end-1997 to over $80 billion today. But the question will remain whether the severe downturn of 1998 was forced by an insensitive and incompetent IMF? Whether the IMF can take credit for the recovery as Dornbusch suggests is also in doubt since Malaysia, which repudiated the IMF, has re-covered. The point is simply that the East Asian fiscal and manufacturing fundamentals are just too strong and these have compressed the crisis period. Alas, the same thing cannot be said about India, where the fiscal system has simply collapsed both at the Centre and the states and where there is now a collective amnesia on the "real" economy, mesmerised as we are by the markets and ICE (information, communication and entertainment). Talk of skating on thin ice.

15/05/2000

◆——◆

COMRADES IN ARMS
The evil that men do lives after them—but sometimes the sons change all that

The past six weeks have seen the death of three outstanding young Indians. Rajesh Pilot was easily the most energetic of politicians and had overcome many odds to carve out a niche for himself. Arvind Das was one of the finest commentators on Bihar and his The Republic of

Bihar (1992) is essential reading for understanding the state. Rangarajan Kumaramangalam was superbly gifted—genetically and intellectually—and was the only man who had photos of Vajpayee and Advani along with statuettes of Lenin and Nehru in his home study!

Of the three, although he had worked intimately with Pilot on Kashmir during 1993-95 and had been captivated by his indomitable courage and dynamism, Kautilya knew Ranga the best. There was also a family link. Ranga's father Mohan and Kautilya's father-in-law K.V. Ramanathan had been part of a team along with Wadud Khan and Hiten Bhaya that set up the Steel Authority of India in 1972, India's earliest attempt at PSU reform.

Kautilya's first encounter with Ranga took place in April 1987 when the former made a presentation on privatisation of Delhi's power distribution system to the then prime minister Rajiv Gandhi. The man who opposed the idea vociferously in the meeting was the MP from Salem who was also leader of the DESU (Delhi Electric Supply Undertaking, as it was then called) Employees Association. The proposal died. Ironically, on January 15, 1999, when a similar presentation was made by Kautilya to the newly elected chief minister of Delhi, the man supporting it most enthusiastically was the Union power minister, the same individual who had shot it down 12 years ago. His receptivity to new ideas was instantaneous: a chat over coffee one morning in mid-January 2000 led to the idea of a memorandum of agreement on power reforms between the Centre and states, with Karnataka becoming the first state to come on board in February. Just before his death, Ranga and Kautilya bemoaned how the newly created electricity regulators had become Bhasmasuras who needed to have their roles more sharply focused.

A second memory is of those momentous days in June-July 1991 when the reforms package was being formulated. The issue was what to do with the MRTP Act, a legacy of Ranga's father. Any company whose assets exceeded Rs 100 crore had to get the government's nod to expand or start new businesses, a process that could take between three and five years—apart from the "greasing" it involved. The debate was whether to increase the threshold limit or abolish the provision altogether. When Ranga and Kautilya met finance minister Manmohan Singh, he advised Ranga thus: "Ask yourself what your father would have done now." Outside the finance minister's room, Ranga remarked: "Yaar, Sardar ne to mujhe phasa diya!" Perhaps that is why he took on his reluctant senior minister, lobbied with the prime minister directly and ushered in a most radical policy change in July 1991.

A third watershed relates to Ranga's brief tenure as Union coal minister. Two individuals—Ranga's father and then coal secretary K.S.R. Chari—were responsible for the nationalisation of India's coal industry between October 1971 and January 1973. However, by 1985 itself Chari had become disillusioned with the way the politicians, the bureaucrats and the trade unions had destroyed the basic objectives of nationalisation. Chari then chaired various committees that recommended major policy changes. Small steps were taken by Manmohan Singh in 1993 to allow private investment for specified captive consumption purposes. P. Chidambaram proposed bold legislation in early 1997 to reform the coal industry but his efforts were thwarted by his own cabinet colleagues. At long last, it was left to Ranga to introduce a bill in Parliament on April 24 this year to undo what his father had done earlier. But the bill faces stiff opposition. Lord Keynes was once berated by a critic for shifting his stance on a particular issue. Exasperated, the greatest economist of the 20th century is supposed to have said: "When presented with facts, I change my mind. What do you do, Sir?" Some months back in the presence of the Karnataka chief minister, it was the trade unionist Ranga who was insisting on the full closure of the hopelessly unviable Bharat Gold Mines at Kolar while the case for keeping it going with a reduced labour force was being made by a liberalisation-wallah, namely Kautilya!

Finally, the sad memory of forenoon coffee on December 6, 1992. Ranga was very confident that the day would pass off peacefully. This was reassuring since he was very much part of P.V. Narasimha Rao's A-Team on Ayodhya. Alas, events proved him totally wrong. Too bad we will never know his version of that dark chapter in our recent history.

11/09/2000

◆——◆——◆

HIGH-YIELDING POLITICIAN
A belated tribute to the political spearhead of India's Green Revolution

C Subramaniam, who passed away on November 8, played a decisive role in transforming Indian agriculture in the mid-1960s and dispelling our begging bowl, basket-case image. Many contributed to launching the Green Revolution, a term coined by Dr William Gaud of the US Department of Agriculture in October 1968, in India: the Rockefeller and Ford Foundations, many Indian and foreign scientists, a few economists and administrators, two Indian prime ministers and one American president and most of all the Punjab farmer. The crisis atmosphere also helped. But CS, as he was called, was the pivot.

I spent a morning with CS at his Chennai residence on April 23, 1983 when he reminisced about those momentous days. Nobody wanted the food and agriculture portfolio in June 1964 when Lal Bahadur Shastri was finalising his ministry. Sanjeeva Reddy had almost accepted but declined at the last minute. Shastri went personally to CS who held the steel and heavy industries portfolio under Nehru. Incidentally, it was during CS' tenure in this ministry that India's first move towards economic liberalism took place, inspired by the Report of Steel Control prepared by a committee chaired by K.N. Raj in 1963.

When CS took over, the nation was already in the throes of an agricultural crisis. We were importing 3-4 million tonnes of wheat annually from the US. One-fifth of America's wheat crop was moving to India. In the 1950s, Indian planning was obsessed with heavy industry and agriculture was seen through land reforms, community development, cooperativisation and motivation.

CS gave a new, threefold thrust to Indian agriculture—technological, economic and organisational. He reorganised the Indian Council of Agricultural Research and, for the first time, appointed a scientist, Dr B.P. Pal, as its head. It was another 40-year-old geneticist at the Indian Agricultural Research Institute, M.S. Swaminathan, who made CS aware that new, highyielding wheat varieties had been developed by Norman Borlaug's team in Mexico and that India must straightaway launch large-scale field demonstrations.

There was stout resistance to the use of these varieties and the new wheat strategy from the Finance Ministry and the Planning Commission. But the situation was getting desperate. CS got Shastri's approval to import 250 tonnes of wheat seeds in 1965. A staggering 18,000 tonnes were imported in 1966. It was the latter that triggered the Green Revolution in wheat. Indian scientists improved upon these varieties.

To provide incentives for the new technology, in August 1964 CS got L.K. Jha, then Shastri's secretary, to chair what came to be known as the Foodgrain Prices Committee. Based on its recommendations, the Agricultural Prices Commission (APC) and the Food Corporation of India (FCI) came into being in January 1965. Noted economist M.L. Dantwala, who had served on Jha's committee, became APC's first chairman. For FCI, CS selected T.A. Pai. The National Seeds Corporation and the Central Warehousing Corporation also came into being at about this time, as did the National Dairy Development Board for which CS backed Dr V. Kurien and allowed him to operate out of Anand, much to the chagrin of his colleagues in Delhi. Kurien was to usher in the White Revolution in India later. CS overruled Biju Patnaik's objections and got B. Sivaraman who had vast field experience in agriculture and irrigation in Orissa as his agriculture secretary in May 1965. If CS provided the big picture, Sivaraman was the details man. His Bitter Sweet is a fascinating blow-by-blow account of the Green Revolution in wheat and rice.

The monsoon failed miserably in 1965 (and in 1966 as well). In November 1965, CS met with Orville Freeman, the US agriculture secretary, in Rome. The two signed the so-called Treaty of Rome. This accord put down on paper what CS had already laun-ched with the support of Shastri. It committed India to end imports of foodgrains by 1971 with more investments in agriculture, irrigation, re-search, seeds, fertilisers and with appropriate economic and marketing policies. In return, the Americans agreed to send more wheat to India—14 million tonnes in 1965 and 1966. Shastri despatched CS to Washington in December 1965. B.K. Nehru wrote in his memoirs, Nice Guys Finish Second, that President Lyndon Johnson told him, "That Subber Mainyam of yours, he is a good feller." These warm sentiments are echoed in the Texan's own memoirs, The Vantage Point.

CS' unwavering belief in science and technology, his unstinted encouragement of education and research, his remarkable ability to pick and back outstanding administrators and professionals, his receptivity to new ideas and his impatience with dogma, all have great contemporary relevance.

                                                                    27/11/2000

—◆——◆—

GLADIATOR ECONOMIST

Hollywood unveils the troubled life of an economics Nobel genius

Russell Crowe, who won the oscar in 2001 for his role in Gladiator, stars in a new film called A Beautiful Mind. The film is based on the life of John Nash who won the Nobel Prize in Economics in 1994 and is derived from a brilliant biography of him by Sylvia Nasar also called A Beautiful Mind, which came out in 1998. Nash had earlier figured in Rebecca Goldstein's novel Mind-Body Problem.

Nash is actually a pure mathematician, an intuitive genius in the Ramanujan mould. He has had just one undergraduate course in international economics. He received his doctorate in mathematics from the renowned Princeton University in 1949 at the age of 21 and his dissertation was only 27 pages long. But that dissertation has had a most profound impact on economics, political science, nuclear strategy and biology.

However, Hollywood would not have made this film had Nash been just a prodigy. He was also a paranoid schizophrenic, a manic-depressive, a man who scaled intellectual heights for a brief while, then plumbed psychological depths for almost three decades and finally with the help of his wife and his peers re-emerged to share the Nobel accolade with John Harsanyi and Reinhard Selten. And just when Nash was returning to normalcy in the 1990s, his son, also a gifted mathematician who got a doctorate without completing school or college, started following in his father's psychotic footsteps.

What gives this man—who went from being brilliant to being hospitalised, treated and given up and then to mysteriously becoming normal—a place in the pantheon of greats? His contributions to athematics at MIT and Princeton, where the great Harish-Chandra was his colleague, have been seminal. But it is his work on game theory that has brought him pervasive fame, although Nash himself considers this his most trivial work. Game theory is a theory of rational human choice and social behaviour based on logic, psychology and mathematics. It burst on the scene dramatically in 1944 with the publication of The Theory of Games and Economic Behaviour by John von Neumann and Oscar Morgenstern. This book dwelt with two-person, zerosum isituations—where one person's win is balanced exactly by the other's lloss. Both cannot win at the same time.

Nash realised that such games of pure opposition have extremely limited applications in the real world where possibilities of compromise also exist and are explored by rivals. He distinguished between non-cooperative games of the type dealt with by Von Neumann and Morgenstern and cooperative games which involve co-operation, confrontation and competition. Every non-cooperative game with any number of players has at least one solution called the Nash equilibrium (an ironic oxy-moron judging from his own life!) point. At a Nash equilibrium point, no player can unilaterally deviate to improve his or her position. Nasar writes, "Where Von Neumann's focus was the group and belief was in world government, Nash zeroed in on the individual ... By formulating the problem of economic competition in the way he did, Nash showed that a decentralised decision-making process could, in fact, be coherent."

Non-cooperative game theory and the Nash equilibrium are now considered the "core analytical methodology" alongside price theory in economic analysis. It is highly abstract and mathematical but has found a number of practical applications. In December 1994 the US Federal Communications Commission used it to auction airwaves for mobile telephony and raked in $7 billion from telecom companies. In the past few years, game theory principles have been used to devise market-based instruments for environmental control. Much earlier in the 1950s and '60s, game theory had been used extensively in the famous RAND Corporation to work out strategies to manage nuclear conflict.

Some of the pioneering work on the application of the game theory to contemporary economics have been done by Indian-born economists. Perhaps, the greatest names here are those of Avinash Dixit, who, like Nash, is at Princeton University and is widely considered to be a potential Nobel laureate, and Pradeep Dubey at the State University of New York, Stony Brook. Bhaskar Dutta and Prakash Chander of the Indian Statistical Institute in Delhi are two other notable names. Both Nash and Selten are coming to Delhi in December 2002 for a conference organised by the Society for the Promotion of Game Theory and its Applications whose president is Subhashis Gangopadhyay, one of India's most accomplished economists.

One of the numerous websites on Nash carries the haunting lines of John Dryden, who wrote in 1681: "Great wits are sure to madness near allied; And thin partitions do their bounds divide." Nash is not alone in this regard. But he is certainly the most unusual.

07/01/2002

BOSE WERE THE DAYS

Bengal's long shadow over Stockholm's Nobel December evening

The six nobel prizes for 2001 had an unusual triple Indian connection. We know that V.S. Naipaul, a Trinidadian of Indian origin, won the literature award. What is much less appreciated is the India factor in two other disciplines as well. George Akerlof, Michael Spence and Joseph Stiglitz shared the honours for Economics for their "analysis of markets with asymmetric inforation". Stiglitz has had noted Indian-born collaborators but it is Akerlof who spent 1967-68 as a visiting don at the Indian Statistical Institute (ISI), Delhi. ISI, started in Kolkata in December 1931 by P.C. Mahalanobis, had acquired an awesome reputation in the 1950s and '60s. Extraordinary names like Norbert Weiner, Jan Tinbergen, Ragnar Frisch, Simon Kuznets, A.N. Kolmogorov, Herman Wold, Karl Pearson, Michael Kalecki, J.B.S. Haldane, Oskar Lange, R.A. Fisher, Harold Hotelling and Nicholas Kaldor were, at different points of time, part of ISI's faculty.

Akerlof was a young 27- year-old coming out to the ISI to work with B.S. Minhas, one of India's most eminent economists. It was the beginning of the wheat revolution and Minhas was studying how the waters from Bhakra Nangal should be released. While at the University of California, Berkeley, in 1966-67, Akerlof had already written the first draft of a paper called The Market for Lemons that was to be completed at ISI, published in 1970 and fetched him the Nobel.

This influential paper deals with one type of market imperfection: when economic agents have unequal access to information. There is a section on rural credit in India. Actually, Akerlof 's theory applies to all credit markets and is the basis of much securities regulation and accounting rules everywhere but, in his own words, the Indian examples are important and poignant and have not lost their relevance. If the moneylender and the bank were to have equal information about their borrowers, they would be in competition and usurious interest rates will not get charged. But moneylenders have more information and thereby have an advantage. If the bank were to charge higher rates, they would only attract "lemons", that is, borrowers who cannot repay. The moneylender is also able to provide timely and adequate credit, which is perhaps more important to the borrower than the interest rate.

The 2001 Nobel Prize in Physics also went to an American trio—Eric Cornell, Wolfgang Ketterle and Carl Wieman for "the achievement of Bose-Einstein conden-sation in dilute gases of alkali atoms, and for early fundamental studies of the properties of the condensate". Thus, 70 years after Albert Einstein built upon the work of Satyendranath Bose and postulated its existence, this new state of matter has finally been observed. Actually, this is the second Nobel award in recent years having to do with Bose-Einstein condensates which is clearly one of the frontier areas of research. The 1997 prize was awarded for techniques that formed the basis for the discovery of Bose-Einstein condensation in rubidium and sodium atoms at temperatures less than one-millionth of a degree above absolute zero (-273 degrees Celsius).

A Bose-Einstein condensate is the coldest form of gas in the universe in which all atoms have lost their individuality and have become indistinguishable from each other. When this has happened, the atoms are said to "Bose condensate" into the lowest possible energy state. The atoms that make up a Bose condensate are, in the words of Cornell and Wieman, "the analogue to the hotons that make up a laser beam", conjuring up visions of applications in areas like precision measurement, lithography, superconductivity, lasers and nanotechnology.

Bose is a most fascinating personality. His academic career was brilliant. In June 1924 while teaching physics at the University of Dacca, he sent a paper describing light as a gas consisting of photons to Einstein. Einstein immediately saw that Bose had "removed a major objection against light quanta". He personally translated it into German and got it published. Einstein went on to write several papers based on Bose's seminal contribution. One branch of statistical mechanics is called Einstein-Bose statistics. Every elementary particle is basically either a fermion (after Enrico Fermi) or a boson named after Bose by Paul Dirac, one of the all-time physics greats. Electrons, protons and neutrons are fermions, while particles of light are bosons. An atom made of an even number of protons, neutrons and electrons is a boson.

The story of ISI and of Bose is a story of an earlier India, an India that nurtured great minds at home, an India whose institutions of higher learning boasted of very distinguished faculty and an India that was the Mecca for world-class academics from abroad. It is also a bygone saga of Bengal at its intellectual zenith. Thinking of Bose, Mahalanobis and their ilk, we can only wistfully wonder, Jaane kahan gaye woh din.

14/01/2002

NEW HAVEN TO HEAVEN

The only economist to have a tax named after him passes away

On March 11, one of the world's truly great and enormously influential economists passed away. Aged 84, James Tobin was still intellectually active at the prestigious Yale University in the US. Incidentally, Yale is named after Elihu Yale, governor of Madras during 1687-1692 who bequeathed his loot to the institution in 1718 after losing his job over a corruption scandal. One of the stars of its economics department for long has been T.N. Srinivasan, among the most brilliant economic minds India has produced.

Tobin was awarded the Nobel Prize in economics in 1981 for his seminal contributions to the understanding of financial markets and their linkages with the "real" economy and also for his theory of portfolio selection by households—for proving, as he said, that you don't put all your eggs in one basket. He was among the chosen few who have fundamentally altered the nature of economic theory, profoundly influenced the practice of economic policy and decisively shaped the course of economic debate.

In 1961, Tobin shot into wider prominence when he became a member of US President John F. Kennedy's Council of Economic Advisers along with Walter Heller and Kermit Gordon. This council had among its staff members Kenneth Arrow who shared the Nobel Prize in 1972, Robert Solow who won the accolade in 1987 and Arthur Okun. It has enjoyed the highest reputation among all such councils and is given credit for having laid the practical foundations of "new economics" based on the works of John Maynard Keynes. This was felt necessary because, as Michael Bernstein puts it in his recent account of economists and public purpose in 20th century America A Perilous Journey, even though a remarkably prosperous decade in the US, the 1950s were punctuated by three recessions. In the early 1960s, American unemployment rates fell sharply from about 7 per cent to 4 per cent. The revival recipe was huge tax cuts. At that time, this appeared heretical because, in the words of Bernstein, it entailed the "first deliberate peacetime indulgence of federal budget deficits".

In 1972, building on a concept originally propounded by Keynes himself, Tobin put forward a proposal to cushion fluctuations in exchange rates that were becoming a matter of serious concern following the abandonment of the fixed exchange-rate system in the winter of 1971. His idea was simple: at each exchange of a currency into another, a small tax could be levied. His motivation was not to have a new revenue-raising device but to have an instrument to curb trafficking in foreign exchange, which he felt would multiply phenomenally with electronic money exchanges. But Tobin's idea generated little enthusiasm for much of the 1970s and 1980s on the ground that in a world of tax havens, it could always be circumvented. Some economists also argued that far from dampening volatility, the levy would discourage growth in forex markets that is essential for lubricating global trade.

The Tobin Tax, as it came to be called, was rescued from the groves of academia by the eruption of currency crises first in Europe in 1992 and 1993 and then in Mexico in 1994. In October 1995, Mahbub-ul-Haq, the eminent Pakistani economist who had been Tobin's student, organised an international meeting in New York under the aegis of the UN. This resulted in a comprehensive book The Tobin Tax: Coping with Financial Volatility, co-edited by Haq. The East Asian crisis of 1997, the Brazilian turmoil of 1998 and the Russian disaster of 1999 all led to renewed support for a Tobin Tax. It has been championed aggressively by the anti-globalisation brigade and NGOs, leading Tobin himself to bemoan that his ideas had been hijacked by those with whose cause he had little sympathy. Ironically, the most powerful and dreaded foreign-exchange trader, George Soros, has also backed the tax.

The tax has invited a positive reaction from European legislatures also, although the US Congress rejected it in 1996. A group of eminent world personalities, including Manmohan Singh, assembled by the UN under the chairmanship of former Mexican president Ernest Zedillo, submitted a report in June 2001 extending cautious support to the Tobin Tax. The International Labour Organisation has just set up a high-level commission to study the social dimensions of globalisation. It is co-chaired by the presidents of Finland and Tanzania and includes Joseph Stiglitz, the 2001 economics Nobel laureate and Deepak Nayyar, vice-chancellor of Delhi University. This commission will also undoubtedly support the Tobin Tax when it submits its report next year.

Tobin was also the only economist, other than John Nash, to figure in a novel—Herman Wouk's The Caine Mutiny (1951) where "a mandarin-like midshipman named Tobit with a domed forehead, measured quiet speech, and a mind like a sponge, was ahead of the field by a spacious percentage". Wouk's thinly veiled reference to his friend cannot be bettered as an epitaph.

25/03/2002

◆———◆

GOODBYE NICE GUY

B.K. Nehru made American underwriting of Indian socialism possible

It is hard to imagine today that there was once a time when India enjoyed a special relationship with the US, when an Indian official had tremendous influence over American politicians, bureaucrats, journalists, socialites and intellectuals, and when an Indian ambassador enjoyed the confidence of American presidents and their aides. Yes, there indeed was such a time when India counted in Washington and when an Indian mattered. That Indian passed away a few days back at the age of 92 virtually unnoticed.

John Lewis, the American economist and a great Indiawallah, once remarked that the edifice of Indian socialism in the 1950s and 1960s was built with massive American aid. It was B.K. Nehru who, in his various official avatars in Washington, made that possible. But there was more to Nehru than America. He had a long tenure in the Finance Ministry in the 1950s, was also governor of Assam and Nagaland (1968-73), high commissioner to the UK (1973-77) and governor of Jammu and Kashmir during 1981-84. Nehru was thus a member of India's governing elite, a tribe that is fast becoming extinct, much to the country's cost.

Bijju, as he was popularly called, was the son of Jawaharlal Nehru's cousin. He became an unlikely Indian hero in Washington. A member of the ICS, he was educated at the London School of Economics (LSE) where he was a favourite of Harold Laski. The LSE along with Cambridge produced an entire generation of Indian political leaders and economic administrators steeped in British statism and Soviet industrialisation. But unusually for a man of his generation and pedigree, Bijju became an Americaphile.

Bijju's extraordinary relationship with the Americans never came n the way of his awe and admiration for his uncle and his rapport with is cousin who became prime minister in January 1966. His special status among the Americans never came in the way of his friendship with and respect for another great Indian official of that generation, also a Kashmiri Pandit, also UK-educated, also an ardent acolyte of India's first prime minister and confidant of his daughter but who was the high priest of "leftist" ideology during 1969-1973—P.N. Haksar. Incidentally, Indira Gandhi used Bijju to build an opening with Ronald Reagan in 1980, just as Rajiv Gandhi was to use Haksar to open a dialogue with the Chinese to pave the way for his historic trip to Beijing in December 1988—showing the importance of "back channels" in diplomacy. Bijju's pro-American image also did not come in the way of Chandra Shekhar offering him the post of India's foreign minister in February 1991.

Bijju was unusual in another respect. Unlike men in Indian public life, he wrote his memoirs and that too in a delightfully self-deprecatory and remarkably racy style providing immense material to students of economic history. His Nice Guys Finish Second was published four years ago and pulls no punches. There is criticism of V.K. Krishna Menon who single-handedly created the international image of Indians as a sanctimonious, arrogant and boorish bunch. There is criticism of how the North-east has been consistently mishandled and misgoverned. Most of all, there is criticism of Indira Gandhi and her political colleagues for needlessly removing Farooq Abdullah in 1984, an event Nehru believed triggered the decline of India in the Valley. In fact, the detailed account of his gubernatorial tenure in Jammu and Kashmir is very tragic, revealing how much more there is to our predicament in that state than cross-border terrorism. But why Bijju had regrets as reflected in the title of his memoirs is unfathomable since he had had such a long and distin-guished innings at the top. Was there regret at his not being appointed secretary-general of the UN in 1961? Was there some bitterness on being "dismissed" as governor of Jammu and Kashmir in 1984 by his cousin to whom he enjoyed unparalleled access? Was there regret that he was not inducted into politics?

In the last two decades of his life, Bijju's pet subject became constitutional reforms. He is strangely silent about this in his memoirs but fortunately P.N. Dhar has a lot to say on it in his book Indira Gandhi, the 'Emergency' and Indian Democracy, published last year. Dhar writes that Bijju's proposals were meant to address the systemic problems of social fragmentation, political instability, competitive populism and low economic growth. His idea was to revitalise local bodies and to replace the Westminster model by the presidential form of democracy. The first is happening but the second remains controversial. It would be tempting to run down Bijju's ideas as the ruminations of the last of the benevolent paternalists. The harsh reality, however, is that Indian democracy gets outstanding marks for delivering on representation and social empowerment but looks increasingly fragile from the point of view of basic governance.

19/11/2001

———◆———

CIVILISING CONFLICT
Huntington's controversial "clash of civilisations" theory is back in the news

There words other than Osama Bin Laden are capturing world headlines these days—"clash of civilisations". This phrase came into pub-lic discourse dramatically with Samuel Huntington's "Clash of Civilisations?" in the summer 1993 issue of Foreign Affairs, published by the New York-based Council of Foreign Relations. Subsequently, the Harvard professor of political science expanded his article into a book The Clash of Civilisations and the Remaking of World Order that came out in 1996.

Huntington's work has been analysed and debated, applauded and heralded, criticised and condemned. September 11, 2001 has brought it back into sharp focus across continents. Huntington defines a civilisation as a culture writ large involving values, norms, institutions and modes of thinking to which successive generations in a given society have attached primary importance. Saying that religion is the defining characteristic of civilisations, Huntington identifies seven contemporary civilisations—Western, Latin American, Sinic, Japanese, Hindu, Islamic and African. He rejects the notion of a Buddhist or Jewish civilisation. He contends that while the lines between civilisations are seldom sharp, they are nonetheless real.

Conflicts can occur within civilisations. But what pre-occupies Huntington is the larger issue of conflicts between and among civilisations, between what he calls "core states" of different civilisations. According to him, the Soviet-Afghan War of 1979-89 was the first war of civilisations while the 1990-91 Gulf War was the second such confrontation. Wars can also occur on a smaller scale across "fault lines" between civilisations, as for instance, in Kashmir. Rich diasporas play a key role in sustaining such conflicts. Having said that future wars are going to be civilisational in nature as a result of growing resistance to the spread of western universalism, Huntington proceeds to give his remedies for peace and harmony. In a multi-civilisational world, he writes, there are three rules that need to be followed. First is the abstention rule: core states must abstain from intervention in conflicts in other civilisations. Second is the joint mediation rule: core states should negotiate with each other to contain or to halt wars between states or groups from their civilisations. Third is the commonalties rule: peoples in all civilisations should search for and attempt to expand the value, institutions and practices they have in common with peoples of other civilisations. Huntington calls for an international institutional order restructuring, based on civilisations as the surest safeguard against a world war.

Huntington devotes considerable attention to the collision between Islam and the West. To be sure, anti-Muslim prejudices in western societies and the policies of western governments, particularly in West Asia, have fuelled great resentment amongst Muslims worldwide, but the problem, Huntington says, is deeper. He argues that the absolute nature of Islam that merges religion and politics, the absence of the concept of non-violence in that faith and the fact that it lacks one or more core states that could effectively mediate conflicts have all combined to make Islam a source of global instability.

While addressing a seminar organised by the Konrad Adenauer Foundation on India in Bonn in May this year, Dietmar Rothermund, the eminent German historian and scholar on India, spoke on how there is a danger that instead of Huntington learning from India, some elements in India will learn from Huntington and make his scheme a self-fulfilling prophecy. While referring to India as a civilisation-state, Rothermund cautioned that such a reference must mean an affirmation of diversity rather than an assent to Huntington's scheme of civilisational blocks.

Huntington visited India in January 1998. His lectures here evoked a jubilant response from RSS-BJP ideologues who saw in his theories a vindication of their own world view. But while recognising that India may well be a case for controverting his theories, we cannot deny the need for an intensified inter-faith interaction on a sustained basis in our society. Secularism must mean confronting bigots, fanatics and zealots of all religions without fear or favour. We can no longer run away from the fact that while we have had a glorious multi-civilisational heritage, that syncretic and composite heritage is under assault from all quarters—majority and minority. Huntington is convinced that a multi-civilisational country can no longer endure as a coherent society. Two of 20th century's multi-civilisational entities—the Soviet Union and Yugoslavia—have withered away. Two remain—the US and India. But our approaches to managing diversity are very different and have to be kept that way if we are to retain the essence of our great civilisation immortalised in Iqbal's moving Saare jahan se accha, Hindustan hamara.

08/10/2001

◆———◆

MORE THAN GLOBALONEY

New scholarship on globalisation raises both cheer and concern

The Distinguished economist Jagdish Bhagwati, while reviewing the widely acclaimed *A Future Perfect: The Challenge and Hidden Promise of Globalisation* by John Micklethwait and Adrian Wooldridge, wondered whether books on globalisation are beginning to be subject to the law of diminishing marginal utility. Bhagwati was writing in *Foreign Affairs* in July/August 2000 when, amidst a vast outpouring, Thomas Friedman's celebrated *The Lexus and the Olive Tree* was also capturing world attention. In recent months, the literature on globalisation has mushroomed even further but Bhagwati's fears are still unfounded.

Globalisation and History by Kevin O'Rourke and Jeffrey Williamson traces the evolution of the 19th century Atlantic economy that was marked by an explosion in trade flows, capital movements and migration. But the 1920s and the 1930s saw a dramatic reversal which the duo, who are well-known economists at University College, Dublin, and at Harvard University respectively, call "deglobalisation". This led to an increase in trade protectionism, a breakdown of international capital markets and an end to mass and easy migration. They reject the conventional view that the deglobalisation of the interwar decades was a consequence of World War I. Instead, they ascribe it to the political backlash in response to the actual or perceived distributional effects of globalisation itself.

Harold James' *The End of Globalisation: Lessons from the Great Depression* is a book of great scholarship. James, a highly distinguished professor of history at Princeton University of the US, examines the world economy in the late 1920s and 1930s and concludes that "globalism fails because humans and institutions they create cannot adequately handle the psychological and institutional consequences of an interconnected world". Institutions created to tackle the problems of globalism themselves become the major channels through which the resentments against globalisation work their destruction.

Dani Rodrik holds a prestigious chair of political economy at Harvard University. He first hit the headlines in 1997 with his provocative *Has Globalisation Gone Too Far?* where he expounded on the political and social back-lashes to the prevailing globalisation paradigm. Now comes *"The Global Governance of Trade As If Development Really Mattered"*. Rodrik believes that import liberalisation is not essential for growth. He argues that the WTO is anti-democratic and that the world trading regime has to shift from a market access to a development perspective. He suggests that globalisation is an outcome, not a prerequisite of a successful growth strategy as evidenced from East Asia and China. He postulates a basic "trilemma": deep international integration, a strong nation-state and vibrant democratic politics cannot coexist and that a country must choose any two of the three.

The WTO has directed the International Labour Organisation (ILO) to continue its studies on the social dimensions of globalisation and the ILO is soon to establish an eminent persons' group on this subject. Based on the experience of Bangladesh, Chile, South Korea, Mauritius, Poland, South Africa and Switzerland, Raymond Torres of the ILO has published *Towards a Socially Sustainable World Economy*. Four areas—education and training, social safety nets, labour laws and industrial relations and core labour standards—are identified as the social pillars that would make the process of globalisation successful. Ajit Ghose, a senior economist at the ILO, has come out with *Global Economic Inequality and International Trade* in which he shows that while inter-country inequality (measured by per capita income) has increased in the past two decades, international inequality (per capita income weighted by population) has actually declined breaking a longterm trend.

The World Bank's characteristically voluminous *Globalisation,*

Growth and Poverty concludes that there are regions where globalisation has reduced poverty. But there are other places where it has clearly had adverse impacts. Many widespread anxieties on the process of globalisation are well-founded. In order to build an inclusive world economy, the report makes seven major recommendations: greater opening of developed country markets, improvement in the investment climate in developing countries, effective delivery of education and health care in the poor nations, social insurance and security, increased development aid, debt relief particularly for African economies and effective global cooperation in environment.

Globalisation is here to stay—indeed, the most globalised community today is that of anti-globalisation protesters! How we leverage the numerous opportunities it throws up and manage the many risks it entails is the real challenge. So far, we have been more successful in the latter than in the former. And getting globalisation to deliver is, ultimately, a matter of effective domestic governance.

11/02/2002

———◆　◆———

ECO-LIGHTS OF INDIA

The memoirs of two of India's greatest names in economics are out

The oral tradition still prevails in *India Access* to official documents remains restricted. There is no habit of keeping personal records. That is why reliable memoirs of public personalities here are rare. This is especially true in economic policy, the remarkably illuminating reminiscences of B.K. Nehru and P.N. Dhar notwithstanding. Now, we have two more in quick succession—The Partial Memoirs of V.K.R.V. Rao edited by his nephew and Glimpses of Indian Economic Policy: An Insider's View by I.G. Patel. Both not only enrich our understanding of these pioneers and the times in which they grew up but also shed new light on the evolution of Indian economic policy.

Rao and Patel are among the most distinguished names not just in Indian but world economics. Rao was one of the first three doctorates in economics from Cambridge University and played a key role in the establishment of the International Development Association, the soft-loan window of the World Bank from which India has gained so much. Patel is a product of both Cambridges, having completed his doctorate at Harvard University. His was one of the important contributions in the creation of a reserve asset by the IMF and he served as director of the London School of Economics in the early 1980s.

Fortunate to be operating under the Nehruvian umbrella, Rao was an indefatigable institution builder. But his progeny are in dire need of massive renewal. The Delhi School of Economics, where Patel himself spent some time in the mid-1960s, has had its glory days but now finds it difficult to attract top-flight teaching and research faculty. The Delhi-based Institute of Economic Growth has also boasted eminent names in the past but it has never fulfilled its role as an effective think tank. The Bangalore-based Institute of Economic and Social Change, like its counterparts in other states, is mired in parochialism and mediocrity. The Indian Council for Social Science Research has fallen prey to prevailing political ideologies. Patel has been director of the Indian Institute of Management (IIM), Ahmedabad. The IIMs, like the IITs, have acquired an awesome reputation entirely because of the quality of their students.

Rao made the transition from academics to politics when he was elected to the Lok Sabha from the now-famous Bellary, first in 1967 and then in 1971. He served as minister for shipping and transport in 1967-69 and then as minister for education in 1969-71. Apparently, his spontaneous ability to offend came in the way of greater glory. The more discreet and urbane Patel could have made a similar shift in June 1991 when he was offered the finance ministership, ahead of Manmohan Singh by P.V. Narasimha Rao and again when he was asked to join the government in 1993. But he said no, choosing to remain in Vadodara.

While Rao was essentially a teacher, organiser and scholar, Patel was a policy mandarin par excellence. He drafted a staggering 14 budgets between 1954 and 1972. It was the example of "IG", as he was known, that inspired a new generation of economists, including Manmohan Singh, Bimal Jalan and Montek Ahluwalia, to join government. But that influx of lateral talent has ceased. Gone are the Pitamber Pants who could inspire the Jagdish Bhagwatis and T.N. Srinivasans, the Lovraj Kumars who could motivate the Nitin Desais and Vijay Kelkars, the Manmohan Singhs who brought in the Deepak Nayyars, the Rakesh Mohans, the Arvind Virmanis and the Shankar Acharyas, and the Abid Hussains who mentored numerous youngsters. The result is that there has been a sharp fall in the quality of economic thinking in government.

The Raos and the Patels have become all-too-rare, men who combined academic scholarship with real-world concerns, economists who imbibed the best of what the world had to offer but who then returned home with a steadfast commitment to establishing and nurturing educational infrastructure, to influencing policy and debate and to serving as role models. It is true that India's economic performance has not matched the brilliance of the Raos and Patels. But that is no reason why their contributions should not be acknowledged. Rao is no longer with us but India desperately needs his reincarnation. Patel, who is a young 78, must be an anguished soul seeing not just the moribund state of the Indian economy but more importantly the ghastly tragedy of Gujarat. Patel is the presiding deity of the Prime Minister's Economic Advisory Council. He can send a powerful signal and message by resigning in protest. Patel is also still active enough to mobilise fellow Gujarati liberal intellectuals from all over the world—Bhikhu Parekh, Meghnad Desai, Jagdish and P.N. Bhagwati, Nitin Desai, Upendra Baxi, Ela Bhatt and Amrita Patel to name just a few—to lead a crusade for a Gujarat restored to its noble traditions of humanism and syncretism, a Gujarat freed from the virus of communal hatred and social polarisation.

01/04/2002

GO IN, DO IT AND GET OUT
Suresh Prabhu prefers a technocrat, not an IAS officer at the helm

Suresh Prabhu is a dynamic minister. This of course, does not make up for the fact that he belongs to the Shiv Sena, a party that epitomises the worst of Indian politics. Prabhu may or may not share Bal Thackeray's rabid social views but he is serving with admirable competence as the Union minister of power. His latest move to induct a private-sector executive, R.V. Shahi, as his top civil servant is a remarkable step. Shahi, who cut his teeth in the public sector NTPC and then managed BSES, the country's leading private-sector power company, is one of the country's most distinguished power engineers. However, this is not the first time that the Power Ministry has had a "technocrat" at its helm: in the early 1980s, Indira Gandhi had inducted as its secretary D.V. Kapur, the man who created and built NTPC in its initial years

There have been three groups of technocrats in government—

economists, scientists and engineers. Economists have served primarily in the Finance Ministry and in the Planning Commission, scientists in scientific departments and engineers in ministries like railways, telecom and industry. Specialised cadres for engineers and economists also exist.

In the past, there have been quite a few instances of eminent public-sector chief executives being inducted into the highest policy-making positions in government. K.S.R. Chari was brought in by Mohan Kumaramangalam when the coal industry was being nationalised in 1971- 72. In the 1970s, noted technologists like Mantosh Sondhi from Bokaro Steel, V. Krishnamurthy from BHEL, S. Varadarajan from IPCL and K.P.P. Nambiar from Keltron became Union secretaries.

But Shahi has been picked up from the private sector for a job that has traditionally not seen professional experts. There have been few occasions in the past when such an induction was made. In the mid-1960s, Lovraj Kumar was weaned away from Burmah Shell by his uncle Dharma Vira and he went on to have a distinguished career in government culminating as petroleum secretary in 1981-83. One of his greatest contributions was to mentor a number of younger professionals in government—Kautilya being one of this fortunate group. In 1972, M.A. Wadud Khan, a former chairman of TOMCO who had earlier been appointed the first chairman of SAIL by Kumaramangalam, was made steel secretary. In the mid-1970s, Indira Gandhi inducted V.G. Rajadhyaksha into the Planning Commission as a member after his tenure as chairman of Hindustan Lever. When he took over as prime minister, Rajiv Gandhi hired P.S. Deodhar, an entrepreneur who had set up his own company Aplab, as chairman of the Electronics Commission. Rajiv's boldest and most productive move was to bring in Sam Pitroda, who energised the system through the various technology missions in 1987-89, a remarkable process that Kautilya was privileged to be part of.

Technocrats can be expected to do well in staff jobs but are they effective in line jobs like that of a secretary? Not necessarily. Scientists with some exceptions have generally been poor administrators. Economists have made a mark as advisers but not as problem-solvers or decision-takers. Engineers have had a better record but then the question is whether being a secretary, pushing files, interacting with the bureaucracy and Parliament and attending countless meetings is the best use of the talent of a Shahi, who has been an outstanding CEO. The skills required for a great CEO are quite different from those for a successful secretary. The tragedy is that in our system, the culture of administration is very seductive and being designated as secretary to the government of India carries the highest prestige even for technocrats who have made outstanding contributions and earned a name for themselves. Many public-sector CEOs in the 1980s pleaded with Rajiv. Gandhi to have themselves designated as ex-officio secretaries to the government of India and have direct access to their minis-ters. Not only did the IAS scuttle this move but even senior ministers opposed the idea vehemently. Politicians prefer to deal with the IAS.

What the government needs most is recirculation and renewal of human resources. That is simply not happening. Professionals do enter but become semi-permanent fixtures, getting ossified as they go along. There is no revolving door through which new talent comes in, makes its contributions over three to five years and then departs, making way for others to follow. Specialisation is at a deep discount and the way the Union Finance Ministry has been managed in the past four years is symptomatic. What is different about Shahi is that at 57, he is not bothered about feathering his nest in government. Of course, there is little that a Union secretary of power can do given that the bankrupt electricity boards are controlled by the states. But to the extent that he can push power sector reforms forward, provide leadership and give youngsters an opportunity to work along with him, Shahi is best qualified.

06/05/2002

XI

Different Takes

This is a very small section containing a few unusual articles that I wrote for sheer pleasure. I wish I had the talent of Stephen Jay Gould who could write as evocatively on paleontology as he could on Joe DiMaggio (and still draw connections between the two!). Alas, he died recently but he will remain an inspiration. My advice to any youngster is to read at least some of his masterpieces, which will be enormously enriching and rewarding. This section is my very small attempt to follow in Gould's footsteps.

This section also reveals my general approach to Kautilya. I wanted the column to be fun—both for the person writing it and for those reading it. Writing on economics can be dry and reading columns written on economics can be exacting. That is because most columnists take themselves too seriously and most columns are meant to impress, not educate and entertain. Ashok Desai's writings in Business Standard come closest to my ideal of what a column should be—calm analytical arguments written in a lucid style and supported by comprehensive data and facts. I hope Kautilya will also be seen in the same light and as aspiring toward a similar objective.

THE MILLENNIUM MADNESS
What is the historical background
to and meaning of Y2K?

The millennium mania is very much on. But what exactly is the millennium all about? Stephen Jay Gould, a distinguished natural scientist at Harvard University, in his Questioning the Millennium points out that millennium originally cropped up in futuristic visions about the end of time and the reappearance of Christ on earth. This is what he calls Millennium as Apocalypse that is derived from the books of Daniel and Revelation in the Testaments. Christian history is dotted with millenarian movements, the more well-known of them being the Seventh Day Adventists and Jehovah's Witnesses. Some of these movements have resulted in mass suicide or genocide.

But from a contemporary perspective, it is Gould's racy account of Millennium as Calendrics that is fascinating. The year 2000 is a leap year. Thanks to the caprices of Pope Gregory (in whose name the modern Gregorian calendar is named) in 1582, an end-of-century leap year occurs only once in 400 years. But this apart, it would be reasonable to presume that 2000 celebrates the 2,000th birth anniversary of Christ. But does it? Gould points out that Dionysius Exiguus, a 6th century monk who had been authorised by Pope John I to prepare a chronology, got his dates hopelessly mixed up. He reckoned Christ's birth three years after the death of Herod which, if the Gospels are to be true, just cannot be right. But worse, Dionysius did not begin time at zero but started reckoning it from one.

The reason for this is simple and Gould only alludes to it. The western world did not, in the 6th century A.D., have the concept of zero. Zero was probably first discussed in Aryabhatta's Aryabhatiya (A.D. 499) and Varahamihira's Pancha Siddhantika (A.D. 505). In History of Indian Science, Technology and Culture: AD 1000-1800 (edited by A. Rahman), Wazir Hasan Abdi writes that more definitively, the concept of zero is to be found in Bhaskara I's commentary on Aryabhatiya and is later elaborated in the great Brahmagupta's work (A.D. 628) and in the writings of Bhaskara II and Mahavira in the 8th and 9th centuries.

Indian mathematics was exported first by the Muslim traders in the early 7th century and later by the Arabs who conquered Sind in

A.D. 712. The Indian system was studied intensely by scholars in the scientifically glittering Abbasid court at Baghdad like Al-Fazari, Yakub Ibn Tarik, Ali-bib-Ahmad Nasavi and most notably the Uzbek/Persian astronomer Al-Khowarizmi. Al-Khowarizmi, heir to the Kushan tradition, is famous for his Kitab Al-jabr w'al-Muqabalah that not only propagated the Indian system but also gave us the name "algebra". The Arabs then took the Indian system to the Spanish centres of learning at Cordoba and Granada. Thereafter, Leonardo Fibonacci of Pisa saw its immense value and wrote his epochal Libor Abbaci in 1202 which introduced Indian mathematics to Europe. Over time, this was to replace the Roman system of numerals.

The other noted populariser of Indian mathematics was the well-known Al-Beruni. Ironically, he was coerced into coming to India by Mahmud of Ghazni in the 1020s. India started the second millennium with Ghazni and is ending it still grappling with the legacy of this warrior who is remembered for his pillage and not for his attempts to patronise Al-Beruni, Firdausi and Avicenna. Two of Al-Beruni's most famous observations still resonate vividly. The first is: Al Hindu, Mushkil Pasand. The second is even more damaging: "(The Indians) are haughty, foolishly vain, self-contained and stolid ... they believe that there is no country like theirs ... no kings like theirs, no science like theirs."

But back to Gould. If we are to follow historical accuracy, the millennium should have occurred, he says, on October 23, 1997. If Dionysius is to be the guide, then the millennium begins on January 1, 2001, a date declared for the landmark by the authoritative UK's Royal Greenwich Observatory and the US's Library of Congress . But since the first decade of this century had only nine years, the year 2000 wins. Of course, 2000 is also a nice. whole number, almost "sensual" in Gould's evocative phrase.

It is India's achievements in mathematics that probably led the noted Oxford historian Felipe-Fernandez Armesto to write in his majestic tour-de-horizon of the past 1,000 years, Millennium: "A history of the first millennium would have to give India enormous weight: the subcontinent housed a single civilisation ... the achievements it produced in art, literature and philosophy were exported, with a moulding impact to China and Islam ... and it was a civilisation in expansion. With bewildering suddenness at about the turn of the millennium, the inspiration seemed to dry up, the vision to turn inward and the coherence to dissolve ... Political dissolution accompanied the cultural decline."

But the don is profoundly mistaken when he also adds: "India has been the Cinderella civilisation of our millennium ... beautiful, gifted, destined for greatness but relegated to the backstairs by those domineering sisters from Islam and Christendom." Islam and Christianity have not only enriched Indian culture but have made us more egalitarian and given us a more meaningful consciousness and sense of the collective.

29/11/1999

◆━━◆

THOSE 100 DAYS AGAIN

The monsoon is predicted to be normal for the
12th consecutive year—thank God!

It is that time of the year once again, the start of the 100 days that make or break India. Sure, the resilience of the Indian economy to withstand monsoon failures has increased. However, even if India harnesses its entire irrigation potential (right now less than three-fifths has been reportedly exploited) about 30 per cent of the country's gross cultivated area will continue to be dependent on the rains.

The India Meteorological Department (IMD) says that we will have the 12th normal south-west monsoon in a row, a not-so-unusual occurrence, contrary to conventional wisdom, when seen over the past century. The definition of "normal", of course, is pretty liberal. It is plus or minus 10 per cent of the long-term average of 88 cm. The forecast is for the country taken as a whole. The IMD divides the nation into 35 meteorological subdivisions. Monsoon can be normal for the country but deficient for a subdivision. The reliability of the forecasting model breaks down at the sub-division level. But this is also where the fore-cast is most relevant. It calls for a lot more rigorous science and mathematics, more so in the context of new developments like global warming. But thanks largely to the vision of Rajiv Gandhi who had the IMD transferred from the Ministry of Civil Aviation to the Department of Science and Technology, climate research is now engaging the attention of our scientific community. In fact, atmospheric science should be on the top of an Indo-US initiative, specially since some of the top atmospheric scientists in the US are Indians like T.N. Krishnamurthy, V. Ramanathan and J. Shukla.

The IMD forecasting model uses highly sophisticated statistical techniques. Its error is plus or minus 4 per cent showing a high degree of reliability. Let us say that the forecast value is 100. What the error range implies is that two-thirds of the time, the forecast value will be between 96 and 104 and 95 per cent of the time it will lie between 92 and 108. Sixteen regional and global parameters are used in the model showing the extent to which the "Indian" monsoon is influenced by what happens else-where across the globe. Of these, six relate to pressure, five to temperature and upper level winds and another five to snow cover and atmospheric oscillations. Some of the global parameters include pressure over Darwin in north Australia and over Argentina, variation of atmospheric pressure between Tahiti and Darwin, sea surface temperature over equatorial south-eastern Pacific, Eurasian snow cover, Northern Hemisphere temperature and pressure, pressure gradient in Europe etc. The "purely" swadeshi parameters, in terms of geography, are central Indian temperature and Himalayan snow.

Considering that our economy is still a substantial gamble on the rains, why is the budget presented before the monsoon? Our financial year runs from April 1 to March 31. This is a British hangover. But a committee was set up in May 1984 under the chairmanship of one of India's all-time great economic administrators, L.K. Jha, to consider whether we should change the financial year. Its report was submitted in April 1985. The Jha Committee looked at four options for the start of the financial year—January 1, April 1, July 1 and October 1—and after a fascinating analysis concluded that India should go in for the January 1-December 31 financial year. Fourteen of the 22 states which gave their views agreed with this change.

The advantage of starting the fiscal year on January 1 is that the government would not only know how the south-west monsoon has fared but will also have a reliable picture on the north-east monsoon's performance. But in spite of the persuasive evidence put forward by Jha in his own inimitably lucid style, the report was buried. The argument given by the no-changers, which incidentally Jha had anticipated, was that April 1 is advantageous because it minimises the inter-ruption in the working season. (This happens on account of the overlap between the time taken for expenditure authorisations during a transition from one year to the other, which is usually three months and the peak monsoon period.) But Jha had argued that it is not just desirable but also perfectly possible to eliminate procedural delays in expenditure authorisations so that the working season would be subject only to the climatic interruption.

When monsoons are normal, we may not feel the pinch. But if for some reason this cycle of good rains is broken, and there is statistical evidence to suggest that the probability of its breaking later this decade cannot be ruled out, then there may well be a case for moving to a January-December financial year and having the national budget presented in the third week of November.

12/06/2000

TIME TO TUNE IN TO FM
Very soon it will be the day of the annual Big B in Delhi

In February 1991 when the congress withdrew its support to the Chandra Shekhar government, it appeared that Yashwant Sinha would have the dubious distinction of being the only finance minister (FM) never to have presented a regular budget. Since then Sinha has come a long way. On February 28, he will present his fifth budget in a row. Last year, he surpassed T.T. Krishnamachari's (TTK) and Pranab Mukherjee's tally of three. This year, he will cross Y.B. Chavan's mark of four. Next year, he could equal Sir C.D. Deshmukh's and Manmohan Singh's record of six consecutive budgets and reach seven in 2004. Morarji Desai would, however, still be on top with eight budgets though in two separate terms.

Free India's first FM was Sir R.K. Shanmukham Chetty, chosen by Jawaharlal Nehru even though he had opposed the Congress. However, Chetty resigned in May 1948 following a furore over his role in protecting a Coimbatore industrialist from investigation for income-tax evasion. Chetty has immortalised himself as the father of the daughter of pioneering dancer Balasaraswati.

Chetty was succeeded by John Mathai, an economist who had worked with the Tatas. Mathai also went prematurely in May 1950 in protest against the creation of the Planning Commission. His son, Ravi, was to later make the IIM Ahmedabad a premier institution. Mathai's successor was Deshmukh who had earlier been the first Indian governor of the Reserve Bank of India. Deshmukh had a distinguished six-year tenure and liked to pepper his budgets with Sanskrit, Tamil and Urdu, reflecting his erudition. Ultimately, he too quit in a huff over the future of Bombay. His most enduring legacy is Delhi's India International Centre.

Among the politicians who followed this technocratic trio—a remarkable tribute to Nehru's eclecticism—TTK and Desai stand out. TTK's budget of May 1957 was a watershed. It introduced the expenditure tax and other taxes recommended by the eminent Cambridge economist Nicholas Kaldor. These were to be accompanied by lower rates of income tax. This did not happen and tax rates zoomed to almost 100 per cent, earning TTK, one of the great builders of industrial India, the sobriquet "Tax, Tax and Kill". Desai was workmanlike, with his February 1967 offering being the only budget to propose a zero deficit. Desai selected H.M. Patel as his FM in March 1977, a vindication for Patel who had quit the ICS over the LIC-Mundhra share controversy which had also claimed TTK almost two decades earlier.

Some prime ministers have also presented budgets as stop-gap FMs—Nehru in February 1958, Indira Gandhi in February 1970 and Rajiv Gandhi in February 1987. Ironically, Mrs Gandhi proposed clubbing the income and wealth of husband and wife for purposes of income and wealth taxation saying "those who are united in heaven should not be put asunder by a mere tax collector". And one of Rajiv's promises which has relevance today—a White Paper on the public sector—never saw the light of day because of great resistance although a reforms blue-print had been prepared by some public-sector CEOs headed by V. Krishnamurthy, then chairman of SAIL.

Till the mid-1970s, the budget focused on financial management. It was C. Subramanian who changed its entire complexion in February 1975 and March 1976 with his emphasis on agriculture, rural development, energy and science and technology. The 1976 Budget was unusual in another respect— it was the first and last to see the direct involvement of a minister of state for finance, Pranab Mukherjee. The March 1985 budget presented by V.P. Singh and reflecting Rajiv's bold views and L.K. Jha's advice signalled a revolution. Alas, political tur-bulence aborted this turn-about two years later.

Manmohan's budgets of July 1991, February 1992 and February 1993 unveiled a whole new vision for India. Reform fatigue set in thereafter, although tax corrections continued. Incidentally, Manmohan, who loved quoting Iqbal, almost didn't make it. Noted economist I.G. Patel, who as an official in the Finance Ministry during 1953-1972 had helped prepare a staggering 14 budgets, was P.V. Narasimha Rao's first choice as FM. But he declined. P. Chidambaram, who was managerially the most capable and who recalled the poet Tiruvalluvar in his speeches like TTK, was also the unluckiest FM. But he left a mark with his February 1997 budget. Sinha's earlier budgets have brought about major changes in excise duties, apart from revealing his penchant for using film titles in his speeches.

Five FMs have come from Tamil Nadu, four from Maharashtra, three from Uttar Pradesh (not counting the PMs), two each from Gujarat and West Bengal and one each from Bihar, Kerala and Punjab/Assam. But nobody has been parochial. The FM's job is the toughest, loneliest and the most thankless. On the whole, North Block has been served well by men of great distinction and competence.

25/02/2002

<hr>

BUDGET, NOT BUDGIVE TIME
The Government's financial year begins on All Fools' Day—should it?

The word "Budget" is derived from the Middle English bouget meaning a wallet that in turn comes from the Old French bougette, a leather bag. But like many English words, it has become part of the Indian lexicon and whether it is Hindi or any of the regional languages, budget is *bajat*.

The Union budget was always presented at 5 p.m. That was an imperial legacy but typically we invented an Indian reason—this is a time when the stock markets are closed. Five o'clock here corresponds to 11.30 a.m. in London when the accounts for India used to be presented in the House of Commons. Yashwant Sinha made a welcome break with this hangover in February 1999. But another colonial practice relating to the budget continues.

On February 28, Sinha will present the Union budget for the financial year 2002-3, that is for the period April 1, 2002 to March 31,

2003. This practice is a gift of the British. who decreed it way back in 1867 so as to be in conformity with their practices. Prior to 1867, the financial year began on May 1, going back over 450 years to the rule of the great Sher Shah Suri, who built the modern Grand Trunk Road linking Peshawar with Kolkata. His choice was linked to the end of the harvest season, April 14, the traditional Hindu New Year in many parts of India. Sher Shah, a largely overlooked figure in Indian history, also introduced the silver coin rupayya, from which we get the word rupee.

Does it make sense to start a financial year in a monsoon-influenced country well before we have any knowledge of what the rain gods have in store for us? This question has agitated successive administrations for over a century now. Many committees have suggested a change. The historic Royal Commission on Indian Currency and Finance, 1914, chaired by Austen Chamberlain and of which John Maynard Keynes himself was a member, did so. So did the Administrative Reforms Commission of 1966.

Most recently, the Committee on Change in Financial Year chaired by the late L.K. Jha, one of India's distinguished economic administrators, submitted its report in April 1985 and was unequivocally in favour of a financial year starting on January 1. Its recommendations received strong support from a vast majority of the state governments and parliamentarians. But nothing happened thereafter and the committee's report was simply buried.

If three basic principles are accepted—that the calendar chosen must be Gregorian, the date chosen must be be the first of a month and the year begins at the start of a generally accepted quarter—then a financial year could begin on January 1, April 1, July 1 or October 1. January 1 coincides with the start of the calendar year and by then the performance of both the south-west and north-east monsoons would be known and their impacts felt. July 1 coincides with the start of the agricultural and co-operative year, while October 1 would fall immediately after the withdrawal of the southwest monsoon.

In addition to the monsoon, the working season factor also has to be considered. Financial authorisations reach the field normally three months after they are made. With an April-March financial year, this means that money will reach in July and then for another three months, till September, works will not go full-swing because of the rains. With a January-December financial year, this hiatus would still be six months—

January to March and July to September—but the work sea-son gets fragmented, though this can be taken care of by eliminating delays in expenditure authorisations. A July-June financial year can give an uninterrupted season of nine months but if this happens, legislatures will have to meet through the summer. This will be resisted. An October-September financial year will also have a working season of six months but the important last quarter, when the pressure to spend mounts, will be relatively slack.

The Royal Commission described the Indian budget as a gamble on the rains. Today, the economic influence of the monsoon may appear less dramatic. But even if all of India's irrigation potential is harnessed (presently about 40 per cent of cultivated area is irrigated), between one-third and two-fifths of cultivated area would still be rainfed. And in the past few years, even with "normal" rainfall in the aggregate, agricultural output has been subject to substantial variations. Thus, a change in the financial year could have more than mere cosmetic value.

India's public finance system has collapsed. Not enough tax and non-tax revenues are being mobilised. There is too much expenditure in the wrong areas. Tax administration is very weak. Accounting procedures are outmoded. These are the priorities waiting to be tackled comprehensively in Part B of the Budget Speech. Unfortunately, Part A, over which the Finance Minister has little direct control, has become more important and the original meaning and significance of the budget has been lost. The nation is paying the price for this shift.

04/03/2002

<hr>

A TIME TO MOVE ON

Alas, after reaching a double century, this column returns to the pavilion

Vijay merchant was found of repeating a story relating to his retirement. Whenever he was asked why he quit prematurely from first-class cricket, his stock reply would be: well, it is better to go with people wondering why, instead of having people clamouring why not. In his many avatars, Kautilya has lived by this Merchantian maxim.

After 200 consecutive columns that started four years ago in April 1998, it is time to sign off. The magazine bosses have scripted an exit policy. There is, of course, no VRS, no golden handshake. Just a corporate decision. No doubt Kautilya will reincarnate himself elsewhere but for now it is farewell two weeks earlier than D-Day when all regular columns are to be dropped.

Why Kautilya for this column, patterned after Bagehot, Lexington and Charlemagne in the world's leading weekly The Economist? Obviously, because his Arthashastra is the earliest available and the first great treatise on practical statecraft going beyond economics, because he is the great master of political economy and because his is the voice of a sherpa. This column was rooted in economics but was not confined to it. This column was by a Congressman. But it never projected a party view—unlike some in the media who are not averse to propagandising on behalf of their political friends. On the contrary, some of the pieces got Kautilya into trouble with his party—the recent encomiums to A.B. Vajpayee while writing his political and moral epitaph being one example. His views on issues like the CTBT and privatisation have been at odds with the official Congress position. This has led to strictures but this columnist is convinced that a larger public interest must be served at all times even at some personal cost.

A typical column idea would begin germinating on a Sunday evening. Research would be done on Monday and Tuesday. Writing would take place on Wednesday with the final touches given on a Thursday. It was a tough discipline to produce something topical, something with durable academic content, something comprehensible to a diverse readership week after week. In some weeks there would be a surfeit of issues to write upon. But at times, it would be difficult to pursue something worthwhile. Sometimes the adrenaline would not stop flowing. However, on occasions those "grey cells" would be weighed down by fatigue. The most difficult part was to conjure up a catchy title to entice readers. But that was fun even if some could not be used—like BALCO Tere Dwar Khada Hai Jogi!

The column has drawn brickbats. Too clinical. Too cold-bloodedly analytical. Mea culpa. Kautilya has found it difficult to write about personalities unless absolutely essential. Here and there a few personal experiences have slipped in but that has been rare. Deliberately so. The column has also believed that there is space in our society for a genuine public intellectual, for a genuinely liberal position based entirely on the merits of the case.

Any regrets, apart from the prescribed departure? Kautilya's economics and that of this magazine are not radically different even though Kautilya does not share the magazine's disdain for the economic legacy of Nehru and Indira Gandhi. For instance, Nehru made India's outstanding success in higher education and in science and technology possible and the lady's greatest achievement was to usher in the Green Revolution. But every once in a while, Kautilya would feel unhappy with the stance taken on political and social issues by the magazine. Without wishing to make a virtue of a necessity, Kautilya must admit that the ambiguous position taken by the magazine on Narendra Modi confronted him with a dilemma: should he continue to write for a publication that he did not see taking a clear stand against the Gujarat chief minister? The magazine's enthusiasm for Murli Manohar Joshi's wild claims on the antiquity of Indian civilisation, its rubbishing of the intellectually brilliant "leftist" historians and its giving credibility to the dubious N.S. Rajarams are other instances when Kautilya has felt uncomfortable. But writing for the country's pre-eminent weekly drowned out all qualms.

Were there any highs? Yes, especially when students would write asking for more details, requesting for more references. Yes, especially when the column got quoted in lectures, papers and even books and drew international attention. Yes, especially when the column spawned follow-up articles in other magazines and newspapers and also led to television discussions.

Were there any embarrassments? Yes,when Kautilya would be ac-costed and congratulated for writing a column for Outlook. Confusion or clairvoyance? Is there a key message? Yes, economic liberalism in a framework of social obscurantism is both unacceptable and unsustainable.

That this magazine could run a semi-scholarly tract for four consecutive years without interference of any kind is a tribute to it. Thank you, INDIA TODAY for making Kautilya possible and for keeping it going for 49 months at a stretch.

13/05/2002

About India Research Press

India Research Press is a collectively run book publisher with support of Authors and Editors. Since our founding in 1999, we have tried to meet the needs of readers who are exploring, or are committed to the politics of change.

Our goal is to publish books that encourage critical thinking and constructive action on the key political, cultural, social, economic and ecological issues shaping life in the Indian Sub-continent and in the world.

In this way, we hope to give expression to a wide diversity of democratic and social movements.

India Research Press publishes Original works-as well as-works under Rights with various University and Academic publishers throughout the world.

The Group now has forty titles to its credit and many titles, scheduled for the next few months.

Since our conception, we have added two new imprints to our existing line of Academic publishing.

The group is proud to introduce its three divisions of publishing....

{ India Research Press
  Academic publishing division.

Swankit Swankit
  General division – Health, Non Fiction and Educational titles.

❋ Tara Press
/TARA press\ *General division – Mass Market including Fiction.*

The group is headed by Anuj Bahri Malhotra, its CEO & Commissioning Manager. He is assisted by an efficient and professional staff of Editors, Administrator and Office Assistants. Born to a bookseller's family, running the most sought after bookshop in the country, Anuj has a long inherited experience in the Indian Book Industry.

Our List of Titles

- **Divided Kashmir : Old Problems, New Opportunities for India, Pakistan and the Kashmiri People.**
  By: Mushtaqur Rahman

- **British Conquest and Dominion of India : Two volume set.**
  By: Sir Penderal Moon

- **India and the Bomb : Public Opinion and Nuclear Options.**
  By: David Courtright & Amitabh Mattoo

- **Rural Labour Relations in India.**
  By: T.J.Byres & Karin Kapadia

- **Architecture of Indian Desert: [Illus in Colour & B/W]**
  By: Kulbhushan & Minakshi Jain

- **Central Asia : A travelers companion.**
  By: Katherine Hopkirk [distribution only]

- **Rogue States : The Rule of Force in World Affairs.**
  By: Noam Chomsky

- **Stolen Harvest : The Hijacking of the Global Food Supply.**
  By: Vandana Shiva

- **Heaven's Child and other Poems**
  By: Sameer Kak

- **Natural Resource Management and Institutional Change. An ODI/IRP joint series.**
  By: Diana Carney and John Farrington

- **Development as process. An ODI/IRP joint series.**
  By: David Mosse, John Farrington and Alan Rew.

- **Quiz Master India. Volume 1**
  By: Sanjay Sharma

- **Quiz Master India. Volume 2**
  By: Sanjay Sharma

- **.......and the answer is a pineapple**
  By: Claudia Hyles

- **Lahore 1947 : The last days of Lahore at Partition**
  By: Ahmed Salim., Intro by : Ian Talbot

- Democracy-a failure, Shefocracy-the solution, for human welfare.
  By: Dr. Rabin Mukherjee
- India-Sri Lanka relations and Sri Lanka's Ethnic Conflict Documents : 1947-2000. [set of 5 volumes]
  By: Dr. Avtar Singh Bhasin
- Security in the New Millenium : Views from South Asia
  By: Rajesh M. Basrur
- The Saffron Book : A study of the Saffron politics.
  By: Prafull Goradia
- Roots of Rhetoric : Politics of Nuclear Weapons in India & Pakistan
  By: Haider K. Nizamani
- Democracy and Dictatorship in South Asia : Dominant Classes and Political Outcomes in India, Pakistan and Bangladesh
  By: Robert W. Stern
- Quiz Master India : A Student's guide to Success [omnibus]
  By: Sanjay Sharma.
- Partition and Gnocide Manifestation of Violence In Punjab
  By : Anders Bjorn Hansen
- Vegetarian Indian Cooking
  By : Manju Kumari Singh
- Sniffing Papa (Fiction)
  By : Inderjeet Badhwar
- Water Wars : Privatisation, Pollution and Profit
  By : Vandana Shiva
- The Muslims of the Indian Sub-continent after the 11th September Attacks
  By : Frédéric Grare
- Beyond Turk and Hindu
  By : David Gilmartin and Bruce B. Lawrence
- Arena of Laughter..........Set of Two Volumes
  By : Sudhir Nath
- SAARC in the Twenty-First Century Towards a Cooperative Future
  By : Dipankar Banerjee

490

Our Forthcoming Titles

- **Industrial Growth in the Punjab since Independe⁻⁻ :
  A Historical Inquiry 1947 to the Present**
  By : Gurpreet Maini
- **Hanklyn-Janklin : A rumble-tumble of Indian Words
  used in everyday English.**
  By: Nigel Hankin
- **Pakistan : In the Face of the Afghan Conflict 1979-1985**
  By : Frédéric Grare
- **The Sustainable Livelihood Series :**
  An ODI/IRP joint series
  Volume One /Volume Two /Volume Three........ [continuing·
  series]
- **Rewriting Indian History**
  By : Francois Gautier
- **Katha Sagar : A collection of Prem Chand's Stories**
  By: R. Gupta
- **No Curtains Yet**
  By: V.K. Madhavan Kutty
- **Adultery and other stories**
  By: Farrukh Dhondy
- **Letters against the War**
  By: Tiziano Terzani
- **India's National Security Annual Review 2002**
  By: Prof. Satish Kumar
- **Cricket The Essentials of the Game**
  By: Sir Richard Hadlee

****

For further information, write to........

India Research Press
Publisher
B-4/22, Safdarjung Enclave, New Delhi – 110 029.
Phone : 4694610; Fax : 4618637
www.indiaresearch press.com   e-mail : bahrisons@vsnl.com

{ India
{ Research
{ Press

Swankit

TARA
press